With a swipe of her artist's bru
of the ordinary things of life—
a devotional guide with memor
find the *divine* in the events of c

—Pat Hart, care pastor, First Assembly of God Church,
Pine Bluff, Arkansas

Have you ever…? Of course you have! *Sheep Ears* is a teacher's manual for life experiences with a Christian perspective. So many times we find ourselves searching for the meaning or the purpose of our own life experiences and adversities—knowing that God has a plan, we search for Scriptures to provide meaning and understanding. When reading *Sheep Ears*, you find yourself relating your own experiences to the ones creatively shared in this book and ultimately finding the meaning that you were searching for. As a Guidance Counselor, I am frequently confronted with young adults searching for "the meaning" of their life experiences, and this provides a great resource and reference guide—a message from God!

—Tammy Cummings-Smith, guidance counselor, Ridgway Christian School; executive director, Seabrook Family Christian Center

Once I picked up the book, I couldn't put it down. *Sheep Ears* takes you on an exciting journey through the author's personal memoirs recounting events in her life where not only listening to God's voice, but also *obeying* His voice made the difference. She is teaching us that by being steadfast and faithful, we listen and obey and vice versa. In this process we train ourselves to be guided by the Good Shepherd in all situations. The challenge is there for all of us, both new believers, as well as those who've been trying for years. Fine-tune our sheep ears, be quiet, listen and obey! A life-long challenge!

—Jennifer Keahey, retired educator

As a pastor, one of the most incredible joys I know is to experience the discovery of hidden gifts within those we love and serve. It was with both surprise and delight that I read the first draft of Sherry's work. I was drawn to every truth by the transparent practicality of her style of writing. As you read through this book, I'm certain that you will be inspired and encouraged by Sherry's real-to-life insights.

—Gary Bell, senior pastor, First Assembly of God,
Pine Bluff, Arkansas

This book lifted my spirit, taught me how to give more freely, and inspired me to obey the voice of our Good Shepherd more than ever. I recommend it with all my heart.

—Gwen Terry, motivational speaker and author

Meeting Sherry during a Christian summer camp a couple of years ago, was a unique yet blessed experience. Her mission to the voiceless was apparent, her enthusiasm palpable and her humility endearing. Our interaction triggered a chain of events that has led to the encryption of these riveting yet compelling stories. The arduous journey of how the various protagonists found their voices and her role in it is attention gripping. It sucks you in. Having a rendezvous with one's essence of existence is something Sherry has done well. This compilation is therefore a good read and I would encourage you to share it with others.

—Robert Muhumuza, MD

Sheep Ears is a compilation of Sherry's real-life stories of her experiences and what happens when you hear and obey God's voice. You will discover how God loves us and uses his sheep (earthly angels) to bless his children and supply their needs (Philippians 4:19). This book is a reminder of the importance of keeping our daily walk with the Lord.

—Arlita "Lita" Garza

Sherry is a modern day disciple. *Sheep Ears* is a new type of testimony in the way that she walks and *hears* His Word. This book shows us all how to listen to God in the way He presents Himself to us personally in our journey—knowing, loving, and listening to Him—*shhhhhhhhh!*

—LaJuana Paris

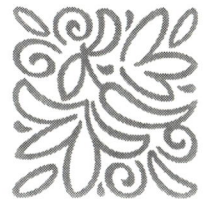

Sheep Ears

Are you guided by the Good Shepherd?

Sherry Witt

WestBow
Press
A Division of Thomas Nelson

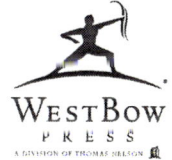

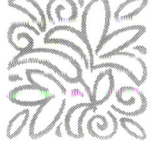

Copyright © 2013 Sherry Witt.

All rights reserved. No part of this book may be used or reproduced by any means, graphic, electronic, or mechanical, including photocopying, recording, taping or by any information storage retrieval system without the written permission of the publisher except in the case of brief quotations embodied in critical articles and reviews.

WestBow Press books may be ordered through booksellers or by contacting:

WestBow Press
A Division of Thomas Nelson
1663 Liberty Drive
Bloomington, IN 47403
www.westbowpress.com
1-(866) 928-1240

Because of the dynamic nature of the Internet, any web addresses or links contained in this book may have changed since publication and may no longer be valid. The views expressed in this work are solely those of the author and do not necessarily reflect the views of the publisher, and the publisher hereby disclaims any responsibility for them.

Any people depicted in stock imagery provided by Thinkstock are models, and such images are being used for illustrative purposes only.

Certain stock imagery © Thinkstock.

ISBN: 978-1-4497-9992-2 (sc)
ISBN: 978-1-4497-9991-5 (hc)
ISBN: 978-1-4497-9993-9 (e)

Library of Congress Control Number: 2013911893

Printed in the United States of America.

WestBow Press rev. date: 8/29/2013

Unless otherwise noted, all Scripture quotations in this publication are from *THE MESSAGE*. Copyright © by Eugene H. Peterson 1993, 1994, 1995, 1996, 2000, 2001, 2002. Used by permission of NavPress Publishing Group.

Scripture quotations are taken from the Amplified® Bible. Copyright© 1954, 1962, 1965, 1967 by The Lockman Foundation. Used by permission.

Scripture quotations are taken from *The Holy Bible, English Standard Version*. Copyright ©2000; 2001 by Crossway Bibles, a division of Good News Publishers. Used by permission. All rights reserved.

GOD'S WORD® Translation is a copyrighted work of God's Word to the Nations. Quotations are used by permission. Copyright 1995 by God's Word to the Nations. All rights reserved.

Scriptures quoted from The Holy Bible, King James Version, public domain.

Scriptures quoted from the New American Standard Bible®, Copyright © 1960, 1962, 1963, 1968, 1971, 1972, 1973, 1975, 1977, 1995 by The Lockman Foundation. Used by permission.

Scripture quoted from the HOLY BIBLE, NEW INTERNATIONAL VERSION®. Copyright © 1973, 1978, 1984 by International Bible Society. Used by permission of Zondervan. All rights reserved.

Scripture taken from the New King James Version. Copyright © 1982 by Thomas Nelson, Inc. Used by permission. All rights reserved.

Scripture quoted from the Holy Bible, New Living Translation, copyright © 1996, 2004, 2007. Used by permission of Tyndale House Publishers, Inc., Wheaton, IL 60189. All rights reserved.

Scripture quotations are taken from *The Living Bible*, copyright ©1971 by Tyndale House Foundation. Used by permission of Tyndale House Publishers, Inc., Carol Stream, Illinois 60188. All rights reserved.

My sheep hear my voice, and I know them, and they follow me.

—*John 10:27 KJV*

*Dedicated to the Good Shepherd who guides me,
Randy, the love of my life,
our fantastic sons—Aaron, Nathan, and Paul,
their beautiful families,
my loving parents, Raymond and Betty Phillips,
and all the sheep who desire to follow the Good Shepherd.*

Table of Contents

Acknowledgments. xiii

Preface xvii

Introduction. xxi

My Family Flock xxiii

Have you ever…
- 1 acted quickly?. 1
- 2 admitted you were wrong? 6
- 3 asked God to pick a friend for you?. 10
- 4 been attacked by dogs?. 15
- 5 been depressed?. 20
- 6 been diagnosed with cancer? 24
- 7 been on a crazy deer hunt? 30
- 8 been recorded? 34
- 9 been told by your son that he was going to cheat on a test? . .39
- 10 been under attack? .43
- 11 been willing? 47
- 12 blinded your right eye? 52
- 13 bought a lemon? 55
- 14 broken your promise? 59
- 15 celebrated a woohoo moment? 62
- 16 controlled your anger?. 67
- 17 crawled under a chair? 72
- 18 cussed like a sailor? .77

19	dealt with a type A personality?	81
20	deceived yourself?	90
21	deprived your kids?	95
22	encountered an angel?	103
23	faced a bully with authority?	109
24	faced your fears?	114
25	felt like giving up?	120
26	felt like you botched it?	127
27	gotten your house in order? (Part 1)	132
28	gotten your house in order? (Part 2)	138
29	had a CD ministry?	144
30	had a game plan?	148
31	had a mission?	154
32	had a nudge?	161
33	had a praying parent?	166
34	had a standby?	170
35	had an opposite day?	177
36	had an unplanned pregnancy?	182
37	had to abruptly change your plans?	186
38	heard a sentence sermon?	193
39	heard God cry?	196
40	heard the voice?	199
41	joined the Sisters' Club?	204
42	known a slow starter?	208
43	learned to be content?	214
44	learned to laugh?	218
45	left a legacy?	223
46	let go of the steering wheel?	228
47	limited God?	231
48	looked through God's eyes?	237
49	loved enough to lose?	243
50	needed a harvest?	248
51	needed a word from God?	254
52	needed an intercessor?	257
53	needed help?	261
54	noticed a flaw?	268

55	overcome a failure?	273
56	overlooked a diamond in the rough?	278
57	planted seeds?	284
58	prayed like a child?	287
59	provoked someone?	293
60	read a different version?	298
61	received a new name?	302
62	refused a gift?	308
63	robbed God?	314
64	said "never"?	319
65	said, "Okay God, talk to me"?	323
66	sat under an overpass?	327
67	seasoned with salt?	331
68	sent your last child to college?	335
69	served two masters?	341
70	sharpened your sword?	346
71	stopped the potter's wheel?	350
72	tamed your tongue?	355
73	used a password? (Part 1)	360
74	used a password? (Part 2)	365
75	wanted to be generous?	370
76	wondered if color matters?	370
77	wondered if God cared about you?	383
78	wondered if there are any good people left in the world?	387
79	wondered if your prayers mattered?	392
80	wondered whose words to believe?	396

Epilogue 403

Bible Version Abbreviations 407

Acknowledgments

First and foremost, I thank God for enabling me to write for Him. He is the sole reason for my book. He is an awesome, way-cool God. I lay my book at His feet and pray that He will say, "Well done, thou good and faithful servant."

Randy, you are the love of my life. I wouldn't be the woman I am if you weren't the man that you are. You give me total freedom to be myself. Thank you for standing behind me through all the story writing, the questions and answers, and especially the tedious editing. You are one in a million-gazillion!

Aaron, Nathan, and Paul, I tremendously appreciate your permission to tell your stories in my book. I have treasured every minute of being your mother and watching you grow from playful little boys to wonderful men with children of your own. I am grateful for the men that you have become. Hopefully the glimpses into our lives will help others along their journey in life, and they will realize that every day truly is an adventure.

My daughters-in-law, their precious parents, and our grandchildren, have made my life overflow with love. You have become the daughters I never had, and my grands are truly *grand*. I'm giving a special shout-out to Laura, Skyler and Ayla (Aaron's family); Sharon, Ethan and Emma (Nathan's family); and Michelle who married Paul after my book was written. We welcome you into our family. Michelle, I am so thankful that you suggested that Paul dance with me at your wedding. It meant the world to me.

Raymond and Betty Phillips, my father and mother, you gave me my strong godly background. It was never shouted or shoved down my throat.

Life was lived with laughter, joy, and by watching as you led by example. Words cannot express my love and appreciation for you.

Gwen Terry, you are my dear friend and the spark plug that got me headed in the right direction on the book. Proverb 25:11 says, "Timely advice is as lovely as golden apples in a silver basket" (LB). If that's the case, I must have a ton of golden apples in an extra large basket after all of your lovely advice. Thanks, thanks, and more thanks.

Clark Terry, when I felt like giving up you inspired me, and all my excuses flew out the window. Like you always say, "Keep on keepin' on."

Brenda Mays and LaJuana Paris, you were terrific cheerleaders and editors. Thanks for your many hours on the phone. You are gems. Your suggestions were invaluable, and your friendships are priceless. Just when I would feel like giving up, you would hold up my arms like Aaron and Hur held up the arms of Moses.

Robert and Eva Muhumuzu, you are my forever friends. I only met you for a short three days, but you changed my life forever when you pushed me to start writing. I hope my stories will inspire people as you have inspired me.

I am also grateful to Pastor Gary Bell for his anointed sermons and invaluable feedback on my book. Words cannot adequately express how wonderful it is to be fed from a man who follows God with his heart, mind, and soul, and is led by the Holy Spirit in every aspect of his life.

Corliss Andrews, you are truly an angel. You encouraged me more than you will ever know with your words, the Bible you gave me, and the special grandmother's love that you gave Skyler and Ayla when I wasn't able to be with them.

Linnie McNabb, you're my very special neighbor and the inspiration for several stories. I will always appreciate that, and I cherish our thirty-three years of growing into close friends.

There are many people who encouraged me when I was at my lowest points. Without my friends' uplifting words and feedback, I don't think I would have finished. God knew just when to send them to me and for that I am eternally grateful: Patricia Jones, Gary Paris, Arlita "Lita" Garza, Jennifer Keahey, Claudia Escudero, Angel and Jason Caudle, Tammy Cummings-Smith, Anna Ashcraft, Alexia Williams, Shannon Blake, Brandy Walls, Tiffany Doolin, and Patricia McCullough.

I am so thankful to my friends who gave me permission to use their names *and* their stories: Mary Jo Watson, Jeff Montgomery, Michael Hickman, Cindy, Travis and Sarah Johnson, Sara Rice-Milner, her daughter Bailey, and her parents, the late Calvin and Willene Rice. I also thank Georgette Wiley, Cheryl Hatley, Judge Jodi Dennis, J'Mille and Kaleb Johnson, Kyron Crutchfield, Carolyn Jackson-Cohn, Cady Hinkle, Monica and Kaneeshia Williams, Dr. John Harris, Pat Hart, Legacy Paris, Patrick Wood, Sha Moody, and numerous other wonderful friends. I also appreciate the families of the late Billy Bock, Sue McNulty, Charles Wood, and Joyce Cole for their willingness to share their stories.

There are many, many other wonderful people in my book whose names and circumstances I changed in order to protect their privacy. I tip my hat to you.

I appreciate Gene White, a.k.a. BGWhyte, who was able to zip my files when they needed to be zipped and merge them when they needed to be merged. I was so honored that you wrote a Christian rap after you read one of my stories, "Have you ever overlooked a diamond in the rough?" and made it your cover song: *Polish Me.* Woohoo!

Gayle Holley, you were amazing as you typed the stories that I wrote out by hand in *eleven* notebooks. You always had the sweetest attitude as I brought you more and more. I'm giving a looong, LOUD shout-out to you, Gayle. YAAAAAAAAAAAAAAAAAAAAAAYYYYY!

No book would be possible without a willing publisher and a fantastic crew. I would like to thank WestBow Press, a division of Thomas Nelson, for the willingness to take a chance on a new author like me. In the past, my book would have only been a dusty manuscript, but you have made book publishing an attainable dream. You guided me in every aspect of the process, until my book was brought to fruition. I'm turning cartwheels in my heart! Woohoo!

I really can do all things through Christ who gives me strength.

Preface

I'd never considered myself to be a writer, so this book took me by more surprise than anyone else. I do love to talk, though, and I'm told that I do so with a great animation. Whenever I told stories to my parents, Raymond and Betty Phillips, they would say, "You ought to write these down." But it all seemed so trivial that I dismissed the thought.

In June of 2010, I attended a Christ-based, nondenominational family camp called Camp Farthest Out (CFO). It was seven hours away in the mountains of Alabama. The lady in charge of selecting the teachers, Jennifer, asked me to teach the children aged six through eleven. Originally, there were to be nine children in my class, but plans changed, and they divided the class so I was left with only one boy and two girls aged ten and eleven. I was disappointed at first, but I gave them my all, and we had a glorious time of bonding and fellowship. I don't know who had more fun, me or the kids. The class was only an hour, so I was allowed to be a camper for the rest of the day.

Mary Jo, a friend of mine who had recommended me to Jennifer, was also a teacher at the camp. In the middle of the week, Mary Jo and I had some down time and decided to take a walk around the campus. As we stopped on the bridge, a hornet zoomed at me as though it had radar. Zap! It stung my left arm, which swelled immediately. The camp nurse made a paste for me to apply along with ice to my arm, but it continued to swell overnight.

The next morning I attended a Bible study with about ten people. As we were wrapping up, someone asked me how my arm was doing. A few grimaced as they looked at my red, swollen flesh but one man, Dr. Robert

Muhumuza, took a special interest. He had just arrived at CFO, joining his wife and kids, who had been there from the start.

"Let me look. Oh, this is not good. You should have antibiotics. No need to take a chance with a staph infection," he said in a beautiful British accent. I filled his prescription at a nearby Walmart. I was impressed that this stranger had such a keen interest in my well-being.

He told me later that he was a gastroenterologist with a practice in Louisiana, but he was originally from Uganda. I *knew* that wasn't a Cajun accent!

Later that night, I sat down with Dr. Muhumuza and his wife, Eva, and started telling them some stories about my life. They asked for more, so I obliged. Ten minutes turned into two hours. We missed the entire service that night, but I believe God had a different agenda for me: that night the seeds for this book were planted.

The next day, Dr. Muhumuza checked my arm and encouraged me to write my stories down. "I don't type," I told him. I thought that was a great excuse, but he was persistent.

"Dragon! You must get the program Dragon. You can speak your stories and it will type for you." He showed me the app on his phone and made me spell the name. I saw him at least ten times more, and each time he encouraged me, "Write your stories down!"

I was baffled. Why was such an esteemed doctor interested in my stories about everyday situations? He informed me that he was working through Savannah Sunrise Foundation (SAS), an organization he had founded, to eradicate HIV/AIDS from Uganda first and then from the world. He gave me a DVD about his impressive mission. Why would this champion of good causes be concerned with me? Didn't he know I was a nobody as far as the world was concerned? I was a teacher's aide, a front-desk receptionist, a mother, and a wife—but a writer? I couldn't imagine.

He was relentless. Enough to make me mention the ridiculous thought of writing to a new acquaintance, Gwen Terry. We were celebrating her birthday at Chili's in Pine Bluff, Arkansas, when I told her, half jesting, about Dr. Muhumuza's proposal. "Do you want me to tell you one of the stories?" I asked her.

"No," she said emphatically. "Write them down." Ugh! That was the last thing I wanted to do. Talking had always been easy, but writing? That took way too long. She softened her approach. "Sherry, if this important man and his wife think you have something worth writing about, then you need to try."

I hurriedly wrote two stories. I didn't purchase Dragon, but wrote them out longhand in a notebook. To my surprise, Gwen liked them. She insisted I write more. Gwen was assisting her husband, Clark Terry, with his autobiography. She was a busy woman, yet she took time to encourage me. I wrote a few more stories, five in all. But they felt plain-Jane to me, nothing out of the ordinary. As I gave Gwen the last batch, I felt a huge weight lift off my shoulders.

"There! I'm glad that's over with! " I said with a big sigh.

Gwen said she could see the stories becoming a book. I argued with her, but finally said, "Maybe a *booklet*, but not a book."

She chuckled. "Okay, then just call it a booklet, but keep writing."

Ideas for new stories kept popping in my head, but the format I was using was all wrong for expansion. Besides, they were just stories. Even though they were true, they had no power.

Around Christmas, Gwen went to Barnes & Noble with her sister, Georgette. She had been praying for me to have a breakthrough on my book(let) and, at the bookstore, she noticed a 365-day daily devotional by Joyce Meyer: *Hearing from God Each Morning.*

As she picked it up, she heard God say, "Give this to Sherry."

She said, "God, what am I supposed to tell her?"

He said, "She'll know what to do. Just give her the book."

Gwen obeyed, and then God opened the floodgates. The minute I looked inside the book, God unveiled His format to me. I had struggled to write my stories like a memoir, but God revealed a better plan: short stories with Scriptures. Not a continuous book with chapters, but short stories mixed with the Word. The next day, in only one hour, God gave me a theme for the story titles and forty-four story subjects besides.

My mind was whirling, but my hands hadn't gotten busy. I was standing in front of the dishwasher on Christmas Eve, 2010, when I heard God say, "If you don't start writing, I'm going to give this to someone else." That lit my fire. My friends and family had been encouraging me, but one word from God changed everything. Ecclesiastes 12:13 says, "The last and final word is this: Fear God. Do what he tells you." I told God I was willing.

In three weeks, I had written about thirty stories. I use the word "I" loosely. My stories would have sounded like this: "We went to the lake. We swam. We went home. It was a good day." But the Holy Spirit came into my stories and directed them. It felt like I was a court reporter and He was dictating my words. "If you don't know what you're doing, pray to the Father. He loves to help. You'll get his help and won't get condescended to when you ask for it. Ask boldly, believingly, without a second thought" (James 1:5). I had no idea what I was doing, but my loving Father helped me, just like He said He would. I believed and He never let me down.

All my stories are true, although some names and details have been changed in order to respect privacy. I may not have gotten everything perfect, but my goal was honesty. The Holy Spirit drew parallels and I was amazed at how they unfolded. I hardly ever knew how each story would end as I wrote them.

Writing has been fun and challenging. It was definitely an adventure. I'm so thankful that God placed people in my life to pull me out from behind the curtain. I had never had the desire to write a book, but God had other plans. I read books by famous authors and felt inadequate, but God has a Scripture even for that: "Don't compare yourself with others. Each of you must take the responsibility for doing the creative best you can with your life" (Galatians 6:5). That is what I've done. I've bared my soul and laid it all out there.

You might wonder where God was throughout your life. I've got news for you: He's been there the whole time. If one person is drawn closer to Christ by this book, then it has been worth the whole process. If more than one person is drawn closer, then it has been doubly worth it.

> Every word you give me is a miracle word—
> How could I help but obey?
> Break open your words; let the light shine out,
> Let ordinary people see the meaning.
> —Psalms 119:129–130

Introduction

What do I mean by "sheep ears"? I'm glad you asked that question. Let me explain. When we go through life, we have many questions: Are there any good people left in the world? Is it okay to cheat on a test? What if I make a mistake? What if I fail? What is the solution to my problem?

Fortunately, we have Someone who will guide us. Jesus said, "I am the Good Shepherd. I know my own sheep and my own sheep know me." He also said, "My sheep recognize my voice; I know them, and they follow me" (John 10:14, 27). We accept Jesus into our heart, read the Bible, and tune our ears to listen to the voice that gently leads us. Our sheep ears develop slowly. We are familiar with the heart of the Shepherd because we have a relationship with Him. When Jesus ascended to heaven, God sent the Holy Spirit to guide us with His prompts.

When you start listening to the loving voice of the Good Shepherd, you may feel awkward. You may miss His direction a few times, but it will get easier. It's a learning process. God will not knock you down or whack you if you think you are hearing from God but misunderstand Him. Joyce Meyer said that when she was first learning to hear God's voice, she was petrified of making a mistake. She said that God told her, "If you miss me, I will find you." He is loving, kind, and patient. Before long you will recognize the Good Shepherd's voice, and your sheep ears will be fully developed.

The Bible may seem difficult to understand, but stick with it, and ask God to give you wisdom to comprehend. Before long your heart will be sensitive, and your life will be better than you would have ever thought possible.

In my book, I share true life stories of how God has guided me in my daily walk with Him. I hope they may help you to realize that God speaks through a child's prayer, a song that touches your heartstrings, and that He directs us, just as we raise our children, with love and patience.

I hope that you enjoy answering the questions and reading the Scriptures that follow each of the chapters, and that they help you to relate to the stories.

My prayer is that after you have read my book, *your* sheep ears will be more developed, and you will discover that the answer to every question you have is in the Bible.

My Family Flock

Sherry Witt, the author

Randy Witt, husband of the author, married thirty-eight years

Aaron Witt, our eldest son

    Laura Witt, Aaron's wife

    Skyler Witt, Aaron's son

    Ayla Witt, Aaron's daughter

Nathan Witt, our middle son

    Sharon Witt, Nathan's wife

    Ethan Witt, Nathan's son

    Emma Witt, Nathan's daughter

Paul Witt, our youngest son

    Michelle Witt, Paul's wife

I

Have you ever acted quickly?

One of the first times that I heard specific instructions from God was in December of 1982. My third son, Paul, was two weeks old. I was pacing back and forth in the living room trying to get him to sleep when I felt an inner voice telling me to take $125 and give it to Cindy Johnson, an acquaintance of mine. "And do it immediately," He said.

God, is that you, or am I hearing my own words? I thought. What was I supposed to do, just call her up and insist she take the money? I didn't even think she needed it. She'd probably feel insulted. *Please don't embarrass me! What if I'm wrong? Then I'll really look foolish! Besides God, I don't even have that much money.*

He said, "Yes, you do. It's in the top drawer of your dresser."

I had forgotten all about that money, but He knew exactly where it was and how much it was! It *had* to be God. I had planned to use it to buy Christmas gifts, but it was more than I actually needed. Now that I knew it really was God directing me, I was determined to complete my assignment. Cindy lived in Conway, Arkansas, about sixty miles away. My husband and I attended the same church as her parents, Travis and Sarah Johnson, so I hoped they wouldn't think I was totally insane. I called them and told them about the urgency.

Travis replied, "Baby, I don't think she needs any money."

I told him that I didn't really think she did either, but I had pretty specific instructions.

He said, "Well in that case, on your word, I will call her and tell her

I'm coming to bring her the money." I was relieved that he didn't ask a lot of questions; I had no answers, just a knowing in my spirit.

I didn't hear anything from them for about a week. I knew I had done the right thing, but I still felt kind of weird about it. When I finally saw Travis, I asked him if he had ever figured out why the money was so urgent.

He apologized for not getting back in touch with me sooner. "Cindy knew a couple in Conway who had just had a baby and she was coming home from the hospital the very day you called. Her friends had just gotten an eviction notice. Unless they could come up with $125, they had nowhere to go. Since we took the money to them that day, they had a place to bring their newborn baby."

I was stunned. I didn't even know the couple with the baby, but God had been aware that Cindy knew them. God also knew He could trust me to get the money to Cindy and that she would take the money to them. God knew that He could trust Travis to believe me and respond quickly. You see, it wasn't just *me* that God had depended on; it was *all* of us. It was an amazing chain of events. God knew everything. We just had to trust His voice.

I had a lot of questions: Why did God pick me? Why didn't He use someone in Conway to give them the money? How did I manage to have that exact amount of extra cash at Christmas time when my own family included three kids, with a newborn? What with our limited income, this last point was in itself a miracle. What if I had waited until the next day to work up the nerve to approach her parents?

I don't know the answers to those questions, but I have my suspicions. Maybe God *had* asked someone in Conway, but they refused. I am guessing that God gave us the surplus and had me set the money aside and forget about it so I would have it on hand for this emergency. I know that giving Sarah this money was not a thought I would have typically had on my own, so it *must* have been God speaking to me. Maybe He picked me because I was willing. Perhaps God was training my sheep ears to hear His voice and to trust Him.

Another incident occurred two years later when I was mowing the backyard of my neighbor across the street. It was three o'clock in the afternoon and about one hundred degrees. I heard that inner voice once again. "Get $125 and give it to Mr. Rice for his daughter, Sara."

I was extremely hot and tired, and I only had five more rows to go. I said, "God, can it wait until I'm through mowing?"

"No."

Not understanding why, but recognizing the voice, I said, "Okay." The amount of money seemed familiar. I remembered the other time I had distinctly heard God, so this time I was a little less resistant.

I went to my house, got the money and took it to Mr. Rice. When I relayed the message I had heard from God, he told me that he appreciated it, but he didn't think that Sara needed any money at this time. I told him I didn't think she needed it either, but would he please call her to come get the money. I shared the previous miracle with Mr. Rice, so I think he was more willing than he would have been otherwise. He promised me he would talk to Sara.

I finished mowing the grass, took a shower, and went back to Mr. Rice's house. I was really curious about why I had needed to act so quickly. When I got there, he looked at me with a quirky smile. I started to apologize for the inconvenience, but he interrupted me. His normally calm demeanor was now animated.

"You won't believe this, but Sara had pawned her wedding ring! It had to be picked up today or be put up for sale at the pawn shop. She was able to get it out of hock before the place closed."

We both sat there in amazement. He hadn't known about the ring, nor had I, but God knew. What if I had been too embarrassed to approach Mr. Rice? What if Mr. Rice had been unwilling to call his daughter? How did I come to have that exact amount of money again? What if I had finished mowing, taken a shower, eaten, rested, and then gone to tell him what I had heard from God? It might have been too late.

I only know that when I hear God's voice inside, I can tell it's Him because the words are peaceful and tell me something I would not have thought of on my own. I may have some doubts, but I feel peace when I commit to doing His will. He will never ask me to do anything contrary to the Scriptures. I don't have to know all the answers; I only need to obey. "Do you think all God wants are sacrifices—empty rituals just for show? He wants you to listen to him! Plain listening is the thing, not staging a lavish religious production" (1 Samuel 15:22).

I once heard someone say that if you hear that inner voice telling you to do something quickly, then it can't be God. But I respectfully disagree. Jesus turned water into wine at a wedding feast (John 2:1–10). What would have happened if they had waited two hours before gathering the water pots? The guests would have gone home and the miracle would have been ineffective. And what about the time Jesus spit into the dust, made a paste with saliva, rubbed it in a blind man's eyes, and told him to wash in the Pool of Siloam? If that man had waited an hour before doing so, he would have ended up with crusty, muddy, still-blind eyes, rather than having had his sight restored.

When opportunity arises and God prompts, please say yes. You never know. Someone's miracle may depend on your quick action.

Questions

1. Has God ever given you specific instructions to quickly obey? If so, what were the instructions?

2. How are *you* able to tell if God is speaking?

3. When God prompts you to action, does it always make sense?

4. What did Mary tell the servants to do at the wedding feast when they ran out of wine? (a)

5. Did Jesus ever give unusual instructions to follow? If so, what? (b)

6. How do you think God feels when you vow to immediately obey Him, yet delay your response? (c)

7. Are you quick to listen, yet slow to obey? Justify your actions. (d)

8. Do we have a promise from God that He will bless us if we obey His commands and do what is pleasing to the Lord? If so, what is it? (e)

Scriptural Answers

(a) "His mother said to the servants, 'Do whatever he tells you'" (John 2:5 NIV).

(b) "Jesus said to the servants, 'Fill the jars with water'; so they filled them to the brim. Then he told them, "Now draw some out and take it to the master of the banquet.' They did so, and the master of the banquet tasted the water that had been turned into wine. He did not realize where it had come from, though the servants who had drawn the water knew. Then he called the bridegroom aside and said, 'Everyone brings out the choice wine first and then the cheaper wine after the guests have had too much to drink; but you have saved the best till now'" (John 2:7–10 NIV).

(c) "When you make a vow to God, do not delay in fulfilling it. He has no pleasure in fools; fulfill your vow" (Ecclesiastes 5:4 NIV).

(d) "My dear brothers, take note of this: Everyone should be quick to listen … Do not merely listen to the word, and so deceive yourselves. Do what it says" (James 1:19, 22 NIV).

(e) "Be careful to obey my commands, so that all will go well with you and your children after you, because you will be doing what is good and pleasing to the Lord your God" (Deuteronomy 12:28 NLT).

2

Have you ever admitted you were wrong?

Is it hard for you to apologize? Don't worry, you're not alone. Most people find it difficult—I'm not sure why, but I suspect it is pride. It used to be pretty hard for me to apologize, but the more I do it, the easier it gets. I think admitting you're wrong falls into the same category as apologizing.

Recently, my husband and I were sitting at the dinner table talking. I don't remember the topic of our conversation, but I jumped to a wrong conclusion. When I discovered that I was wrong, I said, "I'm sorry. I was wrong and you were right." Randy kind of mumbled, "Okay."

Then I said, "You know, that apology stuck in my throat, but I finally got it out." I had a big grin on my face and we both laughed.

Later that evening, he was wrong about something, so I said, "Well, what do you say?" Randy has the cutest boyish grin when he's done something wrong. I really love that look. He finally said, "I was wrong and you were right." We gave each other a hug and had another good laugh.

I think some people are afraid to admit they are wrong because others will think less of them. But the opposite is true. It is freeing to admit you are wrong. Hey, we all mess up. But did you know that if we haven't made things right in our relationships, God won't hear our prayers? It's like there's a thick ozone layer keeping our prayers earthbound so they can't get through. Don't believe me? I love this verse as translated by *The Message*: "If you enter your place of worship and, about to make an offering, you suddenly remember a grudge a friend has against you, abandon your offering, leave immediately, go to this friend and make things right. Then and only then, come back and work things out with God" (Matthew 5:23–24). I've made several trips away from the altar myself. Satan will try to talk you out of it—at least, he has with me. That old P-word, "pride," pops up every now and then. But just wash it down with a big piece of humble pie. Even if you feel that you are 99 percent right, what would it hurt to say, "You *might* be right"?

When I worked at a middle school, I had an issue with some seventh-grade students. Dazmine and several other girls laughed and pointed at my flooded pants (pants that were too short). Instead of ignoring them, I made a big deal about it and gave a long, tedious lecture on how I don't make fun of them, and they shouldn't make fun of me. Blah, blah, blah. I'm sure that's all Dazmine and the other kids in class heard after my first sentence. I knew I should stop; I knew I sounded foolish. I was thinking, *Stop, Sherry, you just need to shut up!* But did I? No.

The apostle Paul said, "I know I am rotten through and through so far as my old sinful nature is concerned. No matter which way I turn I can't make myself do right. I want to, but I can't. When I want to do good, I don't; and when I try to not to do wrong, I do it anyway" (Romans 7:18–19 LB). I guess if Paul could admit when he was wrong, then I can, too.

I saw Dazmine later that day and I admitted that I was wrong to react the way I did. I decided to *really* humble myself and apologize to her and the other girls in front of the class the next day. The whole seventh-grade group graciously accepted my apology. Things got better between us since that day. I think they respected me more because I apologized.

I bet that you, too, will be more respected when you are able to admit you are wrong and apologize. And I guarantee your prayers will be unblocked. Like Joyce Meyer, the renowned television minister, once said, "Being right is highly overrated." Maybe you win your case—but at the cost of your relationship with your spouse, the respect of your students, or your customers at work. We are meant to be peacemakers. Start today. Find the friend who has a grudge against you. In Paul's words, "Make things right." You will find afterward that you walk a little more lightly and that song comes back to you.

Allow yourself to be *f-r-e-e-e-e!*

Sheep Ears   7

QUESTIONS

1. If you are going to "make things right," is it better to do it quickly or to wait for at least a year? (a)

2. Do you think it's harder to apologize to a stranger than a family member? Why or why not?

3. If someone admits they are wrong, should you ignore them or forgive them? (b)

4. When someone has offended you but not apologized, is it okay to repay them with evil? (c)

5. List the people with whom you need to "make things right."

6. Do you believe that a person who refuses to admit his mistakes will ever be successful? (d)

7. How does God want us to live our lives? (e)

SCRIPTURAL ANSWERS

(a) "In light of all this, here's what I want you to do … I want you to get out there and walk—better yet, run!—on the road God called you to travel … And mark that you do this with humility and discipline … alert at noticing differences and quick at mending fences" (Ephesians 4:1–3).

(b) "Be kind and compassionate to one another, forgiving each other, just as in Christ God forgave you" (Ephesians 4:32 NIV).

(c) "Do not repay evil for evil. Be careful to do what is right in the eyes of everybody. If it is possible, as far as it depends on you, live at peace with everyone" (Romans 12:17–18 NIV).

(d) "A man who refuses to admit his mistakes can never be successful.

But if he confesses and forsakes them; he gets another chance" (Proverb 28:13 LB).

(e) "Turn from all known sin and spend your time in doing good. Try to live in peace with everyone" (Psalm 34:14 LB).

3

Have you ever asked God to pick a friend for you?

My best girlfriend in the whole world was Gwendolyn Sue McNulty. We called her Sue. I first got acquainted with her after I was attacked by two dogs. She was the secretary of the school where I worked. When I returned to school after a three-week recovery, she took me to a clothing store and told me to pick out a scarf as a gift of encouragement.

After that trip to the store, we started to bond. We ate lunch together every day at school, went garage-sale hopping, and even went to the dirt track races for a different kind of outing. I helped her polish her silver once a year (it took all day) and at Christmas wrapped all her presents for her (this took about two days). Christmas was her favorite time of year. She kept one tree up year-round and put another one up before Thanksgiving. Her house was always decked out in holiday spirit.

Sue informed me one day that she was having some health problems so she was going to the doctor. She said, "I'll be fine. Most likely it's a bladder infection." But it was cancer. After one of her kidneys was removed, her doctor said everything should be okay. And for a while, it was. Then she told me that her problem had returned. Sue had her other kidney removed and dialysis became her lifeline.

Sue was a very strong woman I truly admired, as well as loved. She continued working, and we still ate lunch together, still enjoyed going to garage sales—but there was always the underlying knowledge that her days were numbered, barring a miracle.

On my fifty-fourth birthday, I called Sue to rib her about forgetting my birthday. She had forgotten it the previous year and asked me to not let it happen again. Earlier that week, on Tuesday, we had had a nice but short visit and told each other "I love you" before we parted. When I called her that Friday night, I didn't expect what her husband said. "I'm sorry, Sue won't be able to talk to you tonight, or any other night. She took a turn for the worse, and I don't think she's going to make it." I was devastated. She was hospitalized and put on a morphine drip to combat her constant pain. I never got to talk with her again.

We had been close friends for twelve years, and I had a big hole in my heart. I knew that Sue was in a better place, free of pain. But I missed her terribly. Six months later, I went through a tough time at work. Sue had always been the one who had consoled and advised me through any crises I might have. That's when her death *really* hit me hard. She was gone. I went into a period of grief that I couldn't shake for about four months.

As I grieved, I prayed. "God, I really miss Sue. I know she's in heaven, but I'm still here and I feel lost. Please send me a godly friend. Pick one out for me, because I know that *you* know who I need, and who needs me. My mom is great, but she lives nine hours away. I love my husband, but sometimes I just need a gal pal. In Jesus's name I pray. Amen."

Several women came in and out of my life, but none of them felt like a godly appointment. I was content to wait, though, because I knew that when God set the friendship up, it would be right. However, I was extremely lonely while I waited. No one but God knew to what degree. I wore a smile on my face but the hole was still there, deep in my heart.

About ten months after Sue passed, I went to Walmart after the Wednesday-night church service. I recognized a lady from church pushing her buggy, and she recognized me. We exchanged a slight wave and said "Hi." About five minutes later, we passed each other again, exchanged another slight wave, and spoke briefly. When this happened a third time, we started laughing. Walmart is so big that it would be hard to find someone in that supersized store even if you were looking for them. And here we had run into each other three times! It was very unusual. *God, is there some reason you want me to see this lady?* I thought.

"Yes. The next time you see her, introduce yourself." So I lingered in

Sheep Ears

the store a little longer than usual. I was hoping to see her again, but it didn't happen.

At the next Wednesday-night service, I spotted her in the pew, remembered my assignment, and stuck out my hand. "Excuse me, but I think I'm supposed to introduce myself to you. My name is Sherry." She told me her name was Gwen. Her name was the short version of Sue's first name. What a coincidence.

I wasn't really sure what to do after that, so I asked her if she wanted me to pray with her about something. She needed some direction about finances, and I wanted to find a place to take my grandchildren swimming that summer. After our prayers, God put a word in my heart to give her. I told her that I had friends who had gotten a reverse mortgage. This eventually led to action that was the answer to her desperate prayer. I thanked God for giving me wisdom and a listening ear. God also found a solution to my swimming issue. I figured that was the end of our association, so I didn't think much more about our encounter.

But God had a different plan. Gwen and I kept noticing each other in church, so we decided to sit together. Things were very casual; we had polite conversations about the weather, the dates of our birthdays, the good sermons Pastor Bell preached. For some reason, her birthday kept sticking in my mind. "Take her out to eat for her birthday, and take her out to a play at The Arts and Science Center," God said.

"God, I barely know her. She's may think I'm a weirdo. She will probably say no, anyway."

"That's all right, just ask." And ask I did. She surprised me when she said yes. Gwen actually seemed happy that I had asked her. *Whew! At least she didn't think I was a fruitcake.*

We went to the play and ate at Chili's afterward. Something happened as we sat there. I was talking to her when God interrupted my thoughts. "Sherry, this is the friend I have picked for you."

Oh, my! I had forgotten my request. God was setting us up for a friendship. I could tell that she felt the same way. We bonded at that meal and have been inseparable ever since. As she explained, "It's like we're two little girls playing in a sandbox, or two friends kicking a can down the street; just happy to be in each other's presence." I can finish her sentences and she can finish mine. It's hard to explain.

She encourages me when I'm down, and I encourage her when she's down. Ours is a spiritual friendship set up by God. "There are 'friends' who pretend to be friends, but there is a friend who sticks closer than a brother" (Proverb 18:24 LB). David had Jonathan, Jesus had Peter, James, and John, and Paul had Timothy. And now I had Gwen. Everyone needs a God-appointed friend.

I have gone into great detail about how we met so that you could see how gradually a friendship begins. There are no bells, whistles, or thunder crashes. Only small nudges.

Do you have a heart that aches for a friend you've lost? Do you wish God would pick a friend for you? It's possible, you know. God says, "Yes, ask anything using my name, and I will do it!" (John 14:14 LB). You can be assured that God is pleased when you ask Him.

Maybe you need a godly husband. Just ask. Maybe you are not able to have children of your own. Ask God. He may have children who need you as much as you need them, praying to be adopted. God will help you find each other. And when God sets it up, you'll know it's right. God may interrupt your thoughts and say, "I picked them for you." Ask in Jesus's name, believe, do good to others, and wait for God to connect you.

"Don't be impatient for the Lord to act! Keep traveling steadily along his pathway and in due season he will honor you with every blessing" (Psalm 37:34 LB). That includes husbands, children, and friends!

Questions

1. Has God ever brought you together supernaturally with a friend? Who is he/she? How do you feel about that friendship? (a)

2. Which is better: a nearby friend or a distant relative? Explain your answer. (b)

3. For what reasons do we need to have godly friends? (c, d)

4. What do you feel are the qualities of a godly friend?

5. Who was David's close friend? (e)

6. Do you believe close friends will be asked to have more responsibility for helping you through hard times? Explain. (f)

7. Do you need a friend, but not know what to pray for? (g)

Scriptural Answers

(a) "Just as lotions and fragrance give sensual delight, a sweet friendship refreshes the soul" (Proverbs 27:9).

(b) "Don't leave your friends or your parents' friends and run home to your family when things get rough. Better a nearby friend than a distant family" (Proverb 27:10).

(c) "The godly give good advice to their friends; the wicked lead them astray" (Proverb 12:26 NLT).

(d) "As iron sharpens iron, so a friend sharpens a friend" (Proverb 27:17 NLT).

(e) "And Jonathan made a covenant with David because he loved him as himself" (1 Samuel 18:3 NIV).

(f) "Jesus saw his mother and the disciple he loved standing near her. He said to his mother, 'Woman here is your son.' Then to the disciple, 'Here is your mother.' From that moment the disciple accepted her as his own mother" (John 19:26–27).

(g) "Don't bargain with God. Be direct. Ask for what you need. This is not a cat-and-mouse, hide-and-seek game we're in" (Luke 11:10).

4
Have you ever been attacked by dogs?

The day started out normally, but it didn't take long for things to go bad. It all began with a desire to drink coffee at my elderly neighbor's house before my work day started.

To give you a little background, Willene's husband had died about two years before. She was retired and alone so I knew it would be hard for her to get out of bed after his passing. I told her that I would come and drink coffee with her every morning before I went to work. She loved the idea, and we cherished the warm cup of java and the small conversations that jump-started each day.

The women's group in her church purchased a beautiful white Spitz dog to serve as her companion. She named him Boaz, and he filled a big gap in her life during this tough time. *He* wasn't the problem. Willene's daughter and granddaughter had moved in with her about a month prior to "that day" with their harlequin Great Dane, Nala, who looked like a small pony, and a Sharpei-mix named Trouble. All three of the dogs stayed inside the small house.

After the entourage arrived, I was a little apprehensive about sticking with the routine, but they all assured me the dogs were like big babies. Sure enough, every morning I knocked lightly at the door and, with newspaper in hand, entered the house to the sweet aroma of coffee. I'd sit in the chair at the kitchen table as Nala the Great Dane would lie underneath me. It was amazing to see such an enormous dog so docile.

I would pet her head to the right of my chair, and to the left, I'd pet her back. Her tail beat rhythmically as we all engaged in conversation, Bailey, Willene's granddaughter, sitting on my left, and Willene sitting on my right.

This was our routine every morning. Ho hum. A boring, mundane story, right? I would have agreed with you—that is, up until the attack.

That day, I picked up the newspaper, like I always did. I threw my cell phone onto the car seat, then I thought, *No, my husband or sons might need me.* So I picked my phone back up and slipped it in my left front pocket. I tapped gently on the storm door as always. This is where the boring story changes. As I took a step into the kitchen and the screen door shut behind me, Nala, the pony dog, bounded at me from the hallway and leaped for my face, her teeth bared.

Everything moved in slow motion, but amazingly, I was able to quickly put up my left arm in front of my face. She ripped the skin of my forearm and blood started pouring out. She barked once; this excited Trouble, who joined the melee. Somehow, I knew to throw the newspaper down in case they felt threatened by me. Somehow, I knew to keep my hands close to my body. I slowly backed out the door, backed through the carport, and edged toward the backyard gate, all the while pursued by the dogs. I thought only of protecting my face and my heart, and trying to keep from falling. They were in such a frenzy that falling would mean certain death for me. They took turns lunging at me and biting me, shredding my pants and puncturing my legs.

I prayed, "Please, God, help me not to feel it when they bite me!" Believe it or not, I *didn't* feel it when they bit me. Later I thought, *What a silly prayer, I should have prayed for them not to bite me!* But when you have only a couple of seconds to pray, you don't worry about accuracy.

I screamed for Willene to get her granddaughter, Bailey, but she was frozen in disbelief and fear with her hands on her face like the *Home Alone* kid after he put on aftershave. Bailey was in the bathroom and unaware of the attack. When she realized what was happening, she ran outside and commanded the dogs to stop. They immediately froze. It was like someone had turned off a frenzy switch. The dogs ran across the street and acted as though nothing had happened. All of this took a matter of minutes, but I guarantee you, it was a *long* few minutes.

I was too upset to drive, so I staggered past the two houses to my home and banged on the door. I had blood all over me, and my pants were shredded. My hands were outstretched. I guess I was in shock because I couldn't utter a word. When my son Paul opened the door, he blurted out, "Mom, what happened? Did you kill someone?!" (I don't know why, but I laugh every time I think how strange I must have looked to him. "Bye, Paul, I'm going to drink coffee." Three minutes later, I returned a bloody zombie.)

So that's what happened. I ended up missing three weeks of work. Some of you might be wondering: Where was God in all this? What about your protective angels? Did the dogs have to be put down? Do you have nightmares? Are you afraid of dogs now?

I know where God was: right there with me. How else did I know to throw the newspaper down so it wouldn't look threatening? My normal response would have been to swat away at the dogs. So how did I know to keep my hands and arms tucked in and not to make defensive swings? How did I know I had to try not to fall? It was because of the inner voice speaking to me, guiding me: the Holy Spirit. "Yet I am always with you; you hold me by my right hand. You guide me with your counsel" (Psalms 73:23–24 NIV). Believe me, I couldn't merely push a pause button, leave to study a book about how to behave in a dog attack, return, and be empowered. God was right there with me, holding my hand and giving me instructions.

Remember that I put my cell phone in my pocket? It seemed an insignificant detail at the time, didn't it? I'm glad I followed that nudge (or counsel, if you will) because I had a ten-inch circular bruise on my leg where the main artery is located. But right in the middle of the bruise was a rectangular, white spot where my phone had protected that important area. I believe that if that artery had been severed, I would have bled to death. Coincidence? No way!

I know you haven't seen my reflexes, but I can assure you that I'm not the fastest woman on the block. There's no way ordinarily that I could have gotten my arm up fast enough on my own power to cover my face. Do you honestly think I could have remained standing with two powerful dogs attacking me? "[God] ordered his angels to guard you wherever you go. If you stumble, they'll catch you; their job is to keep you from falling"

Sheep Ears 17

(Psalms 91:11–12). The injuries could have been much worse. I am thankful for the angels that protected me that day and kept me from falling.

The dogs were put in quarantine for ten days and then released. While they were at the shelter, Willene invited me to her house for supper. I knew she felt bad about the attack. I went because I didn't want her to think that I blamed her. During the meal, Bailey told me that Nala had never attacked anyone before me, so what happened was a shock to everyone.

Do I have nightmares? No. Am I fearful of dogs? No. I have three: one small, one medium, and one large. I walk them regularly. Every now and then, a dog in the neighborhood gets loose and comes at us. God instructs me to say, "In the name of Jesus, go back home!" And they do. "The wise counsel God gives when I'm awake is confirmed by my sleeping heart" (Psalm 16:7).

After the attack, I remembered all the hardships that Joseph goes through in the Bible. When he talks to his brothers, he says, "'Don't be afraid. Am I in the place of God? You intended to harm me, but God intended it for good to accomplish what is now being done … So then, don't be afraid, I will provide for you and your children.' And he reassured them and spoke kindly to them" (Genesis 50:19–21 NIV).

I decided that if that was in the Bible, then I was going to believe it for myself. *God, I don't know how you're going to work this out, but please work it out for good,* I thought. And God did. I got a monetary settlement from the injury. It enabled our son Paul to attend baseball showcase events where he could be scouted by colleges for his athletic ability. He traveled to Arizona, California, Oklahoma, and Illinois, and ended up getting a fantastic scholarship to Baylor University. Paul's coaches told us that they had seen him more often than they had seen the local Texas boys! Thank you, God. You never fail.

Now don't get me wrong. I didn't wake up the morning of the attack and say, "Well, this is the day I will be attacked by dogs, but it's gonna work out because now we'll have money to pay for the showcases." If I had been given a choice in the matter, I would have said, "No, thank you, God, I think I'll pass." But it did happen. The angels, God, and God's Word were there. I came through the fire and I'm here to say, "God never fails!"

Questions

1. Is it possible to remain calm when tragedy strikes? (a)

2. Has God ever given you supernatural peace in a horrible situation? What happened?

3. Has God ever told you to do something unusual (like my putting the cell phone in my pocket) that you later discovered was a divine instruction? (b)

4. Did you follow His voice, or ignore Him? (c)

5. In a crisis, can we expect angels to protect us? (d)

6. As Christians, can we expect God to work things out for our good? (e)

7. Has God ever worked out a tragedy or crisis for your good? If so, write your story down

Scriptural Answers

(a) "When besieged, I'm calm as a baby. When all hell breaks loose, I'm collected and cool" (Psalm 27:3).

(b) "I will instruct you and teach you in the way you should go; I will counsel you and watch over you" (Psalm 32:8 NIV).

(c) "Don't be ornery like a horse or mule that needs bit and bridle to stay on track" (Psalm 32:9).

(d) "God's angel sets up a circle of protection around us while we pray" (Psalm 34:7).

(e) "We know that in all things God works for the good of those who love him, who have been called according to his purpose" (Romans 8:28 NIV).

5
Have you ever been depressed?

When I was around seventeen years old, I went through a period of depression. It lasted about a year. I had many sleepless nights. Tossing and turning in my bed became the norm, not the exception. My upbeat temperament turned sullen. I would soon graduate and didn't know which direction I should follow. *Should I marry Randy, or am I too young to know whether he's the one?* Should I go to college in a different town, or stay and go to the college in my hometown? *It seems like I've been happy, but why am I happy, anyway? Come to think of it, who are my true friends?* I'd attended six different schools and had never really gotten to establish a bonding relationship with anyone. *Poor me. Pitiful Sherry. No reason to be happy, so why even pretend anymore?*

Those were my thoughts. Drowning and wallowing in self-pity was my daily exercise. I prayed for deliverance. "God, help me! I don't know what to do. I can't snap myself out of this confusion." One day, I read a saying that made me think: "Ask yourself if you're happy and you cease to be." I contemplated that simple sentence. *It seems like I used to be happy; but when I try to figure out why I am happy, I can't put my finger on it.* I finally understood: I had been overanalyzing my life. I wasn't trusting God; I was trusting myself. I was completely self-absorbed.

I decided to test my new theory. That night, while I lay in bed, I prayed for everyone I could think of. After going through my list, I began to pray for people in other states, other countries, and for world peace. I thanked God for everything I could think of. I went to sleep and woke up refreshed the next day. *Hmm!* I felt I was on to something. Maybe I'd been thinking about myself too much. I should be looking outward instead of inward. I asked my mom if I could clean the house for her. I also volunteered to wash our car and mow the lawn.

When bedtime came, I started my prayer list all over again, praying for the same people and thanking Him for the same things. I don't think God minded one bit. Another peaceful night. I even found a Scripture in *The Living Bible* that said, "I lie awake at night thinking of you—of how much you have helped me—and how I rejoice through the night beneath the protecting shadow of your wings" (Psalms 63:6–7).

The next week, my dad came to me and said, "Sherry, I found a job for you."

"Really?" I exclaimed. "That's great!"

"There's an elderly woman who needs help around the house and someone to run errands for her. It would only be two days a week."

I couldn't hide my disappointment. "Dad, you know I'm uncomfortable around old people. Why would you think I would like this? You've got to be kidding!"

But guess what? I took the job anyway. I learned to love that little old lady and she loved me. I was afraid of what I didn't understand.

Before I knew it, my depression had disappeared. My questions took care of themselves. I went to college in my hometown. I dated Randy for four years and we have been happily married for thirty-eight years. I don't even worry about asking myself if I'm happy anymore; I am. And I have plenty of friends. These may have seemed like petty things to you, but when you aren't thinking straight, they are monumental. I'm not talking about clinical depression, I mean the kind that is brought about by faulty thinking. Paul said, "Let heaven fill your thoughts; don't spend your time worrying about things down here" (Colossians 3:2 LB).

If you feel yourself slipping like I did, snap yourself out of it. Pray for other people. Be kind to others. The Bible said that Jesus went about doing good. If that's what He did, then it's the least that we should do. If you're sitting on a pew wondering why no one will speak to you, get up and introduce yourself. I imagine that other people are lonely, too. Open the door for someone. If you have some gum in your purse, don't sneak it into your mouth; offer to share it with others. You will reap what you sow.

Face what you fear. You might discover it was all in your head. You might discover you are stronger than you thought. You might find a friend around the corner from the place you used to fear.

> Trust God from the bottom of your heart;
> Don't try to figure out everything on your own.
> Listen to God's voice in everything you do; everywhere you go;
> He's the one who will keep you on track;
> Don't assume that you know it all.
> Run to God! Run from evil!
> —Proverbs 3:5–7

QUESTIONS

1. Have you ever been depressed? If so, how long did it last?

2. If you start to feel depressed or anxious, what should you focus your mind on? (a)

3. Do you feel more depressed when you are tired? Write down how exhaustion affects you. Will God energize you? (b)

4. How can you give your anxiety to God when you need peace? (c, d)

5. How much can you add to your life by worrying? (e)

6. What kind of attitude should we have when we pray to God? (f)

SCRIPTURAL ANSWERS

(a) "Give your entire attention to what God is doing right now, and don't get worked up about what may or may not happen tomorrow. God will help you deal with whatever hard things come up when the time comes" (Matthew 6:34).

(b) "He energizes those who get tired, gives fresh strength to dropouts. For even young people tire and drop out, young folk in their prime stumble and fall. But those who wait upon God get fresh strength. They spread their wings and soar like eagles. They run and don't get tired, they walk and don't lag behind" (Isaiah 41:29–31).

(c) "Cast all your anxiety on Him because he cares for you" (1 Peter 5:7 NIV).

(d) "You will keep in perfect peace him whose mind is steadfast because he trusts in you" (Isaiah 26:3 NIV).

(e) "Who of you by worrying can add a single hour to his life?" (Matthew 6:27 NIV).

(f) "Enter His gates with thanksgiving and His courts with praise" (Psalm 100:4 NASB).

6
Have you ever been diagnosed with cancer?

One year, my husband went in for a routine health exam. We were quite surprised when the nurse called and asked him to return to the doctor's office the next morning. Noticing the terseness in her voice, I asked her if I should come with him. She said, "Yes, I think you should." The next day, Dr. Harris solemnly told us that something unusual had shown up on Randy's lung x-ray. He wanted Randy to see a pulmonary specialist, Dr. Dargo. Dr. Harris didn't use the C-word, but it was implied. Randy and I looked at each other in disbelief. Neither of us had smoked a day in our lives.

At the consultation with Dr. Dargo, he recommended a CAT scan. As I looked at the x-ray image, I recognized a familiar shape. After leaving the doctor's office, I asked Randy if he had noticed anything peculiar about the shape of the abnormal spot.

"No, did you?"

I told him it looked a lot like the cartoon character SpongeBob SquarePants. We both laughed and from then on we called the spot "SpongeBob."

After the results came back, Dr. Dargo wanted to take a PET scan. Another picture of SpongeBob.

We were pretty shocked when the doctor reported that the scan showed "hot activity" (definitely not good). Next, he scheduled a biopsy and a swab of Randy's lungs. I told Dr. Dargo about our nickname, SpongeBob. He gave a slight chuckle, but there was no sparkle in his eyes.

Why weren't we afraid? Scriptures told us, "Be strong and courageous … Do not be afraid or discouraged, for the Lord God, my God, is with you. He will not fail you or forsake you" (1 Chronicles 28:20 NIV).

I guess we were just childlike enough to believe Him. Of course, we prayed and the people in our church prayed for Randy. We recognized that something was there in Randy's lung, but we had peace. This Scripture came alive in our souls: "He will keep in perfect peace all those who trust in him, whose thoughts turn often to the Lord! Trust in the Lord God always, for in the Lord God Jehovah is your everlasting strength" (Isaiah 26:3–4 LB).

The day for the biopsy came. Dr. Dargo told us he would take a snippet of SpongeBob and swab Randy's lung to determine what was going on in there. After he finished the procedures, Dr. Dargo came into the post-op room, looking baffled. Everything moved in a blur because it was so confusing. He spoke in a lot of technical terms that we didn't understand. Then we heard words that we definitely understood. "There was nothing there." That was all we needed to hear.

I threw my hands up in the air, and started hollering. "That's because Jesus healed him!"

"That's not what I'm saying," Dr. Dargo said.

I said, "I know you're not! That's what *I'm* saying!"

With a reserved look, he said, "Well, we still have to get the results back from the lab, so we won't know till then."

I repeated my shout of triumph. "Woohoo! Thank you, Jesus!"

Dr. Dargo seemed exasperated, as though he knew not to argue with a woman. "Well, we'll see."

"We sure will, because the tests will *prove* that he was healed." I thought of the Scripture, "[Jesus] personally carried away our sins in his own body on the cross so we can be dead to sin and live for what is right. You have been healed by his wounds" (1 Peter 2:24 NLT). Not "will be," but "have been." Jesus doesn't have to die daily for our healing; He took care of that in one day. Our only requirement is to believe.

We had to wait six weeks for the results. We slept well in that time. Sure, doubt tried to creep up every now and then. But as my dad had preached while I was growing up, "You can't keep the birds from flying over your head, but you can keep them from building a nest." So the doubt birds flew over, but they were never allowed to build a nest. I heard my husband sing in the shower—proof that he trusted God.

We finally went back to Dr. Dargo's office, and as we waited for him, we reminisced about our old buddy SpongeBob. Not with fear and trepidation, but as though he were a long-forgotten friend. After all, I've heard that the best way to lose an enemy is to make them your friend.

Dr. Dargo swung open the door and immediately began to list the test results. Negative, negative, (turn page) negative, negative. He went on and on. With the last negative, he looked up and said, "Well, Mr. Witt, I don't know what to say except that there was something there and now there's not."

Randy and I both smiled. The doctor repeated what he had said. I guess he thought we hadn't heard him. My husband popped up and said, "Yeah, 'cause you know cancer showed up on all three tests, but now it's *gone!*"

Dr. Dargo replied, "Well, I don't know what to tell you, Mr. Witt. But there was something there, and now it's not." I think he said it about four times before we left his office.

I'm not sure if the doctor ever believed it was God, but it didn't matter. We knew. Randy said, "Sherry, I always felt like God would heal me." Randy's faith was so strong. After that, he prayed for several of his friends who had cancer, and all but one of them were completely healed.

Maybe you've wondered before whether it is God's will for you to be healed. Maybe you have your doubts. Look to Scriptures for the answer. A leper saw Jesus, fell down at his feet and said, "'If you want to, you can cleanse me.' Jesus put out his hand, touched him, and said, 'I want to. Be clean.' Then and there his skin was smooth, the leprosy gone" (Luke 5:12–13). Jesus not only healed the leper, He also restored his decayed skin. Jesus wants you to be healed, too.

Why are some people healed and some people not? I really don't know. If I did know, I would be God. I know what Randy's initial reports said, but we serve a God who is bigger than test results. The Rich Mullins song "Awesome God" resonates: "Our God is an awesome God / He reigns from heaven above / With wisdom, power, and love / Our God is an awesome God."

My best friend, Sue, died of cancer. Today, I attended the funeral of a coworker who lost her battle with cancer. It would be wrong to say that they didn't believe enough or that they were too fearful. The apostle Paul had a "thorn in his flesh." It could have been cancer; it could have been bad eyesight. It could even have been a barking dog. Paul said, "Three times I begged the Lord to take it away from me" (2 Corinthians 12:8 NIV). God in His sovereignty didn't take Paul's thorn away. And no one had more faith than Paul.

I once had a mammogram and received a call to come in for a second screening. Something didn't look right. Maybe it was a shadow, but it was best to make sure. I made the appointment and my son Paul noticed that I didn't seem too concerned. "Mom, aren't you nervous?"

"No, Paul. If I die, I go to heaven. If it's nothing, then I'll thank God. Either way, I win."

He looked at me pensively, said nothing, and turned away. What *could* he say?

I'm reminded of Shadrach, Meshach, and Abednego, who stood up defiantly to King Nebuchadnezzar when he threatened to throw them into a blazing furnace because they would not bow to his statue. "Your threat means nothing to us. If you throw us in the fire, the God we serve can rescue us from your roaring furnace and anything else you might cook up, O King. But even if he doesn't, it wouldn't make a bit of difference, O King. We still wouldn't serve your gods or worship the gold statue you set up" (Daniel 3:16–18).

My pastor, Gary Bell, told us of the story of Horatio Spafford. He wrote the song "It Is Well with My Soul" as he sailed over the spot where his four beautiful daughters drowned when the Steamer Ville de Havre was struck by an iron sailing ship. Listen to the words of the first verse:

When peace, like a river, attendeth my way,
When sorrows like sea billows roll;
Whatever my lot, Thou hast taught me to say,
It is well, it is well with my soul.

We never know how our situations will turn out. Cancer, multiple sclerosis, divorce, miscarriage. God beckons us to pray, and when we pray, to believe. We must be like David and seek God as long as we have breath left in us. David fasted, wept, and prayed as his child fought for his life. His son died, but his faith in God never wavered.

I want to be like King David, Horatio Spafford, and the men thrown into the fiery furnace. God can rescue me, but even if He doesn't, I will trust Him. I will believe in healing as long as there is hope, but even if all is lost, I will still square my shoulders and declare, "Whatever my lot, you have taught me to say that it is well with my soul."

Questions

1. Is it okay to "talk to" an illness? If so, what should you say? (a)

2. Is it proper to ask people in church to pray for you when you're sick? (b)

3. Can your faith in Jesus heal you? Why or why not? (c)

4. If you've accepted Jesus as your Savior, then when you die, will your body be renewed in heaven or broken down? (d)

5. How is it possible to have peace when you are facing a crisis? (e)

6. Can you be at peace with God if your prayer is never answered? Write down your thoughts.

7. Should we only praise God if our prayers are answered? (f)

Scriptural Answers

(a) "[Jesus] stood over her, told the fever to leave—and it left. Before they knew it, she was getting dinner for them" (Luke 4:39).

(b) "Are you hurting? Pray. Do you feel great? Sing. Are you sick? Call the church leaders to pray and anoint you with oil in the name of the Master. Believing-prayer will heal you, and Jesus will put you on your feet. And if you've sinned, you'll be forgiven—healed inside and out" (James 5:13–15).

(c) "In the presence of all the people, she told why she had touched [Jesus] and how she had been instantly healed. Then he said to her, 'Daughter, your faith has healed you. Go in peace'" (Luke 8:47–48 NIV).

(d) "But there's far more to life for us. We're citizens of high heaven! We're waiting the arrival of the Savior, the Master, Jesus Christ, who will transform our earthly bodies into the glorious bodies like his own. He'll make us beautiful and whole" (Philippians 3:20–21).

(e) "The Lord gives strength to his people; the Lord blesses his people with peace" (Psalm 29:11 NIV).

(f) "I will praise the Lord no matter what happens. I will constantly speak of his glories and grace. I will boast of all his kindness to me. Let all who are discouraged take heart. Let us praise the Lord together and exalt his name" (Psalms 34:1–3 LB).

7
Have you ever been on a crazy deer hunt?

My friend told me not to use clichés when I write. The title of this story could have been "Have you ever been on a wild goose chase?" however I accommodated. But you get the point.

One fall day, I felt God give me a direction to get in my car and drive. I tend to heed directions after the incidents with Cindy and Sara. (See "Have you ever acted quickly?"), so I said, "Okay, God." He said, "Drive to the end of the block and turn right." I did so, and then He said, "Turn left at the stoplight. Now go straight and get onto Interstate 530." He told me to get off at the Walmart exit, which was about five miles from my house. Then He instructed me to go to the parking lot and sit in my car.

I couldn't wait to get there. I just knew something big was about to happen. Maybe I would find someone in distress. Maybe I would see a purse left in a buggy and return it to its rightful owner. Maybe I would save a child in the parking lot from being hit by a car.

I watched with anticipation, ever alert to what God wanted me to do. It seemed like things were happening in slow motion as I waited. After about ten minutes, God said, "Okay, get back on I-530 and head for home." This seemed crazy, but I knew it was God. What can I say? I know His voice. "My sheep listen to my voice; I know them and they follow me" (John 10:27 NIV).

How do you know whether it is His voice? How do sheep know their shepherd's voice? It's kind of hard to explain. How do you hear your child calling "Mom" in a crowded mall full of hundreds of other moms? All the others ignore the call while you know that *your* little darling is the one speaking. You spend time with your children; you nurture them, you love them, you even chastise them. I guess that's how you know God's voice. You spend time with Him, you are nurtured by Him, you love Him, you read His Book, and you even take His chastisement. Gradually you are able to identify that gentle whisper in your heart. You just know.

Anyway, getting back to the story, when I was only two blocks from home, God told me to turn into the parking lot of Big Lots and go inside the store. "Go down the first aisle, turn left at the end, go to the end of the store, and turn left again." At this point I was beginning to wonder, but still I heeded the instructions.

In the greeting card section, I ran into Joyce, a former coworker of mine. We struck up a conversation. She told me she was working through some issues after her husband had suddenly died of a heart attack. God brought to my memory some appropriate Scriptures to share with her. I gave her some encouraging words, and then we held hands and prayed. She told me that she felt so much better about her situation and was now at peace about some decisions she was about to make.

I decided to tell her about God's instructions and how it had felt like a "crazy deer hunt" to me. I told her about the trip to Walmart, the comical waiting period, and the trip to Big Lots right around the corner from where I live. It occurred to me that she might think I was cuckoo, but I told her anyway. Her mouth kind of hung open for a second, and I said, "I know. It sounds weird."

Joyce said, "No, you have no idea! I just came from Walmart, and then for some strange reason I came to Big Lots. I *never* come here."

We both laughed and agreed that God had set it up.

Why did God have me going all over the city only to find my friend two blocks from home? Did I miss the connection at Walmart? I really don't know. But I do know that the Bible says, "To obey [the Lord] is better than sacrifice" (1 Samuel 15:22 NIV). Perhaps God was just testing me to see if I could be trusted to hear and obey His commands. "Whether you turn to the right or to the left, your ears will hear a voice behind you, saying, 'This is the way; walk in it'" (Isaiah 30:21 NIV). Since I'm a visual person, maybe God needed to show me.

So the next time it seems God is asking you to do something a little unusual, just try to listen, no matter how bizarre it sounds. You might find a "dear" at the end of the card aisle needing a little encouragement.

Sheep Ears

Questions

1. Have you ever received instructions from God and wondered if it was a test of obedience? (a)

2. How would you feel if you were Noah and God gave you instructions to build the ark?

3. Did Noah obey, even though it seemed strange to build an ark? (b)

4. What visual did God give Elijah in order to illustrate His voice? (c)

5. What made Abraham so special to God? (d)

6. What did Jesus's mother tell the servants to do when the wedding party ran out of wine? (e)

7. Is there a promise for us if we obey God? (f)

8. Write down any new resolutions you have after having read this story.

Scriptural Answers

(a) "They were there to test Israel and see whether they would obey God's commands that were given to their parents through Moses" (Judges 3:4).

(b) "Noah did everything just as God commanded him" (Genesis 6:22 NIV).

(c) "'Go out and stand before me on the mountain,' the Lord told him. And as Elijah stood there, the Lord passed by, and a mighty windstorm hit the mountain. It was such a terrible blast that the rocks were torn loose, but the Lord was not in the wind. After the wind there was an earthquake, but the Lord was not in the earthquake. And after the earthquake there was a fire, but the Lord was not in the fire. And after the fire there was the sound of a gentle whisper" (1 Kings 19:11–12 NLT).

(d) "All nations on Earth will find themselves blessed through your descendants because you obeyed me" (Genesis 22:18).

(e) "His mother said to the servants, 'Whatever He says to you, do it'" (John 2:5 NKJV).

(f) "This is what I told them: 'Obey me and I will be your God, and you will be my people. Only do as I say and all will be well!'" (Jeremiah 7:23 NLT).

8

Have you ever been recorded?

When my children were born, I gave them each a name and supplied the hospital with our personal information so that they could fill out the birth certificates. When my friend adopted a little girl who was two days old, she did the same thing. We were both ecstatic. My children and her child were each given our families' respective surnames. It didn't matter if the babies were born naturally into our families or adopted; their names were recorded in a book, forever to be loved, forever to be a family.

As our children grew, my husband and I collected photos and memorabilia that would help us remember the cute and sometimes not so cute phases in their lives. I love the pictures, but what mainly excites me is their words of affirmation. For example:

"Thanks for being a great role model. Now I can be the best parent because you showed me how."

"Thanks for showing me how to budget. I'm glad you never gave me too much, because I learned how to make my money stretch."

"I hope I can be half the man you are, Dad."

"Mom, thanks for coming to all my ballgames. You cheered for me when things went well, and you cried with me when I failed."

Even the text at 11:24 p.m.—"Love u"—is treasured.

Those words mean more to me than all the picture albums I could ever have assembled. I've saved and savored them all. They were words recorded on paper as well as in my heart.

When you receive Jesus as your Lord and Savior, He records your name in the Book of Life, and your name is tattooed in His hand (Isaiah 49:16

LB). But were you aware that He also has a Book of Remembrance? Listen to this: "Then those who feared and loved the Lord spoke often of him to each other. And he had a Book of Remembrance drawn up in which he recorded the names of those who feared him and loved to think about him" (Malachi 3:16 LB). So God also records our thoughts.

Not only does God like to see us doing good things for people, He also delights in our words of affirmation. Do you talk to others about God's goodness? Do you brag about what a great Father He is? Do you want to be like Him? Are you thankful when He doesn't spoil you by granting your every wish? When you talk to your friends, are you whining about problems, or are you testifying about His favor? I've got news for you: He's listening. And He's recording everything.

Hebrews 11 talks about the heroes of faith in the Old Testament. Did you know that they also cheer for you? Read a little further to Hebrews 12: "Therefore, since we are surrounded by such a great cloud of witnesses, let us throw off everything that hinders and the sin that so easily entangles, and let us run with perseverance the race marked out for us" (Hebrews 12:1 NIV). *The Message* translates the Scripture thus: "All these pioneers who blazed the way, all these veterans cheering us on."

About eight years before I learned about that Scripture, I experienced the feeling of being cheered on. I had just led a young man to Christ, and I *felt* the applause. I cannot explain the feeling except to say that it was euphoric. I thought I had imagined it at first, but once I saw those verses written in black and white in the Bible, I could boldly proclaim that it really does happen. Your heavenly family is cheering for you in heaven.

Has there been a joyous occasion in your family that you have invited friends to come and share with you? Maybe it was celebrating the birth of a child, a graduation, or a wedding, or perhaps winning the state championship in football or performing at a dance recital. In Psalm 20:5, David says, "When you win, we plan to raise the roof and lead the parade with our banners. May all your wishes come true!" In Jesus's parable of the prodigal son, the father says to his servants, "Let's have a feast and celebrate" (Luke 15:23 NIV). You may have recorded your celebrations in pictures or video and posted them on the Internet for everyone to see. Everyone always looks so happy! You save your recordings to remember the good times.

The apostle Paul says, "Laugh with your happy friends when they're happy, share tears when they're down" (Romans 12:15). Not only does God have sympathy, but also, like a family member, He is right there with us through the bad times.

> You have seen me tossing and turning through the night. You have collected all my tears and preserved them in your bottle! You have recorded every one in your book. The very day I call for help, the tide of battle turns. My enemies flee! This one thing I know: God is for me.
>
> —Psalms 56:8–9 LB

God has seen your torment, and He catches your tears. Have you ever wondered what He does with your tears of sadness? I believe He will exchange them. "To all who mourn ... he will give: beauty for ashes; joy instead of mourning; praise instead of heaviness ... Instead of shame and dishonor, you shall have a double portion of prosperity and everlasting joy" (Isaiah 61:3, 7 LB). That sounds like a great exchange to me. When you think you are alone and crying where no one can see you, God is keeping a count so He can give you double for your trouble.

Have you ever been to a family reunion? Invitations are mailed with a request to RSVP. When you arrive, you see Aunt Irene, Grandpa Fred, baby Emma, and nephew Austin. The cooking is "scrumpdelicious." There are games, singing, laughter, and lots of reminiscing. That's exactly what God is planning for us, but it will be the best reunion ever!

> The Master himself will give the command. Archangel thunder! God's trumpet blast! He'll come down from heaven and the dead in Christ will rise—they'll go first. Then the rest of us who are still alive at the time will be caught up with them into the clouds to meet the Master. Oh, we'll be walking on air! And then there will be one huge family reunion with the Master. So reassure one another with these words.
>
> —1 Thessalonians 4:16–18

There are many tender aspects of God. He adopts you and is your proud papa. Want proof? Listen to this beautiful Scripture:

How blessed is God! And what a blessing he is! He's the Father of our Master, Jesus Christ, and takes us to the high places of blessing in him. Long before he laid down earth's foundations, he had us in mind, had settled on us as the focus of his love, to be made whole and holy by his love. Long, long ago he decided to adopt us into his family through Jesus Christ. (What pleasure he took in planning this!) He wanted us to enter into the celebration of his lavish gift-giving by the hand of his beloved Son.

—Ephesians 1:3–6

God records your name in the Book of Life when you are born into His kingdom. He pulls out His album of all precious memories and celebrates our victories. He is not a fuddy-duddy. He throws parties in our honor. He records the nice things that we say and think about Him in the Book of Remembrance. God catches our tears in a bottle with a wonderful payback in mind. He's planning a reunion that is out-of-this-world. Literally.

He has invited all, but not all have accepted the invitation. God has recorded your response. Ask Jesus into your heart, and I'll be seeing you soon at 777 Heaven Boulevard. Papa has a new wardrobe for everyone and there's plenty of room. Bring as many friends with you as you can!

QUESTIONS

1. Do you believe that accepting Jesus into your heart is the only way to have your name recorded in the Book of Life and the only way to get to Heaven? (a)

2. How can you be saved? (b)

3. Have you asked Jesus to forgive your sins and come into your heart?

4. Do you talk to others about Jesus? (c)

5. Why do you think the Bible says that God "adopted us"? (d)

Sheep Ears

6. Does anyone know when Jesus will return to Earth in a cloud to take us to Heaven? (e)

7. What will happen to you if your name is not recorded in the Book of Life? (f)

Scriptural Answers

(a) "Jesus answered, 'I am the way and the truth and the life. No one comes to the Father except through me'" (John 14:6 NIV).

(b) "If you tell others with your own mouth that Jesus Christ is your Lord and believe in your own heart that God has raised him from the dead, you will be saved. For it is by believing in his heart that a man becomes right with God; and with his mouth he tells others of his faith, confirming his salvation" (Romans 10:9–10 LB).

(c) "Then he said, 'Go into the world. Go everywhere and announce the Message of God's good news to one and all'" (Mark 16:15).

(d) "You can tell for sure that you are now fully adopted as his own children because God sent the Spirit of his Son into our lives, crying out, 'Papa! Father!' Doesn't that privilege of intimate conversation with God make it plain that you are not a slave, but a child? And if you are a child, you're also an heir, with complete access to the inheritance" (Galatians 4:6–7).

(e) "And then at last the signal of my coming will appear in the heavens, and there will be deep mourning in all the earth. And the nations of the world will see me arrive in the clouds of heaven, with power and great glory. And I shall send forth my angels with the sound of a mighty trumpet blast, and they shall gather my chosen ones from the farthest ends of the earth and heaven … But no one knows the date and hour when the end will be—not even the angels. No, nor even God's Son. Only the Father knows" (Matthew 24:30–31, 36 LB).

(f) "And if anyone's name was not found recorded in the Book of Life, he was thrown into the Lake of Fire" (Revelation 20:15 LB).

9

Have you ever been told by your son that he was going to cheat on a test?

When my youngest son, Paul, was in the tenth grade, he stopped me in the kitchen and said, "By the way, Mom, James got the answer key to Mrs. Smith's test. He and some of the other guys are looking at the answers and then they're giving them to me. I hope you understand because the test is *so* hard, no one will be able to pass it."

I knew a lot depended on my response so I shot up a quick, silent prayer for guidance. I knew that since he was a teenager, forbidding him to cheat would only fuel the fire. I know God heard me because this was my reply: "Well, Paul, it's your choice what you do. But I would be much prouder of you making a D or F on your test without cheating than I would be of you getting an A or B while cheating. But thank you for letting me know."

Three days later, Paul came to me and said, "Guess what? I made an 88 on that test I told you about."

I said, "That's good," and turned to walk away. Something told me not to ask if he had cheated.

"Hey, Mom," he said, this time with a smile in his voice, "I didn't cheat."

I wheeled around and gave him a big hug. "Oh, Paul, I'm so proud of you! I knew you wouldn't." And I thanked God for His wisdom in letting Paul arrive at the right decision by himself.

"Train a child in the way he should go, and when he is old, he will not turn from it" (Proverb 22:6 NIV). I knew I wouldn't always be with him to make the right choices. I had wanted to rant about the virtues of honesty. I'd felt like screaming, "Cheaters never win and winners never cheat! You will never succeed in life if you cheat!" But then the decision would have been my will, not Paul's. I knew this was training for the future. I just didn't realize how important it would be until four years later, when Paul was a sophomore at Baylor University.

He called me one day and, like a volcano erupting hot lava, spewed rapid-fire: "Mom, you know I've been struggling in one of my classes. Well, I made a 77 on the test and Mr. Williams called me to the front of the class and in a loud voice he accused me of cheating! He said I had only made Ds and Fs in his class and Ray had been making Cs. We both made a 77 with the exact same answers, so he assumed it was *me* who'd cheated. I told him that I stayed up two nights in a row studying for the test. I *begged* him to let us retake the test, even to make it harder. But he refused. I went to the baseball coach and told him what was happening and he said the athletic department would back me up, but if I had cheated, they would take away my scholarship!"

Then there was silence.

Wow! What can you do? You pray. Paul was six and a half hours away, but God was right there with him. I prayed for an advocate. My son went to the department head and told him what had happened. I don't know all the details, but by the grace of God, Mr. Williams decided to give both of them the same test over again. One made 77 percent, the other made 52 percent. Paul got an apology from Mr. Williams. Not in front of the class as he had been chastised, but privately, by e-mail.

Paul called me to let me know the good news. We rejoiced! He kept his good grade and his scholarship, but what should he do about the apology? Was it enough? Should he demand Mr. Williams apologize in front of his classmates? I told him, "No, walk into the class and act like it never happened. Give a polite smile, not a sarcastic one. Keep your head down and do your work." He followed my advice.

I believe Paul's study habits as well as his meek attitude played a big part in the redemption of his grades. "And we know that God causes everything to work together for the good of those who love God and are called according to his purpose for them" (Romans 8:28 NLT). Well, God sure worked things out magnificently!

Paul made a C that day and finished with a C in the class. Later, he asked me why I hadn't asked him if he had cheated. I told him I had known I didn't have to. I remembered that when he was in the tenth grade, he had made the right choice, so I knew his character.

Thank you, God, for giving me wisdom and words to guide Paul in making his own choices, because there did come a time I wasn't there to decide for him. Proverb 22:6 proved to be true.

QUESTIONS

1. Have your children ever told you they were going to do something dishonest? If so, how did you respond?

2. Do you feel that God will give you wisdom for handling situations in which you are falsely accused? (a)

3. Have you seen how your guidance helped your children in their decisions later in their lives? How?

4. Do you thank God for His wisdom in your child-rearing decisions? (b)

5. Do you think that God will put victims back on their feet? (c)

6. Has God stepped in and worked out injustices in your life? How could you tell it was God working? (d)

SCRIPTURAL ANSWERS

(a) "I'll give you the words and wisdom that will reduce all your accusers to stammers and stutters" (Luke 21:15).

(b) "I give you all the credit, God—you got me out of that mess, you didn't let my toes gloat" (Psalm 30:1).

(c) "God makes everything come out right, he puts victims back on their feet" (Psalm 103:6).

(d) "So what makes you think God won't step in and work justice for his chosen people, who continue to cry out for help? Won't he stick up for them? I assure you, he will. He will not drag his feet" (Luke 18:7–8).

10

Have you ever been under attack?

When I began writing this book, I was healthy. I worked two jobs and loved every minute of it. I wrote a few stories in the summer, but I wasn't convinced they were quality pieces. A few dear friends began to encourage me. December 16, 2010, I resigned from my second job which was at Seabrook Family Christian Center. Then, four days later, a strange malady hit me. I had severe pain in my left wrist. It started around 11:00 a.m. and by 3:00 p.m., the pain was excruciating. My friend talked me into going to the chiropractor. I felt somewhat better afterward, but by nightfall, I couldn't move either of my hands.

Around 10:00 a.m. the next day at school, my upper arms started to hurt. By 2:30 p.m., I was in tears. I couldn't lift either arm any further than one inch from my thighs. My coworkers had to push me up into my truck. It felt like I had had ten tetanus shots in both arms, or been beaten with a baseball bat. I couldn't get out of a chair without assistance.

The next day, my hands and arms were better, but it felt like my left foot had been slammed in a car door. Different areas of my body hurt intensely every day. I never knew where the pain would hit next. I knew only to pray, quote Scriptures, and ask friends for prayer. I took some leftover antibiotics prescribed for a wasp sting, probiotics, liquid aloe vera, cod liver oil, and fish oil. I rested and got a hormone shot, but nothing really changed. My husband even told me that he was so upset watching me suffer that he had to pull his truck off the road once because he was crying so hard. He said he was begging God to take my pain away.

I was in the shower one day and I looked up at a sign that I had taped on the wall a long time ago. It said, "Jesus can heal you everywhere you hurt." It was a quote from Joyce Meyer. I thought, *That's right, Jesus can heal me everywhere I hurt!* But then I felt the Holy Spirit say, "No, this is not pain, this is spiritual warfare." Now I was able to look at my situation in a different way.

I remembered the dream I had had four weeks before my strange pain appeared. In the dream, I was standing outside, talking on my cell phone. I said, "I'm leaving Seabrook." A man wearing a black hoodie ran out from around the corner and knocked me down. A second man came from behind him and proceeded to beat me. He ran off and left me lying on the sidewalk. Other men ran past, ignoring me. At the time, I thought the dream was literal. I felt someone was going to attack me at work. I had worked happily there for eleven years without problems, but now I was afraid of leaving the building at night. Besides, I wanted to devote time to my writing.

After the revelation that I was experiencing spiritual warfare, my eyes were opened. The dream meant that after I resigned, I would be attacked, beaten—and then it would pass me by. That told me that Satan didn't want this book written, so he was going to attack me and beat me down, but in the end, it would pass me by. Hallelujah! Thank you, Jesus.

Even before the Holy Spirit informed me of the spiritual warfare, I had been fighting in the spiritual realm. I had told my friend Gwen that the more I hurt, the more I would write with God's sustaining power; if the pain was extra bad, I would write two stories instead of one. That was my way of spitting in the devil's eye. I would not be defeated! I told the devil that the longer the pain lasted, the bigger a story I would write. *Take that, you stupid devil!* With God on my side, Lucifer was not going to win.

For twenty-three days, I suffered. On the morning of the twenty-fourth day, at 7:30 a.m., I was watching *Believer's Voice of Victory* on television. Kenneth Copeland was speaking. He told of a time when the door of his private plane would not unlock. It was impossible to budge the door. He was at the hotel waiting to go to the airport when someone called him about the situation. They asked him to come quickly.

On the way to the airport, he said, "Okay, God, what words do you want me to say?"

God's answer was, "Door open now." Then God gave him a Scripture to say after he said those words: "And we know that all things work together for good to those who love God, to those who are the called according to His purpose" (Romans 8:28 NKJV). He was baffled by the Scripture at first, because it didn't seem to have anything to do with the door. But immediately after he had said the words God asked him to, he received a phone call. His friend had opened the door effortlessly, as though it were brand new. He realized that "all things work together" referred to the cogs on the door working together. He said he never would have thought of that Scripture on his own.

That gave me an extra surge of faith. I asked, "God, what do you want *me* to *say?*" He gave me a Scripture I was not expecting: John 3:16. Then he told me to plug my name into the Scripture. This is how it went: "For God so loved [Sherry], that He gave His only begotten Son, that [when Sherry] believes in Him, [Sherry] should not perish, but [Sherry will] have everlasting life" (NKJV). That was it, the missing piece! God wanted me to make His word personal by replacing "the world," which seems so generic, with "Sherry." I can't tell you how many times I said that verse the "personal" way. Sometimes, I shortened it to just, "I believe." By 8:50 a.m. that morning, I no longer had any pain! Praise God! I spit in your eye, you stupid devil!

I write this story to encourage others who are going through a barrage of attacks. It may be your marriage, it may finances, it may be illness. God has the *exact* Scripture for you to speak. Ask God what He wants you to say. The Scripture may seem odd at first, but God is never wrong. He will reveal the personal meaning of the Scripture to you. The Word is alive. It will breathe fresh manna into your soul. It will defeat the devil! "Don't be weary in prayer; keep at it; watch for God's answers and remember to be thankful when they come" (Colossians 4:2 LB).

Hallelujah, thank you Jesus! I am free!

Questions

1. Do you feel that any of your physical or financial woes could be an attack from Satan? (a)

2. Should you resist the devil or let him have his way with you? (b)

3. Is it Biblical to combat the Devil with Scripture? Support your answer. (c)

4. Is it possible to be happy when you face trials? (d)

5. How can tests and challenges make you stronger? (e)

6. Write down your favorite battle Scriptures.

Scriptural Answers

(a) "Be self-controlled and alert. Your enemy, the devil, prowls around like a roaring lion looking for someone to devour" (1 Peter 5:8 NIV).

(b) "Submit yourselves, then, to God. Resist the devil, and he will flee from you" (James 4:7 NIV).

(c) "Jesus answered [the Devil] by quoting Deuteronomy: 'It takes more than bread to really live'" (Luke 4:4).

(d) "Consider it pure joy, my brothers, whenever you face trials of many kinds, because you know that the testing of your faith develops perseverance. Perseverance must finish its work so that you may be mature and complete, not lacking anything" (James 1:2–4 NIV).

(e) "Not only so, but we also rejoice in our sufferings, because we know that suffering produces perseverance; perseverance, character; and character, hope" (Romans 5:3–4 NIV).

11
Have you ever been willing?

My husband and I were returning from a Thanksgiving trip in Texas when we looked at the gauge and saw the arrow was pointing to E. We stopped at a TravelCenters of America. It was forty degrees and the wind was really kicking up. The windchill factor was thirty degrees. I went inside the building to stretch my legs while Randy filled the gas tank. When he came in the building, he asked me if I had any clothes hangers in the truck. He said, "There's this poor old woman panicking at the pumps. She's wearing a long robe and house slippers and she's going from person to person begging for help because she locked her keys in her car. The door isn't shut tightly. I think I can pry it open and use a clothes hanger to pick up her keys from the seat."

I told him that we didn't have a hanger, but maybe there was one in the store. He promptly asked the cashier and a customer overheard Randy's request. The man said, "Follow me to my car, I have several hangers."

My husband returned to the frantic lady and the customer returned to the store. I was looking through the window, admiring my husband for his chivalrous deed, when I suddenly remembered to thank the stranger for the clothes hanger. He and his wife were just about to turn the corner of the aisle out of sight when I hollered, "By the way, thanks for the hanger. Hopefully, he can make it work."

The man said, "Sure, no problem," then he hesitated. Sheepishly, he added, "You know, unlocking cars is what I do for a living."

"Really? Maybe you could help him," I said excitedly.

"Oh, I don't have my equipment with me," he replied. "You know, the slide bar that will pop the door lock is at my shop."

"Do you live anywhere around here?" I asked, pushing for more information.

"Sure, just across the highway."

I'm sure my mouth hung open for a second as I took his statement in. At this point I was thinking, *Well, why don't you drive the four tenths of a mile and get your tool.* But I didn't want to hear any excuses. I thought, *Even if he gave Randy the tool, Randy wouldn't know how to use it.* I thanked him again for the hanger and turned around to watch my knight in shining armor.

At this point, another man, rather sloppy in appearance and very portly, appeared out of nowhere to help my husband. It only took about five minutes for them to fish out the keys with the shepherd's crook they'd fashioned out of the hanger. I watched as the former damsel in distress threw her arms up in a victorious gesture, clapped her hands excitedly, and hugged them both.

My husband returned and gave me a cute little smile, as if to say, "No big deal." But it was a big deal to me. I remembered something he'd told me about twenty years ago. He had changed a flat tire for an elderly couple who were stranded on the side of the highway. He said, "Sherry, I always stop to help people in trouble because I know that someone will always stop and help you." And they have. I'm so grateful when I see his kind deeds. But there was also another thought going through my head: *The man who unlocked doors for a living was not willing to do the job. Randy and another guy were willing, and they got the job done.*

It reminded me of David's confrontation with Goliath, the Philistine giant. The soldiers in the Israeli troops had lots of equipment: armor, shields, and swords. But they were afraid to fight the giant. David, the shepherd boy, did not like the way Goliath defied God and Israel. Even though he didn't have any fighting gear, he was *willing* to fight.

David fastened on [Saul's] sword over the tunic and tried walking around, because he was not used to them. "I cannot go in these," he said to Saul, "because I am not used to them." So he took them off. Then he took his staff in his hand, chose five smooth stones from the stream, put them in the pouch of his shepherd's bag and with his sling in his hand, approached the Philistine.

—1 Samuel 17:39–40 NIV

David was willing to defend his God and his country, so God gave him the ability to complete the job. "So David triumphed over the Philistine with a sling and a stone; without a sword in his hand he struck down the Philistine and killed him" (1 Samuel 17:50 NIV).

That same day, our son called to tell us what had transpired in his neighborhood. A cute little puppy had escaped through a hole in his neighbor's fence. Being a dog lover, Paul said he could imagine how he would feel if one of his dogs had escaped. He returned the pup to the owner. He said he felt kind of silly, but offered to help the man repair his fence. The man jumped at the offer, but told Paul that he didn't have any equipment or supplies to mend the fence. Paul told the man not to worry. He had some spare lumber and tools they could use to repair the hole. A few hours later, the fence was mended and the puppy was safe. Another knight in shining armor—maybe not physical armor that glitters in the sun, but the spirit of the soldier who rises to the question, "Are you willing?"

I once heard Reverend Happy Caldwell talk about God asking him to form a Christian television station in Arkansas. He said, "God, why are you asking *me*? There are people more qualified than me to do this." God said, "I asked seven other people before I asked you, but none were willing." VTN was born after Reverend Caldwell said yes.

What has God asked you to do? Help a neighbor? Maybe you don't think that's very Biblical, but "[Jesus] went through the country helping people and healing everyone that was beaten down by the Devil. He was able to do all this because God was with him." Another translation says that "He went around doing good"(Acts 10:38 NIV).

Maybe He's asked you to sing or preach. Maybe he wants you to teach a class or write a book. Do you think you're unqualified? God delights in giving ability to people who are underqualified but willing. Moses doubted the Israelites would follow his leadership. He said, "What if they do not believe me or listen to me and say, 'The Lord did not appear to you?' Then the Lord said to him, 'What is that in your hand?' 'A staff,' he replied" (Exodus 4:1–2 NIV). Then Moses used his staff to perform many miracles from God.

Sheep Ears

When Jesus preached all day to thousands of people, He asked Philip where they could go to buy food for the crowd. Philip told Jesus that it would cost a fortune to feed everyone. "Then Andrew, Simon Peter's brother, spoke up. 'There's a youngster here with five barley loaves and a couple of fish! But what good is that with all this mob?'

'Tell everyone to sit down,' Jesus ordered. And all of them—the approximate count of the men only was 5,000—sat down ... Then Jesus took the loaves and gave thanks to God and passed them out to the people. Afterward he did the same with the fish and everyone ate until they were full" (John 6:8–11 LB). Jesus used the small barley loaves and fish in the little boys hands to feed a multitude.

My question is: What do you have that God can use? Has God asked you to do something for Him? Have you made excuses time after time? He may find someone else who is willing, and you might miss the blessings that He had in store for you. Randy had a measly clothes hanger. Who knows? The portly man may have been an angel in disguise sent to aid him in his efforts. David had a stone, Paul had some spare lumber, and Reverend Caldwell said yes. Many people saw the need, but few were willing to do the work. Jesus said, "The harvest is plentiful, but the workers are few" (Luke 10:2 NIV).

Opportunity is all around you, but are you willing to let God use what you have, no matter how small it may seem? Get busy! There's plenty of work to be done, but the workers are few.

Questions

1. How do you think God feels about excuses? (a)

2. Have you ever passed someone in need without stopping to help them? Why or why not? (b)

3. What is a simple rule of thumb for helping someone? (c)

4. Why is it sometimes harder to perform simple tasks than complex ones? (d)

5. Do you feel that Jesus was willing to help people? (e, f)

6. Are you willing to obey your boss when he/she asks you to do a job?

Scriptural Answers

(a) "But [the invited] all alike began to make excuses. The first said, 'I have just bought a field, and I must go and see it. Please excuse me.' Another said, 'I have just bought five yoke of oxen, and I'm on my way to try them out. Please excuse me.' Still another said, 'I just got married, so I can't come.' ... Then the owner of the house became angry and ordered his servant, 'Go out quickly into the streets and alleys of the town and bring in the poor, the crippled, the blind and the lame ... I tell you, not one of those men who were invited will get a taste of my banquet'" (Luke 14:18–21, 24 NIV).

(b) "In fact, if you know the right thing to do and don't do it, that for you is evil" (James 4:17).

(c) "Here is a simple rule-of-thumb guide for behavior: Ask yourself what you want people to do for you, then grab the initiative and do it for them. Add up God's Law and Prophets and this is what you get" (Matthew 7:12).

(d) "But [Naaman's] servants caught up with him and said, 'Father, if the prophet had asked you to do something hard and heroic, wouldn't you have done it? So why not this simple "wash and be clean"?'" (2 Kings 5:13).

(e) "Jesus said to them, 'Children, have you any food?' They answered Him, 'No.' And He said to them, 'Cast the net on the right side of the boat, and you will find some.' So they cast, and now they were not able to draw it in because of the multitude of fish" (John 21:5–6 NKJV).

(f) "[Jesus] went through the country helping people and healing everyone who was beaten down by the Devil. He was able to do all this because God was with him" (Acts 10:38).

12

Have you ever blinded your right eye?

When I was in high school, we were required to read *The Scarlet Letter* by Nathaniel Hawthorne. It told of a young woman, Hester Prynne, who became pregnant by a man she would not publicly name. The townspeople made her wear the letter A on her dress everywhere she went. The A stood for adultery.

Our society has become so complacent that people now laugh and make jokes not only about adultery, but also about pornography, thievery, and lying. I wonder if people would take these things more seriously if there were obvious consequences, like those for Hester Prynne. What if, for a two-week period, the offending part of your body changed color? For example, if you lied, your tongue would turn black. If you stole, your hand would turn purple. If you committed adultery, a red A would blaze on your chest. If you were jealous, your face would turn green. If you looked at pornography, your pupils would be illuminated by a white P. I imagine that these hidden sins would come to a screeching halt.

God sees everything we do, so who do we think we're fooling? We may fool ourselves and we may fool our neighbors, but we can never fool God. Want to know what Jesus had to say?

> If you want to live a morally pure life, here's what you have to do: You have to blind your right eye the moment you catch it in a lustful leer. You have to choose to live one-eyed or else be dumped on a moral

trash pile. And you have to chop off your right hand the moment you notice it raised threateningly. Better a bloody stump than your entire being discarded for good in the dump.

—Matthew 5:29–30

Those are very strong words, but they were Jesus's words, not mine. Does He really want us to blind our eyes or cut off our hands? I imagine He overemphasized so He could shock us into realizing that you have to cut yourself off from sin in the beginning, when it's just a thought. Like my grandma used to say, "Nip it in the bud."

Don't worry, your tongue's not going to turn black if you lie, you don't have to blind yourself if you look lustfully at another person, and your face won't turn green if you are insanely jealous. But you might want to reconsider the next time the temptation pops into your head. James says, "Happy is the man who doesn't give in and do wrong when he is tempted, for afterwards he will get as his reward the crown of life that God has promised those who love him" (James 1:12 LB).

I want to be happy and I hope you do, too. Let's get the crown!

Questions

1. Have you ever tried to hide your sins from God? How did that work for you? (a)

2. Which sins can be hidden from God? (b)

3. Hypothetically speaking, do you feel that color-coding sins would deter desires? Express your thoughts.

4. If we try to conceal our sins, will we prosper? (c)

5. Why should we confess our sins to God? (d)

6. Do you feel that God can see the intent of your heart? (e)

Scriptural Answers

(a) "Nothing in all creation is hidden from God's sight. Everything is uncovered and laid bare before the eyes of him to whom we must give account" (Hebrews 4:13 NIV).

(b) "Nobody gets by with anything, no one plays fast and loose with [God]" (Psalm 76:12).

(c) "He who conceals his sins does not prosper, but whoever confesses and renounces them finds mercy" (Proverb 28:13 NIV).

(d) "If we confess our sins, [God] is faithful and just and will forgive us our sins and purify us from all unrighteousness" (1 John 1:9 NIV).

(e) "Even hell holds no secrets from God—do you think he can't read human hearts?" (Proverb 15:11).

13
Have you ever bought a lemon?

One year, my husband and I bought a beautiful truck. We were so proud of it. Everything about it seemed great. It had leather seats, a Bose radio, and all the bells and whistles. You couldn't ask for a better vehicle. We went around showing it to our friends and giving them rides. It was a one-owner; that sealed the deal. Just to be safe, we bought the extended warranty. We probably wouldn't need it, but since it wasn't brand new, we thought that it would be a smart move.

Two months later, we heard a groan in the rear of the truck. While replacing the driver's side rear wheel bearing, the mechanic noticed a funny hesitation in the transmission. After those repairs, we thought we were through—but then we heard another noise from the front end. And what was that fluid dripping from the pan? Did the air conditioning work as well as it should?

We could no longer deny the fact that we had bought a lemon. It looked great on the outside and it was a comfortable ride, but underneath, where things weren't so obvious and only time could tell, it was sour.

Have you ever met someone you thought was a beautiful person? They said all the right things, you introduced them to your friends, and you were proud to be in their company. They quoted Scriptures, attended church, and testified about great miracles. You bought their act. But after a while, you heard some groaning. *That didn't sound right.* You overlooked it, but a few months later you heard them verbally trashing their spouse. They made snide remarks about the church people who couldn't make time for the mission trip. On their rearview mirror, they quickly flick the handicapped tag that was meant for their ailing mom. They say that the waiter was inept, so no tip! Drip, drip, drip, drip—just like that lemon we bought. Sure, everyone has bad days, but if you consistently find that the sweet fruit you expected leaves a sour taste, you may feel like your friend destroyed the trust you had in God.

A holy man was sent to deliver a horrible message to Jeroboam. God instructed the holy man, "Don't eat a crumb, don't drink a drop, and don't go back the way you came." (1 Kings 13:9). The holy man obeyed, and along the way, another man came out to meet him. "He said, 'I am also a prophet, just like you. And an angel came to me with a message from God: "Bring him home with you, and give him a good meal!"' But the man was lying. So the holy man went home with him and they had a meal together" (1 Kings 13:18–19). The holy man ended up being killed by a lion right down the road from where he had fellowshipped with his so-called friend, the prophet. The bottom line is that he believed the friend instead of heeding God's instructions. His "friend" was a liar and a hypocrite.

It's easy to see a hypocrite in the church and say, "Ha! I knew it! They're all alike!" and then cry yourself to sleep, cursing God. "I can never trust a Christian again. That's what I get for buying into their sanctimonious garbage." But God doesn't want you to look at people. He wants you to look at Him, the all-knowing, ever-loving God of the universe who is the same yesterday, today, and forever.

I've got news for you. Hypocrites are everywhere. They're on Wall Street, they're in the pew next to you, and they're at your job. But don't let that persuade you to take your eyes off Almighty God. Fortunately, we have a guarantor who will heal anything that is broken in our lives—the stings of a hypocrite, physical abuse, cancer, heart disease. Just as the warranty on our vehicle was bumper-to-bumper, "God can heal you everywhere you hurt," as Joyce Meyer said.

I'm not afraid to trust my vehicle any more. It can be fixed. The mechanic handles all the problems. I've also learned to focus on God instead of worrying about the hypocrites that boggle my mind. All it takes is one long look in the mirror to bring me down to earth. I leave the judgment up to God. "Don't pick on people, jump on their failures, criticize their faults—unless, of course, you want the same treatment. That critical spirit has a way of boomeranging" (Matthew 7:1–2).

Paul says, "You ran well; who hindered you from obeying the truth? This persuasion did not come from him who calls you" (Galatians 5:7–8 NKJV). Our job is to stay out of the judgment seat, keep our eyes on God, and serve Him with the joy that we had before we were distracted.

Joseph was treated horribly by his brothers. He endured thirteen years of hardship at their expense. However, he had an awesome attitude. "But Joseph told them, 'Don't be afraid of me. Am I God, to judge and punish you? As far as I am concerned, God turned into good what you meant for evil, for he brought me to this high position I have today so that I could save the lives of many people'" (Genesis 50:19–20 LB).

Lemonade for lemons, mercy for transgressions, beauty for ashes: a great exchange.

QUESTIONS

1. Has a hypocrite ever made you doubt God? Write down your feelings. (a)

2. Do you feel that hypocrites will face judgment? (b)

3. God will welcome hypocrites into heaven. True or false? (c)

4. Have you ever felt like a hypocrite in front of your kids or your spouse? Write down your feelings.

5. Is it good to tolerate hypocrisy in your life? (d)

6. Why is it so easy to point out others' faults yet ignore our own? Explain. (e)

7. Have you ever discovered that a close friend was a hypocrite? How did you feel? (f)

8. Do you believe God wants you to forgive him/her? Why or why not? (g)

Scriptural Answers

(a) "You were running superbly! Who cut in on you, deflecting you from the true course of obedience? This detour doesn't come from the One who called you into the race in the first place" (Galatians 5:7–8).

(b) "But the one who is upsetting you, whoever he is, will bear the divine judgment" (Galatians 5:10).

(c) "Not everyone who says to me, 'Lord, Lord,' will enter the kingdom of heaven, but only he who does the will of my Father who is in heaven. Many will say to me on that day, 'Lord, Lord, did we not prophesy in your name, and in your name drive out demons and perform many miracles?' Then I will tell them plainly, 'I never knew you. Away from me, you evildoers!'" (Matthew 7:21–23 NIV).

(d) "Therefore, rid yourselves of all malice and all deceit, hypocrisy, envy, and slander of every kind" (1 Peter 2:1 NIV).

(e) "How can you say to your brother, 'Brother, let me take the speck out of your eye,' when you yourself fail to see the plank in your own eye? You hypocrite, first take the plank out of your eye, and then you will see clearly to remove the speck from your brother's eye" (Luke 6:42 NIV).

(f) "All my life I've been charmed by his speech, never dreaming he'd turn on me. His words, which were music to my ears, turned to daggers in my heart" (Psalm 55:21).

(g) "Your heavenly Father will forgive you if you forgive those who sin against you; but if you refuse to forgive them, he will not forgive you (Matthew 6:14–15 LB).

14

Have you ever broken your promise?

When my brother and I were young, our dad promised to take us camping. Summer came and went with no camping trip.

"Maybe next year," he said. But next year was the same.

The third year, we made him put it in writing: "I promise to take Steve and Sherry camping this summer." He even signed his name, and we put the note in an encyclopedia for safekeeping. This time we just *knew* he would keep his promise.

But he never did.

I learned a lot of things from my dad, most of them positive—but I also learned from the negative. "Keep your word even if it costs you" (Psalm 15:5).

When my kids were growing up, I tried to remember the hurt of my dad's broken promise. If I couldn't do something, I wouldn't promise it. If I could do it, then I would promise it and keep my promise, even if keeping my word was inconvenient. Promises are important to your kids, but they're also important to your friends and your fellow workers.

Have you ever promised to call your friend, but failed to do so? Have you ever made a date but not shown up, nor given an explanation? Did your friend clear their schedule only to be ignored? Have you ever promised your boss you would have a report done by Friday, then stayed home and pretended to be sick? Have you told a customer their truck would be fixed on Thursday, knowing full well that you were going on vacation

Wednesday? These promises may seem harmless, but your reputation is based upon your word, your promise.

If you wonder why your business is dwindling, or you wonder why your friends aren't as excited as they used to be when you set up a date, you might want to ask yourself, "Do I keep my word?" Are your kids disinterested when you promise them the moon and then deliver a deflated ball? Turn the page on your sloppy promises. Be a person of your word. Instead of a bucket list of things to do before you die, how about a promise jar? Make good on your promises, even when it costs you.

By the way, years later, my wonderful husband took me and all three of our kids camping in a tiny pup tent, and we had a glorious time. I believe God provided a way for my heart's desire to be fulfilled and I believe he will fulfill your desires if you are not bitter and delight yourself in the Lord.

Questions

1. Has anyone ever broken their promise to you? How did you feel?

2. Have you made promises to someone and then failed to follow through? What did you promise? How do you think they felt?

3. Are there consequences to a broken promise? (a)

4. Do you feel that Christians are accountable to God to keep their promises? (b)

5. Should we keep vows we make to God or will He let us off the hook? (c)

6. Is it better to make a vow and break it or never to make a vow? Explain. (d)

7. Is it possible for God to break a promise? (e)

8. Is there a promise in the Bible where God says that He will give us the desires of our heart? If so, what is the condition? (f)

Scriptural Answers

(a) "Then, I [Nehemiah] called the priests together and made them promise to keep their word. Then I emptied my pockets, turning them inside out, and said, 'So may God empty the pockets and house of everyone who doesn't keep this promise—turned inside out and emptied'" (Nehemiah 5:12–13).

(b) "You have kept your promise because you are righteous" (Nehemiah 9:8 NIV).

(c) "When you make a vow to God, your God, don't put off keeping it; God, your God, expects you to keep it and if you don't you're guilty" (Deuteronomy 23:21).

(d) "It is better not to vow than to make a vow and not fulfill it" (Ecclesiastes 5:5 NIV).

(e) "When God wanted to guarantee his promises, he gave his word, a rock-solid guarantee—God can't break his word. And because his word cannot change, the promise is likewise unchangeable" (Hebrews 6:18).

(f) "Delight yourself in the Lord and he will give you the desires of your heart (Psalm 37:4 NIV).

Sheep Ears

15

Have you ever celebrated a woohoo moment?

The next to last day of school, Mrs. Thompson's sixth-grade math class played a kickball game against Mrs. Choy's seventh graders. I was Mrs. Thompson's fourth-period assistant, so that was my team. I've coached baseball, soccer, and basketball youth teams, but participating in sports has never been my forte.

As each student stood at home plate, a pitcher gave them a multiplication problem. If they got it right they could kick the ball; if they got it wrong, they were out. I never realized how competitive Mrs. Thompson was until I heard her give the class her pep talk. "Now listen, guys, Mrs. Choy's team beat us last period. Now we need to even the score."

The students picked up on her enthusiasm. One student tried to stretch one base into two bases. "Out!" screamed the student umpire. The next kid also tried. "Out!" Then someone got on base and we squeaked in a run. Now we needed to protect the lead. Hormones and growth spurts start to set in around the seventh grade, so our sixth-grade students were definitely outmatched in size.

Oh, no, here it comes, I thought. We managed to hold them because two students were thrown out at first and the third student gave the wrong answer to the multiplication problem. It was three up, and three down.

We didn't get a run in our inning, but we still needed to keep the other team from scoring. The bell was about to ring, so this was it. I stood behind shortstop but in front of left field. Mrs. Choy's class had two outs with a runner on third. It was time to make it or break it.

I don't remember who kicked the ball, but it went high in the air. Really high. *Oh no*, I thought, *it's headed in my direction.* I thought about stepping aside to let the ball bounce because I'd never be able to catch it. Usually a kid ran to take over, but not this time. Everyone froze. I felt their stares. I thought, *It's just me and the ball. God, please help me.*

I stuck out my arms. I didn't even have to move my feet. I had seen kids catch the ball but forget to bring their elbows in so the ball went straight through their arms and thudded onto the ground. I quickly brought my elbows in right before I caught it. Woohoo! The kids started whooping and hollering. "Mrs. Witt, you did it!" I've never gotten so many high fives in my life. I looked over at Mrs. Thompson and she was hopping up and down clapping her hands. My arms and chest stung for a long time, but it didn't matter to me. The important thing was that I hadn't let the class down.

I've attended all sorts of sporting events in my lifetime, seen all sorts of heroes. But that was the first time *I* was the hero. It was a great feeling. We celebrated what I call a "woohoo moment."

Another woohoo moment in my life involved coffee. I love to drink coffee in the morning. It's a nice thing that I do for myself. I prefer liquid creamers, so at the grocery store I love to scan the refrigerator case for new creamer flavors. One day, I saw a container that said "limited edition." I looked at the label and felt like I heard angel harps playing: Cinnabon by International Delight. I had to try it. They also had Almond Joy. I picked up two Cinnabon and one Almond Joy. I wasn't about to miss out on a limited edition! At home, I tasted the Almond Joy first. *Mmm. It can't get any better than this.* The next day, I tried the Cinnabon. It tasted okay, but not the way I'd expected. Then I tried adding a little more. *Ahh, perfect!* I don't know who created that flavor, but I would like to meet them and give them a hug.

I've even watched my ten-year-old dog, Brownie, experience one of these beautiful moments. When I walk my three dogs in the 100-degree weather, Brownie, a bloodhound and beagle mix gets bogged down by her thick, heavy fur. Brownie weighs thirty-seven pounds and is only fifteen inches tall, but twenty-four inches long with a fifteen inch tail. One summer, I took her to the groomer to be shaved. They left nothing but a tuft of fur on the end of Brownie's tail, making it look like a lion's tail. She looked really adorable. It may have been my imagination, but she looked like she was smiling when I picked her up. As I took her for a walk, she raised one of her hind legs really high and it looked like she happily skipped on three legs, as her tail wagged rhythmically like a metronome on a fast tempo. Her body language was a picture of celebration. Woohoo! Woohoo! Woohoo!

Some other moments I've enjoyed are the smeared magenta hues of a sunset, the unexpected aroma of a gardenia bush, the beauty and the smell of my salmon-colored roses in the backyard. I also love to get on the ramp to the highway near my house just to look at the deep green shades of the crops that line my path. I've experienced the exhilaration of hearing that Laura, Aaron's wife, was pregnant with our first grandchild, the shock when Nathan won a car in the awards ceremony his senior year in high school, and the rush of adrenaline when Paul and his college team created a dog pile after the last out that determined they were going to Omaha for the College World Series. Woooooohooooo!

James 1:17 says, "Every good thing given and every perfect gift is from above" (NASB). I've listened to reports of people who say they've visited heaven and returned to earth. They say that colors are deeper, smells are more fragrant, and that there is indescribable music. I can't wait to experience the biggest woohoo moment ever. The joy we experience here is like a tiny drop in the largest ocean, only a taste of what's to come. When my small mind says, *It doesn't get any better than this,* I imagine that God smiles and says, "Just wait until you see the good stuff."

Jesus told a parable of a woman who had ten coins but lost one. She turned the house upside down looking for her lost coin. Jesus said, "And when she finds it you can be sure she'll call her friends and neighbors: 'Celebrate with me! I found my lost coin!'" (Luke 15:9). A woohoo moment worthy of joyous celebration.

Right now, though, I thank God for my woohoo moments as I travel through life. He is under no obligation to answer even my small request to catch a ball on a dusty playground in ninety-eight-degree weather for an insignificant game. The Cinnabon creamer, the three-legged skip of a freshly shorn dog, a majestic sunset, the sweet fragrance of a home grown rose—the list could go on forever. I'm sure you have your own stories. Let us never take for granted the little joys He sends each day.

Take a minute to thank your Heavenly Father. David said, "But let me run loose and free, celebrating God's great work" (Psalm 35:9). Embrace your woohoo moments and celebrate.

Questions

1. List your favorite woohoo moments?

2. Write down your thoughts about James 1:17 NASB: "Every good thing and every perfect gift is from above."

3. Is it godly to celebrate holidays? (a)

4. Have you ever noticed an animal being joyful, like Brownie after she was shorn? (b)

5. Can you allow yourself to be so overjoyed by God's righteousness that you are able to celebrate Him without inhibition, like you've seen others doing? Why or why not? (c)

6. Is it possible to be afraid yet filled with joy? (d)

7. David was a man after God's heart. How did he celebrate? (e)

Scriptural Answers

(a) "The king now commanded the people. 'Celebrate the Passover to God, your God, exactly as directed in this Book of the Covenant'" (2 Kings 23:21).

(b) "The wings of the ostrich flap joyfully, but they cannot compare with the pinions and feathers of the stork" (Job 39:13 NIV).

(c) "But for you who revere my name, the sun of righteousness will rise with healing in its wings. And you will go out and leap like calves released from the stall" (Malachi 4:2 NIV).

(d) "So the women hurried away from the tomb, afraid yet filled with joy, and ran to tell [Jesus's] disciples" (Matthew 28:8 NIV).

(e) "Blessed be God—he heard me praying. He proved he's on my side; I've thrown my lot in with him. Now I'm jumping for joy, and shouting and singing my thanks to him" (Psalms 28:6–7).

16

Have you ever controlled your anger?

When my son Paul was fifteen years old, his all-star baseball team was in the 1998 Junior Babe Ruth World Series. There was a photographer onsite named Jeff who would, for a fee, take pictures of your son. I signed up for the first game and he took several good action shots of Paul at shortstop. I was pleased with them.

Paul was going to pitch in the next game, so I signed up once again. I emphasized to Jeff the fact that this may be Paul's only chance to pitch. "So make sure you get some good ones," I said, as I walked away.

We won the game and I couldn't wait to look at the photos. But Jeff's jaw dropped when he saw me. He said, "I'm sorry, Mrs. Witt. Somehow I forgot to shoot him pitching. I have some nice shots of him batting, though." I had really wanted pictures of him pitching, but I smiled through my disappointment. "Maybe he'll get to pitch again," he said.

I thought, *Yeah right. His arm has been hurt for three months. That's not going to happen.*

But two days later, Paul's arm recovered and he was scheduled to pitch again. I went straight to Jeff. "Don't forget! He's pitching again. Get some good ones." I was confident that Jeff would get plenty, maybe more than usual since he messed up the last time. I didn't even bother to take any photos with my small-lensed, low-budget camera. Paul would have looked like an ant from that far away, anyway.

We won that game, too. I zipped on over to Jeff, excited to see the pictures. As I approached Jeff's booth, his jaw dropped even more than it had the last time. "I am *sooo* sorry. Somehow I forgot again."

My mind was really whirling at that point. Believe me, no Scriptures popped in my head. I didn't feel any special anointing to testify. All I felt was anger. How could he forget—not once, but twice? This could have been Paul's only chance to participate in a tournament this prestigious. There would be no more pitching. All those thoughts went through my head, but my mouth froze. This time it was *my* jaw that hung open. I'm pretty transparent with my facial expressions, so I'm sure he figured out what I was feeling. I wanted to explode, but I knew that wouldn't change anything.

Jeff offered to take pictures of my son on the mound after everyone left the field. Even though Paul was exhausted from the 100-degree heat, he agreed. Jeff sent the photos to us in the mail, and I must say, they turned out to be fantastic. Jeff felt really terrible about the situation; he made up for it by not charging us for the pictures.

When, in Paul's junior and senior years, his high school team, the Pine Bluff Zebras, played in the state tournament in Fayetteville, Arkansas, Jeff took the pictures. We smiled and exchanged knowing waves as we passed each other. All was forgiven and we were in good standing with one another.

In 2005, Paul's senior year in college, the Baylor Bears made it to the College World Series in Omaha, Nebraska. It was the goal of all teams to make this trip. We couldn't believe it! I took my camera along to get some candid shots, but I didn't worry about game shots because I figured they would have photographers for hire at this illustrious tournament. I figured wrong. I talked to about eight different people working the event and finally understood: you're on your own.

Well, at least I brought my own camera, I thought. But when I took my first picture, something in it jammed. It was broken, it was busted, and I was disgusted. I couldn't let that ruin all the fun. At least I was there to enjoy the game in person. "God, please put it in someone's heart to take a few photos that they will share with me," I prayed.

The game ended and we won! I went into the stands behind the Baylor dugout to congratulate the team. As I turned to go back up the steps, I was greeted by a familiar face. "Hey! Do you remember me?" I was shocked to see Jeff!

He proceeded to tell me how he had kept up with Paul throughout his baseball career. When he found out Paul's team had made it to Omaha, he bought tickets to the Series—nothing was going to keep him away. I listened as he excitedly talked on and on. It was as if it he were talking about his own son whom he was proud of. But his next statements floored me. "By the way, I hope you don't mind, but I took a few extra pictures of Paul. I'll send them to you later. Do you still live at the same address?"

Believe me, I started bawling right there on the steps of the bleachers. He had no idea what I had been going through that day, just trying to get a few memorable pictures. "Of course you can take pictures! Take all you want!" I said through my tears.

"You know, Mrs. Witt, I always felt bad about my mistake in '98."

He started to say more, but I held up my hand. "Stop beating yourself up. I forgave you a long time ago." We both laughed.

I thought back to that day when Paul was fifteen. I admit that I had been angry that Jeff didn't take the pictures I wanted, but I'd had a choice as to how to respond. Should I blow up and make a fool of myself, or keep my emotions under control? The Bible says "Control your temper, for anger labels you a fool" (Ecclesiastes 7:9 NLT). That means that we are allowed to experience our emotions—we just need to keep them under control.

I remember Mary and Martha in the Bible. Imagine how they felt when their brother Lazarus died. Lazarus had been dead for four days when Jesus arrived. Jesus loved them, yet He waited until Lazarus was stinking in the tomb. What kind of friend was this? Heal strangers, but ignore your friends. You know they must have been angry, but are you aware that Jesus was angry, too? "When Jesus saw her sobbing and the Jews with her sobbing, a deep anger welled up within him" (John 11:34). He told Martha that her brother would be raised up, but she didn't understand.

Others had questions about Jesus not healing Lazarus. "Then Jesus, the anger again welling up within him, arrived at the tomb" (John 11:38). We know that Jesus *did* raise Lazarus from the dead. However, it is important to remember that Jesus was angry because the people didn't believe he would do it. But He didn't let His anger rule him. He could have said, "If you're going to act like that, he can just *stay* in the grave!" Get mad, but don't be a fool about it. Express displeasure, but don't dwell on it.

Consider the Canaanite woman who approached Jesus. Her daughter needed to be healed. "[Jesus] said, 'It's not right to take bread out of children's mouths and throw it to dogs'" (Matthew 15:26). The woman could have gotten all huffy, said, "Well, I never!" and stormed off, missing a blessing. However, "She was quick: 'You're right, Master, but beggar dogs do get scraps from the master's table.' Jesus gave in, 'Oh, woman, your faith is something else. What you want is what you get!' Right then her daughter became well" (Matthew 15:27–28). I'm sure the woman was angry, but she controlled herself, and thus got what she wanted: healing.

It's easy to blow a future blessing with a stupid response. We are the only ones who determine our own responses. I'm glad I didn't voice how I felt that day with Jeff. Maybe God was testing me.

Would you like to know the rest of the World Series story? About a month after we got back home, I received a package in the mail: Ninety-nine free, beautiful, professional pictures of Paul in the games! It was more than I could have asked for in my wildest dreams. Two weeks later, Jeff sent two collages of action shots from the World Series. As they say in the MasterCard commercials, "Priceless."

The next time you feel you are justified in your anger, you probably are. But consider how you react, because it could be a test. The one who has angered you could be the one who will later bring the blessings. I've got proof!

QUESTIONS

1. Were there times in your life that you felt you were justified in being angry? (a)

2. Name three times you've experienced this.

3. Were any kids watching? Were you proud of your response or ashamed?

4. Do you feel that harsh words will stir up anger? (b)

5. Even when you have a right to be angry, people are watching your

reactions. Do you feel that it would destroy your Christian witness if they watch you explode? Why or why not? (c)

6. What is the best response to give when we are angry? (d, e)

7. Do you feel that losing your temper delights the Devil? Explain your answer. (f)

Scriptural Answers

(a) "Go ahead and be angry. You do well to be angry—but don't use your anger as fuel for revenge. And don't stay angry. Don't go to bed angry. Don't give the Devil that kind of foothold in your life" (Ephesians 4:26–27).

(b) "A gentle answer turns away wrath, but a harsh word stirs up anger" (Proverb 15:1 NIV).

(c) "Do not cause anyone to stumble" (1 Corinthians 10:32 NIV).

(d) A man of knowledge uses words with restraint and a man of understanding is even-tempered" (Proverb 17:27 NIV).

(e) "Bridle your anger, trash your wrath, cool your pipes—it only makes things worse" (Psalm 37:8).

(f) "Keep a cool head. Stay alert. The Devil is poised to pounce, and would like nothing better than to catch you napping" (1 Peter 5:8).

17

Have you ever crawled under a chair?

When I was seven years old, my dad had a radio spot on which he preached a sermon and sometimes sang songs. One day he had a bright idea and asked me to sing on the show. Back in the good old days, radio was the main form of entertainment. I couldn't wait to be famous. We went to the studio and I gave my best shot at the song "Mansion Over the Hilltop."

But when they played it back, I was mortified! *How can that be me? I sound like a country bumpkin.* "Please, please, please don't play that on the air," I begged. I crawled under the chair and my dad and the man at the radio station had to pull me out. They were laughing, but I didn't think it was one bit funny. They played my song on the radio; however, I had no more thoughts of fame after my infamous debut.

You can imagine my fear when my friend, Gwen, recently asked me to appear with her on the web series *OBKB* with Bill Cosby. Gwen and her husband, Clark Terry, were long time friends of Bill and Camille Cosby, and Bill had selected the University of Arkansas at Pine Bluff to tape a show. On the show he interviewed guests and asked questions that sometimes confused them, but made for a lot of laughter. There was no guessing what he would talk to guests about—this made the idea even more intimidating. I remembered what Joyce Meyer preached: "Even if you're afraid, you can still *do* it afraid." In Isaiah, God says, "Don't panic, I'm with you. There's no need to fear for I'm your God. I'll give you strength, I'll help you. I'll hold you steady; keep a firm grip on you" (Isaiah 41:10). I had a flashback of hearing my radio song and thought, *Oh well, at least I won't be singing.* I told Gwen that I would appear on the show three weeks later.

In the "greenroom," which was really a converted restroom, Gwen and I held hands and prayed that we would give honor to God, only say what He wanted us to say, and keep our mouths shut if we weren't supposed to say something. I nervously watched the door, waiting for it to swing open and have the runner tell us that we could come to the stage. She laughed when she saw me sweating. Gwen wasn't afraid at all, but I was looking for a chair to crawl under.

We went onstage and Mr. Cosby asked us about our friendship. That was an easy subject. Next, he asked me about a town I used to live in, and I mentioned a song my mom and dad wrote when they were bored. All of a sudden, I heard myself sing "There's a Snake" in front of a live audience. Then I made a funny face that made me look like I had four chins, and Gwen did her Bucky Beaver face. We covered some other subjects, and then he had us make some closing remarks, wisdom from our days on earth.

We left the stage and hugged each other. We recounted things that we each regretted having done. "Why did I sing that song?" "Why did I make that horrible face?" "I'm not sure I conveyed what I was trying to say." "I should have looked into the camera when he asked us to talk to the audience."

The man who was removing our microphones said, "I don't know what you ladies are talking about. What you said was great!" So maybe it wasn't so bad. At least I'd confronted my fears and my friend was proud of me.

But over the next two weeks, I kept mulling it over and over in my mind. *Why did I sing that ridiculous song? I have the worst singing voice! Why did I make that crazy face? I must have looked like an idiot!*

Then, one day, God answered me: "I needed to see if you would be a fool for me."

Well, God, I guess I passed that test with flying colors. I laughed. It dawned on me that God might ask me again to do things that felt embarrassing to me. Even if it seemed foolish, my willingness to perform might free others to be uninhibited, since I was far from perfect.

And God did.

A year later, God had me teach nineteen ninth graders all sixty-six books of the Bible by singing a song—with my terrible voice. Many times they joined in with me as I sang. Believe me, we didn't sound like the Mormon Tabernacle Choir, but we all had fun, and they learned the names of the books with ease. No one seemed intimidated. Sometimes I use my four-chin face to make kids laugh when they are taking themselves too seriously. Now I understand God's reasoning a little better.

Ezekiel said, "The Spirit lifted me and took me away. I went bitterly and angrily. I didn't want to go. But God had me in his grip" (Ezekiel 3:14). Do you know what God asked Ezekiel to do? He wanted Ezekiel to warn the Israelites about their sins. God commanded him to eat a book that tasted like honey, to build a model of a military siege, "then get an iron skillet and place it upright between you and the city,"(4:3) and then lie on his left side for 390 days. This was to symbolize how long they would be punished: one day for each year they had sinned. God said, "I will tie you up with ropes, tie you so you can't move or turn over until you have finished the days of the siege"(Ezekiel 4:8).

Then God asked him to prepare a special type of bread to eat for that entire time. But here is the clincher: He said, "Bake the muffins out in the open where everyone can see you using dried human dung for fuel" (Ezekiel 4:12). Ezekiel really threw a fit about that, so God said he could use cow dung. I'm sure that wasn't a huge consolation to Ezekiel. He must have felt stupid. You caught his protest: "I went bitterly and angrily. I did not want to go." But Ezekiel did what he was told in spite of how he felt. He was definitely a fool for God.

God might even ask Sherry, the little girl who once crawled under a chair, to appear on a show with Bill Cosby, or to publish a book for the world to read. In 1 Corinthians Paul says, "Brothers, think of what you were when you were called. Not many of you were wise by human standards; not many were influential; not many were of noble birth. But God chose the foolish things of the world to shame the wise; God chose the weak things of the world to shame the strong" (1 Corinthians 1:26–27 NIV).

So even though Gwen and I didn't make the final edit of *OBKB*, I guess I was qualified. That Scripture also qualified me to be an author. Just call me a fool for God.

Do you feel inadequate or unqualified to do the job that God has set before you? Maybe you need to read 1 Corinthians 1:26–27 again. I bet you're more qualified than you thought. So get out from under that chair or wherever you've been hiding. God has something for you to do, too. It can't be anything worse than what He asked of poor old Ezekiel!

Questions

1. Has God ever asked you to do something for Him that you were afraid to do? What was it?

2. Did you ask anyone to pray with you? Whom did you ask? (a)

3. Do you believe that God will help you overcome your fears? (b)

4. Can you trust God with your fears? (c)

5. Do you panic when you have to face a challenge? Is there help to be found anywhere? (d)

6. If you have rubbery knees, what can you say to yourself? (e)

Scriptural Answers

(a) "Pray also for me that whenever I open my mouth, words may be given me so that I fearlessly make known the mystery of the gospel" (Ephesians 6:19 NIV).

(b) "Light, space, zest—that's God! So, with him on my side, I'm fearless, afraid of no one and nothing" (Psalm 27:1).

(c) "When I am afraid, I will trust in you" (Psalm 56:3 NIV).

(d) "Don't panic. I'm with you. There's no need to fear for I'm your God. I'll give you strength, keep a firm grip on you" (Isaiah 41:10).

(e) "Energize the limp hands, strengthen the rubbery knees. Tell fearful souls, 'Courage! Take heart! God is here, right here'" (Isaiah 35:3–4).

18

Have you ever cussed like a sailor?

In the sixth grade, I started to hang out with the in crowd. It felt wonderful to be popular. We laughed behind the teacher's back as we gave her the one-finger salute. Curse words became easier and easier to say. It felt empowering at first.

But after a short season of euphoric thrill, my young heart began to feel conflicted. I knew this was not how a Christian should act. My parents didn't know about my internal battle; only God and I did. I started praying to God. "If you'll just get me out of this situation, I promise I won't ever want to be popular again. God, please help my parents move from this town." I felt like a fresh start in a new town would free me from my temptations.

Amazingly, about a week later, my parents announced that we would be moving from our small town of Warren, Arkansas, to the big city of Memphis, Tennessee. I couldn't believe it. I think my parents were surprised by my positive reaction. They knew I loved my friends and they had thought it would be hard for me to leave them. However, they didn't know what was going on underneath the surface.

True to my promise, I never hung out with the popular kids at my new school. I had already tried that and hadn't liked the way I'd behaved. I guess you could say I didn't trust myself.

About eighteen years later, I befriended a neighbor who was a proficient "cusser." Calvin had had a heart attack several years prior to my meeting him and was retired from the workforce. He walked through the neighborhood for his health, and since I did, too, we ended up taking many walks together. After hearing Calvin pepper his speech with expletives, I fell easily into the same mode. I guess I thought it made him feel more comfortable. He was a Christian and I was a Christian, and we talked about God a lot. It never dawned on me how bad my vocabulary had gotten until one day he said, "Sherry, you cuss like a sailor! I don't think I like the way you talk."

Boy, oh boy! That was a reality check. My mind flashed back to the promise I'd made as a sixth grader to God, when I had asked Him to forgive me. My conversations got an instant conversion. That is, until Paul, who was away at college, called to tell me some bad news. I am embarrassed to say I felt that an expletive would be appropriate for expressing my emotions. I was wrong.

"Mom, you've never cussed before, why would you do it now?" were his jarring words. That was another reality check from God that came through my son.

What does the Bible have to say about our words? "Don't talk dirty or silly. That kind of talk doesn't fit our style. Thanksgiving is our dialect" (Ephesians 5:4). The apostle Paul says, "Watch the way you talk. Let nothing foul or dirty come out of your mouth. Say only what helps, each word a gift" (Ephesians 4:29).

I have a friend who once came near death. She was taken to a place where every vile and cutting thing that she had ever said flashed before her. It broke her heart and changed her life. I could see how it had affected her. Still, I was amazed when I read Matthew 12:36–37. I had read this verse many times before, but never fully grasped its impact: "Let me tell you something: Every one of these careless words is going to haunt you. There will be a time of Reckoning. Words are powerful; take them seriously. Words can be your salvation. Words can also be your damnation."

Those powerful reality checks came out of Jesus's mouth, not my neighbor's or son's. I don't think Jesus was only talking about cuss words, but also words that are said in a jeering manner. Cruel words that finish with, "I was only joking." Careless words that mean, "You'll never amount to anything. Can't you do anything right?" Haughty words that insinuate all others are incompetent and you are the only smart one. And gossip.

Jesus also said, "There's nothing done or said that can't be forgiven" (Matthew 12:31). A day of Reckoning is coming and I want my slate to be clean. Don't you? Let thanksgiving be our dialect.

Questions

1. Explain your view on profanity and careless words coming from a Christian's mouth. (a)

2. Has God ever chastised you for doing something that you knew was wrong? If so, did He use other people to point out your problem?

3. Why do you believe God will correct us if we stray from Him? (b)

4. Do you frown on cussing but feel that white lies and gossip are permissible? Explain your opinion. (c)

5. Even though the tongue is small, can it do damage? Write down your thoughts. (d)

6. Is a change in behavior possible? Find a Scripture to support your answer. (e)

Scriptural Answers

(a) "Guard your tongue from profanity and no more lying through your teeth" (Psalm 34:13).

(b) "Young man, do not resent it when God chastens and corrects you, for his punishment is proof of his love. Just as a father punishes a son he delights in to make him better, so the Lord corrects you" (Proverbs 3:11–12 LB).

(c) "Keep vigilant watch over your heart; that's where life starts. Don't talk out of both sides of your mouth; avoid careless banter, white lies, and gossip" (Proverbs 4:23–24).

(d) "Likewise the tongue is a small part of the body, but it makes great boasts. Consider what a great forest is set on fire by a small spark" (James 3:5 NIV).

(e) "For I can do everything with the help of Christ who gives me the strength I need" (Philippians 4:13 NLT).

19
Have you ever dealt with a type A personality?

Dogs each have different personalities. Some dogs are docile, some needy, some hyper, some dominant. If these characteristics are left unchecked, they could become major problems in a household. If you've ever seen the television show *The Dog Whisperer,* you'll know what I mean. Whenever Cesar Milan helps a family with their dog problem, he emphasizes the fact that owners are usually the problem because they don't understand how to deal with their dogs' personalities.

I'm talking about dogs because, as a dog owner, that's the best way I can explain a type A personality. Type A personalities are dominant, strong-willed. An alpha dog rules the house and intimidates everyone else. This might be a simplification, but it is basically how a type A personality acts.

According to the online encyclopedia *Wikipedia*, the type A and type B personality theory was developed in the 1950s by cardiologists Meyer Friedman and Ray Rosenman. People with type A personalities are often high-achieving workaholics who multitask, push themselves with deadlines, and hate delays and ambivalence. Their behavior is expressed in three major symptoms: free-floating hostility, a competitive drive, and an achievement driven mentality. In contrast, type B personalities generally live at a lower stress level. When faced with competition, they do not mind losing and either enjoy the game or back down.

In the work force, type A personalities are the go-getters, the kind of people corporations seek out. They are the lawyers, the office managers, the salesmen of high-profile medical devices. Businesses thrive on them because they are earthshakers. But what are these people like as children? Who would want to deal with a hostile, competitive, achievement-driven child at home, in school, or on the basketball court? Combine the type A personality with hormones and you have, as the kids say, a hot mess.

That's what our household felt. Paul was my type A personality. I always knew he was different from anyone else in our family. I remember one incident when he was two years old. His brothers, ages five and seven, were playing soccer in the backyard, and I was on a ladder filming them. Paul screamed, "Me wanna play!" They told him, "You're too little!" which made him even more furious. After bantering back and forth with them, Paul darted straight for the ball, tapped it away with his foot, got control, and dribbled it around the yard, his head thrown back laughing while they tried to catch him. I stopped filming and just watched. I could tell you of many more incidents, but suffice it to say, he always took charge.

I had to spend a lot of time corralling his free spirit. I even sat Aaron and Nathan down once and apologized for having to devote so much of my time to Paul. He was different and he required a lot of handling. By the time he turned twelve, I guess you could say our household was a fully-fledged hot mess.

I didn't go to *The Dog Whisperer*. I went to God, the child whisperer. I thought my husband and I must have made mistakes with Paul. I prayed, "God, I don't know what to do. Please give me guidance. I know his spirit doesn't need to be broken, but God, I know you'll never be pleased with Paul unless things get under control."

God asked, "Do you trust me?"

I said, "Yes, God, I trust you."

"Then let me have him."

I pretended that I had Paul in my hands and I threw him up to God. I said, "God, do what you want with him, because I'm at the end of my rope." But I knew I had to "Be still before the Lord and wait patiently for him; do not fret when men succeed in their ways, when they carry out their wicked schemes" while God worked in his young life (Psalm 37:7 NIV).

So over the next year and a half, Paul went to the school of hard knocks. God orchestrated three important events in his life. I hurt for him, because I saw him hurting, but I knew God was at work molding him into the man He wanted Paul to become.

Incident 1: Paul had a classmate named Brandon who had a sort of redneck gang. They didn't have guns or anything; they were just big guys for their age with bully mentalities. Someone told Brandon that Paul had made some ugly remarks about Brandon's girlfriend.

One afternoon, Brandon went to the mall with his friends. When Brandon and his buddies saw Paul there, they started running after him, with a slew of profanities. They chased him through the mall and out the door. Thank goodness Paul had some speed, because he ran the mile home in record time. They were much slower, so they never caught up to him.

That's all that happened, but it kept him from going to the mall for a year. Paul claimed that he had never said anything about Brandon's girlfriend, but just like Joseph in the Bible, he still had to flee for his twelve-year-old life.

Incident 2: When Paul was in seventh grade, he played in a basketball league that consisted of seventh, eighth, and ninth graders. In one game, he made a three-pointer right over the outstretched hands of another player, John. That was bad enough, but Paul also gave John one of his in-your-face haughty grins that said, "That's right, and I'll do it every time, sucker!" It was just a look, but that was all it took. "Pride goes before destruction, and a haughty spirit before a fall" (Proverb 16:18 AB). I saw the look and John saw the look, but most importantly, God saw the spirit of the look. Paul had gotten overconfident and edged over the line into arrogance.

From that moment on, Paul was a hunted man by John and his crew. They were the preppy type. When they played soccer against each other in the local recreational league, they would aim for Paul, not the ball. He told me they doubled up behind him and said, "You'd better watch your back, 'cause we're coming for you." There were lots of curse words peppered in the threats.

When Paul entered the eighth grade and they were in the tenth grade, I had to drop him off at school exactly when the bell rang, because they would sometimes leave their campus and patrol his school trying to hunt him down. I would be waiting at the curb when school was over, ready to pick him up immediately so he could avoid their wrath.

Paul would come in and say, "Mom, we have to move. We can't live here anymore." I told him that wasn't an option. My heart ached for my son. I prayed for him. I knew that look hadn't been worth all this torment. However, I had given Paul to God, and I was confident that He was teaching Paul in a way that I never could.

Finally, about a year and a half later, Paul walked into the house and said, "Mom, get the Bible out. See what it says. I can't live like this anymore."

My heart leaped. I knew that God would bring this trouble to a close now that Paul was seeking Him. I asked God for His wisdom. "Paul, I'm not going to find the Scriptures—you are."

"But Mom, I don't know where anything is!"

"Just open the Bible and read out loud," I replied. I had no idea what he would turn to, but God had given me His direction. Paul read from Jeremiah 26. It went something like this: "Bad things will happen to you because of your evil heart. I have sent people to warn you and you haven't listened. This, and more will happen if you don't repent. If you repent, I will cancel the punishment against you." He looked up, wide-eyed, and so did I! God didn't mince His words. I said, "Paul, what do you think that means?" He needed to figure it out for himself.

Slowly and with a lot of thought, he said, "I think I need to go to John and apologize." Whew, what a revelation!

I called John's mom and told her what had been happening. She'd had no idea about the things that had been going on. She promised that it wouldn't happen anymore and said it wouldn't be necessary to speak face-to-face. I explained that Paul wanted to apologize in person. She said she would talk to her husband and call me back later. Eventually, she called to say her husband was bringing John over to our house. I had met her husband before. He was about 6'3" and looked kind of like the Hulk. I'm sure to Paul, he looked more like Goliath.

While we were waiting for them to arrive, Paul got a little nervous. "Mom, what am I going to say? Help me!"

"Tell John that you know why he is mad at you. That he has a right to be upset, and that you don't blame John or his buddies for following you around. Tell them you learned your lesson and want to ask for their forgiveness."

And Paul said exactly what I had advised him to say. John's dad asked, "John, what do you think? Do you forgive him?"

John thought for a second, and then said, "Yes, I do."

"What about your buddies? Are you going to call them off, too?" his dad asked.

"Yes, it won't ever happen again." And it didn't.

Paul looked about seven feet tall to me that day. He did what many grown-ups fail to do in their lifetimes: he swallowed his pride and asked for forgiveness.

Incident 3: A couple of months after Incident 2 began, things came to a head at our house. For the umpteenth time, Paul was ragging on Nathan, our type-B middle son. "You're sorry. You can't touch me. I'm too fast for you. You're weak." All of this was said in front of Paul's friend, Michael. They both laughed at Nathan. I heard the remarks and fussed at Paul. Nathan went to his room in grievous silence, and Paul and Michael left to ride their bikes.

I went to my swing outside and started talking to God. "Please tell me what to do. I've paddled Paul, I've grounded him, and I've talked to him until I'm blue in the face. There's got to be a solution."

God said, "There is. Let them fight."

"Are you serious? Nathan is too big! It won't be a fair fight."

"Exactly."

God gave me specific instructions about how to carry out His plan, just as in Psalms He says, "I will instruct you and teach you in the way which you should go; I will counsel you with My eye upon you" (Psalm 32:8 NASB). I thought, "God, I sure hope you're right."

First, I talked to Nathan. I asked his forgiveness for letting the situation get out of hand. I could see the relief in his face when I told him that God had given me instructions, and shock as I outlined the plan and told him there were to be no broken bones or hits to the face. Nathan isn't a violent person, anyway; I had to talk him into doing it. He reluctantly agreed.

As soon as Paul and Michael returned and walked in the door, I asked Paul to come sit down. He had his usual smirk on his face. "Paul, you're always telling Nathan how great you are, how you're stronger and faster than him. Well, I'm going to give you a chance to prove it today."

"What are you talking about?" he exclaimed.

"I'm going to let you and Nathan fight."

Sheep Ears

"That's crazy! He's bigger than me!" At age fifteen, Nathan was 5'9"; Paul, at age twelve, was 5'2".

"What does that matter? Are you scared? You're always saying you can beat him. Here's your chance."

Paul yelled, "Mom, what are you doing?"

I looked at Michael and said, "Does it look to *you* like he's scared?"

Michael nodded. "Sure does."

At that, Paul scowled. "Okay, I'll fight."

God had impressed me to go to all the neighbors beforehand and inform them of what was going to happen. I didn't want anyone to call the police. I picked my friend's yard for the fight because it had soft grass and no trees. Michael and I stood on the sidewalk, and Nathan and Paul went to the center of the "ring." I had a feeling some of the neighbors were peeking through their curtains, but I wasn't sure.

I explained the rules: they had one and a half minutes to fight and they had to stay in the perimeter of the yard. Paul didn't know that I had given Nathan the rule about no face-hitting/no broken bones."

I looked at my watch. "Get ready, get set, go!" Paul ran as fast as he could to the driveway and I called time-out. "Hey, what are you doing? No running! You gotta stay in there and fight!"

"That's no fair! He's bigger than me!"

"But you keep saying you can whoop him. Now fight! You have one minute, twenty-eight seconds." I looked at my watch, shouted, "Go!" and they started again. Nathan grabbed Paul by the arm and flung him to the ground. Paul yelled, "Ow, that hurt!"

Again I called time out. "What's wrong?"

"That hurt!"

"And?"

"Nothing."

"Okay, one minute, twenty-five seconds left. Ready, set, go!"

Nathan stood there waiting for Paul to strike. He said, "Hit me, Paul, hit me!" Paul made a half-jab and Nathan once again grabbed Paul and slung him to the ground.

"Ow, that hurt!" Paul yelled indignantly.

This time it was Nathan who called time out. "Mom, I'm through. That's enough!"

"But you still have a minute and twenty seconds left. You need to finish this."

"No, Mom, no more," was Nathan's response.

Paul and I sat down on the swing and Nathan stood as I gave my speech. "Paul, from now on, any time Nathan hears anything negative from you, he gets one minute and twenty seconds back in the ring with you. All he has to say is, 'Mom, I need my time back,' and he's got it. Do you fully understand that?"

"Yes ma'am."

"Nathan, do you understand?"

"Yes ma'am."

"Okay then, we're done." They shook hands, and as they walked off, I said, "Now remember, Paul, he has—"

"I know, Mom, a minute and twenty seconds." This time there was no smirk on his face.

Only time would tell if Paul had gotten the point. Everything went pretty well for about a month. Then one day I heard Paul getting revved up again. I hollered to Nathan from the other room, "Nathan, do you want your minute and twenty seconds?"

I heard Paul say, "Never mind." And that was the end of it.

The minute and twenty seconds was never mentioned again. Things changed in our household. Paul now respected Nathan, not because he started the fight, but because he had ended it. I believe Paul saw that superiority does not come from physical strength, but from mental meekness. I've heard meekness defined as strength under control—that was Nathan. I call him my "Quiet Thunder."

I really admired Nathan that day. I had no idea what would happen, but God knew. He looked in Nathan's heart and saw forgiveness and mercy. Nathan forgave me for not correcting the problem sooner. He also showed mercy to Paul. God knew that Nathan could be trusted. That day in the temple when Jesus erupted in anger at the people doing trade in the temple at Jerusalem and overturned tables, He was making a point: Don't abuse God's temple. And that day in my neighbor's front yard, God had a message: Paul, don't abuse your brother. Point made.

Nathan was Paul's best man in his wedding. Paul was Nathan's best man in his wedding, and also the godfather to Nathan's beloved son,

Sheep Ears

Ethan. Amazing! Nathan told me that he had talked to Paul about the incident fourteen years later. Nathan had been remorseful and apologized for the fight. Guess what Paul said? "I don't know what you're talking about. I don't even remember." I know he must have remembered, but that was just his way of saying the matter was forgiven and forgotten.

When we have transgressed against God and sought forgiveness, and when we apologize once more, that is His reply: "I don't know what you're talking about. I don't even remember." "I, even I, am the one who wipes out your transgressions for my own sake, And I will not remember your sins" (Isaiah 43:25 NASB). Thank you, Jesus.

Paul went to the school of hard knocks, mentally and physically. It was hard on me and it was hard on him. If you met him now, you would think, "What an awesome, yet humble guy!" It would have been easy back then to rescue him from those hardships, but would his lesson have been learned? Probably not. I'm not saying this same method will work for everyone; I am saying that it is important to seek God. He has the answer to your problems. "Trust in the Lord with all your heart and lean not on your own understanding; In all your ways acknowledge him, and he will make your paths straight" (Proverbs 3:5–6 NIV).

But you'd better be willing to let go and let God do his work. When he asks you to step up, do so even if it's hard. You will be amazed by the results, just as I am amazed by my type-A son now under control, and my meek type-B son, redeemed. "The Lord redeems the soul of His servants, and none of those who trust in Him shall be condemned" (Psalm 34:22 NKJV). Yea, and amen.

Questions

1. Have you ever felt like you were at the end of your rope about something? Describe your dilemma and express your emotions.

2. Is that a good place to be? Explain. (a)

3. Do you feel it's easier to turn to God when your pride is shattered? Why? (b)

4. Do you feel like the school of hard knocks is necessary if you can't learn the easy way? (c)

5. We correct our children because we love them. Do you feel that God corrects us because he loves us? Explain. (d, e)

6. Have you ever considered that the problems in your life could be caused by having the wrong spirit? Write down your thoughts.

7. What did Jesus have to say about the meek people in the world? (f)

Scriptural Answers

(a) "You're blessed when you're at the end of your rope. With less of you there is more of God" (Matthew 5:3).

(b) "I learned God-worship when my pride was shattered. Heart-shattered lives ready for love don't for a moment escape God's notice" (Psalm 51:17).

(c) "It's a school of hard knocks for those who leave God's path" (Proverb 15:10).

(d) "God is fair and just; He corrects the misdirected; Sends them in the right direction" (Psalm 25:8).

(e) "But don't, dear friends, resent God's discipline; don't sulk under His loving correction. It's the child He loves that God corrects; a Father's delight is behind all this" (Proverbs 3:11–12).

(f) "Blessed are the meek; for they shall inherit the earth" (Matthew 5:5 KJV).

20
Have you ever deceived yourself?

My great uncle Maynard was in the Navy and was the captain of his sharpshooting rifle team. He was a heavy smoker. Many years ago, people weren't aware of the dangers of smoking, and it was a popular thing to do. His team competed against other teams for medals and they were always among the best. One day a man told Uncle Maynard that if he quit smoking, his aim would be more accurate.

My uncle argued, "You've got to be kidding. Smoking calms me down. If I quit, my hands would be all over the place. I might even miss the target."

Still, the man's suggestion was such a ridiculous, far-fetched notion to my uncle that he decided to try it. The first time Uncle Maynard competed after he quit smoking, he felt like his hands shook horrendously. The guys on his team hollered, "Just hold your rifle up, man!" They were falling over laughing at him. I imagine he wanted to light up right then but felt that as he had gone this far, he might as well give it a chance. So he slowly lifted the rifle and fired off the most perfect round he had ever shot!

No one was laughing any more. The men shook their heads in disbelief, silent with reverent awe. Not much was said about Uncle Maynard and his cigarettes that day, but by the next competition, Uncle Maynard was not the only man who had stopped smoking; his whole team had quit. When the rifle team went ashore and ate at restaurants, they stacked up all the ashtrays and set them aside because no one needed them anymore. The men were totally and unanimously convinced.

After my dad shared that story with me, I was never, ever tempted to smoke.

You see, it's easy to deceive yourself. "I need cigarettes to calm down." "I need a glass of wine so I can sing beautifully." "I need a line of cocaine before I go on stage." "If I put only one dollar in the tithing envelope, people will never know. They'll think my entire tithe is in there." God gives you your talent and your money. Trust Him with everything you have.

Have you ever watched *Let's Make a Deal?* Imagine this scene: Jesse has already won a brand-new Volkswagen and a sixty-inch LCD television, but he is lured by what's behind curtain number three. He wavers back and forth, he hears the crowd screaming, and he decides to take a chance. The beautiful girl is smiling, tantalizing his senses, and he reasons to himself, "It's probably a Jaguar, a speed boat, a Bahamas cruise, and $60,000. I saw it happen last week on the show. I came here with nothing, so I'm going to take a chance!"

Jesse shouts, "I pick curtain number three!" The audience screams with exhilaration. Slowly the curtains part, and the beautiful model is standing there with only a donkey and a year's worth of chips. The crowd groans and then laughs. Jesse is disgusted with himself. *How could I have been so deceived? Why did I listen to them? I had enough, but I was greedy. Stupid, stupid, stupid!*

Perhaps you want to get ahead in your company and you rationalize that Jacob tricked his brother, Esau, and got the birthright. He also deceived his father and received the family blessing. God continued to love and bless him. *If Jacob did it, then so can I.* But are you aware that Jacob spent over twenty years in a different land hiding from his brother because of that deceit? He was also betrayed time and again by his father-in law, Laban.

Are you trying to justify adultery and rationalize that David was a man after God's heart? *God forgave him and He'll forgive me, too.* But David's actions had consequences. His adultery led to him plotting to murder Bathsheba's husband, Uriah, by sending him to the front line and then commanding the troops to withdraw, allowing the enemy to kill him.

David was confronted by Nathan. "Then David confessed, 'I've sinned against God.' Nathan pronounced, 'Yes, but that's not the last word. God forgives your sin, you won't die for it. But because of your blasphemous behavior, the son born to you will die'" (2 Samuel 12:13–14). David's son died. Bathsheba conceived again and they named that child Solomon, so God continued to bless David after the mess.

But David gave in to temptation when he lusted after Bathsheba. We deceive ourselves if we think we can justify actions that go against what we know in our hearts is right. "Be not deceived, God is not mocked" (Galatians 6:7 KJV). In *The Message*, this passage is translated as, "Don't be misled: No one makes a fool of God."

We make excuses for poor decisions. "It calms my nerves." "They made me do it." "I need to get ahead at work." "I can't resist the temptation." Excuses like these may sound plausible or justifiable, but they lead to sin. We're human and we're going to fail sometimes, but maybe if you think about your actions you can avoid making serious mistakes. I've felt the stings of being deceived myself. We're all in the same deceitful boat.

Hopefully, your new resolution is to nix the excuses. God is *not* mocked. "[Moses] chose to be mistreated along with the people of God rather than to enjoy the fleeting pleasures of sin for a short time" (Hebrews 11:25 NIV). That's the kind of strength we should want.

Change is hard, but until we look into our soul's mirror with eyes wide open and acknowledge that we *want* to change, things will remain the same. God will give us the desire and the ability to change. In Romans 7, Paul gives a beautiful account of his inner battle, the fight between good and evil that we all face. Here is his conclusion:

> So you see how it is: My new life tells me to do right, but the old nature that is still inside me loves to sin. Oh, what a terrible predicament I'm in! Who will free me from my slavery to this deadly lower nature? Thank God! It has been done by Jesus Christ our Lord. He has set me free.
>
> —Romans 7:24–25 LB

Jesus raised the dead, He healed cripples, He mended hearts. Your problems are not too hard for Him. Lay them at the cross and leave them there. Then you will be free indeed. Surely He didn't die in vain.

QUESTIONS

1. Do you justify your bad habits and sins or do you confess them to God? Write down how you feel when you don't confess. (a)

2. Do you feel that confessing your failures to God will result in forgiveness? (b)

3. Is it possible for us to be like we have never sinned in God's eyes? Explain. (c, d)

4. Putting on airs to hang out with popular sinful people is a temptation for many. Do you agree or disagree? How should we act? (e)

5. As a Christian, should you take on immoral ways just to be acceptable to your peers? (f)

6. Have you ever deceived yourself?

SCRIPTURAL ANSWERS

(a) "When I kept it all inside, my bones turned to powder, my words became daylong groans. The pressure never let up; all the juices of my life dried up. Then I let it all out; I said, 'I'll make a clean breast of my failures to God'" (Psalms 32:3–5).

(b) "Suddenly the pressure was gone—my guilt dissolved, and my sin disappeared" (Psalm 32:5).

(c) "For I will forgive their wickedness and will remember their sins no more" (Hebrews 8:12 NIV).

(d) "'Come now, let us reason together,' says the Lord. 'Though your sins are like scarlet, they shall be as white as snow; though they are red as crimson, they shall be like wool'" (Isaiah 1:18 NIV)

(e) "So be content with who you are, and don't put on airs" (1 Peter 5:6).

(f) "Those who belong to Christ Jesus have crucified the sinful nature with its passions and desires" (Galatians 5:24 NIV).

21

Have you ever deprived your kids?

When our three sons were living at home I often wondered if they felt deprived. I look back now, though, and I realize that it was good not to have too much.

When it was time to get school clothes for my sons, one child got new clothes one week, another got them two weeks later, and the third son got new clothes the next week. I explained to them that we couldn't afford to buy everything at once and they understood. Each year I switched up the order of the first buyer; I was always fair. They each knew their day to be first would come, it taught them not to covet. I never heard one complaint. I was grateful for that.

Our sons were avid hunters; we ate about seven deer a year. They felt pride when their skills put meat on our table. We ate most meals at home instead of blowing money we didn't have at restaurants. They learned to take pride in provision, and they learned that family meals at home were important.

We had five people in our three-bedroom, one-bathroom house. We staggered shower times and "other" visits and it all seemed to work out. I cannot remember one time that anyone ever fussed over the bathroom. In fact, when one of our sons was purchasing his house, his wife questioned the fact that there was only one bathroom. His reply was, "Hey, my entire life we had five people in one house with only one bathroom and we didn't have any problems. It's not that big of a deal." They learned patience and consideration.

One by one, our friends moved to more affluent neighborhoods. One of our sons asked if we could move, too. We were making payments on his truck, so I told him, "Sure, but we'd have to sell your truck in order to make the house payments." Moving was never mentioned again. He learned to value living within his means. He also learned to make wise choices.

When Paul was in high school he got twenty dollars a week to use for his gas and lunch money. He knew what a sacrifice it was for us to give him this amount, so he ate at First United Methodist for two bucks every Tuesday, and every Wednesday he ate at Arthur's Bar-B-Que to get a jumbo sandwich for half price. He conserved his gas by not driving all over town. He never complained, although some of his friends got $100 per week as their allowance, because he knew it was the best we could do. He learned to be content.

In high school, our sons had jobs. Aaron worked at Walmart and Paul worked at The Light House, a lighting store. Nathan refereed and umpired games at our local boys and girls club and worked for a lawn care service. We were not able to put much money in their pockets, so they worked to earn spending money. Consequently, they had the *desire* to work. "The desire of the lazy man kills him, for his hands refuse to labor" (Proverb 21:25 NKJV).

When Paul went to college, he got a credit card in his own name. We told him to use the card only for gas for his truck, and we paid the bill. Since he had a baseball scholarship he had to keep up his studies along with attending long practices and a heavy schedule of games, so he couldn't work. After his graduation, he made all his bill payments in a timely manner, which helped his credit rating. He learned to budget.

Paul's truck was an awesome, older model Toyota. It had a four-inch lift, giant tires, a winch, nerf bars, and big speakers: everything a young guy could want. But during his second year in college, it kept breaking down on his six-hour trips home. I don't believe it was meant for long distance traveling. After the fifth breakdown led to a repair bill of over $600, I explained to him how the cost of maintenance for his truck was high compared to what it would be for a reliable, economical car. Paul was in the deer woods. He agreed and gave his reluctant permission via text for me to sell the truck. I cried, my husband cried, and Paul cried. He didn't even get to tell it good-bye.

The dealership gave us an unbelievable trade-in amount and we bought him a used maroon Grand Am, but it was a far cry from a cool "guy truck." The players on his baseball team ridiculed him, but Paul never got angry with us. He said, "Mom, I realize my truck kept breaking down, so I know why we had to sell it, and I'm grateful I still have a vehicle, but I sure do miss it."

I said, "Paul, I know you're sad. Tell God how you feel. I believe that He'll make things right for you one day, if you keep the right attitude." Lamentations 3:25–27 says, "God proves to be good to the man who passionately waits, to the woman who diligently seeks. It's a good thing to quietly hope, quietly hope for help from God. It's a good thing when you're young to stick it out through the hard times."

Paul may have had his doubts, but he never brought them up. We said a prayer and left it in God's hands. He learned self-sacrifice. And guess what? He now owns a brand-new Texas Edition Silverado and has already put a lift kit on it. He saw the faithfulness of God.

Do you think your kids are deprived? That's not a bad thing, because they might learn a lot of great qualities along the way. Are you giving them too much? You might want to rethink what you're doing. "What good would it do to get everything you want and lose you, the real you?" (Luke 9:25). It's good to make sure you have your priorities straight.

You might be reading this in your easy chair thinking to yourself, "You don't have to worry about my kids, Sherry. We didn't have much, so that was never an issue at my house." I'd like to make an analogy that might help you see things in a different perspective.

We are God's children, but did you ever complain about how deprived you were? "It's not fair! Yvonne got a whole new wardrobe but I've been wearing these rags for five years." God might have given you a whole new wardrobe next month, but because of a wrong attitude, decided to wait a little longer before giving it to you. In fact, you might never get your due. Be happy for other people when they get theirs. Yours might be right around the corner.

Pray for God to give you creative ways to contribute to the household

Sheep Ears

income if you're running short of funds. He may give you an idea that could make you a millionaire. Then use wisdom to spend and invest your money in a prudent manner. Solomon talks about how we can learn from the industrious ant:

> Nobody has to tell [the ant] what to do. All summer it stores up food; at harvest it stockpiles provisions. So how long are you going to laze around doing nothing? How long before you get out of bed? A nap here, a nap there, a day off here, a day off there, sit back, take it easy—do you know what comes next? Just this: You can look forward to a dirt-poor life, poverty your permanent houseguest!
> —Proverbs 6:7–12

The apostle Paul said, "I know what it is to be in need, and I know what it is to have plenty. I have learned the secret of being content in any and every situation, whether well fed or hungry, whether living in plenty or in want" (Philippians 4:12 NIV). That's how I want to be.

Paul's statement brings to mind a birthday party I attended for a beautiful girl named Legacy. Her parents requested that each adult guest bring her, instead of a gift, a letter containing a word of wisdom. It was her thirteenth birthday, which in a way marked her passage into adulthood, kind of like a Bat Mitzvah. As each guest read their nuggets of wisdom, I thought how wise her parents were; they valued the experience of people who had been down the path that their daughter was only beginning to travel. Legacy patiently listened to and hugged each reader. And guess what? Every single person had brought a gift, too. I thought back to King Solomon requesting wisdom. God was so pleased by this that he gave Solomon not only extreme wisdom, but riches, too.

I overheard Legacy's mother, LaJuana, telling the other guests about Legacy's ninth birthday party. The candles were lit, the song was sung, and they had told Legacy to make a wish and blow out the candles. They waited and waited until the candles were melting into the cake. Finally LaJuana had asked, "What's wrong? Why aren't you blowing out the candles?" Legacy said, "I have nothing to wish for. I have the love of my mommy and daddy and that's all I need." Out of the mouths of babes. That's why Jesus said we must become childlike. I love Legacy's wisdom. I wonder if God is craving to hear us say, "I love you; I have no more needs."

All this time we thought we were deprived, but God was teaching us lessons. Embrace God and He really will give you the desires of your heart.

Happy Birthday!

Dear Legacy,

Congratulations to you and best wishes on your thirteenth birthday! Most parents have birthday parties for their children where the partygoers are expected to bring presents. However, your parents have asked for nuggets of wisdom. The advice you get today from your loved ones will outlast any material gifts you could receive, so hold the words close to your heart.

I will give you keys of wisdom that have helped me throughout my life. I hope they will help you on *your* journey.

- Don't sweat the small stuff. (Don't make little issues into big problems.)
- Look for others in need and you will never be needy.
- Always honor and obey your parents.
- Give to God, give to others, and give to yourself.
- Don't pout.
- Forgive yourself if you mess up.
- Set goals and never give up.
- Read the Bible.
- Ask yourself if you're happy, and you cease to be happy. (Don't overanalyze.)
- Never cheat; you only cheat yourself.
- Be patient.
- Laugh loudly and strongly every day. Laugh with others, not at them.

Last, but not least:

- Love God with all your heart, mind, and soul.

Trust God from the bottom of your heart;
don't try to figure out everything on your own.

Listen to God's voice in everything
you do, everywhere you go;
He's the one who will keep you on track;
Don't assume that you know it all.
Run to God! Run from evil.

—Proverbs 3:5–7

That was King Solomon's advice and it sounds pretty good to me! *Happy birthday, Legacy!*

Love,

Sherry Witt

Questions

1. Are you comfortable talking to God and discussing your concerns? Why or why not? (a)

2. Is there a difference between wants and needs? Explain your answer from God's viewpoint.

3. Do you think it is a good idea for kids to have jobs? Why or why not? (b)

4. Is it easy or hard for you to join Legacy in saying, "I don't need a thing"? (c)

5. Do you feel that it is easy to get caught up in material things? (d)

6. Do you feel that wants can turn into greed? Explain. (e)

Scriptural Answers

(a) "Open up before God, keep nothing back; he'll do whatever needs to be done" (Psalm 37:5).

(b) "Let the thief no longer steal, but rather let him labor, doing honest work with his own hands, so that he may have something to share with someone in need" (Ephesians 4:28 ESV).

(c) "God, my Shepherd! I don't need a thing" (Psalm 23:1).

(d) "What good is it for a man to gain the whole world, and yet lose or forfeit his very self?" (Luke 9:25 NIV).

(e) "Then he said to them, 'Watch out! Be on your guard against all kinds of greed; a man's life does not consist in the abundance of his possessions'" (Luke 12:15 NIV).

22

Have you ever encountered an angel?

I think an angel came to my door about twenty-five years ago. Am I positive? No, but he sure was suspicious.

A young man about nineteen or twenty years old knocked on my door. He was selling books and had a black suitcase in his hand. He asked to come in. Normally, I wouldn't let a stranger in my home, but for some reason I felt at ease with him. He sat down and promptly told me that he was hungry and asked if I could give him any food. It was several days until Randy's next paycheck, and we were getting by on the bare essentials. At first I said, "No," but then I remembered that I did have some peanut butter and bread. He said that would be fine. I also gave him some lemonade. After he ate, he seemed very grateful and stood to leave. As I closed the door behind him, I thought, *Hey, he didn't even try to sell me any books. That seems strange.* All of a sudden I remembered the Scripture, "Be ready with a meal or a bed when it's needed. Why, some have extended hospitality to angels without ever knowing it!" (Hebrews 13:2). I flung open the door. I ran to the sidewalk and anxiously looked around for the salesman. He was nowhere to be seen, and there hadn't been enough time for him to get inside another house.

Some people would trivialize the encounter, but not me. I was glad that I had given him the meal. I don't believe it was important *what* I'd given him, but just that I gave. Isn't that the way God is? He doesn't really care what you give; He just tests you to see if you're willing.

Nowadays, I wouldn't recommend letting a stranger into your home. But have you ever seen a lonely look on a person in church and invited them out to lunch? Sometimes companionship means more than ordering the Ultimate Feast from Red Lobster in a booth by yourself.

Can you imagine what it's like to have three kids under five years of age and to wish you could afford to eat out? You could make a meal out possible for a struggling family. Think about how much it would mean to them and forget about that necklace you were going to buy for yourself at JCPenney. It may be that you extend hospitality to an angel without even knowing it.

Proverb 31 gives a description of a worthy woman. You might want to read it sometime. This is the verse I want to draw attention to: "She's quick to assist anyone in need, reaches out to help the poor" (Proverb 31:20). You see, you could be an angel in disguise to someone in need.

Angels do much more than test our hearts, though. They protect us. They hearken to God's bidding. "When I was desperate, I called out, and God got me out of a tight spot. God's angel sets up a circle of protection around us while we pray" (Psalms 34:6–7). I can tell you of four instances when God miraculously got me out of a tight spot, and the only explanation was not road assistance, but angel assistance.

Incident 1: I was twenty-one years old and driving in an unfamiliar part of town. Add to that the good hard cry I was having and a tree branch partially covering a stop sign and you have a bad driving situation. I ran through the stop sign at the exact same time a lady was driving through the intersection. *Blam!* I never saw her. We collided and my car went onto the sidewalk, over some steps, and through a tree. Yes, that's right. I said *through* a tree. Did I feel it? No. This was before we were required by law to wear seatbelts. I hit my tailbone on the passenger armrest, came back to the driver's side, and I tried to raise myself up off the floorboard to grab the steering wheel.

I remember that I said, "Please, God, help me to stop." And instantly the car stopped. It really was instantaneous, like when you hit the pause button on the television. Silent and effortlessly, the car stopped. When I got out, I looked at where our cars had collided, where I had chipped the cement off the sidewalk, and where I had landed. There was no logical explanation. *I went through the tree.* I had an undeniable realization that

God wasn't through with me on this earth yet. I was humbled. I know I should have died. But I was thankful for my protective angels.

Incident 2: When Nathan, my middle son, was in his third year of college baseball, I traveled to one of his out-of-state games. It took me about three hours to drive there. I watched them play two back-to-back nine-inning games, and then I had to drive the three hours back home. The coach let Nathan ride in the car with me instead of in the school van. We were both tired, but he was *exhausted* from catching for eighteen straight innings. I drove for two hours while he rested. I was starting to go cross-eyed when he said, "I'm rested, mom. I'll drive. You look really sleepy."

I was glad to hear those words. We switched seats and I leaned back in mine to rest. I'm not sure how much time elapsed, but I woke up to weird bumping noises. It was dark and the headlights of our car illuminated the weeds as we drove swiftly through a dry, overgrown field. The sounds were amplified. *Swish, swish, swish, thump, thump, swish!* Everything looked black and white.

Nathan had fallen asleep right in the middle of a humongous curve by Hardin Farms in Grady, Arkansas. We both woke up at about the same time. He tried to gain control of the car—we were heading straight for some raised railroad tracks. I heard a voice say, "It's okay. I've got everything under control." It sounded like Nathan's voice, but it felt like an angel's voice. It was very soothing. Nathan didn't panic, and neither did I. He steered the car back to the shoulder and we stopped to regroup and assess the damage. Everything was fine. We headed back home. We definitely weren't sleepy anymore! I think we could have driven to California and back at that point.

What if there had been a car in our path? What if we had stayed asleep? We might have ramped the train tracks like stunt drivers and gotten airborne. It could have been ugly, but God in His mercy sent angels to protect us. "He will command his angels concerning you to guard you in all your ways; they will lift you up in their hands, so that you will not strike your foot against a stone" (Psalms 91.11–12 NIV). Or, in our case, so we wouldn't flip, crash, and burn. I know that we were spared. Thanks, angels!

Incident 3: My husband and I were driving to watch Paul play baseball in Waco, Texas. It had begun to rain hard that afternoon, but it hadn't

Sheep Ears 105

felt dangerous to drive, so we'd kept traveling. Randy had the cruise control set and we were listening to a Joyce Meyer CD. All of a sudden, we hydroplaned. We headed straight for the grass median. The median was V-shaped: a sharp slope downward, then a sharp incline. Things happened quickly, yet also as if in slow motion. I grabbed the dashboard. We were sliding sideways. Mud was hitting my window like rapid-fire darts. I said, "God will protect us, God will protect us." I have no doubt that God heard.

I was bracing for the flip as Randy tried to get control of the car. He has always loved NASCAR racing, and at that moment he was better than Richard Petty, Dale Earnhardt, and Davey Allison all rolled into one. We never flipped, although we should have because we skidded sideways in the grass in the median for about forty feet. The car slowed down as we reached the opposite lane of traffic. Randy steered the car to the shoulder.

Five seconds later, an eighteen-wheeler and seven cars blew past us. I don't know how I had the presence of mind to count, but I did. Our little, red Grand Am shook as the force of the air whipped around us. *Whew!* We got out of the car and checked for damage. The back passenger tire had grass wedged between it and the rim, and the grill was busted, but that was all. Thank God it wasn't worse. We turned the car around and went a half mile back to Mount Vernon, where a mechanic dug the mud out of the rims. Then we headed back down the highway toward the game in Waco.

How did we survive? We should have flipped. We were calm. We could have panicked. If it had happened five seconds later, we could have been a disastrous wreck on the highway. *Why were we spared, while others died?* I don't know. But I do know that we were grateful for the angels who guided us and calmed us that day.

Incident 4: This isn't the biggest incident that has ever happened to me, but it is still significant. I was leaving the shopping center near my home, turning left. There's a median there that has bushes which partially block one's view of oncoming cars. I couldn't see the car that was coming, but my angel did. Suddenly, it seemed like an invisible force grabbed my steering wheel and made a hard left. Both vehicles stopped parallel to each other. The woman in the other car didn't look too happy. I could tell by the way her face contorted, mouthing angry words. But all I felt was relief. I never saw her coming, so how did I know to turn my steering wheel? I believe that I have angels all around me.

Some people might say I'm lucky, but not me; I would say I'm blessed. God's angels parted the tree, they woke Nathan up when he fell asleep, they brought Randy those NASCAR skills, and they steered me away from danger. I believe that one even asked me for food on a hot summer's afternoon.

Take time to reflect on similar incidents in your life. Perhaps you received divine intervention and took the rescue for granted. Maybe your child couldn't find his shoes and it delayed your trip, but as you proceeded on your journey, you passed a wreck that could have involved you, if you'd been earlier. Maybe you were looking for your cell phone before heading out the door, and then noticed the pan of grease on the burner that you had forgotten to turn off. You might have planned to be gone for three hours. Be grateful for the lost phone. You could have returned to a charred home.

Our family doesn't have a monopoly on angels, of course. There are plenty of angels for everyone. Call on God. He'll send them your way, and they will be there faster than the twinkle of His eye. Believe me! Angels are constantly at work, beckoning to God's voice. We are not to worship the angels, but our God who made them.

Look around. Count your blessings. See what the Lord has done. And always give thanks.

QUESTIONS

1. Write about a time you may have encountered or been rescued by an angel.

2. Do you feel that God will send angels ahead of us? (a)

3. Should we praise the angels, or our God who created the angels? (b)

4. If angels can restrain lions, do you feel that they could restrain an animal that attacked you? (c)

5. Do you think that angels communicate with God? (d)

6. Can angels talk to us? Wake us up? (e)

7. Who mediates between us and God: Jesus or the angels? (f)

8. Do you feel that you have been an angel to someone in need? How?

Scriptural Answers

(a) "I am sending an angel ahead of you to guard you along the way and to bring you to the place I have prepared" (Exodus 23:20 NIV).

(b) "Then Nebuchadnezzar said, 'Praise be to the God of Shadrach, Meshach, and Abednego, who has sent his angel and rescued his servants!'" (Daniel 3:28 NIV).

(c) "My God sent his angel and he shut the mouths of the lions. They have not hurt me, because I was found innocent in his sight. Nor have I ever done any wrong before you, O king" (Daniel 6:22 NIV).

(d) "Watch that you don't treat a single one of these childlike believers arrogantly. You realize, don't you, that their personal angels are constantly in touch with my Father in heaven?" (Matthew 18:10).

(e) "Suddenly an angel of the Lord appeared and a light shone in the cell. He struck Peter on the side and woke him up. 'Quick, get up!' he said, and the chains fell off Peter's wrists" (Acts 12:7 NIV).

(f) "For there is one God and one mediator between God and men, the man Christ Jesus, who gave himself as a ransom for all men" (1 Timothy 2:5–6 NIV).

23
Have you ever faced a bully with authority?

When my mild middle-child, Nathan, was in the third grade, he suddenly developed headaches and stomachaches. These symptoms seemed to get more severe as each school day began. When he got home, they disappeared, only to appear again the next day. Nothing Saturday. Nothing Sunday. But on Monday it started all over again.

I figured that something must be going on at school, and after a long probing talk, I finally got the answer: Orville. Orville was the third-grade playground bully. Nathan told me that Orville went around the school yard at recess picking on kids and starting fights that he usually won. Orville was constantly in trouble, but nothing fazed him.

My momma-bear instincts came out and I marched straight to the principal's office. Mr. Chambers informed me that Orville's mother had been notified and that Orville had been punished and paddled, but nothing affected his Goliath-like personality.

I prayed to God for wisdom and He gave me a solution. I informed Mr. Chambers that I was going to give Nathan permission to retaliate if he was approached (or more likely, attacked) by Orville at recess. Nathan was not to start the fight, but he was going to finish it. Nathan heard me telling this to the principal, and I must admit, I saw him stand a little taller with a slight grin on his face. Mr. Chambers told me since they had exhausted all their ideas, he would not punish Nathan if there was a ruckus. Then I went to Nathan's teacher and told her of the plan. She was also agreeable. She was tired of the bullying, too. Nathan heard this conversation as well.

The next morning when we left our home, he looked a lot more confident. You see, he was no longer afraid of the repercussions of his actions. He now had authority backing him up: his mom, his principal, and his teacher. I waved to my son as I left him at school. I was a little bit proud, but a little bit scared. What if Nathan backed down? What if Nathan got whooped? What if he doubted the support of his principal and teacher? But there was no turning back now.

So I went home and waited. It seemed like twenty-four hours passed before my child got home that day. I was sitting outside in the swing when I finally saw him coming down the sidewalk. *Well, he doesn't look like he's limping. That's a good sign!*

As he came up the driveway, he said in his happy-go-lucky voice, "Hi, Mom! How was your day?"

"It was fine, but what about you? Anything happen with Orville?"

"Oh, I beat him up," was his nonchalant reply.

He passed me and headed for the door. "Wait a minute, Nathan. What happened?"

"Well, don't worry Mom. Orville started the fight, but I finished it. I knocked him down, sat on his belly, then I hit him on his face with both fists. When I got up and walked away, everybody was cheering for me."

"Did you get in trouble?"

"Nope. Hey, Mom, what's there to eat?"

The next morning, Nathan did not have a stomachache or a headache. In fact, I seem to remember him skipping a little as he left for school.

When he arrived home in the afternoon, he said, "Hey Mom, you won't believe what happened today!"

"What?" I asked with a little trepidation.

"Orville went to beat up Steven and Steven hollered, 'Go get Nathan!' When Orville heard that, he got off Steven and ran!"

And that is the last I ever heard of Orville. There were no other problems then or later in their school years. Nowadays schools have no-bullying policies, so I am issuing a disclaimer: I don't recommend anyone repeat what I did. However, it does make my point.

Satan is a bully. He intimidates you, he taunts you, and he beats you up. You can try to reason with him, but it won't work. You need authority, and that comes from the word of God, that is, the Bible. Is Satan giving you fits? Do you have headaches and stomachaches trying to avoid him? Do you need authority? Listen to how David handled Goliath:

> David answered, "You come at me with sword and spear and battle-ax. I come to you in the name of God-of-the-Angel-Armies, the God of Israel's troops, whom you curse and mock. This very day God is handing you over to me. I'm about to kill you, cut off your head and serve up your body and the bodies of your Philistine buddies to the crows and coyotes. The whole earth will know that there's an extraordinary God in Israel. And everyone gathered here will learn that God doesn't save by means of sword or spear. The battle belongs to God—he's handing you to us on a platter!"
> —1 Samuel 17:45–47

Does David sound like a wimp? No. And don't *you* sound like one either. Dare to defy Satan. Come at him in God's authority. Nathan would have gotten himself in big trouble if he had said, "Orville, I am going to fight you today because my little brother told me to." Orville might have left Nathan lying in the dust. But Nathan knew who was backing him up.

Do you know who's backing you up? When you have an illness, do you say, "Satan, the doctor told me I have a disease. I know you're doing this, so just leave me alone, will ya?" No! Your best defense is to find a Scripture like this: "But he was pierced for our transgressions, he was crushed for our iniquities; the punishment that brought us peace was upon him, and by his wounds we are healed" (Isaiah 53:5 NIV). Not "were" healed, but "are" healed!

If I need wisdom or guidance, I don't just read a good book, I read *the Book.* "Trust in the Lord with all your heart and lean not to your own understanding; in all your ways acknowledge him, and he will make your paths straight" (Proverbs 3:5–6 NIV). If I have a really big issue, I'll write every relevant Scripture I can find down on notebook paper; then when I start to doubt, I reread the verses and my faith builds. This is my authority. I have God's words to back up my fight, and so do you. Don't shake at the edge of the playground or hide underneath your covers at home. God-of-the-Angel-Armies has your back. You can confidently stand taller knowing whose shadow you stand underneath.

So go ahead and be like Nathan and David. Face your foe. He's bluffing. You have authority. You belong to the extraordinary God-of-the-Angel-Armies.

Questions

1. Write about a similar incident you faced with your child.

2. How did you handle it?

3. Do you feel that God will shelter you from bullies if you call on Him? (a)

4. Can you trust God to set everything right with your enemies? (b)

5. How do you feel after someone stands up for you? Discuss. (c)

6. Sometimes it's frightening when the Devil taunts. How should you respond? (d)

7. Policemen have authority and a boss has authority, but do you have authority over evil spirits, disease, and sickness? Who gave you that authority? (e)

Scriptural Answers

(a) "I call to you, God, because I'm sure of an answer. So—answer! bend your ear! listen sharp! ... Take in your frightened children who are running from the neighborhood bullies straight to you" (Psalms 17:6–7).

(b) "The day my enemies turned tail and ran, they stumbled on you and fell on their faces. You took over and set everything right; when I needed you, you were there, taking charge" (Psalms 9:3–4).

(c) "Because you've always stood up for me, I'm free to run and play" (Psalm 63:7).

(d) "So let God work his will in you. Yell a loud no to the Devil and watch him scamper. Say a quiet yes to God and he'll be there in no time" (James 4:7).

(e) "[Jesus] called his twelve disciples to him and gave them authority to drive out evil spirits and to heal every disease and sickness" (Matthew 10:1 NIV).

24

Have you ever faced your fears?

I recently had the dewclaws removed from my dog Mollie. The dewclaws are small, unnecessary toes on a dog's front legs. My veterinarian, Dr. Grissom, told me that a dog can easily injure its eyes if it scratches them with its dewclaws, so I decided to have Mollie's taken off to prevent possible future damage. Mollie, a Belgian Malinois mix, was a little over a year old and weighed fifty-five pounds at the time. The surgery ended up being a lot more extensive than I had imagined, since dewclaws are usually removed when the puppy is three days old and its cartilage is still soft. Dr. Grissom cut four-inch incisions in each of Mollie's front paws, removed the dewclaws, then stitched the incisions closed with steel sutures.

Mollie seemed to be in some pain, but she took it like a trooper. Four days after the surgery, I thought a quick jaunt around the block would lift her spirits since she was accustomed to a daily walk. I was right. She perked up and her legs looked fine.

The following day, we started on another quick trip around the block, but things weren't as peaceful as the day before. We passed by a yard with a three-foot wooden privacy fence that divided two properties. The fence blocked my view and I couldn't see who or what was in the front yard. Suddenly, two dogs, a Labrador Retriever and a pit bull, ran toward us. They weren't on leashes, so they came freely bounding toward Mollie. I really don't think they intended any harm; they just wanted to sniff. But Mollie had been chased by a Lab in the past, and she was petrified. She bucked and snorted until she came out of her collar, then she took off like she was being chased by a mountain lion and a wild hog. Man, she turned on the turbo boosters!

She ran down the street and then bolted the length of an elementary schoolyard. She crossed another street before she even slowed down. The other two dogs stopped at the end of the first block. I kept yelling, "Mollie, stop! Mollie!" But to no avail. She didn't hear anything I said. I guess her inner voice was warning, "Danger! Danger! Get out of here quickly!"

Finally, I remembered to tweet. I can't whistle loudly, so I've trained her to come to me when I roll my tongue and give a really loud tweet. She recognized the sharp trill and stopped in her tracks. When she realized she was no longer being chased, she came to me.

I looked at her wounds and my heart sank. Blood was dripping down both paws. I was mad at myself for taking her out too soon. The wounds were not healed enough. I should have waited longer. I had no idea that those dogs would be running loose, but they couldn't be blamed. By that afternoon, Mollie had licked her sores so forcefully that I had to take her back to Dr. Grissom. He said one stitch was busted, two were coming loose. He gave me ointment, pain pills, and antibiotics.

The next day, Mollie had busted out of her other two stitches from all the licking. I took her back to the vet and he rebandaged her leg and put a protective e-collar on her neck to prevent further damage due to her vigorous self-medicating licking. Now she could heal properly.

People respond to their fears just like Mollie did. They run from their fears instead of running to God. I was Mollie's master. I wanted to help her but she ran from me. Like Mollie, we try to cure our own problems and only make things worse. We should instead ask God for his help. Maybe the solution is to face what you've been running from and let God do His work in you.

God was preparing Moses to lead the Israelites out of Egyptian bondage. But Moses saw an Egyptian treating an Israelite unjustly, and in anger, he killed the Egyptian. He thought no one was looking. However, the next day, Moses tried to convince someone to stop fighting and make peace. "The one who started the fight said, 'Who put you in charge of us? Are you going to kill me like you killed that Egyptian yesterday?' When Moses heard that, realizing that the word was out, he ran for his life and lived in exile over in Midian" (Acts 7:27–29).

Moses ran from his fears. But God had a different solution. Forty years later, God spoke to Moses: "I have come down to rescue them. So now come! I will send you back to Egypt [as My messenger]" (Acts 7:34 AB). God's original plan for Moses to rescue the Israelites never changed. It took him forty years, but Moses finally faced the very place he had fled. This time there was success: Moses led the Israelites out of bondage from the Egyptians.

I wanted to help Mollie face her fears. I wanted her to be comfortable around other dogs. We registered in an eight-week course of obedience training. Mollie also had a fear of getting into cars. It was a major ordeal to accomplish this. I had to pick up her front paws and place them on the seat, then grab her by the hind legs and shove while my husband grabbed the leash from the other side of the car. He pulled as I shoved. Finally, exhausted, I could shut the door and begin the trek. By the time we got to the class, let's just say the towels that lined the back seat were saturated.

The next problem was getting her through the door to the building. I was glad that her collar was snug and that I had a tight grip on her because her instinct was to bail. I reeled her back in. The first thing she did was find cover under a wooden table. The instructor, John Segars, talked about the class while she shivered in seclusion. The other dogs sat by their owners, but not Mollie. If it were possible to dig through concrete, she would have dug her way to China.

There were lots of rambunctious dogs barking and tugging at their owners' leashes. I'll be honest: I wasn't sure if this was a good idea. I had been attacked by two dogs in the past, and I could imagine one or more of the dogs breaking loose from their owners and charging not only Mollie, but also me. However, I was there to help Mollie. That's what kept me in the class.

Slowly but surely, Mollie and I became more comfortable. She started socializing with some of the smaller dogs, then graduated to the larger dogs. There were two Rottweilers that were especially intimidating, but their owners had good control of them. Each Rott wore a prong collar. Prong collars, or pinch collars as they are sometimes called, help with correction by startling the dog. At the fifth class, we went up to the Rotts a few times, and I talked casually while Mollie got up the nerve to take a few sniffs. Believe me, that was a major accomplishment.

By the sixth lesson, I no longer needed my husband's assistance getting Mollie into the car. I just opened the door and she hopped in. Mollie walked into the classroom without balking, and she no longer feared socializing with her fellow classmates. She had valiantly faced her fears. I must admit that I felt more at ease, too.

Twenty dogs started the class, but by testing day, there were only twelve canines left. The two Rotts won first and second place in the obedience competition. I'm proud to say that Mollie took a third-place ribbon. John turned around and told the other participants what a feat this was for Mollie because of her extreme anxiety. They gave her a resounding round of applause and I felt I was about to explode from joy and pride.

John informed us of an extra two-day session of training to become a Canine Good Citizen®. The training entailed ten potentially stressful tests, including intermingling with a crowd, and separation from me. A large metal pole was also slammed to the concrete floor after your dog passed the instructor to test the dog's reaction. This one worried me.

Only four dogs returned for the first extra session: the two Rottweilers, a German Shepherd, and Mollie. To be honest, Mollie didn't do so well. She was jumpy after the noisy pole-slamming. The instructor informed us that prong collars weren't allowed for the test, which made the Rottweiler owners cringe. A possible recipe for disaster.

The day of the official test came. It was freezing and raining, and I had had a rough day at work. The other dogs wouldn't be wearing their prong collars. Everything in me screamed, "Don't go! It's not worth it!" The slamming pole was the best rationalization I could come up with to not go. It seemed cruel. But I kept feeling a quiet gnawing in my heart. *Just go. Trust Mollie.*

We got in the car and I had a mental battle even as I drove. *Go home, go test, go home, go test.* Suddenly, I realized I was in the parking lot, the point of decision. Mollie and I walked in with pretended confidence. The German Shepherd hadn't come, so it was just the two beefy Rottweilers and Mollie.

Mollie and I went first. She was amazing! She passed with flying colors. Everyone gave her a standing ovation. She had faced her fears and overcome them: walking in a crowded area, the unpronged rambunctious Rotts, the slamming pole. All of it. John said, "I have to admit, when I saw her in the last session, I wouldn't have given you a plug nickel for her to pass the test."

Have you ever run from your fears? Is your heart hurting? Go to God and let Him make you whole again. "Don't panic. I'm with you. There's no need to fear for I'm your God. I'll give you strength. I'll help you. I'll hold you steady. Keep a firm grip on you" (Isaiah 41:10). God will help you. Just as I helped Mollie, He will help you. He helped Moses face his fears, and He will help you. Go to the only One who can take your pain away. Quit trying to self-medicate. Go to the healer who created your heart. Jesus said, "Don't run from suffering; embrace it. Follow me and I'll show you how. Self-help is no help at all" (Luke 9:24).

The next time you face a problem that makes you want to run, consider the other option: facing your fears. Don't panic, because God will give you strength. He will help you.

Mollie and I couldn't have passed the test unless we were willing to take it. And what about Moses? For all we know, the Israelites would still be in Egypt if Moses hadn't faced his fear.

How do you know whether you can pass your test unless you are willing to face *your* fears? The new job, the shadow on the mammogram, the tax audit, the parent with dementia, the bulimic teenager. They are all rational fears, but God wants to help you. There are people in the stands waiting to give you a standing ovation for your courage. But it's your decision. If you don't face your fears, you will never know total victory.

QUESTIONS

1. Write down any fears that you are afraid to face.

2. Do you feel that God is with you when you are afraid or do you think He leaves you? Explain. (a)

3. Will God give you victory? (b)

4. God will only help certain people. True or false? Explain. (c)

5. When you are afraid and you don't think you're able to face your fears, what Scriptures can you quote? (d, e)

6. Do you fear death? What Scripture could help you with this? (f)

Scriptural Answers

(a) "I am the God of Abraham, your Father; don't fear a thing, because I'm with you" (Genesis 26:24).

(b) "He shall say: 'Hear, O Israel, today you are going into battle against your enemies. Do not be fainthearted or afraid; do not be terrified or give way to panic before them. For the Lord your God is the One who goes with you to fight for you against your enemies to give you victory" (Deuteronomy 20:3–4 NIV).

(c) "It's exactly the same no matter what a person's religious background may be: the same God for all of us, acting the same incredible generous way to everyone who calls out for help. Everyone who calls, 'Help, God!' gets help" (Romans 10:12–13).

(d) "I can do everything through him who gives me strength" (Philippians 4:13 NIV).

(e) "When I am afraid, I will trust in you. In God, whose word I praise, in God I trust; I will not be afraid. What can mortal man do to me?" (Psalms 56:3–4 NIV).

(f) "Yea, though I walk through the valley of the shadow of death, I will fear no evil: For You are with me; Your rod and Your staff, they comfort me" (Psalm 23:4 NKJV).

25
Have you ever felt like giving up?

Do you like to pick up a book, skim over the first part, then go to the back of the book and read the last chapter? I'm one of those people and perhaps you are, too. So I'll skip to the end and tell you that my son Paul played baseball for the Baylor Bears. In 2005, his senior year, he started all seventy games at shortstop and established a Baylor single-season record with 218 assists, which means that he turned 218 double plays. Baylor went to the College World Series in Omaha, Nebraska, that year and he knocked in the winning run to beat Tulane, who was ranked first in the nation. He received a World Series ring. The Florida Marlins drafted him in the fifteenth round and he played in the minor leagues for three years.

That's the good part. Now let me take you to the beginning of his baseball career.

We knew there was something special about Paul's abilities in baseball when he turned a triple play by himself in T-ball as a five-year-old. We couldn't speak. How could a five-year-old think to execute a double play, much less a triple play? I guess you could say he was given a gift.

Fast-forward to the summer before his sophomore year in high school. Paul's all-star team played in the finals of the Junior Babe Ruth World Series in our hometown. My husband, Randy, was the coach. Paul pitched two complete games and played shortstop in the other games. They played against California, Washington, Kentucky, Louisiana, and Florida. Their team came in second, which was unbelievable for a local team, and Paul won MVP of the tournament. In a way, you might say he was a local hero.

Everywhere we went, we would hear shouts of "Congratulations!" "Good job!" and "Way to go!" Although Paul was confident, I was pleased that he didn't let all the fame go to his head.

He lettered in basketball that year, and when that season was over, he went straight to baseball. He hopped on the bus with the team and rode forty miles to play against Dumas High School. I don't remember all the details, but he pitched a five-inning shut-out game, which means that the other team didn't even score. I believe he got three hits. As he boarded the bus afterward, he waved and flashed me one of his thanks-for-coming grins.

But a different son got off the bus. He was sullen when he got in the car. I tried to recount some of the good points of the game, but all I got was silence. When we got home, he burst into a tirade. "Mom, the coach cursed and ridiculed me the whole trip back. He made me sit by him where everyone could hear and ranted for thirty minutes. He said, 'Where in the h--- did you learn to pitch like that? Did your blankety-blank-blank dad teach you? That's the worst hitting I've ever seen in my blankety-blank life!'" I told Paul that I guessed Coach Bock was just trying to keep him humble. Privately I questioned his method, but Coach Bock had received so many national awards for coaching, who was I to doubt him? After all, Coach Bock was the 1992 American Baseball Coaches' Association "National Baseball Coach of the Year," and he was also voted Collegiate Baseball's "Coach of the Century."

Week after week passed with Paul coming home from practice and retreating to his room. I wasn't sure if he was just tired or trying to hold everything in. I was told by another parent that on one particular afternoon practice, several coaches had laughed at and ridiculed Paul when he was in the pitching cage for two hours. I hurt for him, but God restrained me from initiating a conversation about all the injustice. About a week later, he walked in the door and announced that he would be quitting baseball. "It's too much to handle. Coach Bock isn't fair. No one should have to put up with this mess. All I've done is my best and all I get is cussing!"

I knew that what I said next would be crucial. I shot up one of my quick two-second prayers. "God help me!"

I boldly said, "Paul, I'm not going to Coach Bock and tell him to leave you alone. I'm not even going to pray that he leaves you alone."

Sheep Ears

He looked shocked. He took a long gulp of air and said, "You're not?"

"No, I'm going to pray that you learn how to handle his criticism. If you ever want to play college ball or professional ball, you will have to learn how to hear the harsh words."

Wow! Where did that come from? Only God could have given me strength to say that. "Pray that I'll know what to say and have the courage to say it at the right time" (Ephesians 6:19).

Paul never complained after that. I'm sure the barrage of criticism didn't stop, but now I believe Paul looked at the situation differently.

Fast-forward to the summer after Paul's senior year in high school. He played American Legion baseball and hit fourteen home runs. He was not normally a power hitter, so this took everyone by surprise. He went to Baylor University for the first hitting practice, excited to show off his power swing. He bounced three balls off the outfield fence. Pleased with himself and believing the coach would also be pleased, he confidently walked over to the coach. He patted Paul on the back and said, "That's good Paul, but we want you to hit like this …"

The coach went on to change every single thing about Paul's batting. Paul was so confused, he could hardly focus his eyes on the ball anymore. They also moved him to second base, a position he had only played once before. He called home wanting to complain, but we told him to listen to whatever they told him to do. "Paul, the Baylor coaches gave you the scholarship and disobedience would surely take it away."

I'm so glad Paul had to adjust his thinking in high school. What if my action then had been to rescue my darling son from the wrath of Bock? Paul would have become a prima donna. Parents don't realize how they hurt their children by rescuing them. Isn't that the way it is with us? We want God to rescue us, but God wants us to grow. "We can rejoice … when we run into problems and trials for we know that they are good for us—they help us learn to be patient. And patience develops strength of character in us and helps us trust God more each time we use it until finally our hope and faith are strong and steady" (Romans 5:3–4 LB).

So Paul grew some more during his freshman year at college. He adapted and things went pretty smoothly for a while. At this point, I was glad that Coach Bock had been so hard on Paul, otherwise he would have argued with his college coaches and looked foolish. He would have felt justified as he remained stubbornly defiant. His playing time would have eventually diminished, and Paul and his pride would have sat indignantly on the bench.

When Baylor played Vanderbilt, a man met us beside the bleachers. "Hey, aren't you from Pine Bluff? Did you play for Coach Bock?"

"Yes," Paul answered.

"I'll bet he was extra hard on you, wasn't he?"

"Sure was."

"That's what I figured. He was always the hardest on the ones who had potential."

There were about five seconds of silence before Paul spoke. You could tell by the look on his face that he was having an epiphany. This time his words were slow in coming, as though he needed to absorb the moment. "Yes, he really was tough on me, and I thought it was the worst time of my life. But looking back, if it weren't for Coach Bock, I wouldn't be the player I am today." Who would have thought *those* words would ever come out of Paul's mouth? But he was right. The adversity had made him stronger.

During his sophomore year at Baylor, Paul was moved to third base. People commented that he played like Brooks Robinson—a natural. "This is the first time we've ever had a true third baseman," they said.

Then came the Texas A&M game.

Baylor faced Texas A&M at their field. We were excited to play our across-state rival. I'm not sure which inning it happened in, but Paul made an error. I think he threw the ball over the first baseman's head. They flashed an E on the board. Before we knew it, he had made another error. *That's okay. Settle down*, I thought. The ball was once again hit to Paul. I heard someone scream, "Oh no, not another one!"

I got out of my seat, moved away from the other Baylor parents, and walked closer to the field. I was standing behind the A&M fans, but they didn't know who I was. I watched as he ran up close to the pitcher's mound and side-armed it to first. The first baseman was pulled off the bag and the runner was safe. In pro-ball, I've seen them time after time count that as a hit due to the difficulty of the play. Maybe they would call it a hit here. Everyone went silent as the crowd looked at the scoreboard. They erupted in unison as an E flashed. They jeered at my son. I hurt for him. I prayed for the game to finish with no more problems. But that didn't happen. The crowd was preying on his errors just as I was praying for his ability.

Someone bunted and once again he ran up, almost to home plate, side-armed the ball, and again the throw was a little off. *Surely they won't count this an error.* No mercy. As another E flashed, I watched as the 6,000 fans mocked him, gave each other high fives, and made him the brunt of their jokes. I know this is not an equal comparison, but I felt like Mary watching her son, Jesus, being mocked, laughed at, the brunt of everyone's jokes.

My husband and I were stunned. The game was over and we slipped out of the stadium. As the team boarded the bus to go home, Paul looked at us with forlorn eyes. Our ever-confident happy-go-lucky son was beaten. Nothing would comfort him now. He told us later that his teammates were forgiving but his play went downhill from then on. We heard no more references to Brooks Robinson. He didn't want to hear encouragement. So we prayed. All the trials he had come through had made him strong, but could he pass this test? "Then, when that happens, we are able to hold our heads high no matter what happens and know that all is well" (Romans 5:5 LB). Paul was in God's hands.

The coach ended up removing him from the games at the end of the year. This was a learning process that hurt. But his junior year was a highlight. He excelled at second base and his hitting improved. Baylor even posted on the Internet an amazing defensive play that Paul made against Nebraska.[1] The next time Baylor played Texas A&M, he called me. "Mom, please pray for me, I'm kinda nervous. I'm afraid they will razz me."

Believe me, I *had* been praying—all year. He was fearful that the Texas A&M fans would continue last year's heckling because of the five errors. However, the crowd seemed oblivious to him. All his torment had been in his head. He made no errors in centerfield that day. Hurrah! Thank you, God. He was redeemed. In fact, Paul concluded his junior season without making an error in the final twenty-eight games, spanning 133 chances.

His senior year, he played shortstop against them and made seven

---

1 http://www.baylortv.com/video.php?id=000585

perfect plays, with a bases loaded double play in the bottom of the eighth inning with Baylor up by a run. And—well, you know the rest of the story.

Was I happy about the adversity he faced? Coach Bock, the hitting coach, the five errors, the jeering crowd. How could I say yes as a loving mother? But I can say that I'm glad that he went through it because of the character of the man I see at the end. As David said, "I learned God-worship when my pride was shattered" (Psalm 51:17).

Paul was always the first one to forgive a teammate's error after that. He would give him a pat on the back and say, "Hey, it couldn't be as bad as *me*!" They would laugh and get back in the game.

Before the World Series, a reporter from our hometown newspaper wanted to interview Paul. I wondered what Paul would say. Would he mention the problems he'd had, or would he hide them? After all, Baylor was in Texas and we lived in Arkansas. Probably no one would know about them, anyway. When the story was printed, it was on the first page of the sports section. Paul had hidden nothing about his errors. It was the blatant truth. Now that's a sign of a true man of character. I don't know whether I would have been brave enough to do that!

Have you ever been knocked down and tempted to give up? The apostle Paul said, "I have fought the good fight, I have finished the race, I have kept the faith" (2 Timothy 4:7 NIV). Have you given up? Have you heard the jeers? Get back up! Fight the good fight! You may not have a World Series around the corner, but you will have your victory!

> We are pressed on every side by troubles, but not crushed and broken. We are perplexed because we don't know why things happen as they do, but we don't give up and quit. We are hunted down, but God never abandons us. We get knocked down, but we get up again and keep going.
> —2 Corinthians 4:8–9 LB

You may be tempted to give up on your dream, but don't do it. Remember my son, Paul. Please, I exhort you: *Never give up!*

Questions

1. Have you ever gone from hero to zero? What emotions did you have?

2. How did this affect your compassion for others who struggle? (a)

3. Can you look back on your times of testing as training for future trials? How? (b)

4. When obstacles block your path, do you feel that giving up is an option? (c)

5. Should we celebrate when we are victorious? (d)

6. When Satan tries to destroy you, what's a good Scripture to throw in his face? (e)

Scriptural Answers

(a) "Simon, I've prayed for you in particular that you not give in or give out. When you have come through the time of testing, turn to your companions and give them a fresh start" (Luke 22:32).

(b) "God is educating you; that's why you must never drop out. He's treating you as dear children. This trouble you're in isn't punishment; it's training, the normal experience of children" (Hebrews 12:7).

(c) "I'm staying on your trail; I'm putting one foot in front of the other. I'm not giving up" (Psalm 17:5).

(d) "We will shout for joy when you are victorious and will lift up our banners in the name of our God. May the Lord grant all your requests" (Psalm 20:5 NIV).

(e) "Do not rejoice against me, O my enemy, for though I fall, I will rise again!" (Micah 7:8 LB).

26

Have you ever felt like you botched it?

When I was working as a teacher's assistant, there was a student in my class named Kia. Her eyes sparkled. She had such a sweet spirit. It was hard not to like Kia. She had a physical disability that limited her body movement, and it was a little hard to understand her when she spoke. However, she read well, she was a good student, and she was generally well liked in the school. She was one of my favorite students.

I worked with her a lot because it was hard for her to keep up due to her limited motor skills. Eventually, the teacher and I felt she was becoming too dependent on me. After Christmas vacation, we both decided that I should back off a little so we could see what Kia was capable of on her own.

When she raised her hand for help, I would say, "Kia, try to do it yourself." I noticed that her eyes looked very sad, but I thought that was because she wanted me by her side all the time.

In April, while the other kids were taking standardized tests, I was with Kia and the other special-needs kids in the school. She had asked me to copy some Miley Cyrus song lyrics from the Internet for her. We were laughing and talking, and I playfully called her "Kia Tia."

She became solemn and said, "That was my sister's name. Tia."

"Was? Do you mean she's not alive anymore?"

"No. She was killed in a car wreck this past December, right after Christmas."

My heart sank. *How did I miss this?* All the time I was weaning her from me, she had been suffering. I should have taken the time to talk to her. I had recognized the sad eyes. Woulda, coulda, shoulda. Regrets.

I told her how sad I was for her and her sister. She explained that a drunk driver had crossed the center line on the road and hit Tia's car head-on.

The teacher pulled the article up on the Internet. There it was in black and white. I had really botched it. Even though I felt horrible about the way I had treated her—trying to put distance between us—I got myself back on the right road and I apologized to her.

Kia forgave me. Kia taught me. I learned a great lesson: don't judge too quickly. Investigate.

There is another incident that I felt like I botched. One Friday, I had just had my eyebrows waxed. I thought, *I should go see Mary and tell her how much she means to me.* Mary was the secretary where Randy used to work. But she was more than a secretary, she was my friend. However, with stupid pride about my appearance, I thought, *No, not now; my eyebrows are beet-red and I look like a clown.*

The next week, on Thursday, I opened the newspaper and, to my dismay, saw Mary's obituary. She had died of a heart attack. Woulda, coulda, shoulda. I cried so hard that my back went out and I couldn't walk for three days. They were tears of regret. I had known I should go last week—but stupid pride! I had thought it was just a passing thought, but now I realized that God was prompting me. I can never go back to Mary, but I can make sure I obey the next time I feel a cue. I can also encourage you to do the same.

When you see someone with sad eyes, talk to that person. When you feel prompted to visit someone, go—no matter what you look like—or call them. Live without regrets. Sometimes a hug, a handshake, or a smile is enough. Don't miss the small voice that cues you to act. And forgive yourself if you do miss the voice. Moses, David, Peter, and the apostle Paul got another chance. David said, "Clean the slate, God, so we can start the day fresh! Keep me from stupid sins" (Psalm 19:13). There are times that we blow it, but we have the chance to redeem ourselves.

About a year ago, I was training my friend Carolyn to substitute for me at my front-desk job. We had worked together about three times and totally enjoyed each other's company. Saturday would be our last session before she launched out on her own. But something changed that day. It started at 9:00 a.m. and ended at 3:00 p.m. I would say this; she would say that. Then vice versa. Pop! Sizzle! No need for details, just take my word for it. There were stinging remarks and little explosions. It was not characteristic of either one of us. There was no excuse nor real explanation for it. When the day ended, both of us were left with knots in our stomachs, but we gave each other faint smiles as we parted.

Have you ever been having a great day when suddenly everything changes? For instance, you're having a nice family outing on the Fourth of July. The kids are popping firecrackers. "Look, mom! Watch this one!" They light a bottle rocket. It instantly goes off and everyone starts hopping and jumping. It hisses like a snake, lands on someone's pant leg, then explodes. The pants are burned and so is the skin. Everyone has an adrenaline surge, and then it's over. *What just happened?* That's what that Saturday felt like, except with emotions, not fireworks.

Carolyn and I saw each other over the course of the year, but things weren't the same. We even sat together once in church, but it felt like icicles hung off the pew.

One Wednesday night, Pastor Bell preached a sermon entitled, "Loving Those You'd Rather Hate." It was a great sermon. It stirred up a lot of memories for both of us. I saw Carolyn at Walmart the next day. She gave me a slight hug. "Wasn't that a wonderful sermon?" She started to make an attempt at rectifying our past, but I jumped in and began justifying my end of the tiff. Everything kind of went sour from there. We backed up, looked puzzled, and then parted.

I went home and prayed about it. "God, I didn't do very well. It caught me by surprise to see her and I wasn't prepared. I wanted to tell her that I was sorry. I wanted to apologize. I blew it. I guess Satan wants to beat us both down, but I want to make it right with her. What do I do?"

God told me to put everything I had just said in a note to Carolyn. "Take her a lily that will bloom every year. And do it before you chicken out," He said. That got me laughing!

So that's what I did. Carolyn wasn't home, but I placed the plant and card on her doorstep. Later that day, she called and left the most joyful

Sheep Ears 129

message I have ever heard. It's been there three months and I still listen to it every now and then because it makes me smile.

So you see, we may botch things, but many times, we get a chance to redeem ourselves. Take advantage while you can, because one day it may be too late.

Questions

1. Have you ever felt like you botched it? Write down your thoughts about that incident.

2. Is it possible for us to make errors that we are unaware of? Should we ask forgiveness for those errors? (a)

3. Peter denied Jesus three times. How did Peter feel about doing so? (b)

4. An angel made it clear that Jesus forgave Peter. True or false? (c)

5. Did Peter forgive himself and have a strong ministry after that? (d)

6. How do you feel when you realize you have botched a relationship? (e)

7. Do you feel that God wants us to mend our relationships or to continue holding a grudge? (f)

Scriptural Answers

(a) "Who can discern his errors? Forgive my hidden faults" (Psalm 19:12 NIV).

(b) "[Peter] went out and cried and cried and cried" (Luke 22:62).

(c) "But go, tell his disciples and Peter, 'He is going ahead of you into Galilee'" (Mark 16:7 NIV).

(d) "Those who accepted [Peter's] message were baptized, and about three thousand were added to their number that day" (Acts 2:41 NIV).

(e) "When I saw this, what turmoil filled my heart! I saw myself so stupid and so ignorant; I must seem like an animal to you, O God. But even so, you love me! You are holding my right hand!" (Psalms 73:21–23 LB).

(f) "I urge Euodia and Syntyche to iron out their differences and make up. God doesn't want his children holding grudges" (Philippians 4:2).

27

Have you ever gotten your house in order?

Part 1

Two of our grandchildren, Skyler and Ayla, stayed with us for four weeks in the summer of 2011. Randy and I cherished this precious time with them, especially since they lived eight and a half hours away and we desired more than little snippets of visits. Their stay also gave their parents, Laura and Aaron, a nice little break too.

Since I had begun working on my book, I wondered whether I should try to continue doing so while they were visiting. I asked God about it and He said, "No writing the book while they are with you. Watch and listen closely, because you might miss their messages." I was excited about my assignment.

I couldn't wait to get started on their innocent-but-wise insights that I had observed. However, I gave myself a day to recuperate after they went home, then I went back to the stories. *Let me see, which one should I start with?* "God, you've directed every story. What do you have in mind?"

"Get your house in order," was what I heard.

"What if I forget what they said? My mind is overflowing."

But I heard those five words again: "Get your house in order."

Of course our home was a wreck, but keeping a tidy house during their visit had been the last thing on my mind. Spending time with them was of utmost importance, that and pouring our love and God's Word into their lives. We'd had oodles of fun! The nine-year-old boy and a four-year-old girl had blasted my house (not so tidy to begin with) into a full-blown play area. Every room was affected. Not just inside, but outside, too. Typhoon Skyler and Hurricane Ayla had hit hard. But laughter had filled the house and there were no regrets.

So, at God's direction, I began to get my house in order. Saturday, I cleaned the kitchen and bathroom. Sunday, I puttered around the house. I received a call from my other daughter-in-law, Sharon, who lived in Utah. She informed me that they would be coming to visit next year. Knowing what a meticulous housekeeper she was, I gave a slight shudder. "Well, we're coming and that's that. No excuses. You've been warned. So get your house in order, woman." She giggled infectiously, we chatted a while longer, then we hung up. Hmm. Her words had a familiar ring.

Monday I worked on our three bedrooms. Tuesday I mowed the grass and thoroughly revamped the back porch. It seemed odd, but somehow her call made me more focused than before. Sure, they weren't coming for a year, and I knew the house would get cluttered again, but her call gave me a goal. Wednesday I started wondering: Is something about to happen to my husband or me? My insurance policies were good. We had a will made out. Was getting my house in order a hint of impending doom? I wanted to write, but God never changed his instructions. So I worked on the den. Thursday I continued working on that area, and at 3:00 p.m., it finally dawned on me—duh! It was now so obvious. God wanted me to write a story about getting your house in order. Not your physical house, but your *spiritual* house. *Ah, now I see.*

We are never promised tomorrow. A teenager drowns in a lake. A twenty-two-year-old man visits my neighbor on Friday, then tragically dies in a car wreck on Sunday. Children play with a pistol, the trigger is touched, an eye is lost, and a life is changed forever. "Just as man is destined to die once, and after that to face judgment, so Christ was sacrificed once to take away the sins of many people; and he will appear a second time, not to bear sin, but to bring salvation to those who are waiting for him" (Hebrews 9:27–28 NIV).

We don't know when we're going to die, but we must be ready. Once we die, there are no do-overs. Our second chances will be gone. You must have your spiritual house in order. Have you asked Jesus into your heart? That's first and foremost. You'll never see heaven without having Jesus as your Lord and Savior. Your heart may be cleansed, but along the way, clutter may accumulate—not things like newspapers, old mail, or dirty socks, but spiritual clutter—things like envy, greed, and unforgiveness.

The power of forgiveness is what's on my heart now, so I'll go to my grandkids for an illustrated sermon. I noticed that the power switch on the television in one of our bedrooms was broken. It was the television that Skyler was prone to watching. He was my prime suspect, but just to be fair, I called both kids in to me. "All right, I know the power switch is broken. We can still use the remote to turn the television on and off. But I want to know, which one of you broke it?"

In unison, they both innocently replied, "We don't know." Ayla looked straight at me, Skyler averted his eyes—always a tell-tale sign.

"Just admit it! The TV still works, so I'm not *that* mad. Just admit it." I guess my bulging eyes and popping veins spoke louder than my words. (Hey, I never said I was perfect.) Skyler's lip trembled a little, and I was convinced of his guilt. He stood in the corner and I gave him time to confess. "Okay Sky, I know you did it, just tell me *how*."

He shrugged, then finally made up a "tool of destruction."

He's lying!" Ayla shouted. "If he moves, I'm going to zap him with my red laser light." Eager to help me administer justice, she was holding a toy that shot out a red beam.

He continued to plead his innocence for a while, but eventually told me what had really happened. He had pushed a pencil onto the switch until both pencil and switch broke. Out of the corner of my eye, I noticed Ayla listening from the hallway.

Tears filled the bottoms of his eyes as he confessed. He said he was sorry, but I wanted to make sure he knew why he was repenting. "Tell me why in a sentence," I said.

"I'm sorry, Grandma Sherry. I broke the TV and I lied."

My instinct was to punish him, but I felt God speak to me in that millisecond of decision. "Little eyes and ears are watching you and hearing you. Model Me."

My mind flashed back to sins that I had committed. God in His mercy forgave me for things far worse than a broken button on a television. Jesus told a parable about an unmerciful servant who was forgiven millions of dollars of debt that he owed to a king. Then the servant promptly found a man who owed him a few dollars, choked him, and demanded immediate repayment. The king found out and chastised him:

> "Shouldn't you have had mercy on your fellow servant just as I had on you?" In anger his master turned him over to the jailers to be tortured, until he should pay back all he owed. This is how my heavenly Father will treat each of you unless you forgive your brother from your heart.
> —Matthew 18:33–35 NIV

Mercy flooded the room. "Skyler, do you know what I'm going to do now?"

"No," he answered as his knees jiggled and his lip quivered.

"I'm going to forgive you. And I want you to understand that I love you no matter how bad you act. Next time, please tell me the truth the first time."

As I said that, he leapt into my arms, grabbed my neck, and hugged me so hard I had to beg for air. Then, in an instant, he dropped to his knees. With his hands clasped, he said, "Let's pray." That really got to me, because I realized how often I have apologized to a person but forgotten to ask for God's forgiveness. "Please help me," he pleaded. Together, we prayed as he asked God to forgive him for breaking the television and for lying. All was forgiven. However, there were consequences to his deed: no watching *that* television for three days.

Later that night, I announced we would be going to the movies. Ayla screamed and Skyler flipped on the bed. Believe me, he accepted his forgiveness and never looked back.

At church two days later, Skyler picked out a piece of chocolate cake with sprinkles on it for Ayla. He gingerly carried it to the car, and she squealed with excitement as we drove home. Skyler, wanting to feel important, insisted on carrying the cake into the house. But three steps out of the car, it plopped right onto the dirt and grass. The icing and sprinkles bit the dust.

Ayla was already in the kitchen when he handed her the icingless cake. "I'm sorry, Ayla." Her normal response would be to stomp her foot and come running to me with tears in her eyes to tell on him. But she surprised both of us.

"I forgive you, Sky."

That little boy came whooping and hollering into the den. "She forgives me! She forgives me! Grandma Sherry, Ayla forgives me!" I realized that was how I had felt in the past when I had been forgiven. I broke down and cried.

We must always be aware that little eyes and ears are watching and listening, waiting for our response. They hear us on the phone, they hear how we talk to our spouses, they watch us from the hallway. I know in my heart that I came very close to blowing a lesson that God had in mind for my grandkids, a lesson not only about being forgiven, but also about forgiving.

Enjoy your life and help others enjoy their lives, too. Get your house in order. Forgiveness is very important. Model the Father because your children are modeling you.

Questions

1. Do you feel that it's Biblical to discipline your kids? Support your answer. (a)

2. Do your kids (or your spouse) have any tell-tale signs of lying? What are they? (b)

3. Have you ever felt like you committed the perfect crime, yet felt transparent before God? (c)

4. Do you fail to forgive others when they fall short, even though God has forgiven you of your sins? Justify your answer. (d)

5. How should we handle forgiveness? (e)

6. Do you feel that you model God's spirit to your kids? Give examples. (f)

7. Do you hope that your child will imitate you? (g)

8. Jesus imitates the Father. True or false? (h)

Scriptural Answers

(a) "Discipline your children; you'll be glad you did—they'll turn out delightful to live with" (Proverb 29:17).

(b) "A shifty eye betrays an evil intention; a clenched jaw signals trouble ahead" (Proverb 16:30).

(c) "They say to each other, 'No one can catch us, no one can detect our perfect crime.' The Detective detects the mystery in the dark of the cellar heart" (Psalm 64:6).

(d) "They turned a deaf ear, they refused to remember the miracles you had done for them; they turned stubborn ... And you, a forgiving God, gracious and compassionate, incredibly patient, with tons of love—you didn't dump them ... you in your amazing compassion didn't walk off and leave them in the desert" (Nehemiah 9:17, 19).

(e) "Be gentle and ready to forgive; never hold grudges. Remember, the Lord forgave you, so you must forgive others (Colossians 3:13 LB).

(f) "Watch what God does, and then you do it, like children who learn proper behavior from their parents. Mostly what God does is love. Keep company with him and learn a life of love. Observe how Christ loved us. His love was not cautious but extravagant. He didn't love in order to get something from us but to give everything of himself to us. Love like that" (Ephesians 5:1–2).

(g) "Imitate me, just as I also imitate Christ" (1 Corinthians 11:1 NKJV).

(h) "Jesus explained himself at length. 'I'm telling you this straight. The Son can't independently do a thing, only what he sees the Father doing, what the Father does, the Son does. The Father loves the Son and includes him in everything he is doing'" (John 5:19–20).

28
Have you ever gotten your house in order?

Part 2

My grandkids and I went to the Pines Mall in our city. It has a playground area where kids can romp and play with each other while their parents (and grandparents) sit down and catch their breath. After about ten minutes, Ayla ran up to me and said, "Skyler made that boy sad."

I quickly called Sky over to me and asked him what had happened. He said, "I was just playing." I needed to make sure. So I urged the little boy to come to me. He must have thought he was in trouble because he resisted approaching at first; however he finally came to me. He said, "Yes, Skyler did hurt my stomach."

The little boy's brother insisted, "They were just playing."

But Skyler needed to own up to the consequences of his behavior. Skyler apologized, the boy accepted his apology, and they shook hands. They continued playing together, only this time I noticed Skyler was much more careful around his newfound friend.

Do you ever wonder how many times we are supposed to forgive people? The obnoxious coworker, the neighbor who acts like a jerk, the spouse who can't ever meet your standards. Peter, Jesus's disciple, had the same thought. "Peter got up the nerve to ask, 'Master, how many times do I forgive a brother or sister who hurts me? Seven?' Jesus replied, "Seven!

Hardly. Try seventy times seven'" (Matthew 18:21–22). So that settles it: We must always forgive.

Little kids can figure this out, but why is it so hard for adults? Could pride and arrogance be two reasons? Solomon said: "If anyone respects and fears God, he will hate evil. For wisdom hates pride, arrogance, corruption, and deceit of every kind" (Proverb 8:13 LB).

Sometimes we may be quick to forgive others but won't let ourselves off the hook. Give yourself a break. Accept forgiveness. Quit being ashamed of yourself. God has work for you to do. Be like a child. "Blessed are the pure in heart, for they shall see God" (Matthew 5:8 KJV). Who are the pure in heart? Those who keep life simple without hidden agendas. Jesus said, "Whoever becomes simple and elemental again, like this child, will rank high in God's kingdom" (Matthew 18:5).

There's also the matter of consequences. I've observed people on television go to visit in prison the person who murdered their loved ones. They forgave the murderer, even befriended him in some cases. However, the murderer will still stay locked up. Even though forgiveness is pure, consequences must be administered.

One episode of Joni Lamb's television show, *Joni*, showed clips of Jews who suffered unthinkable injustices in the Holocaust. Many Jews said that their healing came when they were able to forgive the people who had murdered their families. They were able to forgive, but they will never be able to see their loved ones on this side of heaven again.

There were also clips showing the families of the murderers crying in agony and sorrow over the tragedies that their predecessors caused. Those families forgave their murdering ancestors, but forgiveness could not bring back those previous generations lost forever. I had never thought of that particular aspect of the Holocaust before. I knew their sorrow was genuine as I watched them groan in remorse.

Here is an excerpt from the speech that Bart Bonikowski, a Polish-Canadian assistant professor of sociology at Harvard University, gave at the 2003 March of Remembrance and Hope, an educational leadership program that teaches about the dangers of intolerance through the study of the Holocaust:

> Against the backdrop of barbed wire fences and ruins of crematoria, the survivors were getting ready to light the candles for Kaddish. Each

stepped forward and read out the names of his or her family members who perished at the hands of the Nazis. One woman approached the microphone but was unable to speak. She stood in front of us and cried. Another survivor came up to her and said. 'Wait, don't cry. Look! Look at them! They are here for you!' She realized that with me were hundreds of young people who wanted to learn, who wanted to remember, who wanted to prevent things like this from happening in the future ... And then, maybe, just maybe will we be able to say "never again."

I've given you examples of forgiveness: a four-year-old and a nine-year-old, Jewish captives forgiving Nazi murderers, and descendants of those Nazis forgiving their ancestors. These examples may seem vastly different on the surface, but really, there is no difference. Forgiveness is forgiveness. Just like a white lie is still a lie.

Sometimes I sin against God and confess, but it's hard for me to accept His forgiveness. I have a better grasp of forgiveness when I relate to Skyler for breaking part of my television; I forgive Skyler because I love him. God is love. He forgives me because He loves me.

> We all did it, all of us doing what we feel like doing, when we felt like doing it, all of us in the same boat. It's a wonder God didn't lose his temper and do away with the whole lot of us. Instead immense in mercy and with an incredible love, he embraced us. He took our sin-dead lives and made us alive in Christ. He did all this on his own, with no help from us! Then he picked us up and set us down in highest heaven in company with Jesus, our Messiah.
>
> —Ephesians 2:3–7

It was grace that I didn't deserve.

The little boy at the mall had the power to forgive Skyler. The Jews had the power to forgive the Nazis. The Nazi families had the power to forgive their predecessors. God has the power to forgive us. Who do you have the power to forgive? Maybe it's your parents, maybe a sibling, maybe a once-close friend. What's required of us is to forgive. Let Judge Jehovah take care of the consequences. Time exaggerates everything. Let's be quick to forgive.

In prayer there is a connection between what God does and what you do. You can't get forgiveness from God, for instance, without also forgiving others. If you refuse to do your part, you cut yourself off from God's part.

—Matthew 6:14–15

And that's not good.

You will never have complete joy in your life until you grasp this concept. Think of Skyler's reaction when Ayla forgave him for dropping her cake. It may have seemed like a small incident, but to him, it meant everything. He loves her, and she loves him. She never mentioned the cake again. We need to follow her lead. That's why Jesus asked us to become like children. They forgive and forget.

We have no idea what tomorrow holds, but it's always best to allow the Holy Spirit to make a clean sweep. John the Baptist exhorted,

The main character in this drama, to whom I'm a mere stagehand, will ignite the kingdom life, a fire, the Holy Spirit within you, changing you from the inside out. He's going to clean house—make a clean sweep of your lives. He'll place everything true in its proper place before God, everything false He'll put out with the trash to be burned.

—Luke 3:16–17

God has given us the power to forgive. No excuses—we have been warned. Let's get our house in order.

Questions

1. Heaven will be filled with people who have asked Jesus into their hearts and asked Him to forgive them of their sins. Do you believe that unforgiveness for others when they sin against you is permissible? (a)

2. When you clean your house, you get rid of unnecessary junk. When a boss "cleans house," should they fire unnecessary employees? Why or why not? (b)

3. Could unforgiveness be considered a sin that God wants cleaned out of your heart? Write down your thoughts.

4. Do you think God will tolerate sin? (c)

5. What was Jesus's response to the Roman soldiers who crucified Him? (d)

6. Is it possible for God to forgive you of past sins? (e ,f)

7. If God has forgiven you, can you still serve Him or are you tarnished and rejected? (g)

8. When you know you should forgive, yet refuse to do so, does God understand? (h)

9. Whom do you need to forgive?

Scriptural Answers

(a) "Keep us forgiven with you and forgiving others" (Matthew 6:12).

(b) "What do you think the owner of the vineyard will do? Right. He'll come and clean house. Then he'll assign the care of the vineyard to others" (Luke 20:15).

(c) "God, I love living with you, your house glows with your glory. When it's time for spring cleaning, don't sweep me out with the quacks and crooks" (Psalms 26:8–9).

(d) "Then said Jesus, Father, forgive them; for they know not what they do" (Luke 23:34 KJV).

(e) "Where is the god who can compare with you—wiping the slate clean of guilt. Turning a blind eye, a deaf ear, to the past sins of your purged and precious people" (Micah 7:18).

(f) "I, even I, am he who blots out your transgressions, for my own sake, and remembers your sins no more" (Isaiah 43:25 NIV).

(g) "But one thing I do: forgetting what is behind and straining to what is ahead" (Philippians 3:13 NIV).

(h) "But if you sin knowing full well what you're doing, that's a different story entirely. Merely hearing God's law is a waste of your time if you don't do what he commands. Doing, not hearing, is what makes the difference with God" (Romans 2:13).

29

Have you ever had a CD ministry?

I don't have the best singing voice and I've never preached a sermon, so you may well raise your eyebrows in disbelief when I say that I have a CD ministry. Well, maybe not in the way you're thinking. I don't know if you've ever heard of Joyce Meyer—if you haven't, you ought to check her out. She is a woman with a powerful ministry. My husband and I donate to it every month, and they send us her sermon series on CDs, which I play in my car.

One day, it dawned on me that I had shelves of her CD sermons that I had already listened to now gathering dust. I started sharing them with people at church and work, and with anyone to whom God led me to share. Joyce preaches on television, but I find that listening to her CDs in my car is like mini tune-ups between stops; it really makes a difference. She's funny and she's serious. She once said that God enabled her to give us a whipping while we laugh at ourselves.

I also share CDs from Joel Osteen, Robert Morris, Jesse Duplantis, and my own pastor, Gary Bell. Whichever CDs the Lord leads me to share are the ones I give.

I was recently talking to a seventh grader named Kavon at the school where I work. I wasn't aware that he was the son of someone to whom I had given a CD series. But he knew me. He said, "Hey, Mrs. Witt, I really like the Joyce Meyer CDs. She's funny."

I talked to his mom the next time I saw her and told her about my conversation with Kavon. "Oh yes," Wenona said, as her eyes lit up. "When we ride in the car, he has no other choice." I like that! What a strong mom.

Some people might think they would have to go to China, Russia, or Antarctica in order to have a ministry. But your mission field could be right in your own neighborhood or job site, or at the Walmart in aisle eight. Share whatever you have, whether it be a CD series, a song track, or an encouraging word.

Perhaps you have volumes of books lying around which avid readers would love to get their hands on, but can't afford to purchase. There are people who would never read a nonfiction book but would be agreeable to reading a Christian fiction book. My personal favorite is *Redeeming Love* by Francine Rivers. Basically, the book is an allegory of Hosea in the Bible but in a western setting.

Your ministry could be walking around the block with your newly widowed next-door neighbor, or treating her to a meal at Chili's. People all around you are lonely. How can they see God if you turn a deaf ear to their hurting? "Go to the lost, confused people right here in the neighborhood. Tell them that the kingdom is here. Bring health to the sick. Raise the dead. Touch the untouchables. Kick out the demons. You have been treated generously, so live generously" (Matthew 10:6–8).

One Saturday, I was talking to a friend about the Joyce Meyer CDs that I share and she said, "You know what, if they're *that* good, I'd like to listen to one."

I ran in the house, said a quick prayer for wisdom in choosing the right one, and brought her a CD entitled "Never Give up." She looked at it kind of funny, staring for a second. I thought, "Oh no, I have offended her." But she took it and drove away.

About ten minutes later, she called me and asked, "Can you tell me why you chose *this* series?"

I replied, "It was what God impressed on me to give you. Why? Is there something wrong?"

"You don't realize this, but I was planning to hand in my resignation at work on Monday."

I texted her the next day to see what her plans were about her job. She said, "Thank you for sharing that CD with me! I'm coming back to work. I will not be defeated."

I thanked God that I was there for her that day. I am thankful that Joyce Meyer made the CDs and that I had them to share, and I'm glad that they no longer sit on my shelf gathering dust.

So this is my CD ministry. I share my CDs with other people who in turn share them with their moms, their daughters, their friends. There is no time limit on the lending; I eventually get the CDs back. People tell me how much they are lifted up by the sermons as they drive to their destinations. If you see someone laughing or crying as you pass them in your car, they may be listening to one of these awesome people of God.

What kind of ministry do you have? You don't have to have a degree from a college, but you must have a willing heart that searches for lost, confused people in your world. Perhaps you have been sharing your resources for some time but never realized the impact you have made.

"[Jesus] said to his disciples, 'The harvest is plentiful, but the workers are few'" (Matthew 9:37 NIV). On judgment day, I want God to say to me, "Well done, thou good and faithful servant"—don't you? Do something, lest you do nothing.

Questions

1. What resources or talents do you have that could be shared with others?

2. Do you believe God expects us to work for Him? (a)

3. Do you consider the needs of those around you or do you prefer to be alone in the world? (b)

4. If you work hard to buy your books, CDs, music, clothes, you have the right to keep them all to yourself. True or false? Give reasons for your answer.

5. How would you respond if God asked you to share them? (c)

6. Are we accountable to God for our actions? Explain. (d)

7. If you are afraid to start any type of ministry, what is the first thing you should do? (e)

8. What kind of ministry could you start?

Scriptural Answers

(a) "He creates each of us by Christ Jesus to join him in the work he does, the good work he has gotten ready for us to do, work we had better be doing" (Ephesians 2:10).

(b) "Each of you should look not only to your own interests, but also to the interests of others" (Philippians 2:4 NIV).

(c) "Make sure you don't take things for granted and go slack in working for the common good; share what you have with others. God takes particular pleasure in acts of worship—a different kind of "sacrifice"—that takes place in kitchens and work places and on the streets" (Hebrews 13:16).

(d) "So then, each of us will give an account of himself to God" (Romans 14:12 NIV).

(e) "Commit everything you do to the Lord. Trust him to help you do it, and he will" (Psalm 37:5 LB).

30

Have you ever had a game plan?

My first experience with basketball was in the third grade at the YMCA in Warren, Arkansas. I remember it like it was yesterday. The name of the team was the Crows and our shirts were black. (Who in their right mind would name a third-grade girls team the Crows?) I didn't know anything about the game. The coach put me in for exactly one minute each half of the game. I dreaded when she put me in and I was happy and relieved when she took me out. I had no idea which way to run, so I ran in the direction of the black shirts. All of a sudden, they would change direction, so I would change direction too. "Oh, no, why are they changing?" Once again, I would reverse my run.

Looking back, I'm sure it was hilarious to watch. But you know what? My parents never got mad at me or put me through grueling private sessions to improve my skills. I never felt inadequate and they always took me for ice cream afterward. When it was time for our next game, I was ready for my one minute of fame. You can see how clueless I was.

Fast-forward thirty-six years: I was asked by the athletic director at Seabrook Family Christian Center in Pine Bluff to coach my son Paul's recreational basketball team. The team consisted of fifth- and sixth-grade boys, a very competitive age group. The director had appointed all the other coaches except one. Paul was only a fourth grader, but because of his advanced skills, they asked him to play in a higher grade bracket. My mind flashed back to my own third-grade experience. So I said, "No, thank you. You don't realize it, but I don't even understand the game." I told him about my one-minute ordeals, we had a good laugh, and he proceeded to try to get someone else. Two days later the director approached me again, desperate. And I mean really desperate! I finally conceded, and I became the official coach of the Hoosiers.

Not willing to give coaching a half-hearted effort, I prayed and asked God for the best way to have a competitive team. He gave me a great game plan.

First, I needed good advice. I went to the best coach I knew, Heulen, and listened intently as he gave me some great pointers on how to be an effective coach. Next, I retrieved my World Book Encyclopedia and got a pretty good grip on the rules of the game and some helpful ideas about offensive and defensive plays. There were no computers in those days, by the way.

Privately, I talked to my son and told him my game plan for him: As a point guard, his only job for the first quarter was to assist all other players on his team. I told him I believed that if he didn't take my advice, the other players would hate him. I felt they would resent his presence on the team since he was the youngest player, for one thing. No one likes a prima donna. Another reason was that his mom, of all people, was coaching. I told him to first help each teammate score, then for all other quarters, he was allowed to score. None of the other players knew this plan, and I instructed him to keep it a secret. To my surprise, he quickly agreed.

Last of all, I talked to the players. I said, "As you know, I'm new to coaching basketball, so I would appreciate it if you gave me advice on the rules every now and then, so I don't embarrass myself."

They all broke into ready grins and gave big sighs after my comment. "Sure coach, we'll be glad to help you," Grant said. I guess they were relieved to know that I recognized my shortcomings.

We worked fundamentals in practice: jump shots, lay-ups, and passes. These were all the fundamentals I had missed as a Crow back in elementary school. I never had to explain to the Hoosiers which direction to run, but if anyone had been confused, I definitely had the answer!

The preseason tournament rolled around and I was nervous. I imagined that my son took some ribbing because his "mommy" was coaching. How embarrassing it must have been for him since most coaches at that level are men. But you know what? If he did, he never let me know.

The ball was tipped to Paul. He snagged the ball, waited for an opening,

Sheep Ears   149

and then passed it to David. Boom, easy bank shot. The other team got the ball. One of our players bumped it, Paul quickly recovered the ball, and ran down the court. Everyone expected a quick lay-up; however, no one was more surprised than Jason when he got a bounce pass from Paul and easily scored.

The whole quarter went like that. Player after player scored, except Paul. When the buzzer rang, they all ran over to the bench with the biggest grins on their faces. They were patting Paul on the back, and any doubts about "Why is this kid on our team?" vanished. He was able to score after that. He learned to enjoy giving away the ball as much, if not more, than getting the ball and scoring himself. The guys were more than willing to tell me what to do when I was confused about when to substitute the players in the game. The team began to bond. We even thought of a catchy motto: "Hoosiers are not loosiers."

We surprised everyone by winning the preseason tournament. Everything worked out just fine.

About five games into the season, we were playing a tough opponent. Paul had several open shots that he didn't take. The teams had learned to guard the other players instead of double-teaming him, which left him open. I called a time-out and said, "Paul, you're wide open! Why are you not shooting?"

He whispered, "Don't you remember what you told me? You said not to shoot in the first quarter."

Talk about obedience. Wow! I gathered my thoughts and said, "Oh yeah. Well, everyone's happy now, so you can shoot if you're open." After that, Paul shot when he was open and he passed when he needed to. He had total freedom.

We ended up winning first place that season. I coached one more season, then I ended my basketball coaching career. Other people stepped up to coach after that, and I was glad that I had confronted my weakness.

I've gone into great detail about a story that may seem insignificant. I wondered about this myself, but as the story unfolded and I recounted the details, I began to see a parallel to God and his game plan for us.

God doesn't care if you don't start out strong. Remember how Gideon felt when the Lord asked him to lead the army? "'Lord,' Gideon asked, 'how can I save Israel? My clan is the weakest … and I am the least in my family'" (Judges 6:15 NIV). He wants you to ask Him for advice. "Listen to advice and accept instruction, and in the end you will be wise" (Proverb 19:20 NIV). He will give you people like your pastor and godly teachers to guide you. He'll give you other chances for success and He'll encourage you not to be afraid of your past. Remember Moses (a murderer in Exodus 2:11–12) and David (an adulterer in 2 Samuel 11:2–5). They turned out to become great leaders.

God provides His Book, the Bible, so you can learn all you need to know about Him. "He guides me in paths of righteousness for His name's sake" (Psalm 23:3 NIV).

God wants everyone to enter into heaven. "For God so loved the world, that He gave His only begotten Son, that whoever believes in Him shall not perish, but have eternal life" (John 3:16 NASB).

You may feel fear sometimes, but you can do things while you are afraid. "Be strong and let your heart take courage, all you who hope in the Lord" (Psalm 31:24 NASB).

God wants us to be givers, not takers. I like how *The Message* phrases it: "You'll not likely go wrong here if you keep remembering that our Master said, 'You're far happier giving than getting'" (Acts 20:35).

And last, but not least, God wants you to be obedient. He may give you a personal plan not to be shared with other people. Don't question Him. Just obey. "And this is love; that we walk in obedience to his commands" (2 John 1:6 NIV). Remember what happened in Genesis 37:5, when Joseph revealed his dreams to his brothers? Sometimes it's better to remain silent. God may be holding you back for a reason. He may eventually give you freedom to show your talents. When the time is right, he'll let you shine.

I guess I learned more than I realized about God while I was coaching. You know what? I'm glad I coached. Don't be afraid to tackle a job in which you don't feel confident. Just as He did for me, He'll guide you through your toughest challenges. Just ask Him. He may have a story for *you* to write one day.

Questions

1. Has God ever given you a plan for anything (your education, launching a business, paying off your bills)? What was it?

2. Did you ask wise people for counsel or did you rely on your own smarts? (a)

3. Have you ever felt like you should keep a Godly revelation to yourself instead of telling others about it? (b)

4. Do you believe that God will promote you if you wait for His timing? (c)

5. Putting yourself first is always a good idea. True or false? Explain. (d)

6. When you have experience in an area, should you help others with your knowledge or tell them to learn the hard way? (e)

7. If someone tries to keep you from accomplishing your plans, what should you do? (f)

Scriptural Answers

(a) "It's better to be wise than strong; intelligence outranks muscle any day. Strategic planning is the key to warfare; to win, you need a lot of good counsel" (Proverbs 24:5–6).

(b) "Mary kept all these things to herself, holding them dear, deep within herself" (Luke 2:19).

(c) "Wait passionately for God, don't leave the path. He'll give you your place in the sun" (Psalm 37:34).

(d) "Don't push your way to the front; don't sweet-talk your way to the top. Put yourself aside, and help others get ahead" (Philippians 2:3).

(e) "Don't be obsessed with getting your own advantage. Forget yourselves long enough to lend a helping hand" (Philippians 2:4).

(f) "Don't be afraid of them. Put your minds on the Master, great and awesome" (Nehemiah 4:14).

31

Have you ever had a mission?

Back in 1994, my husband and I had a 1982 Buick LeSabre that was still running. However, it was on its last legs. We reluctantly purchased a used Grand Prix with payments totaling a whopping $190 a month. With our income and outgoing expenses, that put us $190 in the hole, but there were no other options.

I was teaching three-year-olds at Marvin Street Baptist Church, an all-white daycare. About a month earlier, I had gotten upset with the job and applied to the Pine Bluff school district to be an instructional assistant. The next day, I thought, "What in the world was I thinking? I love this job!" But the first week of the school year, I received a call asking me to come for an interview for the new job. I had heard that they paid more than my current job, and after all, I did have a new-to-me car with a payment that I couldn't afford.

So I went for the interview and it seemed to go well. I told them that if they did want me, I would have to give my current employer two weeks' notice. I prayed, "Well, God, this job pays $190 more than the other job. That's the exact amount of our car payment, but please give me direction because I don't want the job if it's not Your will." A few nights later, I had a dream. I was standing behind someone who was looking at ten job applications on the floor. They pointed to mine and said, "That's the one we want more than anyone."

The next day at the daycare, I received a call from the Pine Bluff school district. They said, "We've looked at all the applications, and we want *you* more than anyone else." I couldn't believe it! Almost the exact same words as in my dream! But there was one catch: it was Thursday and they needed me at work on Monday. I reminded them about my two weeks' notice, but they encouraged me to talk to my boss, May.

With knees shaking, I went into May's office and told her the situation. I almost fell over when she said, "You'd better take it! And see if there's an opening for me!"

I called the school district and told them that I would report for work on Monday. As I got into the car that we could now afford, I prayed again. "God, you orchestrated everything about this situation, so you must have a mission. Could you tell me what it is?"

He answered me, not audibly, but in my spirit. "I want you to let black kids know that there are still good white people."

I said, "Is that it?"

He said, "Yes, that's it."

Knowing that I was leaving an all-white daycare to work in a predominantly black school, I recalled my mother and I walking into Ederington's Department Store when I was seven years old. I was just learning to read and was practicing my skills. At the back of the store were two water fountains. One was marked "Whites Only," and the other, "Colored Only." I asked my mom what it meant, and when she explained, I was sad. I told her that it was wrong and she replied, "Yes, it's wrong." I remembered the terrible feeling I had when she told me, and I remembered being relieved when integration began when I was in the sixth grade.

Antavion Washington was the first black student to attend our elementary school in Warren. We were at sixth-grade reading level and he was at third. I was happy he had become our classmate.

Now that I was facing a new job, I had reservations. I felt afraid. You know how you are sometimes afraid of a situation, but you know it's the right thing to do? Well, like Joyce Meyer says, "Do it afraid!" I wasn't afraid of the kids; I was afraid that they wouldn't accept me. Not only was I white, but I was also green. I had never been really close to many black people. Still, I knew that I had a mission. So with a little trepidation, I reported at Carver Elementary.

One of the first things I remember is walking down the sidewalk my first week at school, and seeing a kid run past me with a large two-inch by four-inch scrape on his arm. It seemed like time froze for a few seconds while God talked to me. "This black child's scrape looks just like your white child's scrape: bright pink." This may not seem like much to you, but it was an epiphany to me. *Color is only skin deep.* A picture is worth a thousand words, and at that moment, I saw the picture! There was no difference except in perception.

That first year, there was a girl in kindergarten named Martha. She looked at me and the other white teacher, Mrs. Keahey. Then she put her hands on her hips and in a defiant voice said, "My momma said white people are bad and black people are proud." At that point, I knew I was definitely in the right place for the mission that God had given me.

Well, it didn't take long for this "anti-white" little girl to start warming up to us. At first, I observed Martha watching Mrs. Keahey and I work with the other kids. She saw that we could be trusted so she gradually allowed us to assist her with *her* work. Before we knew it, she was giving us hugs like her original statement was a faraway, long-forgotten thought. I thanked God because I knew that my assignment was simple, yet far-reaching.

I think the biggest compliment I've ever gotten was from Mrs. Jones, the black teacher I worked with for twelve years. She said, "Mrs. Witt, I've seen you in all situations, and you're always the same. You've had some bad times in your life but you never let it show. Whether the kids act horrible or great. Whether they're rich or poor. It's obvious you don't see color."

Matthew 5:14–16 says, "You are the world's light—a city on a hill, glowing in the night for all to see. Don't hide your light! Let it shine for all; let your good deeds glow for all to see, so that they will praise your heavenly Father" (LB). My prayer was that as the students saw me, they also saw Christ.

One year, a sixth-grader named Kemonte announced to the class that he was moving to a city in northern Arkansas because his mom didn't think our town was safe due to crime. I cringed because I knew that he was moving to a predominantly white town that was antagonistic toward blacks. I said a quick prayer for Kemonte and sighed to myself. I thought, *He'll be back.*

In about three weeks, he *was* back. This time his bright eyes were clouded and sad. The teacher called him over privately to discuss what had happened. I couldn't hear everything, but I did hear the words "stab" and "pencil." Over the next two weeks, I could tell that he had changed. He now resented me and would not obey anything I said. I felt I knew what had probably happened to him, but I wasn't sure.

One day, the teacher was absent and they couldn't find a substitute. Since instructional assistants were allowed to fill in, I conducted the class. Kemonte was particularly awful that day. After reprimanding him four or five times, I wrote him up with an office referral, a sure paddling. I hated to do it, but he was disrupting the class terribly.

After ten minutes, he returned to the classroom. He told me that the principal wasn't in and the office would call for him later.

It was apparent that his attitude had improved because he now answered all questions with enthusiasm. I found out later that a teacher had talked to him. I don't know what was said, but apparently it made an impact. I think all the students were shocked and confused about his abrupt change. After the bell rang, I called him to the front. "Kemonte, I noticed a complete change in your attitude. You behaved much better since you returned and you answered questions with enthusiasm. I'm cancelling the referral. If they call you to the office, give them this note that says, 'Cancelled.'"

He looked at me wide-eyed, then he lowered his eyes and quietly said, "Thank you, Mrs. Witt."

He turned to go, but I called him back. "Kemonte, I don't know what happened when you moved, but I have a feeling it was bad. Did they call you the N-word?"

With eyes still lowered, he said, "Yes."

"I'm sorry that happened. There are a lot of ignorant people in the world, but I am not one of them. There are a lot of people like me who are sad about mean people. My daughter-in-law is from Africa, and she and my son have a beautiful child named Ethan. I love them more than anything."

He looked at the picture on my desk, his eyebrows raised. "You mean *that's* your son's wife?"

"Yes, I love her and I love you. Not everyone is like the people you saw in that town. I can't change how they've hurt you, but I can let you know that not everyone is like that. Are we okay?"

With that, we shook hands and he walked out the door. I was so happy that God had put me there. The seeds that the enemy had planted of hate, prejudice, and malice were squashed. Had I not been there, who would have shown him the other side? I thank God that for generations, Kemonte will tell his seed, "No. The white people are not all bad. I know."

The next day, Kemonte walked animatedly from side to side into the classroom, grinning from ear-to-ear with his arms spread-eagled. "Mrs. Wiiittt!" And with that, he embraced me and rocked back and forth, letting all his hate go. Things changed in the classroom. He looked at me differently, and I looked at him differently. I was thankful that this young black child could so easily forgive. My hope was that I could maybe make a difference not just to Kemonte, but to generations after him.

Mrs. Jones told me that she had watched a reunion of the Little Rock Nine on *Oprah*. Those nine students had crossed segregation lines in an effort to attend Central High School in 1957. The white tormentors who had been cruel to them beyond measure now had such remorse. Mrs. Jones said they were crying and asking for forgiveness. They said that they had only repeated what they had heard at home. They were ashamed of the way they had treated the black students. What a tragedy.

That's why I believe God had me work at the black school. If the kids are taught bigotry at home or are forced to face it in their daily situations, how will they know anything different if there is no one there to show them?

My prayer is to see people through God's eyes, to look past all barriers and to see the spirit that God created in all of us. I don't want to see what *I* see, but what *God* sees. Actually, I thought I was making a difference in the students' lives, but it was the other way around: they made a difference in my life. What a revelation! When you start helping others, you are the one who is more blessed. God knew exactly what He was doing.

My hope is that by sharing my experiences, you, too, will learn to think and respond outside your comfort zone. It's not really that scary; it's an adventure! But are you willing?

Questions

1. Has a dream ever given you clear guidance? What was it? (a)

2. Have you ever been intimidated by a mission that God assigned you to do? (b)

3. Did you persuade God to change His mind? (c)

4. Has anyone ever stood up for you when you were in a hostile environment? Write about your experience. (d)

5. Has their influence on you helped you to be more sympathetic to outsiders? (e)

6. Have you ever asked God what your mission was? What has God told you?

7. Do you live a life worthy of His calling? (f)

Scriptural Answers

(a) "The Master spoke to him in a vision: 'Ananias.' 'Yes, Master,' he answered. 'Get up and go over to Straight Avenue. Ask at the house of Judas for a man from Tarsus. His name is Saul. He's there praying. He has just had a dream in which he saw a man named Ananias enter the house and lay hands on him so he could see again'" (Acts 9:10–12).

(b) "Ananias protested, 'Master, You can't be serious. Everybody's talking about [Saul] and the terrible things he's been doing, his reign of terror against your people in Jerusalem! And now he's shown up with papers from the Chief Priest that give him license to do the same to us'" (Acts 9:13–14).

(c) "But the Master said, 'Don't argue. Go!'" (Acts 9:15).

(d) "Back in Jerusalem [Saul] tried to join the disciples, but they were all afraid of him. They didn't trust him one bit. Then Barnabas took him under his wing. He introduced [Saul] to the apostles and stood up for him" (Acts 9:26–27).

(e) "This is why I, Paul [Saul], am in jail for Christ, having taken up the cause of you outsiders, so-called. I take it that you're familiar with the part I was given in God's plan for including everybody. I got the inside story on this from God himself" (Ephesians 3:1–3).

(f) "As a prisoner for the Lord, then, I urge you to live a life worthy of the calling you have received" (Ephesians 4:1 NIV).

32

Have you ever had a nudge?

When our oldest son, Aaron, was eighteen months old, we tried moving him from his crib to a small bed, but he was having trouble adjusting. He would awaken during the night and whimper, wanting to get in bed with us. One of us (usually me) would go into the room and console him if he didn't settle down in a few minutes. One night he did his usual whimper but I didn't think much about it. My husband nudged me and said, "Sherry, why don't you go check on him?" I was really tired, but since Randy didn't usually suggest this, I thought I had better go check on Aaron.

When I went to Aaron's room, I was shocked. In his sleep, he had rolled off the bed. Somehow a cord attached to his "moo-cow" toy had wrapped around his neck. It was so tight that I had to turn the light on to be able to see to get it off. Talk about holding your baby boy close and giving thanks to God and to my husband for the nudge! You'd better believe that I did.

I had another nudge when Aaron was sixteen years old. This time, however, it wasn't a physical nudge, but a spiritual one. I kept feeling a strong urge to pray for him. It lasted for about a week and I couldn't shake the feeling. I didn't know what the problem was, but I knew I should intercede for him. To intercede means, in its simplest form, to pray on behalf of someone else. The apostle Paul says, "I urge, then, first of all, that requests, prayers, intercession, and thanksgiving be made for everyone" (1 Timothy 2:1 NIV).

Every time I got the chance, I prayed for his safety, his health, and anything else that crossed my mind. One night there was ice on the roads, and he called to say that he and his girlfriend were coming to our house. I told them to be careful. I never thought to tell him not to drive on the overpasses. Since he was an inexperienced teenage driver, I should have. Never assume anything.

When Aaron and his girlfriend walked into the house, they were wide-eyed and obviously shaken up. He had driven on an icy overpass, lost control of the truck, hit the cement walls and bounced back and forth across the freeway. At that particular spot, the overpass was about forty feet above the railroad tracks with no grass embankment whatsoever. His truck was banged up, but they were unharmed. I know this may seem funny, but that was the happiest I have ever been after a wreck. I immediately felt released from the burden I had been feeling for him.

I'm so thankful that I followed the nudge to pray an intercession prayer for Aaron. I believe the angels were dispersed to surround and protect him when I interceded for him. "For He will command his angels concerning you to guard you in all your ways" (Psalm 91:11 NIV). Amen to that!

Another nudge happened one year when I noticed a young man in the seventh grade whose name was Raul. He did poorly in school, but I noticed that when he went to the library, he checked out a book on Greek mythology. It was definitely not a book for the faint-hearted. I started talking to him and found him to be highly intelligent, but living in a troubled home. One particular day, he told me that the police had arrested him because someone reported that he slept with a knife under his pillow. Raul told me that he had threatened his stepfather, who was constantly telling Raul that he would kill him. Raul was afraid every night.

During my conference time, I was reading my Bible and God nudged me to get up, right that minute, make copies of some pages in the Bible, and give them to Raul. I asked God if it was okay to do it tomorrow, but He said no. I copied the pages quickly and then looked up Raul's schedule so I could find him. I caught him just as the bell rang to change classes, and I asked him if he would mind if I gave him some Scriptures. He was very receptive. I told him to keep the pages with him and read them when he felt afraid.

Some of the Scriptures that I highlighted were: "Listen to my pleading, Lord! Be merciful and send the help I need … For if my father and mother should abandon me, you would welcome and comfort me. Tell me what to do, O Lord, and make it plain because I am surrounded by waiting enemies" (Psalms 27:7, 10–11 LB). When Raul read them, his eyes teared up. It was a very tender moment.

I told Raul that I believed one day in the future when he was a grown man, he would run into me somewhere, hug me, and say, "Hey, Mrs. Witt, remember me? I'm Raul, and I came back to tell you that you made a difference in my life. Those Scriptures helped me have faith that God would get me through the tough times. I'm helping people now! I'm a policeman now (or a fireman, or maybe even a preacher). Thanks for believing in me."

He grinned from ear to ear when I said that.

He wasn't at school the next day, and I never saw him again. It's been about seven years now, and I still haven't heard from him. But I believe that one day I will see him once again with that big grin on his face and a great redemptive story to tell me.

I often wonder what would have happened if I hadn't promptly done what God asked me to do. What if I had waited until the next day? I would not have been able to give him the message of encouragement that God had for him. What would have happened if I had ignored the nudge to intercede for Aaron before his truck wreck? The angels might not have been there to guard him. What if I had waited until the next hour to check on Aaron in his bedroom when he was a toddler? It would have been too late. These are the important lessons God taught me about acting quickly when He nudges us.

Opportunities would have passed; the windows would have closed. When opportunity arises and God nudges you, please say yes. You never know when the decisions you make will have an eternal difference.

I'm still praying for Raul.

Questions

1. Do you believe God will open your ears so you can hear when He nudges you? (a)

2. When you have fear in your heart, how do you handle the situation? (b)

3. Do you feel that God is a safe house for battered people? (c)

4. Can God turn a terrible life around and use that experience to help someone else? (d)

5. Have you ever felt the nudge to pray for someone when you were thinking of them? (e)

6. As a Christian, should we just pray for people that are going through a tough time, or should we stop what we are doing and encourage them? Write down your thoughts. (f)

7. Write down the times when you felt that God nudged you. How did you respond?

Scriptural Answers

(a) "You've opened my ears so I can listen" (Psalm 40:6).

(b) "Do not be anxious about anything, but in everything by prayer and petition, with thanksgiving, present your requests to God" (Philippians 4:6 NIV).

(c) "God's a safe-house for the battered, a sanctuary during bad times. The moment you arrive, you relax; you're never sorry you knocked" (Psalms 9:9–10).

(d) "God of all healing counsel! He comes alongside us when we go through hard times, and before you know it, He brings us alongside someone else who is going through hard times so that we can be there for that person just as God was there for us" (2 Corinthians 1:3–4).

(e) "Every time we think of you, we thank God for you. Day and night you're in our prayers … It is clear to us, friends, that God not only loves you very much but also has put his hand on you for something special. When the Message we preached came to you, it wasn't just words. Something happened in you. The Holy Spirit put steel in your convictions" (1 Thessalonians 1:2, 4).

(f) "The Master, God, has given me a well-taught tongue, so I know how to encourage tired people. He wakes me up in the morning, wakes me up, opens my ears to listen as one ready to take orders. The Master, God, opened my ears, and I didn't go back to sleep, didn't pull the covers back over my head. I followed orders" (Isaiah 50:4–5).

33
Have you ever had a praying parent?

My dad, Raymond Phillips, is an eighty-two-year-old retired minister. He's blind in one eye from a botched cataract surgery, but with his gift of perfect pitch, he's still able to tune pianos (and is the best at it, in my opinion). But, as far as I'm concerned, the most important title he has ever had is that of "praying parent." He told me that he gets up every morning at 4:00 a.m. to pray for all of his kids, grandkids, and great-grandkids.

But on a more personal level, he said that he thanks God every day for opening my ears to hear His voice and for giving me an obedient heart. Without my dad's prayers, this book would most likely not exist. Dad's consistent daily prayers helped to mold me into who I have become: a willing servant of the Most High God.

One time, in my younger days, before I had matured in God's work, I arrogantly told my dad, "Hey, everything is going great. You can let up on the prayers. I think I've got this." I can *see* that you're grinning now. Maybe you've once said something as defiant as this. What a ridiculous statement!

Well, as you can imagine, the next few days were weird. I felt a void, a hole. I seemed to get angry about small things that didn't normally bother me; other drivers on the road, my husband, my kids, the lady at the bank, my dogs, and every single person at work seemed to annoy me.

I thought, *Whoa, what's happening here?* It finally dawned on me that it might have to do with what I had said to my dad. I made a frantic call.

"Hey, Dad, you remember our conversation about praying for me ... well, forget I ever said that! Forgive me! I took your staying prayers for granted. I promise you that those words will never come out of my mouth ever again." He gave a slight chuckle, and things went back to normal in my life.

I'm not sure if my kids or grandkids realized how fortunate they are to have a praying grandfather. To my father, I say, "Thank you, Dad. It's better to be the best role model than to be the best lecturer. You always say that you're amazed by me, but Dad, I'm amazed by you! You may not be the richest man on the planet, but you have passed on to me the richest heritage." David said, "For thou, O God hast heard my vows: thou hast given me the heritage of those that fear thy name" (Psalm 61:5 KJV). And that is how I feel, too.

Are you aware that Jesus prays for us? John 17 talks of Jesus praying for his followers: "My prayer is not that you take them out of the world but that you protect them from the evil one (John 17:15 NIV). "I'm praying not only for them but also for those who will believe in me" (John 17:20). I hope you didn't miss that. If you did, I'll repeat it with my own emphasis added: "for those who *will* believe." That means future children and grandchildren: you and me!

My father said that he loves me with a love that will never waiver. How much more does Jesus love us?

> Do you think anyone is going to be able to drive a wedge between us and Christ's love for us? There is no way! Not trouble, not hard times, not hatred, not hunger, not homelessness, not bullying threats, not backstabbing, not even the worst sins ... None of this fazes us because Jesus loves us. I'm absolutely convinced that nothing—nothing living or dead, angelic or demons, today or tomorrow, high or low, thinkable or unthinkable—absolutely nothing can get between us and God's love because of the way that Jesus our Master has embraced us.
> —Romans 8:35–39

Now I have a question: Who are you praying for? Do you have children and grandchildren who need your prayers? Do you love them with a love that will never waiver? You may say, "I don't have any children." Have you noticed any kids playing around the neighborhood? Is there a school nearby? What about the children who attend your church? Perhaps you could pray for a new Christian.

Someone needs your prayers. Believe me when I tell you: You will make a tremendous difference in their lives if you pray for them. Jesus is praying for us, and He is our perfect example.

Questions

1. Have you ever felt God's favor leave you because you became arrogant? (a)

2. What is a good way to pray for your children or new Christians? (b, c)

3. Is it important to give your children a rich Christian heritage? Explain. (d)

4. Should we pray for a God-listening heart? Why? (e)

5. Do you feel that when we ask for the right thing from God, He will reward us with many blessings? Give your thoughts. (f)

6. Why should we desire the prayers of a righteous man? (g)

7. Whom do you pray for?

Scriptural Answers

(a) "When things were going great I crowed, 'I've got it made. I'm God's favorite. He made me King of the Mountain.' Then you looked the other way and I fell to pieces" (Psalms 30:6–7).

(b) "I couldn't stop thanking God for you—every time I prayed ... but I do more than thank. I ask—ask the God of our Master, Jesus Christ, the God of glory—to make you intelligent and discerning in knowing him personally, your eyes focused and clear, so that you can see exactly what it is he is calling you to do … endless energy, boundless strength!" (Ephesians 1:16–19).

(c) "So ever since we first heard about you we have kept on praying and asking God to help you understand what he wants you to do; asking him to make you wise about spiritual things; and asking that the way you live will always please the Lord and honor him, so that you will always be doing good, kind things for others, while all the time you are learning to know God better and better" (Colossians 1:9–10 LB).

(d) "Solomon said, 'You were extravagantly generous in love with David, my father, and he lived faithfully in your presence, his relationships were just and his heart right. And you have persisted in this great and generous love by giving him—and this very day!—a son to sit on his throne'" (1 Kings 3:6).

(e) "Here's what I want: Give me a God-listening heart so I can lead your people well, discerning the difference between good and evil. For who on their own is capable of leading your glorious people?" (1 Kings 3:9).

(f) "God, the Master, was delighted with Solomon's response. And God said to him, 'Because you have asked for this and haven't grasped after a long life, or riches, or the doom of your enemies, but you have asked for the ability to lead and govern well, I'll give you a wise and mature heart … As a bonus, I'm giving you both the wealth and glory you didn't ask for—there's not a king anywhere who will come up to your mark" (1 Kings 3:10–13).

(g) "The prayer of a righteous man is powerful and effective" (James 5:16 NIV).

34
Have you ever had a standby?

What is a standby? According to Bing Dictionary, a standby is a person or thing readily available: somebody or something that can always be relied on to be available and useful, especially if needed as a substitute or in an emergency. That brings me to what everyone knows to be a faithful companion: the dog. I became an ardent dog lover only recently. My mom didn't care for dogs at all, and consequently, we didn't have any when I was growing up. I allowed my kids to have them, but I never got attached.

When my son Nathan moved to Indiana, we inherited his two dogs (both rescues): Jackie, a rat terrier and Chihuahua mix, and Brownie, a beagle and bloodhound mix. I tried for several weeks to give them away, but no one was interested. I rationalized in my mind that my mom and dad eventually became avid dog lovers, so maybe I would adjust, too. *We don't really live in the safest neighborhood, and come to think of it, Jackie would be the perfect indoor burglar alarm, and Brownie would be the perfect outdoor alarm with her deep, ferocious bark. I love to walk and they would be perfect walking companions, the perfect defenders in every way.* So Jackie and Brownie became our new companions.

Jackie is very animated. When my husband and I arrive home, she never, and I mean *never,* fails to bolt out of the door, jumping as high as her body can possibly go. She even uses her head to pull her body higher, looking like Charlie Brown's pet dog Snoopy when she reaches her peak. We could have been gone for only five minutes—when we return, we get the same joyful dance. We laugh and say, "Jackie, we haven't been gone long, why are you so happy?" But she doesn't care. She loves us and that's all that matters to her.

One day Jackie came up to me. She looked different; she was droopy and her breathing was labored. She hates lying on her back, but this time she allowed me to cradle her in my arms like a baby. She's more attached to Randy, so it surprised me that she came to me. As I stroked her, she looked into my eyes as if to say, "You've been a good friend, but this is good-bye."

It took me by surprise. I cried for that little girl. Randy and I started praying for her. I called Nathan and asked him to pray, too. Then I had an idea. "Randy, go ring the doorbell; that always perks her up."

At the sound of the doorbell, Jackie bolted out of my arms and ran, ever on guard, to defend our house. A couple of minutes later, she drooped and we thought, "Oh no, we're losing her."

"Randy, go ring the doorbell again!" He rang it, and once again, Jackie bolted. It was like her little brain overrode her own pain, thinking, "I must defend, I must defend!"

"Good girl, Jackie!" we exclaimed. And she never drooped again. We eventually determined that she might have touched some ant repellant that Randy had sprayed on the floor. We believe that our prayers and her desire to alert and protect her family were two things that brought her back from death's door. She had a purpose in life. That was the day I really bonded with Jackie. Who knew that she loved me so much that she would come to *me* when she was at death's door?

When I had an illness and moved to different areas of the house to sleep, she would find me and sit with me in silence as I tried to make it through the night. I wouldn't realize it until the next morning when I got up; but there she was beside me, having quietly watched over me all through the night. She had left the comfort of her own bed to be my comforter. I know it's not possible, but I wondered if she was praying for me. As I sit writing this book, I look down, and there she is. It's like she wants to encourage me. She's my standby.

I felt our little two-dog family was complete until one day I had a strange thought: *I would really like to have a German Shepherd.* Where did that come from? I didn't think any more about it until two weeks later. On Saturday, a young neighbor, Kyron, was looking for his German Shepherd puppy that had escaped from his yard. Sunday morning, I was walking Jackie and Brownie when I saw a stray dog.

I checked with Kyron but he said that he had already found his dog. *This must be a different dog.* She looked like a German Shepherd from her markings, but it was hard to tell because she was so scrawny, frail, and frightened. I talked to the boys in the neighborhood and they said she had been roaming in the area for three weeks. No one knew who she belonged to.

"Why don't you take her, Mrs. Witt?" the boys said in unison.

"Oh, no. I've got all I can handle here with these two dogs." But the second those words were out of my mouth, I recalled my thoughts from two weeks earlier. And she *did* look like a German Shepherd.

I surprised myself with my next words. "Well, I could, but I have no way of getting her home."

Michael, a strapping six-foot-tall young man, said, "If you want her, Mrs. Witt, I'll help you." And he did. First he worked patiently with her to get a leash around her neck. Since she was unfamiliar with us and the leash, Michael said, "I'll carry her home, if you really want her." That nixed all my excuses.

Michael held her in his arms, secure against his chest, while we walked the four blocks to my home. Then he instructed me to give her some food. While she ate, he maneuvered a stick around and into the bowl. This was to determine if she was food aggressive, which meant that she would attack others if they approached her food bowl. She was so starved that she had to lie down to eat. I could feel each and every bone on her ribcage, but the stick didn't bother her. I named her Mollie.

I called excitedly to tell my husband about our new German Shepherd puppy. Randy wasn't as eager as I was. When he saw her, he said, "Sherry, she's a mutt!" But she wasn't a mutt to me; she was Mollie, a dog sent from God, because she was in my thoughts two weeks before she appeared. I remembered reading, "for your Father knows what you need before you ask him" (Matthew 6:8 NIV). The veterinarian said she was four months old when we found her, so I knew that God had been thinking of what (or whom) I needed before I even had the thought.

The second day we had her, I said, "Sit," and she sat. I had never, ever had a dog obey my command before—I was amazed! I decided to see how much more she was capable of over the next few weeks. I would work with her on one day and the next day she could hear and obey. First, I worked on a handshake, followed by a high five. Next, we worked on "lie down" followed by "lie down and crawl." When I walk her, she stops at the intersections if I give the command. She ignores all pedestrians, car noises, dog barks, and every other noise imaginable. She only has eyes for me. When I stop to talk to the kids in the neighborhood, I let Mollie perform her obedience tricks. If anyone else gives the commands, though, she acts like a deaf-mute.

When I leave for work, she runs to the gate to watch me leave, her tail in a slow, sad wag. When I return, there she is, waiting for me like a mailman, faithful in the rain, sleet, or snow. She often drags her pillow to the gate if my return takes longer than expected. Before I can turn the car ignition off, her body rises, her tail whips in the air like the flag of a returning conqueror, and she is ready to greet me at the door.

I hide treats around the house and tell her, "find them!" She won't quit until she finds everything. If I am gathering fallen branches outside, I hand them to her and she puts them in a pile. She works alongside me. I love that dog! She's my Mollie. My faithful, loyal, reliable companion. My standby.

One day, I watched a television show which had a Belgian Malinois that looked just like Mollie. I looked the breed up on the Internet and I believe this is the breed that Mollie is, a shepherd-type dog, but, apparently, more valuable. I've seen Belgian Malinois puppies listed for over one thousand dollars—a far cry from a mutt! By the way, it didn't take long for my husband to fall head over heels in love with Mollie, and vice versa. When she comes inside, she alternates running between Randy and me for a good rubdown, careful that neither one of us is jealous for her attention. She was, and still is, a special dog sent from heaven.

Now, you might be wondering how any of this could possibly tie in with God? I'm glad you asked. If you have access to the Internet, I'd like you to go to Wendy J. Francisco's website (www.godanddog.org) to watch her short animated film, *GoD and DoG*, about the parallel between her dog and God. When I watched the video, it helped me to view my dogs through different eyes, so I will make my own feeble attempt to do the same.

Sheep Ears

Jesus said, "And I will ask the Father, and He will give you another Comforter [Counselor, Helper, Intercessor, Advocate, Strengthener, and Standby], that He may remain with you forever—the Spirit of Truth, Whom the world cannot receive ... because it does not see Him or know and recognize Him. But you know and recognize Him for He lives with you [constantly] and will be in you" (John 14:16–17 AB). At first I thought "standby" was an odd word, but now that I know its definition, I can see why the translators picked that word.

The Holy Spirit is faithful. Everywhere I walk, He is there with me. He is one who can always be relied on. If I'm traveling through an illness, if I'm home by myself, if I'm walking through a dangerous neighborhood, if I'm going where I've never gone before, He's there. "Even though I walk through the shadow of death, I will fear no evil, for you are with me; your rod and your staff, they comfort me" (Psalm 23:4 NIV). When Satan comes against me, God will defend me; by His Word and by His Spirit.

When I look at myself, I can see the person who was once weak and lonely. Yet God picked me up, held me in His arms, and carried me in His bosom. I was undeserving, yet He saw something in me that was worth saving. Some may have said, "Unworthy, not clean, mutt," but God called me "His Own." He gave me a name: "Redeemed." He was willing to sacrifice His Son so that I could live freely. He nurtured me and trained me in His ways. I hear Him and obey. My eyes and ears are trained to Him only. I will not be distracted, for He rescued me. I anxiously wait for Jesus's second coming. I complete the jobs He assigns me.

It is a joy to have such a kind, loving Master. I will be faithful until I lay down my head and go to meet Him in the sky. I thank God that I have learned the Holy Spirit's characteristics and have become familiar with them by watching and learning from my sweet, loving, ever-faithful, standbyish dogs.

"When you call on me, when you come and pray to me, I'll listen. When you come looking for me, you'll find me. Yes, when you get serious about finding me and want it more than anything else, I'll make sure you won't be disappointed" (Jeremiah 29:12–14). The Ultimate Standby.

Are you looking for God? He's waiting for you, just like my dogs run out the door or run to the gate. He's waiting for your return. He will always welcome you. His heart beats faster when you call His name. Leap into his arms and let Him hold you. You are more valuable than you could ever fathom.

The Holy Spirit is your standby. He loves you and He calls you by name.

QUESTIONS

1. Has a friend, relative, or pet ever stood by you when you felt rejected or alone? Who were they?

2. Did their comfort and guidance help you to relate to the closeness of the Holy Spirit? Explain the comparison.

3. Have you ever felt like physically running to God? (a)

4. Has it ever felt like the Holy Spirit strengthened you and caressed you? (b)

5. Why did Jesus have to go away? (c)

6. Who will guide us on earth since Jesus is in heaven? (d)

7. Do you stand by your friends when they face trials, or do you leave them alone so they can learn to be tough? (e)

SCRIPTURAL ANSWERS

(a) "I've already run for dear life straight to the arms of God" (Psalm 11:1).

(b) "You protect me with salvation-armor; you hold me up with a firm hand, caress me with your gentle ways. You cleared the ground under me so my footing was firm" (Psalms 18:35–36).

(c) "But I tell you the truth: It is good that I am going away. Unless I go away, the Counselor will not come to you; but if I go, I will send him to you. When he comes, he will convict the world of guilt in regard to sin and righteousness and judgment" (John 16:7–8 NIV).

(d) "But when the Friend comes, the Spirit of the Truth, he will take you by the hand and guide you into all the truth there is. He won't draw attention to himself, but will make sense out of what is about to happen and, indeed, out of all that I have done and said. He will honor me; he will take away from me and deliver it to you" (John 16:13–14).

(e) "Friends come and friends go, but a true friend sticks by you like family" (Proverb 18:24).

35

Have you ever had an opposite day?

When I was a kid, my brother and I would play "opposite day." We didn't tell our parents what we were doing, but they eventually figured it out. "I hate you" meant "I love you." "I'm dumb" meant "I'm smart." Maybe you have played that game, too.

Has it ever seemed to you that God has opposite days when He doesn't fill you in on what He's doing? He's done it to me. I went to work at a new job and one particular lady, I'll call her Alice, took an instant dislike to me. She snubbed me and made fun of me behind my back. Nothing I could do was right. When I walked into the room, even her demeanor would change. She had made up her mind that I was the enemy from the first day I walked in the door.

After working with her for over two years, nothing changed. That is, until God gave me an opposite-day instruction. My husband had been given a forty-dollar gift card at work, and I was excited. "I could really use that, Randy! Thanks!"

I was planning how to spend it when God said, "Why don't you give it to someone else and bless them?" Several people came to mind, but when I asked God who I should give it to, He said, "Alice." *Whoa, I didn't see that one coming.*

So Alice got the card. I think she was actually more surprised than I was. After that, Alice seemed to look at me differently. I could tell that she no longer thought I was the enemy. "Our Scriptures tell us that if you see your enemy hungry, go buy that person lunch [or a gift card], or if he's thirsty, get him a drink. Your generosity will surprise him with goodness. Don't let evil get the best of you; get the best of evil by doing good" (Romans 12:20–21). God sure had the right idea, because the invisible barrier that had blocked a healthy relationship was broken, and we actually became friends.

In 2005, I came down with a severe foot problem called plantar fasciitis, or fallen arches. I would wake up in pain in the morning. After stretching my feet, the pain got better, but by noon they would start to hurt again. By bedtime, the pain was crippling. I would have to hold on to furniture to make my way to the bedroom. I went to the podiatrist and he gave me a shot, but it didn't help. He gave me inserts for my shoes, which didn't help either. I went to a specialty store and had $400 inserts made for my shoes. They helped a bit, but my feet still hurt. Naturally, I prayed for my feet, but there were no instant cures.

God, however, had another one of his opposite-day instructions: "Mow Linnie's yard."

I thought, *God, are you sure you mean that? My feet hurt intensely after I mow my yard. That will finish me off. I mean, I need to know if that's really what you want me to do.*

"Yes, and edge her yard, too. And do her yard before you do yours. Your feet will eventually be healed." So I followed God's opposite-day instructions. One year turned into three years with no change. In fact, my feet got worse.

That third summer, God instructed me to go swimming. *Now, that's more like it, God! I love to swim!* But once I got there, He told me to hop like a bunny rabbit around the pool. Talk about embarrassing! *I wanted to swim, and now you want me to hop?* Oh well, my feet weren't any better, and I knew I would never think of anything that silly on my own, so it had to be God giving one of his opposite-day instructions. So I hopped and mowed all summer long. And guess what? By the end of the summer, I was completely cured! Thank you, Jesus. "I will instruct you and teach you in the way which you should go; I will counsel you with My eye upon you" (Psalm 32:8 NASB).

"So that really *was* you, God. You and Your instructions don't make sense to me sometimes, but I know you're always right."

It's been three years since my healing and my feet are still completely well. In fact, I walked my dogs for an hour and a half today and I think I wore *them* out. By the way, I still mow my neighbor's grass. Not because I have to, but because I want to. It's my offering of thanks to my Lord and King.

I also had an opposite-day incident with our truck. My husband and I had a 1993 Dodge Dakota, which we loved. We named her Nelly Belle. There was one problem, though. Sometimes the transmission wouldn't shift into the last gear on the highway. When that happened, its highest speed was only forty-five mph. That was a little embarrassing. As people passed us on the highway I always looked straight ahead because I anticipated unfriendly glares. We wanted to look for a newer pickup, but we couldn't sell the truck in good conscience because of this problem. Still, for puttering around town and hauling things, it was perfect. We had a car for our usual transportation and the slow truck was our second vehicle.

One day a lady came to my Sunday school class to testify about how God had saved her and given her a job. She had one problem: she had no way to get to work. You guessed it. God said to my spirit, "Let her use your truck."

I was shocked. "God, I was really hoping for a *new* truck and now, not only will we not get that, you also want us to let her use our Nelly Belle?"

I heard nothing more from God, so I figured that was the end of the conversation. God was not persuaded.

That didn't seem right. It was the opposite of what I wanted, but the instructions were unmistakable. I didn't even know this woman. For all I knew, she was going to skip town and I would never see her or the truck again. But I knew what God had said, so she got the truck. My husband wasn't as excited as I was. After all, it was also his hunting truck, and he hadn't heard of opposite-day before. Nevertheless, he went along with it.

The lady kept the truck for several months, and then gave it back to us when she could afford her own vehicle. She was very grateful. We kept the truck for another year. I still felt like we should get a new one, but what should we do with old Nelly Belle?

God had a plan.

You might remember cash for clunkers, a federal program wherein you could trade in an older vehicle for a brand-new one. You would get a $4,500 trade-in allowance if you purchased a more gas efficient vehicle. So that's what we did. We got a brand-new 2009 Pontiac Vibe that had a $3,000 rebate on it. With the trade-in allowance, this added up to a total of $7,500 off the sticker price of a new car! "I never saw that one coming either, God! We never could have gotten that good a deal if we had done it our way! You are a way cool God!"

Now you may be saying, Wait, I thought you said you wanted a truck, not a car. God worked that out, too! We kept the Vibe for a year and a half, then traded it in for a 2003 Silverado 4x4 truck. Almost a year later, we traded that in for a brand-new, Dodge Ram 4x4 Laramie hot off the assembly line. It's an awesome truck!

That's right, God arranges things better than you even imagine in your wildest dreams. Now my husband has the best hunting truck ever. Almost every time he drives it, he calls me to tell me how much he loves it. I'll be honest: I love it, too. We never would have gotten such a great deal if we hadn't followed God's instructions, which seemed opposite to what was logical.

I think God has quite a sense of humor. Why else would He have me give a gift card to an enemy, mow grass and hop like a bunny when my feet were about to explode, or let a stranger borrow our truck when we needed to trade it in for a new one? God's ways are not our ways. He thinks differently than we do. Sometimes His answers are a lot slower in coming than we'd like, but He is *always* right. Even when He asks you to do the opposite of what you expect, you might want to consider doing it His way. It may be opposite day.

QUESTIONS

1. Write down any instructions you have had from God that seemed like they were the opposite of what you would logically do.

2. Did Jesus preach anything opposite to the world's philosophy? (a)

3. Jesus was the disciples' master, yet He washed their feet. Why? (b)

4. Is it possible to give away, yet gain? (c)

5. In Matthew 5:38–48, Jesus tells us not to hit back when someone strikes us; if someone sues you for the shirt on your back, gift wrap your best coat and give it to them; love your enemy. When someone gives us a hard time, we should pray for them. This is opposite of our nature. Why should we do these things? (d)

6. When you can't figure out what God is up to, what should you do? (e)

Scriptural Answers

(a) "This is the Great Reversal: the last in line put at the head of the line, and the so-called first ending up last" (Luke 13:30).

(b) "So if I, the Master and Teacher, washed your feet, you must now wash each other's feet. I've laid down a pattern for you. What I've done, you do. I'm only pointing out the obvious. A servant is not ranked above his master; an employee doesn't give orders to the employer" (John 13:14–16).

(c) "One man gives freely, yet gains even more; another withholds unduly, but comes to poverty. A generous man will prosper; he who refreshes others will be refreshed" (Proverbs 11:24–25 NIV).

(d) "If all you do is love the lovable, do you expect a bonus? Anybody can do that ... In a word, what I'm saying is, Grow up. You're Kingdom subjects. Now live like it. Live out your God-created identity. Live generously and graciously toward others, the way God lives toward you" (Matthew 5:46, 48).

(e) "Lean on, trust in, and be confident in the Lord with all your heart and mind and do not rely on your own insight or understanding. In all your ways know, recognize, and acknowledge Him, and He will direct and make straight and plain your paths" (Proverbs 3:5–6 AB).

36

Have you ever had an unplanned pregnancy?

I distinctly remember Nathan's second birthday. Our little family went to the park, fed the ducks, had a picnic, and played on the slides and swings. I remember taking a picture of Randy and Nathan and thinking, *Tomorrow I'm taking a pregnancy test and our whole world could change. We already have two kids and that's enough.*

The next day came, I took the test, and you guessed it: positive. I called Randy and expressed my displeasure, to put it nicely, then hung up the phone quite forcefully. I immediately heard God say, "You didn't plan for this child, but I did." He went on to tell me more, but that's enough for you to understand why I called Randy back, apologized, and embraced my child-to-be with joy.

You might say, "That's nice, Sherry, but God never told me that." Listen to this:

> Oh yes, you shaped me first inside, then out;
> you formed me in my mother's womb.
> I thank you, High God—you're breathtaking!
> Body and soul, I am marvelously made!
> I worship in adoration—what a creation!
> You know me inside and out,
> you know every bone in my body;
> You know exactly how I was made, bit by bit,

how I was sculpted from nothing into something.
Like an open book, you watched me grow from
conception to birth;
all the stages of my life were spread out before you.
The days of my life all prepared
before I'd even lived one day.

—Psalms 139:13–16

That is absolutely beautiful. Did you catch that? "You watched me grow from conception to birth." Not after the first breath, but from conception. Think about that for a while.

Now, you may say, "I *can't* raise this child! I was raped!" or "I'm only thirteen years old." You may have some other reason to be upset. God still has plans for your children. He has watched them grow since their conception. The days of their lives have been prepared by Almighty God. "For I know the plans I have for you says the Lord. They are plans for good and not for evil, to give you a future and a hope" (Jeremiah 29:11 LB).

There is a man whose mother was raped when she was in her forties, yet she still gave birth to him. Today he is a mighty man of God and a champion of the hurting, starving children in Africa. He has a program on television that you may have heard of: *Life Today With James Robison*. He was definitely not planned, but God has used James as a champion of the children. Satan had a scheme which I'll call plan E for evil. God had a better plan which I'll call plan G for good. God's plan trumps Satan's plan every time.

My son Paul was unplanned, but he has positively broadened our lives beyond measure. James Robison's life has touched millions of other lives. God has big plans for every child that is conceived.

He has a great future planned for *your* children, too. They will make an impact on the world. It's definitely something to think about.

QUESTIONS

1. Can you think of anyone in the Bible who had an unplanned pregnancy? Who? (a)

Sheep Ears   183

2. Do you believe Mary and Joseph had difficulty handling this surprise? Discuss problems they may have encountered. (b)

3. How did God reveal Jesus's conception and birth to Joseph? (c)

4. Even though Mary and Joseph did not plan for the birth of Jesus, do you believe God had plans for Him? (d)

5. Are children a gift from God only if they are planned? Express your thoughts. (e)

6. Does God know us before we are formed in our mother's womb? (f)

Scriptural Answers

(a) "But the angel assured her, 'Mary, you have nothing to fear. God has a surprise for you: You will become pregnant and give birth to a son and call his name Jesus'" (Luke 1:30–31).

(b) "Mary was engaged to be married to Joseph. Before they came to the marriage bed, Joseph discovered she was pregnant. (It was by the Holy Spirit, but he didn't know that.) Joseph, chagrined but noble, determined to take care of things quietly so Mary would not be disgraced" (Matthew 1:18–19).

(c) "While he was trying to figure a way out, he had a dream. God's angel spoke in the dream: 'Joseph, son of David, don't hesitate to get married. Mary's pregnancy is Spirit-conceived. God's Holy Spirit has made her pregnant'" (Matthew 1:20).

(d) "She will bring a son to birth, and when she does you, Joseph, will name him Jesus—'God saves'—because he will save his people from their sins" (Matthew 1:21).

(e) "Don't you see that children are God's best gift? the fruit of the womb his generous legacy? Like a warrior's fistful of arrows are the children of a vigorous youth. Oh, how blessed are your parents, with your quivers full of children!" (Psalms 127:3–5).

(f) "The Lord said to me, 'I knew you before you were formed within your mother's womb; before you were born I sanctified you and appointed you as my spokesman to the world'" (Jeremiah 1:4–5 LB).

37
Have you ever had to abruptly change your plans?

I woke up on August 22, 2011, in a great mood. Normally, I wake up and linger awhile in bed, but not that day. I decided to walk my dog, Mollie, at 7:00 a.m. because there was an unusual break in the summer heat. It seemed that I heard every bird in the neighborhood chirping. A gentle breeze blew against my face, and I thanked God for the beautiful day. If I had to pick a song to represent it, I would have chosen the one from *Oklahoma*: "Oh, what a beautiful morning, oh what a beautiful day. I've got a beautiful feeling everything's going my way."

I planned to write once I got back home—one, maybe two stories. I felt so inspired and light-hearted that day. I guess I was daydreaming when suddenly my left foot squarely hit an uneven spot on the sidewalk. I stumbled forward to try to regain my balance, but to no avail. My hands landed on the sidewalk near the middle of my body. As my scientifically-minded son Nathan later explained, this created a fulcrum. Therefore, my head hit the concrete at an accelerated rate.

A humongous goose egg was developing on my right eyebrow and forehead, and I had a long bloody scrape down my right temple. The heels of my hands were raw from the sidewalk. I rolled onto the soft grass of a yard and lay there as I regained my composure. Mollie curled up on the grass beside me as if to say, "Don't worry. I'll wait here until you're ready to get up."

I staggered to my feet, knowing that I needed to apply ice to my head as quickly as possible. I was only a block from home. "I can do this," I kept saying to myself. "God help me." I felt blood flowing, but I didn't want to scare myself, so I ignored it. Two kids passed me on their way to school, and the expressions on their faces when they saw me told me it was bad. Closer to my house, a neighbor zoomed past me in her car and then circled back. "Are you alright?" She worked out of town and I didn't want to make her late, so I told her I would be okay.

As soon as I got home, I quickly put Mollie in the backyard and grabbed some ice for the knot on my head. I also applied aloe vera to my scrapes. Then I went to my next-door neighbor Linnie for help. She took me to my family physician, Dr. Harris, who applied butterfly stitches to the gash beside my eye and gave me a prescription for painkillers. "It will probably leave a scar," he said, "but it will look like a laugh line. You can move your eye now, but if that changes, don't even call me. Go straight to the emergency room."

My plans had abruptly changed that day. No stories, no more singing. Just a horrible-looking black eye. I was at work by noon. I applied ice off and on that day, but the grimace on customers' faces told me that I didn't look so hot.

The next day, I returned to Dr. Harris. My face and eyelid were black, purple, and blue, and I couldn't open my eye. My sores were weeping, and my face had swollen so much that the butterfly stitches had popped off. People thought I had been in a car wreck.

Since I could still move my eye, I thought it was okay for me to attend a wake that night for Versie Spearman, who was the mother of one of my friends. I made some comments for her in front of a small audience at the funeral home chapel, never thinking about how my face looked. I just talked about how nice Ms. Versie was, and how sorry I felt about her passing.

An acquaintance of mine, Juanita, was there. I have known her for twenty years, but, she later told me, she didn't recognize me at the wake that night until she heard me introducing myself to someone.

Almost two weeks later, on September 4, 2011, at 4:47 p.m., I experienced another abrupt change. I received a text from my son Aaron: "Big fire like 4 miles away. Pray for us, please. We're getting ready don't call yet."

Aaron and his wife, Laura, worked in Bastrop, Texas, but they lived between Bastrop and Smithville, where their children, Skyler and Ayla, attended school. Laura's parents, Corliss and Andy, lived next door. I found out later that while that message was being sent to me, both families were grabbing essential items to flee for their lives. They had only minutes to evacuate. That fateful day, they planned to go to work the next morning as usual. The kids had their homework in their backpacks ready for school. But their plans changed dramatically by sunset.

The cell phone towers in the area burned down, so communication was practically nonexistent. We relied on Internet reports to keep us informed, and we asked family and friends to send fervent prayers for God's protection. A particular Scripture gave me great comfort: "When you pass through the waters, I will be with you; and when you pass through the rivers, they will not sweep over you. When you walk through the fire, you will not be burned; the flames will not set you ablaze" (Isaiah 43:2 NIV). Hours later, we learned they had made it safely down the winding road of the mountain where they lived. We rejoiced that God had spared them. Thinking they would head back home the next morning, they spent the night with some friends in Smithville. But again, those plans didn't come to pass. Things got worse. The fire kept spreading, coming closer to where they were staying, so they headed to Waco, Texas, to stay with my son Paul, who lived over a hundred miles away. They stayed with him for a week, not knowing if their house would still be standing when they returned.

To their dismay, the fire destroyed their home and all their worldly possessions. It was two months before they would be able to sleep in their own house again.

One week later, the television and newspapers reminded us of the day that abruptly changed the United States: September 11, 2001. A decade later, no one has forgotten. We still honor the lives lost and the heroes who came to rescue the trapped people. I heard of a man who was late to work that infamous day because his son asked him for a ride to school. That side trip saved his life, but over forty of his coworkers perished.

Probably no one that day woke up thinking, *My life will change today. It will never be the same.* I'm sure the courageous people on Flight 93 had had no idea that the glorious morning they greeted that day would be their last on earth, or that they would sacrifice themselves so that others could live.

I had a dear friend who was going through a terrible divorce. Her spouse wanted out, and this broke her heart. She stayed with us for two weeks. I grieved as I watched her get on her flight back home. Her last words before boarding were, "I have no reason to wake up in the morning."

As I prayed for her, God gave me words of encouragement. He said, "I will cause her to rise from the ashes like the phoenix." I didn't know what that meant, but hearing those words felt good. I looked up "phoenix" on Wiki Answers and found this: "In mythology, a phoenix is an immortal bird that when it dies, bursts into flames, and is reborn from its own ashes. To 'rise from the ashes of the phoenix' means to make a miraculous comeback." That reminded me of some powerful Scriptures in Isaiah that I love.

> The spirit of the Lord is upon me, because the Lord has anointed me to bring good news to the suffering and afflicted. He has sent me to comfort the broken-hearted, to announce liberty to captives and to open the eyes of the blind. He has sent me to tell those who mourn that the time of God's favor to them has come, and the day of his wrath to their enemies. To all who mourn in Israel he will give: beauty for ashes; joy instead of mourning; praise instead of heaviness. For God has planted them like strong and graceful oaks for his own glory.
>
> —Isaiah 61:1–3 LB

What do you do when things suddenly change in your life? You adapt. You look to God to restore, rebuild, and return your joy. Satan wants to wreck your face, your marriage, your home, and your country. Peter warns:

> Be careful—watch out for attacks from Satan, your great enemy. He prowls around like a hungry, roaring lion, looking for some victim to tear apart. Stand firm when he attacks. Trust the Lord; and remember that other Christians all around the world are going through these sufferings, too.

> After you have suffered a little while, our God, who is full of kindness through Christ, will give you His eternal glory. He personally will come and pick you up, and set you firmly in place, and make you stronger than ever.
>
> —1 Peter 5:8–10 LB

A physical miracle happened with my face after that fall on the sidewalk. My accident occurred on a Monday, and my wounds oozed until Friday, when they formed a huge scab. Sunday, while worshiping in the song service, I felt something strange, like electrical impulses prickling in a circular motion on my cheekbone. The sensation lasted about six minutes. I looked at my friend and asked, "Are you praying for me?"

She shrugged and said, "Sorry, no."

A few minutes later, the impulses started again, but this time they lasted about two minutes. Out of the corner of my eye, I saw my scab start popping off. Half of the scab came off that day, and by Monday, the whole scab had come off. One week after my fall, my face was healed. There was still a bump on my forehead, but the scar was miraculously gone, totally gone.

It was a miracle! People who knew what had happened to me were amazed. Where the scar had been was what looked and felt like brand-new, baby-soft skin. Three and a half weeks after my fall, the heels of my hands were still scuffed and healing, but not my face, which really mattered.

I couldn't write for the three days that I couldn't open my eye, but I asked God to make my stories stronger than ever. Satan thought he was going to trip me up by making me give up writing, but he was wrong.

My friend has recovered from her divorce and she has a new love in her life. I was glad when she told me she was happier than ever before.

Aaron's family and in-laws eventually rebuilt. We thank God that they escaped with their lives. There could have been funerals. They value each other now more than ever. They have not only a new home but also a new outlook. Corliss, my son's mother-in-law, told me that she had collected dolls from many foreign countries. They were off-limits to her daughter, Laura, when she was growing up, because she was afraid that fingerprints would deposit oil which might slowly deteriorate the dolls. She was saving them for Ayla, her granddaughter. She thought Ayla would appreciate them better when she was older.

However, Ayla was five and never even got to *see* the dolls. I asked Corliss if she would have changed the no-touch policy if she had somehow known the fire would occur. "Yes," she replied emphatically. "Ayla would have played with them every single day." We should listen to her words. We never know what tomorrow brings.

The word "rebuild" was printed on a banner at Ground Zero after the 9/11 tragedy. The words "double portion" are imprinted on my heart. That is what God promises me after my trials: the unexpected, unwelcome changes that affect my life will not last forever. Here is God's promise: "Instead of shame and dishonor, you shall have a double portion of prosperity and everlasting joy" (Isaiah 61:7 LB). That gives me hope.

If you are thinking that you have no reason to get up in the morning, or if you think the changes in your life are overwhelming, you are wrong. That is what Satan wants you to believe. As long as your hope is in God and you trust His Word, you will overcome.

Change does not have to destroy you. It can and will make you better. Allow people to comfort you and help you along the way. Don't be afraid to rebuild, because a double blessing may be waiting for you. Like the phoenix rising from the ashes, God has a miraculous comeback in store for you.

Don't despair. Just believe.

QUESTIONS

1. What is the most abrupt change you have ever had to face?

2. At the time, did it seem overwhelming?

Describe your circumstances six months later:

Two years later?

3. Which Scriptures helped you the most? (a, b)

4. Do you have a fear of sudden disasters that would change your life? Write down your concerns. (c)

5. Do you feel that a crisis would show what you are made of? (d)

6. Instead of worrying, what should you do? (e)

Scriptural Answers

(a) "Have mercy on me, O God have mercy on me, for in you my soul takes refuge. I will take refuge in the shadow of your wings until the disaster has passed" (Psalm 57:1 NIV).

(b) "The Lord himself goes before you and will be with you; he will never leave you nor forsake you. Do not be afraid; do not be discouraged" (Deuteronomy 31:8 NIV).

(c) "Have no fear of sudden disaster or of the ruin that overtakes the wicked, for the Lord will be your confidence and will keep your foot from being snared" (Proverbs 3:25–26 NIV).

(d) "If you fall to pieces in a crisis, there wasn't much to you in the first place" (Proverb 24:10).

(e) "Don't fret or worry. Instead of worrying pray. Let petitions and praises shape your worries into prayers, letting God know your concerns. Before you know it, a sense of God's wholeness, everything coming together for good, will come and settle you down. It is wonderful what happens when Christ displaces worry at the center of your life" (Philippians 4:6–7).

38

Have you ever heard a sentence sermon?

My definition of a "sentence sermon" is a sentence that impacts you for life, although that impact may be oblivious to the one speaking the words. I'll give you three examples.

I remember way back when I was in the second grade in Warren, Arkansas. It was winter and I was sick and staying in at recess. The church that I went to didn't allow girls to wear pants, so I had to wear a dress with pants underneath. That was before they had the cute leggings that they have today. What I wore that day was ugly, bulky trousers. Two other girls started making fun of me. The teacher reprimanded them, "Don't make fun of Sherry; she's only doing what her mother told her to do." It was such a small gesture, but forty-eight years later, I still remember that kind teacher. I will never forget how special it made me feel to have someone defend me.

When I was in the seventh grade, I was new to a school in Nashville, Tennessee. A popular girl came up to me and said, "Sherry, you have a beautiful smile, but I hardly ever *see* you smile." That was the whole conversation, but boy what an impact it had on me! "Beautiful smile" was really all I heard. I guess that's all I needed to hear. I started smiling that day and I haven't stopped. I guess that's why I like to compliment people on their smiles: because it meant so much to me.

I don't remember that teacher's name or that seventh grade girl's name, but I do remember the way they made me feel. That's what I want to be:

a defender, an encourager, someone who doesn't go around with lofty sermons that people tune out so all they hear is "blah, blah, blah." A sentence-sermon preacher, if you will. You can be one, too.

Maya Angelou once said, "I've learned that people will forget what you said, people will forget what you did, but people will never forget how you made them feel." Solomon said, "Everyone enjoys giving good advice, and how wonderful it is to be able to say the right thing at the right time" (Proverb 15:23 LB).

My next example came from my teenage son Paul who gave me good advice when he said the right thing at the right time. I warn you, though, that not all sentence sermons are uplifting; some hurt a little. He may not remember the incident, but I do because his words still resonate in my spirit whenever I'm tempted to go there again.

Are you ready for his words of wisdom? Here is the sentence in all its simplicity: "Mom, you're not very attractive when you pout." That's all he said. I didn't realize what I was doing until he pointed it out. He showed me mercy, because when *I* see a fault, I am tempted to give long lectures. In most cases, though, a lecture will only make the listener tune you out.

I looked at him and said, "Paul, you're right." I may slip up every now and then, but for the most part, I'm cured. Thank you, Paul, for your sentence sermon. It impacted me.

"Fools are headstrong and do what they like; wise people take advice" (Proverb 12:15). Which do you want to be? Listen to yourself the next time you hear a criticism. It might give you a clue. And when you feel like giving a lecture, believe it or not, less is more.

Questions

1. Write down sentence sermons that people have preached to you that impacted you for a lifetime.

2. Whom do you respect more, someone who gives you criticism in one sentence, or a two hour lecture? Explain. (a)

3. How do you feel when a friend gives you the right word at the right time? (b)

4. If you refuse good advice, what could happen? (c)

5. Have you ever pouted or seen others pout? (d)

6. You may get what you want when you pout, but you may not like the consequences. Write down your thoughts.

7. When we talk to others, is it wise to tell it like it is and let the chips fall where they may, or should we walk in love? (e)

8. Give an example of a sentence sermon that Jesus preached. (f)

Scriptural Answers

(a) "It's the straightforward who gets his respect" (Proverb 3:32).

(b) "The right word at the right time is like a custom-made piece of jewelry. And a wise friend's timely reprimand is like a gold ring slipped on your finger" (Proverbs 25:11–12).

(c) "Refuse good advice and watch your plans fail; take good counsel and watch them succeed" (Proverb 15:22).

(d) "Ahab went home in a black mood, sulking over Naboth the Jezreelite's words, 'I'll never turn over the family inheritance to you.' He went to bed, stuffed his face in his pillow, and refused to eat" (1 Kings 21:4).

(e) "God wants us to grow up, to know the whole truth and tell it in love—like Christ in everything" (Ephesians 4:15).

(f) "When they kept on questioning [Jesus], he straightened up and said to them, 'If any one of you is without sin, let him be the first to throw a stone at her'" (John 8:7 NIV).

39
Have you ever heard God cry?

I awoke at 1:30 a.m. this morning. It's March 28, 2011. I said, "I love you, God."

He said, "I'm sad."

"Why are you sad, God?" I asked.

"Because people don't believe Me."

"What do they not believe, God?" There was silence. I felt like He was crying. "Why are you sad? What do they not believe?"

"Jesus, my Son, is coming soon, but they don't believe Me. People are worried about paying bills, vacations, their jobs, and they've forgotten about Me. If each person led just one more into salvation, there would be so many more in heaven. But who is going to do *my* work? I really like the movie *Pay It Forward*, where one person does a favor for three other people, who must each themselves pay the action forward to three more people. My kingdom works the same way. It's not so overwhelming if you think about it one person at a time. I'm watching, you know. Oh, there are plenty of opportunities, but people are afraid. Why are they afraid?"

"I don't know, God."

"Well, that's why I'm sad. Will you let them know?"

"Yes, God, I'll let them know."

And that was it. I cried as God cried.

His message is for everyone. Are we doing enough? Probably not. Jesus is coming soon, but whom are we taking with us to heaven? What really makes God happy? Is it prayer, praise, or obedience? All of these things are important, but many people are still lost. I wonder how many opportunities I have missed? Jesus said to His disciples, "The harvest is plentiful but the workers are few. Ask the Lord of the harvest, therefore, to send out workers into his harvest field" (Matthew 9:37–38 NIV).

There are more earthquakes, tsunamis, floods, and tornadoes than ever before. The earth is groaning for our Lord's return. But are *we* groaning? Are we serious about His return? Share the Good News with someone. Set them free. "So if the Son sets you free, you will be free indeed" (John 8:36 NIV). "But as for those who serve the Lord, he will redeem them; everyone who takes refuge in him will be freely pardoned" (Psalm 34:22 LB). *The Message* puts it this way: "God pays for each slave's freedom; no one who runs to him loses out."

Do you know someone who is in bondage and needs to be free? Are they a slave to drugs, pornography, or debt? You have the keys to the jail that they are imprisoned in. Jesus is the answer. Jesus is *their* answer. Are you going to tell them how to get their freedom, or are you scared to speak? God is watching. We should be fearful of Him, not of them.

"Investigate my life, O God, find out everything about me; cross-examine and test me, get a clear picture of what I'm about; see for yourself whether I've done anything wrong—then guide me on the road to eternal life" (Psalms 139:23–24). Let God search out your heart. He'll guide you and He'll be gentle.

Yes, God, I am guilty myself. I need to show people the way to You. I need You to guide me and I am willing. You aren't willing for anyone to perish without everlasting life and I shouldn't be either. Help me to overcome my fears. Help me to put a smile on Your face as I bring more people to You.

Are you willing, too? That's good, because there are lots of lost souls. Let's take as many as we can with us. Let's get our priorities straight and put that smile back on God's face.

Questions

1. Do you believe God has emotions? Give examples. (a, b)

2. Does God really watch us? (c)

3. Is Jesus really coming in a cloud? (d, e)

4. We will never have to give an account of ourselves to God. True or false? (f)

5. When will we talk to God about our words on earth? (g)

6. Are you willing to talk to others about Jesus? Why or why not?

Scriptural Answers

(a) "Don't grieve God. Don't break his heart. His Holy Spirit, moving and breathing in you, is the most intimate part of your life, making you fit for himself. Don't take such a gift for granted" (Ephesians 4:30).

(b) "God saw that human evil was out of control. People thought evil, imagined evil—evil, evil, evil from morning to night. God was sorry that he had made the human race in the first place; it broke his heart" (Genesis 6:5–6).

(c) "You see, we are not like the many hucksters who preach for personal profit. We preach the word of God with sincerity and with Christ's authority, knowing that God is watching us" (2 Corinthians 2:17 NLT).

(d) "Sing hymns to God; all heaven, sing out; clear the way for the coming of Cloud-Rider. Enjoy God, cheer when you see him!" (Psalm 68:4).

(e) "At that time they will see the Son of Man coming in a cloud with power and great glory. When these things begin to take place, stand up and lift up your heads, because your redemption is drawing near" (Luke 21:27–28 NIV).

(f) "Yes, each of us will give an account of himself to God" (Romans 14:12 LB).

(g) "I tell you this, that you must give account on Judgment Day for every idle word you speak. Your words now reflect your fate then: either you will be justified by them or you will be condemned" (Matthew 12:36–37).

40

Have you ever heard the voice?

When my son Paul played baseball at Baylor, the games started at noon on Sundays. The game this particular day was over at 5:00 p.m. It takes six and a half hours to drive back home, so it was probably around midnight by the time I was on the home stretch. The last forty miles were not on the interstate, but on a two-lane, winding road with trees everywhere.

I had my cruise control on and was going about sixty mph when I heard a voice in my spirit. "I want you to take the cruise control off." I thought that seemed strange, but I did it anyway. Next I heard, "Now slow down." I slowed down to about forty mph. Within five minutes I came over a hill and saw a big deer that had stopped on my side of the road. It was calmly looking at me. As I slowed down a little more, the deer straightened its head and walked to the other side. I reset my cruise control and finished the trip.

Believe me, I was wide awake after that! I was so excited to know that I had been given such perfect instructions. I'm glad the Holy Spirit didn't wait until I was right on the deer to scream and scare me out of my wits. He was gentle. "Whether you turn to the right or to the left, your ears will hear a voice behind you saying, 'This is the way; walk in it'" (Isaiah 30:21 NIV). Or in my case, take off the cruise and slow down.

I can't help but think of my dogs when I hear that Scripture. When I walk the dogs on a leash, I walk behind them. When I say "stop," they stop. When I say "let's go," they go. If I'm going to let them enter the house or receive a treat, I say "wait," and they wait. If I want to change the direction we're walking, I simply say, "this way." Their ears are trained to my voice; they ignore everyone else. I don't beat them with a stick. They don't obey me because they're afraid of me, but because they love me. I don't scream at the top of my lungs; I give gentle instructions. That's how the Holy Spirit is: gentle with His instructions.

I would also say the Holy Spirit is similar to a GPS (Global Positioning System) for your vehicle. The GPS navigates you from where you are to where you want to be. It gives you commands that are simple. However, you must read the manual in order to get the maximum benefit. If you take a side trip, it must recalculate, and it will set you back on your course. When you arrive, the voice says, "You have reached your destination."

That's the simplest way to explain the Holy Spirit. He navigates me through my world. He is my personal GCS (Guiding Comfort System). Jesus said,

> If you love me, obey me; and I will ask the Father and He will give you another Comforter, and He will never leave you. He is the Holy Spirit; the Spirit who leads into all truth. The world at large cannot receive Him, for it isn't looking for Him and doesn't recognize Him. But you do, for He lives with you now and some day shall be in you. No, I will not abandon you or leave you as orphans in the storm—I will come to you. In just a little while I will be gone from the world, but I will still be present with you. For I will live again—and you will too.
>
> —John 14:15–19 LB

Isn't that beautiful?! When Jesus left this earth, He provided a way for us to navigate through this world: the Holy Spirit. I have been Spirit-filled since I was twelve years old and He has guided me my whole life. But I had to repeatedly read the Bible, His manual, to fill my spirit with knowledge. You train your ears to His voice by reading the Word.

There are other imitating voices that will confuse you if you don't know who to listen for. Learn to recognize the Master's voice. When you hear the Holy Spirit speaking to your inner spirit, there should be no conflict with the Bible or confusion in your mind. "For God is not a God of confusion but of peace" (1 Corinthians 14:33 NASB). Jesus said, "My sheep listen to my voice; I know them and they follow me" (John 10:27 NIV). We develop sheep ears that are tuned to the Good Shepherd's voice.

The Holy Spirit comforted me when three of my friends died from cancer. He counseled me when I didn't know how to handle my kids, He was a helper when I needed a game plan, He was an intercessor when I didn't know how to pray. He was an advocate when I felt deserted and He strengthened me when every fiber of my being screamed, "Give up!" He guides me when I don't know which direction to go, and if I get lost along the way, He will find and redirect me.

He is the Spirit of Truth and He will guide. Read God's Manual. Listen to the Voice. You will reach your destination.

Questions

1. Can you understand the thoughts from God if you aren't a Christian? (a)

2. Does the spiritual man have insight into God's mind. (b)

3. Does God talk to us in a loud, scary voice, or in a whisper? (c)

4. Do you believe the Lord will talk to us and give us specific instructions? (d)

5. What has God said to you?

6. Some people believe that God will only talk to them in church. What do you think? (e)

7. How does God guide us? (f)

8. Has someone ever told you that they had heard from God, but you thought it didn't feel right? How do you handle this situation? (g, h)

Scriptural Answers

(a) "The man who isn't a Christian can't understand and can't accept these thoughts from God, which the Holy Spirit teaches us. They sound foolish to him, because only those who have the Holy Spirit within them can understand what the Holy Spirit means. Others just can't take it in" (1 Corinthians 2:14 LB).

(b) "The spiritual man has insight into everything, and that bothers and baffles the man of the world, who can't understand him at all. How could he? For certainly he has never been one to know the Lord's thoughts, or to discuss them with him, or to move the hands of God by prayer. But, strange as it seems, we Christians actually do have within us a portion of the very thoughts and mind of Christ" (1 Corinthians 2:15–16 LB).

(c) "A hurricane ripped through the mountains and shattered the rocks before God, but God wasn't to be found in the wind; after the wind an earthquake; and after the earthquake fire, but God wasn't in the fire; and after the fire a gentle and quiet whisper" (1 Kings 19:11–12).

(d) "The Lord said to Joshua, 'Jericho and its king and all its mighty warriors are already defeated, for I have given them to you! Your entire army is to walk around the city once a day for six days, followed by seven priests walking ahead of the Ark, each carrying a trumpet made from a ram's horn. On the seventh day you are to walk around the city seven times, with the priests blowing their trumpets. Then, when they give one long, loud blast, all the people are to give a mighty shout and the walls of the city will fall down; then move in upon the city from every direction" (Joshua 6:2–5 LB).

(e) "Listen for God's voice in everything you do, everywhere you go; he's the one who will keep you on track" (Proverb 3:6).

(f) "You will keep on guiding me all my life with your wisdom and counsel, and afterwards receive me into the glories of heaven!" (Psalm 73:24 LB).

(g) "Don't suppress the Spirit, and don't stifle those who have a word from the Master. On the other hand, don't be gullible. Check out everything, and keep only what's good. Throw out anything tainted with evil" (1 Thessalonians 5:19–22).

(h) "Dearly loved friends, don't always believe everything you hear just because someone says it is a message from God: test it first to see if it really is. For there are many false teachers around" (1 John 4:1 LB).

41
Have you ever joined the Sisters' Club?

It was sixty-one degrees Fahrenheit, a perfect fall morning for walking my dog Mollie. I like to meander through different neighborhoods so we don't get bored. A few weeks before, I had made a mental note that the two elderly women who normally sit on their porches in the early morning weren't there. I occasionally saw them while walking Mollie, but I didn't know their names. I just knew that they looked friendly and they always made me smile.

This particular day I proposed to walk down their street and give our usual greeting. My intention was to walk a rectangular path which would make me pass their houses on my return trip.

As I approached 11th Street heading toward 8th Street, I had a desire to take a left instead of proceeding forward. I thought, *What does it matter which route I go? I'll still get there.* I had another strange thought: *Turn left.* At this point I realized it must be the Holy Spirit talking to me, so I stopped arguing. *Maybe there's a big dog around the corner. Thanks for the tip.*

Two steps later, I heard, "Go and talk to the lady in the first house."

"Okay God, but what do you want me to say?" I heard nothing.

I was a block away and could tell that the woman was not on her porch. "God, it's 7:45 a.m., and this black woman might be scared if I knock on her door. I have a large dog with me and that may scare her and her little dog out of their wits. If this is really You directing my path, please have her open the door when I get there."

When Mollie and I approached her house, we stopped at the curb directly in front of her door. At the exact same time, she opened her screen door as if on cue from a movie director.

I had a big grin on my face because I couldn't contain my excitement. God was up to something. "Hello, Ma'am! How are you doing today?"

"Oh, I guess I'm okay. I've been in the hospital for four weeks. I had a brain stroke and I've been in a wheelchair and on a walker. It happened on my brain stem."

I heard what she was saying, but at the same time, I was listening for God's voice. This time, He spoke. "Just tell her everything's going to be okay."

And that's exactly what I told her. We conversed about how wonderful God was to have me bring a message of encouragement this day. I told her how I ended up at her door. We were amazed that she had even come to the front door. She had been on the back porch doing laundry and had hobbled to the front porch. She couldn't figure out why she had made the slow journey to open the front door until my greeting. We laughed at how you can never figure out what God is up to, so you might as well just listen and obey. We took turns bragging about God.

I shared with her how my husband had been healed from cancer and how God could give her a brand-new brain stem. "If God could create the universe, then it's not that hard for Him to create a new brain stem and a total recovery."

Our spirits soared and tears brimmed in our eyes as we joined together in prayer over this God-ordained encounter. I don't think I told her anything she didn't already know; I just confirmed her already strong faith. Because I had been obedient, I had found a new sister in Christ: Sister Louvina, otherwise known as Baby Doll. We were so happy! It was as if we had been friends forever.

I'm embarrassed to say that I had passed by this beautiful lady year after year without taking the time to really know her. But I can promise you that I will be stopping at her house again, and I won't have to be personally asked by God to do so.

Who in your neighborhood would love for you to stop by and chat a while? Ask God to point them out. If God asks you to turn left when you planned on going straight, He might have a God-ordained encounter for you.

> We must continue to hold firmly to our declaration of faith. We must also consider how to encourage each other to show love and good things. We should not stop gathering together with other believers, as some of you are doing. Instead, we must continue to encourage each other even more as we see the day of the Lord coming.
> —Hebrews 10:23–25 GWT

Beautifully said. Now join the club! By the way, I hear there's a Brothers' Club, too.

Questions

1. Are there people in your neighborhood whom you haven't met yet? Would it be possible to meet them?

2. According to Jesus, the most important commandment is to "Love the Lord your God with all your heart." What is the second most important commandment? (a)

3. Should we imitate God? (b)

4. Do you think Jesus showed us how God loves us? (c)

5. As Christians, should we fellowship with each other or keep to ourselves? (d)

6. If we are to love our neighbors and imitate God, should we encourage each other as we go through trials? How? (e)

7. How often should we encourage each other? (f)

8. Who is your brother, sister, and mother? (g)

Scriptural Answers

(a) "The second is this: 'Love your neighbor as yourself.' There is no commandment greater than these" (Mark 12:31 NIV).

(b) "Be imitators of God therefore, as dearly loved children and live a life of love, just as Christ loved us and gave himself up for us as a fragrant offering and sacrifice to God" (Ephesians 5:1–2 NIV).

(c) "I've loved you the way my Father has loved me. Make yourselves at home in my love. If you keep my commands, you'll remain intimately at home in my love. That's what I've done—kept my Father's commands and made myself at home in his love" (John 15:9–10).

(d) "Be sure to welcome our friend Phoebe in the way of the Master, with all the generous hospitality we Christians are famous for ... She deserves anything you can do for her. She's helped many a person, including me" (Romans 16:1–2).

(e) "Let's see how inventive we can be in encouraging love and helping out, not avoiding worshiping together as some do but spurring each other on, especially as we see the big Day approaching" (Hebrews 10:25).

(f) "But encourage one another daily" (Hebrews 3:13 NIV).

(g) "[Jesus] added, 'Anyone who obeys my Father in heaven is my brother, sister, and mother!'" (Matthew 12:50 LB).

42

Have you ever known a slow starter?

My pastor, Gary Bell, told our congregation about a Chinese bamboo tree that grows in the Far East. Once the seed is planted, it must be watered and fertilized for four years, but you will see no inkling of growth during that time. In the fifth year, the ground breaks and the tree's growth is phenomenal, sometimes reaching a height of ninety feet in as little as five weeks.

I thought of the perseverance of people willing to take a chance planting this tree. What if they lived with a pessimist? Can you imagine the type of conversation that might go on in the household?

The pessimistic one, I'll call her Mabel, might say, "Why do you keep watering that seed? It's been two whole years! You're making a fool out of yourself!"

The optimistic one, I'll call him George, might say, "I still believe the tree will grow. You worry about your problems; I'll worry about the tree."

The third year, Mabel might say, "This is embarrassing! The neighbors planted a nice Chinese elm tree and it grew three feet each year. It's nine feet tall now! What do you have to say for yourself?"

George would then say, "This tree is different. Not all trees progress at the same rate. Just wait, you'll see."

The fourth year, Mabel would demand, her arms crossed, "Just give up! I'm *still* not seeing any results!"

George would calmly reply, "Don't you remember the story of the tortoise and the hare? Slow and steady wins the race. Some things mature slower. Just believe."

But that fifth year—look out! George would run into the house breathless. "Mabel, come here! You've gotta see this tree!"

At that point, Mabel would shrug her shoulders and say, "Wow, I guess I was wrong."

Just like the Chinese bamboo tree, my husband, Randy, was a slow starter. Back in the old days they didn't have kindergarten. He told me he remembers his first grade teacher telling him to color a picture. He grabbed all of his crayons in one hand and drew big circles. Instead of showing him how to do it right, she yelled at him. He didn't know what he had done wrong. He passed the first grade, but they held him back because they said he was immature.

God blessed Randy throughout his school years, because by the time he reached high school he was taking and excelling in advanced courses. Randy's teacher had predicted that he would be a hoodlum by the time he grew up. His teacher was wrong. He was a slow starter, but today you would never know that fact. Now, he is a fantastic heating and air service man who is a leader in the company where he works. This may sound prejudiced, but I would say he is the best in our city, maybe in the nation. Who would ever have thought that rascally, hyperactive, immature little boy would turn into a man whom doctors, lawyers, schools, and restaurants call when they have a heating or cooling problem.

My grandson, Skyler, is also a slow starter. He has been in speech therapy since he was three years old. The speech therapist told his parents, Aaron and Laura, that Skyler had invented his own language. When Skyler was asked to repeat an unclear response, he could duplicate it perfectly. His speech sounded similar to a foreign language.

I remember walking into Walmart with Skyler when he was in the first grade. We ran into one of his classmates. After talking for a couple of minutes, Ricardo, noticing my frustrated expression, interrupted Skyler in midsentence and said to me, "It's okay, I can understand him." I was amazed that Ricardo had no trouble understanding Skyler, even though I and other adults in his life had been clueless.

Skyler had to repeat the first grade—not because he failed, but because they felt he was too immature. Hmm. I think he's a chip off his papaw's block.

As a matter of fact, there was a certain genius who had a similarly challenging start to his life. You might have heard of him: Albert Einstein. Thomas Sowell wrote a book called *Einstein Syndrome: Bright Children Who Talk Late.* According to *Wikipedia,*

> This book investigates the phenomenon of late-talking children, frequently misdiagnosed with autism or pervasive developmental disorder ... the book and its contributing researchers make a case for the theory that some children develop unevenly (asynchronous development) for a period in childhood due to rapid and extraordinary development in the analytical functions of the brain. This may temporarily "rob resources" from neighboring functions such as language development.

In a nutshell, Skyler may be a genius! Not too bad for a slow starter, huh?

When I was in the first grade, my books went something like this:

See Dick. See Dick run.
See Jane. See Jane run.
See Spot. See Spot run.

My slow start with an early reading primer has not hindered me from reading and comprehending anything I want to read now. It may seem like an unbelievably basic beginning, but I really wish we could go back to those days. Back then, the teachers were not in a hurry, rushing through lessons, trying to meet each day's prescribed criteria. What's the rush, anyway?

One of Skyler's first-grade spelling words was "foundation." No wonder kids are having trouble. They skip over the basics and have them flying fighter jets when they have only just begun to ride a tricycle. They need to *build* a solid foundation, not *spell* foundation.

The Bible says, "Does anyone dare despise this day of small beginnings?" (Zechariah 4:10). I don't think it would be too much of a stretch to say, "Don't despise the day of a slow start."

You could say that Jesus Christ had a slow start. He knew that He had a mission on this earth, yet didn't begin His ministry until He was thirty years old. During that waiting period, He was a lowly carpenter. He had not only a slow beginning, but a small beginning. He accomplished His mission in three and a half years. Most people would have been chomping at the bit. "This is taking too long. I'm ready now. I was born for this."

We live in a microwaving, gotta-have-it-now society, but is that always for the best? Ever try to cook a pot of stew in the microwave? I doubt it, although I did once try to cook a twenty-pound turkey in one. I don't think it ever got done. If I remember correctly, it was a bloody, rubbery mess. Stew needs to simmer, and turkeys need to cook slowly. We need to be patient. "Don't be impatient for the Lord to act" (Psalm 37:34 LB). Allow God time to work out the issues in your life.

At the age of nine, Skyler is only forty-seven inches tall and he weighs forty-two pounds. Every morning he rushes to the scales and the door frame hoping and praying for some sign of growth. It hasn't happened in a long time, yet he still believes. And he waits.

Perhaps your career has taken longer than you thought it would to develop, and you're about to stop watering the seed that you planted many years ago. Don't quit now; there's a little green sprout poking out of the ground. Your marketing campaign may be about to go viral and thrive, just like the ninety-foot Chinese bamboo.

Maybe you're struggling to potty train your child. Relax. By the time little Johnny graduates high school, no one will remember that it took him four years to get out of training pants. Remember the Einstein Syndrome? Well, there may very well be a Johnny Syndrome. Lighten up!

Don't obsess about the slow starts in your life. Maturing is a slow process. The best wine takes decades to age, and you are far better than the most fragrant wine.

There's an interesting story in the Bible about a three-year drought. God told the prophet Elijah that he was about to make it rain. Elijah believed God and went to the top of Mount Carmel, where he prayed intensely. Then he instructed his servant to look toward the sea. The servant saw nothing, but Elijah sent him back seven times. "And sure enough, the seventh time he said, 'Oh yes, a cloud! But very small, no bigger than someone's hand, rising out of the sea' ... Things happened fast. The sky

Sheep Ears

grew black with wind-driven clouds and then a huge cloudburst of rain" (1 Kings 18:44, 46).

God gave Elijah a word. He believed God's word, he persevered, he saw a speck of hope, and then things happened quickly.

Please don't be discouraged when your little Chinese bamboo children take a little longer than others to mature. I imagine that their roots are maturing under the surface where no one can see them except the awesome God who formed them. God has His own timing and it's always perfect.

I can't wait to see how Skyler turns out. I have no doubt that he will excel at something awesome. He may be a slow starter, but that's okay. I heard about the Chinese bamboo, I saw Randy, I read about Einstein, and I believe with strong faith in Skyler. I have seen his slivers of genius as he plays video games, and I wonder if this will be his forte. I've been amazed by how he turned our yard into a full-fledged war zone as he organized six neighborhood boys into troops. I envision him leading ground troops to lay siege of an enemy force, or possibly protecting the president one day.

One day, things will happen quickly for Skyler. Look out, world, here he comes!

QUESTIONS

1. Have you ever known anyone who seemed slow at things that were easy for you, yet surpassed your skills in another area? Who were they? What skills did they develop?

2. There was a time in the Bible that God told the Israelites to wait five years before they ate the fruit of a tree. Why did He have them wait? (a)

3. Have you ever felt like a mess, unable to discover where you belong in life? Write down your thoughts. (b)

4. When you have waited a long time for any sign of progress, is it best to give up, or to stay with God? Explain. (c)

5. When you know that others have struggled and overcome, does it give you hope for yourself? (d)

6. In your opinion, does it help if someone believes in you when you are struggling? (e)

Scriptural Answers

(a) "When you enter the land and plant any kind of fruit tree, don't eat the fruit for three years, consider it inedible. By the fourth year its fruit is holy, an offering of praise to God. Beginning in the fifth year you can eat its fruit; you'll have richer harvests this way. I am God, your God" (Leviticus 19:23–25).

(b) "And me? I'm a mess. I'm nothing and have nothing: make something of me. You can do it, you've got what it takes—but God, don't put if off" (Psalm 40:17).

(c) "Stay with God! Take heart. Don't quit. I'll say it again: stay with God" (Psalm 27:14).

(d) "And now he shows me off—evidence of his endless patience—to those who are right on the edge of trusting him forever" (1 Timothy 1:16).

(e) "There has never been the slightest doubt in my mind that the God who started this great work in you would keep at it and bring it to a flourishing finish on the very day Christ Jesus appears" (Philippians 1:6).

43

Have you ever learned to be content?

My grandkids, Skyler and Ayla, ages nine and four respectively, came to visit me and my husband for several weeks in the summer. Normally, I would spare no expense for their entertainment. We usually go out as often as we can without even worrying about the money. This past summer, I had a different philosophy: Let's see how much fun we can have while spending the least amount of money.

That spring, I shopped around at a few garage sales and found each of the kids a bicycle and a scooter for only twenty dollars. I also found a play piano, Play-Doh accessories, and quality play clothes at twenty-five cents each. A small wading pool and some water blasters were added to the mix. I located a Slip 'n Slide for under thirteen dollars. I couldn't believe they still made those things! I recall hours of fun watching my sons play on that slippery yellow plastic. I had tried to make one myself the previous summer out of an old shower curtain. Trust me: it's better to buy their product. All of these bargain items combined to form a great foundation for summer fun.

Every day we did something special. One day we washed our car and truck. That transitioned into cannonball blasts into the front yard "swimming hole" created by the overflowing water. Our neighbor Linnie had a pile of sand beside her house, so she picked out the weeds, gave the kids spoons and fireplace shovels, old Folgers coffee cans, and plastic water bottles. They made numerous trips from the bathroom sink to the sand pile as they filled up their containers with water. I must admit they created the most magnificent waterfall and lake ever. And it was totally free.

In the mornings we walked the dogs and they rode on their bikes and scooters. Many days, we ate at McDonald's, then they played on the playground until they were exhausted. I take that back. They never got exhausted, but I sure did. We also went to the Railroad Museum and the Delta Nature Center, which were free and educational. Skyler and Ayla attended Vacation Bible School at two different churches. They loved to learn about God, especially when the teachers made it fun for them.

Even though summer is my husband's busiest time of year, he always made time for them. They squealed when they saw his service truck pull up in the driveway. Ayla would grab her latest artwork to show him, and Skyler would grab his guns. He and Papaw would run around the yard chasing and throwing plastic water bottle bombs at each other. We had special times that I hope Skyler and Ayla will always remember. One day I'd like to take them to Six Flags Over Texas theme park.

I don't have a suffer-and-be-blessed mentality. I just want to stress the fact that even if your budget is tight, there are many options for having fun. Be creative. Memories don't have a dollar sign in front of them. Contentment does not depend on how much money you spend. You could spend one hundred dollars on a Christmas present only to have the child play for hours on end with the box it came in. Children have God-given imagination; we just need to allow them the freedom to use it.

One fall Saturday my husband and I were sitting on our lawn swing under our live oak tree and Randy commented, "This has been the best day I've had in a long time." Do you know what we had done? We ate a leisurely breakfast at Hardees and then visited his friend Wayne who had been off work for three weeks. That was Randy's best day: no high-pressure expensive trips, but just a simple, relaxing day. Jesus said, "Don't load yourselves up with equipment. Keep it simple; you are the equipment" (Luke 9:3).

Society has brainwashed us into thinking we need more expensive toys and more complex electronics, but in my opinion, we need to get back to the basics. Enjoy life beyond the electronic beeps, the e-mails, Facebook, and Twitters. I'm not just addressing the kids now.

In Paul's message to the Philippians, he said, "I know what it is to be in need, and I know what it is to have plenty. I have learned the secret of being content in any and every situation, whether well fed or hungry, whether living in plenty or in want. I can do everything through him who gives me strength" (Philippians 4:12–13 NIV). The secret that Paul discovered was the ability to be content in Christ.

I have no doubt that Skyler and Ayla had fun this summer. I did, too. I urge you not to be consumed by buying bigger and better things. Learn how to be content with the simple things in life. That's advice for everyone, including myself. Time spent with loved ones is what everyone craves. As they say, the best things in life are free.

Questions

1. When you vacation, do you have to stay at the most luxurious hotels, or could you be content with modest accommodations? (a)

2. Do you know people who are obsessed with getting more and more material things? Is that a godly attitude? (b)

3. Is it possible to live a full life that is simple? (c)

4. If you have trouble with selfish ambition, how should you adjust your thinking? (d)

5. Can God help your heart when you are discontent? (e)

6. What often happens when you live a rich lifestyle? (f)

Scriptural Answers

(a) "When you enter a town or village, don't insist on staying in a luxury inn. Get a modest place with some modest people and be content there until you leave" (Matthew 10:11).

(b) "Don't be obsessed with getting more material things. Be relaxed with what you have. Since God assured us, 'I'll never let you down, never walk off and leave you'" (Hebrews 13:5).

(c) "A pretentious, showy life is an empty life; a plain and simple life is a full life" (Proverb 13:7).

(d) "Do nothing out of selfish ambition or vain conceit, but in humility consider others better than yourselves" (Philippians 2:3 NIV).

(e) "I'll give you a new heart; put a new spirit in you. I'll remove the stone heart from your body and replace it with a heart that's God-willed, not self-willed" (Ezekiel 36:26).

(f) "A simple life in the Fear-of-God is better than a rich life with a ton of headaches" (Proverb 15:16).

44

Have you ever learned to laugh?

I was raised in a house full of laughter. My dad always told corny jokes and my mom chimed in. Whenever my husband and I made the nine-hour trip to my parents' house, my sister, Michelle, came over and we would have a laugh feast. Sometimes we didn't even know what was so funny, but we would laugh in unison at the exact same time. We have an awesome rapport.

My husband, Randy, was raised in a more serious atmosphere. He told me that he loved to visit my parents because he enjoyed watching us laugh so much. It wasn't natural for him, though. After his comment, I realized how fortunate I was to have been raised with such free-flowing humor, and I prayed for God to show me a way to teach Randy to enjoy life like we did.

We were on a trip to Texas when I realized this would be the perfect time for a lesson in Laughter 101, since he couldn't escape the classroom. I said, "Randy, would you like to learn how to laugh like my family does?"

He said, "Sherry, I can't do it."

"I'll tell you something funny, and I want you to laugh." I did, but he didn't even crack a smile. *Okay, let's try again.* I made another attempt at a joke, but again, nothing. This was some of my best stuff, so I knew it was good material. On my next joke, I asked him to fake a laugh, even if it was a quiet one. So out came a small chortle—but his eyes were sad. I hadn't realized how hard this would be for him. I could see that he wanted to do it, but it was difficult. It was like learning a new language; you have to do it gradually, with lots of repetition.

Next, I encouraged him to give a good loud laugh no matter how silly he felt. He actually took my advice and it surprised us both. So I giggled and he spontaneously started a genuine full laugh, which tickled me more than ever. I busted out laughing and he went into a full-fledged belly laugh. You know the kind I'm talking about. The kind that makes your spirit soar. His eyes lit up and the sadness was broken.

While he was still in that frame of mind, we bantered back and forth the whole trip with wise cracks and funny faces. Sometimes, I would have to remind him to laugh, but he's a fast learner. By the end of the trip, he got his certificate that said he passed the course. Just joking, ha ha!

David laughed. He said, "When the Lord brought back the captives to Zion, we were like men who dreamed. Our mouths were filled with laughter, our tongues with songs of joy. Then it was said among the nations, 'The Lord has done great things for them'" (Psalms 126:1–2 NIV). If you are a Christian, what better witness of being happy can we give to the world than laughter and a cheerful countenance? Solomon said, "A cheerful heart brings a smile to your face; a sad heart makes it hard to get through the day … A miserable heart means a miserable life; a cheerful heart fills the day with song" (Proverbs 15:13, 15). Our attitude and demeanor really do make a difference in our lives and the lives of those around us.

Of course, we must be wise. There is "a right time to cry and another to laugh" (Ecclesiastes 3:4). You wouldn't want to walk into a hospital room laughing, or walk onto the scene of an automobile accident cracking jokes. I'm just talking about a general lifestyle of joy.

Have you ever met strangers whom you could tell were Christians by their countenance, the smiles on their face, and the light in their eyes? I have, and I'm sure you have, too. On the other hand, have you ever met someone who professed to be a Christian, but looked like they drank pickle juice for breakfast every morning? It seems contradictory, doesn't it?

Maybe you've never thought about your countenance, and you wish you had someone to give you lessons. I've got some ideas for you: watch funny shows on television. Some favorites of mine are *The Dick Van Dyke Show*, *America's Funniest Videos*, and *The Cosby Show*. Jesse Duplantis has

Sheep Ears

some fantastic CDs filled with hours of humor in his sermons. I might warn you, though: have plenty of tissues ready. You can also watch funny movies or read joke books. When I get my monthly copy of *Reader's Digest*, I go straight to the joke section. Same with the newspaper: I go straight to the comics. And have you noticed the best commercials are the funny ones?

I have heard of people diagnosed with cancer who go to the video store, rent funny movies, and play them one after another to get healing in their bones. Solomon said, "A happy heart is good medicine and a cheerful mind works healing, but a broken spirit dries up the bones" (Proverb 17:22 AB).

One day I walked into the classroom and saw a student in a very foul mood. Nothing I said would get her out of her funk, so I looked at what I was wearing that day: purple pants, purple vest, purple jacket. "Hey, look at me, I look like Barney! 'I love you, you love me, we're a great big family,'" I sang as the other kids joined in. "Now if you can't laugh at me, you're hopeless." I tried to look serious, but the twinkle in my eyes were a sure giveaway. She broke into the cutest giggles, and all her frustrations vanished. Sometimes it's good to laugh at yourself. It gives other people freedom to laugh at themselves, too.

What do people see when they look at you? Do you look like you attend The First Church of the Sanctified Pickle? Or do they see the joy of the Lord permeating every fiber of your being? When the law was read and explained to the Israelites, they wept because of their sorrow for their disobedience. But Nehemiah stopped them. This is what he said: "Go home and prepare a feast, holiday food and drink; and share it with those who don't have anything. This day is holy to God. Don't feel bad. The joy of God is your strength" (Nehemiah 8:10).

So that's my message to you: the *joy* of God is your strength. Let your joy shine so that others will see it. Jesus said, "You are the light of the world. A city on a hill cannot be hidden. Neither do people light a lamp and put it under a bowl. Instead they put it on its stand, and it gives light to everyone in the house" (Matthew 5:14–15 NIV).

Be a light to your world. Laugh a little. Show people the joy in your life with the look on your face. They'll figure it out.

QUESTIONS

1. Do you take the time to laugh? Do you feel it's important?

2. If you are happy inside, do you believe your countenance will show it? (a)

3. Do you sleep better when your heart is glad? Why? (b)

4. Have you ever laughed so hard you felt like your bones were laughing? When? (c)

5. Is it possible to feel complete joy? How? (d)

6. If we follow God's instructions for life, will we find joy or pain? Why? (e)

7. What do you think the Lord laughs at? (f)

SCRIPTURAL ANSWERS

(a) "A happy heart makes the face cheerful" (Proverb 15:13 NIV).

(b) "Therefore my heart is glad and my tongue rejoices; my body will rest secure" (Psalm 16:9 NIV).

(c) "Every bone in my body laughing, singing, 'God, there's no one like you'" (Psalm 35:10).

(d) "For the Lord your God will bless you in all your harvest and in all the work of your hands, and your joy will be complete" (Deuteronomy 16:15 NIV).

(e) "The revelation of God is whole and pulls our lives together. The signposts of God are clear and point out the right road. The life-maps of God are right, showing the way to joy" (Psalms 19:7–8).

(f) "The wicked plot against the righteous and gnash their teeth at them; but the Lord laughs at the wicked, for he knows their day is coming" (Psalms 37:12–13 NIV).

45
Have you ever left a legacy?

If I had one wish for a legacy for my sons, it would be one of giving generously. Now you may wonder, what exactly is a legacy? I looked it up the old-fashioned way, in my dictionary. It defines "legacy" as money or other property left to a person by someone who has died (an inheritance), or something figurative that has been handed down from an ancestor or a predecessor.

I prefer definition number two, since we don't have a lot of money to leave to our kids. But we do have something to hand down: generosity. There are many ways to show generosity, like giving of your time, your talent, or your money. It is our responsibility as parents to let our children *see* our generous spirit. You already know that preaching won't work, so you must show them—not with a lecture, but with actions.

I recall one day when my sons were in elementary school. I had picked them up at school and we were in a hurry to get somewhere—soccer practice, I think. I noticed an elderly gentleman lying on the sidewalk around the corner from our house. I pulled my car over and we got out to talk to the man. It was apparent he was lost, confused, and hungry. I had my kids stay with him for about five minutes while I drove the two blocks home to get him a sandwich and some water. The man didn't know who he was or where he lived, but he did have a bus pass. We got him into the car and took him to the bus stop. When the bus driver saw the man, he immediately knew who he was. The driver assured us that he would take the man home safely. The whole ordeal took about fifteen minutes. Instead of telling my kids to help people, I showed them. No words, just action.

One day my youngest son, frustrated by another kind deed he observed, said, "Mom, why are you always so *nice* to people?" I told him that it was the right thing to do, and that it pleased God. But in my heart I smiled, because I knew he was beginning to *see* the meaning of generosity.

My husband coached our boys in all sorts of sports while they were growing up. He worked in heating and air conditioning and commercial refrigeration, putting in long hot hours, but he always made time for the boys. He would work until just before their practices (or games) and then stop everything to go to the event. Often, he would stay out afterward until one, two, or sometimes three o'clock in the morning to finish his job. I didn't think the boys fully realized or appreciated his sacrifice, but the cards he got on Father's Day and the letters he received upon their graduations testify of their love for Randy. They said that they wanted to be just like him. Eventually, they understood his generous gift of his time.

He never gave them lectures during their rebellious days, although he could have. They might have gone something like this: "I can't believe you're talking to me like that! Did you know that I stayed up until 3:00 a.m. just to finish working because of your game last night! And this is how you treat me?!" But you never heard anything like that come out of his mouth. He was rock solid. He never complained. He showed by his actions, not his words, how to be generous with his time and how to help someone even in the middle of a hectic day at work.

One year when our son Paul was in college, he was so broke that the only way he could afford to buy us gifts for Christmas was if we gave him money. I told him that instead of spending money on us, the best gift he could give would be to show kindness to strangers. He quickly agreed. I wasn't sure if he was happier about not having to spend money, or about the challenge. It was three weeks before Christmas and I made up my mind I wasn't going to mention it again.

Paul didn't come home for Christmas that year, but I did receive a call. "Hey, Mom, you remember what you wanted me to do for Christmas? Well, I did thirteen good things for people." My heart felt like it was about to explode with joy. I asked him to tell me about three of them. He said, "I went to McDonald's and bought a meal for a vagrant, and I offered a girl student my coat because she was shivering." To be honest, I don't remember the third deed, but it doesn't really matter. I was thrilled because I could hear the joy in his voice. He got the point and I think he was hooked.

One summer, Paul played baseball in Hays, Kansas. He met a guy named Kory who played baseball at a junior college in another state. At Kory's school, they had to buy their own bats, but at Paul's college they gave their players one new bat per year. These were valued at around $150. Paul said, "Mom, I hope you don't mind, but I gave Kory my bat from last year. He couldn't afford a good one."

I started to protest, because I knew how emotionally attached he got to his bats, but isn't that what generosity really is? What does it matter, if it costs you nothing? I was glad I didn't flunk my own lesson. So I smiled and said, "Yes, Paul, that's great!"

Another time, Paul's brother Aaron was running short on cash, so Paul sent him $200. "A brother is born to help in time of need" (Proverb 17:17 LB). I texted Paul to let him know how proud I was of him. Guess what he texted back? "I know. I wanted to be like you." Now that's what I'm talking about!

One day, my twenty-five-year-old washing machine broke down. At that point in our lives, we were struggling financially. Our son Nathan called me and asked me to meet him at Sears. When I hung up the phone, I broke down and cried. I knew what was coming. When I got there, he said, "Mom, pick out what you want." He didn't tell me to get the cheapest one, either. He also bought the extended warranty. I cried again in the store. Not just because we needed a washing machine, but because my awesome son had realized the spirit of generosity. Allow your kids to be generous to you. That's important. Don't refuse their help when you really need it, or it may stop the flow that you desire.

My oldest son, Aaron, developed diabetes when he was nineteen years old. Do you know what his comment was? "I'm glad it was me and not Nathan or Paul. I don't think they would be able to handle it." To me, that was a generous spirit because he was willing to take the illness on himself instead of his brothers. Putting others first. Unselfish. To me, that's generous.

Aaron and his wife, Laura, have two children: nine-year-old Skyler, and five-year-old Ayla. They live eight and a half hours away from us, which makes it really hard for Randy and me to spend much time with them. We are privileged to keep them at our house for several weeks in the summer. It is the highlight of our year. It's hard on my son and his wife because they go through a lot of anguish, missing their kids. But they are generous with Skyler and Ayla because they know the joy the kids bring us. For that, I thank them.

"Don't you see that children are God's best gift? ... his generous legacy?" (Psalm 127:3). I like the way that reads, but I also like my own paraphrase: Children are your generous legacy. You see, generosity is a matter of the heart. It's not something taught from a book, but learned through the senses: seeing, hearing, feeling, touching (and maybe smelling, too).

The most awesome text I've ever received in my life came from my daughter-in-law Sharon (Nathan's wife). Ethan, their son, was nine months old at the time. "I just finished listening to Randy Travis's 'Three Wooden Crosses' and I wanted to thank you for raising Nathan right. He has turned out to be a wonderful friend, husband, and father. This inspires me to be a good mother so my son can be just as worthy. With that in mind, I must thank the Phillips and previous Witts for Sherry and Pops. It's not what you take when you leave this world behind you. It's what you leave behind that matters. I hope to give Ethan a good start like you have given your kids." Now that's a legacy, folks!

"If our powerful God had not provided us a legacy of living children, we would have ended up like ghost towns" (Romans 9:29). What legacy are you passing down to your children? They'll be grown before you know it. Make those precious days count, with no regrets. They truly are your living legacy.

Questions

1. Do you believe our actions speak louder than our words? (a)

2. Has anyone influenced you by their actions? How did it affect you?

3. Generosity will leave you broke and your children will be cursed. True or false? Explain your answer. (b)

4. Does generosity beget generosity? Does stinginess beget stinginess? (c, d)

5. Do you believe that refusing a handout from someone deprives them of the blessing that comes from generosity? (e)

6. Do you think it means more to people when your generosity is a sacrifice? Why or why not? (f)

7. Are you a good or bad example for your kids and grandkids? Whom do they admire?

8. What is your legacy?

Scriptural Answers

(a) "Your cleansed and obedient life, not your words, will bear witness to what I have done" (Luke 5:14).

(b) "I was young and now I am old, yet I have never seen the righteous forsaken or their children begging bread. They are always generous and lend freely; their children will be blessed" (Psalms 37:25–26 NIV).

(c) "Give away your life; you'll find life given back, but not merely given back—given back with bonus and blessing. Giving, not getting is the way. Generosity begets generosity" (Luke 6:38).

(d) "Generous gets it all in the end; stingy is cut off at the pass" (Psalm 37:22).

(e) "Not that I'm looking for handouts, but I do want you to experience the blessing that issues from generosity" (Philippians 4:17).

(f) "But [David] said to Araunah, 'No, I've got to buy [the threshing floor to build an altar] for a good price; I'm not going to offer God, my God, sacrifices that are no sacrifice'" (2 Samuel 24:24).

46

Have you ever let go of the steering wheel?

I don't care too much for hunting. However, riding a four-wheeler is exhilarating. In the fall, I go with my husband to put out corn seed. For you who aren't familiar with hunting, that's what you do to lure the deer. I love to accompany Randy on these trips. We each have our own four-wheeler, so off we go to the woods. He has hunted with the Big Creek Hunting Club on a 3,000-acre lease for over thirty years.

Randy always wants me to lead so the debris won't get in my eyes, but I refuse. Why? Not because I'm stubborn, but because I would get lost. The trees all look alike. The path that is so obvious to him is not obvious to me. When Randy is in front, we can go at warp speed—at least it seems that way to me. I admire how he leads with such confidence. But the path I would choose in the woods is not even a path; it's just a side trail.

Now wouldn't it be silly if I tried to show off and take my friend Lita, who has never been in the woods or on a four-wheeler, all by myself? I can imagine helicopters circling and search dogs looking for us for days, and we would only be half a mile from the gate, lying on soft leaves, shivering, only to find out poison ivy was our bed of choice. I know you are laughing because that's ridiculous.

I once had a dream that I was driving a car when, all of a sudden, I went blind. I cried out to God, "Please, God, help me! I can't see!!" Immediately, I let go of the steering wheel, God took over, and the car was safely controlled. My sight returned, then I grabbed the steering wheel and resumed driving. As my dream continued, I became blind again. I screamed to God, "Please, God save me! I can't do this! Save me!" And once again I let go of the steering wheel and God took over. This time I was blind for a longer time, but again I regained my sight and I was safe. After the ordeal, I said, "That was good! Thank you Jesus!" Then I woke up.

As I follow my husband in the woods, I can also see what it is like to follow God. Randy goes before me. I can't always tell where he's going, but he's been this way before. As we ride, I don't ask, "Hey, are you sure you're going the right way? This doesn't look right! When are you going to let me lead?" I just follow.

But how easily we say to God, "Hey, are you sure you're guiding me the right way? This doesn't look right! When are you going to let me lead?" It sounds silly when you put it like that, but hey, we've all done it. This is what Jesus had to say about it: "Anyone who intends to come with me has to let me lead. You're not in the driver's seat—I am" (Luke 9:23). Sound familiar?

In my dream, I believe that God was showing me that I should trust Him to guide me in life and "live by faith, not by sight" (2 Corinthians 5:7 NIV). "Whoever trusts in the Lord is kept safe" (Proverb 29:25 NIV). In the woods, it's smarter to follow my wonderful husband, and in my life situations, it's smarter to follow my wonderful God. I willingly let Him steer my life.

Are you lost and can't find your way? Free yourself and let go of the steering wheel. Trust God. And when your crisis is over, you will truly say, "That was good! Thank you, Jesus!"

Questions

1. God will guide us if we ask Him. True or false? (a)

2. How do you think God would feel if you prayed to Him, yet wouldn't listen to His answer? (b)

3. How did God guide the Israelites? (c)

4. How are we guided today? (d)

5. Have you ever called on God when you were in distress? Did he answer? (e)

6. Even though we always want a quick answer, do we sometimes have to wait? (f)

7. It is easy to brag when we forget to give the glory to God. True or false? (g)

Scriptural Answers

(a) "Show me your ways, O Lord, teach me your paths; guide me in your truth and teach me, for you are God my Savior, and my hope is in you all day long" (Psalms 25:4–5 NIV).

(b) "God has no use for the prayers of the people who won't listen to him" (Proverb 28:9).

(c) "By day the Lord went ahead of them in a pillar of cloud to guide them on their way and by night in a pillar of fire to give them light" (Exodus 13:21 NIV).

(d) "When he, the Spirit of truth, comes, he will guide you into all truth. He will not speak on his own; he will speak only what he hears, and he will tell you what is yet to come" (John 16:13 NIV).

(e) "Do not hide your face from me when I'm in distress. Turn your ear to me; when I call, answer me quickly" (Psalm 102:2 NIV).

(f) "What I do, God, is wait for you, wait for my Lord, my God—you will answer!" (Psalm 38:15).

(g) "All we do is trust him enough to let him do it. It's God's gift from start to finish! We don't play the major role. If we did, we'd probably go around bragging that we'd done the whole thing!" (Ephesians 2:8–9).

47

Have you ever limited God?

My son Paul was applying for a job that would have the potential to increase his salary up to six times what he was currently making. He said that it was a long shot, but he still applied. There were several major obstacles that could have stopped the process. He got very frustrated with me because every time he told me about a new hurdle, I would counter with a positive response.

"Impossible. It cannot happen," were his words. He finally got so frustrated with me that he yelled, "Quit being so optimistic! This will never work out!"

I said, "Paul, I can't help it; that's the way I am."

He got quiet then said, "I gotta go," and hung up.

I didn't feel like it was the time for a lecture on all the challenges in his life that God had brought him through, but it caused me to reflect. I remembered the times that God had changed things in Paul's life that had seemed impossible to *possible*.

I recalled that when he was thirteen, his right pitching elbow was crackling like a fried pork rind when you crunch down on it. We didn't know what was wrong but we knew that this couldn't be good. A chiropractor, Dr. Tommy Ray, overheard us talking about it after one of Paul's games and he offered to examine Paul's arm in the parking lot. Dr. Ray told us not to worry because he thought he could fix the problem. He asked us to come to his office the next day. Dr. Ray said the stress of throwing curve balls had misaligned the elbow joint, but he could manipulate it back into place. He grabbed Paul's wrist and pushed upward on his elbow with great force until it popped. This was painful for Paul, and it was also painful to watch, but we believed in the doctor.

I tried to pay Dr. Ray but he said, "No, I just want him to get better." So we kept going to his office, and Paul's elbow got better and better. It took a while for the muscles to form properly around the joint to keep it in place, but the crackling disappeared. We went for about thirty treatments, and Dr. Ray never charged a penny. Thank you *so* much, Dr. Tommy Ray!

Isn't that the way God does it? He puts people in your path to help you through life. At thirteen years of age, the elbow crackle didn't seem like such a big deal, but God knew Paul would get a college education for playing baseball, so He sent someone to correct the problem before it got out of hand. Left unattended, his elbow would have deteriorated and high school ball might have been as far as he got. We had to trust Dr. Ray even though it looked impossible to fix. Thank you, Almighty God!

Another time we felt the awesome power of God was when Paul was a sophomore in high school. He was playing basketball and went up for a rebound. Another guy's elbow clobbered him on the bridge of his nose. Paul told me that there was a terrible cracking noise, and we feared that his nose was broken.

We went to Dr. Stephen Shorts, an ear, nose, and throat specialist who said that Paul's nose was not broken but the cartilage was separated. I believe he said it was a deviated septum. That may not be the exact diagnosis, but I remember the doctor's prognosis: "In a few years, he will start having problems. He will start snoring, and breathing will be difficult."

We walked out of the office, and I said, "Paul, I don't think that will ever happen. God will heal your nose." He didn't say anything, but I imagine from the look on his face that he was thinking, *Yeah, right.*

That same summer, on the first day that the swimming pool opened, Paul jumped off a twenty-foot tower into the water and his eardrums burst. Another trip to Dr. Shorts. No swimming for the rest of the summer. Dr. Shorts said, "Let them heal."

Then, in the fall, we went to a baseball showcase in Chicago. Afterward, a lot of the boys were going to the Sears Tower, so we went, too. The elevator zoomed 110 floors up to the top of the building like lightning. It felt like we were in a vacuum seal and the air was being sucked out of our bodies. Paul dropped to the floor in excruciating pain. I screamed, "Oh, no! We forgot about your ears!"

When we got back home, we went to see Dr. Shorts. He said, "Well, Paul, you've really got some damage now. Your eardrums burst again and I don't know that they will ever recover. In about ten years the scar tissue will be so bad that you will probably have to wear a hearing aid."

We left his office and got in the car. I said, "Paul, I don't think that will ever happen. God will heal you." He said nothing but I'm guessing he was thinking, *Cuckoo*.

During Paul's senior year, we made another trip to Dr. Shorts. I don't even remember why we went, but I do remember what the doctor saw when he examined Paul's right ear. He backed his chair up, furrowed his brow, then took another look.

I said, "Is something wrong?"

"No, I just need to check his other ear." So he checked Paul's right ear. Another perplexed look. "You gotta see this!" he said in disbelief. He let me look in Paul's ear.

"What am I looking at, Doc?"

"You are looking at beautiful, perfectly pink, brand-new-looking ears!"

"Wow! That's amazing." I thought, *No wonder Paul kept hearing us when we whispered*. Recently he had seemed to have Superman ears. Then I said, "Hey, why don't you check out his nose?"

"That's just what I'm about to do!" he replied with a determined look.

He looked into Paul's nose and then rolled back his chair once more, only this time, he couldn't control his excitement. "You gotta look at *this*!" Dr. Shorts showed me a faint, microscopic line where Paul's nose had completely healed. There was no damage at all! He had new ears *and* a new nose. God is way cool. I got goose bumps all over my body.

So you see why I have trouble limiting God. Who knows what can happen in our lives if we only believe? And not with a Pollyanna-ish, only-look-on-the-bright-side kind of belief, but a God-founded, God-proven belief that anything, and I mean *anything*, is possible with God. I don't even want to limit Him. The angel Gabriel came to Mary and said, "And did you know that your cousin Elizabeth conceived a son, old as she is? Everyone called her barren, and here she is six months pregnant! Nothing, you see, is impossible with God" (Luke 1:36–37).

Now I ask you, did God part the Red Sea? Did He save Daniel from the ravenous lions? Did Jesus raise the dead, heal blind eyes, and walk on water? Did He heal my son's ears, nose, and elbow? Yes, yes, and yes!

God is listening to what you say. Do you have faith in the doctor's report, or are you do you have faith in God's Word?

"For [God] Himself has said, I will not in any way fail you nor give you up nor leave you without support. [I will] not, [I will] not, [I will] not in any degree leave you helpless, nor forsake nor let [you] down! [Assuredly not!]" (Hebrews 13:5 AB). I can't help but cry every time I read that passage. I can hardly see to write, but I'll press on. God will never leave you without support. He needs you to believe in Him, though. Jesus says, "Have faith in God" (Mark 11:22).

So yes, Paul, I am optimistic. I know that God will work out every problem you have in life. If you don't get this job, He'll give you one that's far better. God specializes in the impossible.

There's a song The Martins sang a while back called "Dream Big."

Oh, I love the word impossible, cause that's what God does best.
So, just reach for the improbable and He will do the rest.

That really hits my heart. When we say, "That's impossible," He's ready to work. He loves those words because when we reach that point of impossibility within our minds, He grins and says, "With Me, nothing is impossible."

God heals by Himself. Sometimes He heals through other people. He also sends people into our paths to make divine connections. Sometimes He says, "Wait," and sometimes He says no." But His power is limitless. His resources, His mercy, His love, His forgiveness, His healing of body and soul: nothing is held back. Our only limiting of Him is through our unbelief. The words "can't," "won't," "but," and "impossible" should be stricken from our vocabulary. God says, "I AM," and that is enough. (Exodus 3:14)

The next time you're tempted to say, "Impossible!" don't worry, because that's what God does best!

Questions

1. Has God ever performed a miracle in your life? Have you witnessed a miracle in someone else's life? What happened?

2. Do you believe that you need faith in God to receive a miracle? (a)

3. Would you consider the following impossible? Walking through a sea? (b) Throwing a stick into bitter water to make if sweet? (c) Making all the walls around a city fall flat? (d) Raising a man who has been dead and stinking for four days from the dead? (e)

4. When things seem impossible, what should you do? (f)

5. How much faith do we need? (g)

6. Do you think God can use your trials to reveal Himself to you? Explain.

7. Whom has God sent to help you with a problem? Have you thanked them?

8. List everything that you think is too hard for God to do. (h)

9. Should we doubt God? (i)

Scriptural Answers

(a) "Then he touched their eyes and said, 'According to your faith will it be done to you; and their sight was restored" (Matthew 9:29–30 NIV).

(b) "And the Israelites went through the sea on dry ground, with a wall of water on their right and on their left" (Exodus 14:22 NIV).

(c) "So Moses cried out in prayer to God. God pointed him to a stick of wood. Moses threw it into the water and the water turned sweet" (Exodus 15:25).

(d) "By faith, the Israelites marched around the walls of Jericho for seven days and the walls fell flat" (Hebrews 11:30).

(e) "Jesus called in a loud voice, 'Lazarus, come out!' The dead man came out, his hands and feet wrapped in strips of linen, and a cloth around his face. Jesus said to them, 'Take off the grave clothes and let him go'" (John 11:43–44 NIV).

(f) "'Have faith in God,' Jesus answered" (Mark 11:22 NIV)

(g) "He replied, 'If you have faith as small as a mustard seed, you can say to this mulberry tree, "Be uprooted and planted in the sea," and it will obey you'" (Luke 17:6 NIV).

(h) "Ah, Lord God! Behold, You have made the heavens and the earth by Your great power and outstretched arm. There is nothing too hard for You" (Jeremiah 32:17 NKJV).

(i) "Then give him this message, 'Blessed are those who don't doubt me'" (Matthew 11:6 LB).

48

Have you ever looked through God's eyes?

While working with some seventh graders in public school one year, I kept seeing isolated students with sad faces, no friends, and no social skills. I heard God saying, "Look at their sad eyes." Actually He kept bugging me. I finally said, "Yes, God. I see all the sad faces, but what do you want me to do about it?"

No answer.

I said, "If you want me to do something, you need to give me a plan."

Well, He did! If you don't want an answer, don't ask.

God told me to start a club at lunch time once a week. He told me to write invitations on cards asking the students to join the club and RSVP. These students were the ones who didn't get invited to parties, were picked last for games, and were loners. The idea was that they would have a special written invitation to keep and know that for once in their lives, that they were the chosen, the invited.

I talked it over with Mrs. Jones, the teacher I worked with, and she really liked the idea. She said that I needed to go through the principal, Ms. Hatley. Ms. Hatley loved the idea, but she said that I needed to have a name for the club and a maximum of twelve kids for six weeks. Thus the RSVP Club was born. I was so thankful to Ms. Hatley. I believe that she saw the sad eyes, too.

The chosen students were called up to the front of the classroom in front of all the other students so that everyone would be aware of the club.

I told the selected students that they were the chosen ones, but it was their choice if they wanted to participate. They all accepted.

Wednesday, our selected club day, rolled around. My husband, Randy, umpired baseball games, and by faith, I told God that I would use only the money from the games to buy pizza for the club. No baseball games, no pizza. The students were to bring their own drinks. Well, that first Wednesday was pretty awkward. The food was good, but the students weren't used to talking to each other or anybody else. Their socialization skills were very lacking.

I asked each one of them to tell the other club members where they would like to go for a dream trip, and that sort of broke the ice. It was hard to tell if they liked sharing that or not because they were so stripped of emotion and hope. It was like they feared having hope. I told them that we would repeat the club meeting next week, but I didn't know if they would come back or not.

The next Wednesday rolled around and guess who showed up? All of the invited kids. They came in pretty deadpan, and I thought, *God, you started this, now you gotta give me some more ideas because I feel like I'm flopping.* Once again, God came through. He gave me the idea to hold a contest to see who could do the best thing for someone else over the next week. The members would be the judges, with ten dollars going to first place, five dollars to second, and several one-dollar prizes. As I explained it to them, they got a little twinkle in their eyes. But only a little.

I felt I knew what God was doing. I thought, *God, You're using me to teach them that they have to reach out and help someone else before they can feel their own worth. These kids were so insecure that they could only look inward, but this might force them to look outward.*

On the third week, the members actually came in excited. After our usual yummy pizza—thanks again to Randy's umpiring—I had the members write down their good deeds for the week. I wrote the acts of kindness on the board at the front of the room for voting purposes, but I kept their names a secret.

One of them mowed his neighbor's yard, one babysat for her brothers, and another gave twenty-dollar earrings to his mother. The list went on and on, but one deed caught my eye: he said he had tutored an F-student outside of the club and helped bring their grade up to a B. This especially touched my heart because I knew that this was totally out of his comfort zone. They had all reached out to others, but his gesture involved repeated efforts with a lot of time invested.

Well, I knew whom I would have voted for, but I wasn't sure whom the members would pick. Kids are often wowed by dollar signs, so I figured they would vote for the twenty-dollar gift. I underestimated those wonderful kids! You guessed it: my personal pick won. They erupted in immediate applause and all patted the young man on the back.

It looked like those supposedly rejected misfits had the right idea. They realized that they were actually becoming friends with each other. The silence was broken, and slowly, they started gaining their confidence. Mrs. Jones told me that she noticed the students in the RSVP Club were starting to show their confidence in the classroom, and I knew God's plan was working.

The next week, they all brought reports of good things that they had done during the previous week. They came up with some impressive deeds, and I was so proud of them. I knew there was something else that we needed to do, but I couldn't figure it out. Once again, I asked God for wisdom, and as you know, God never fails.

The next week, I followed God's suggestion and had the RSVP Club play games—Monopoly, Scrabble, Old Maid—anything to develop social skills. It was amazing to watch the students slowly come out of their shells.

The other students in the class started asking to come to the meetings. But I told them, "I'm sorry, you have to be invited." The cool kids, the athletes, and the brainy ones all wanted to come. The tantalizing aroma of pizza would waft into the classroom, and it was almost more than the others could take. They begged, "Please let us come!"

The RSVP members heard them but only smiled. For once, *they* were the chosen ones. Jesus said, "You did not choose me, but I chose you" (John 15:16 NIV). I felt that Jesus had chosen the RSVP Club members. And God showed me in this six-week period how to look at people through God's eyes. Jesus chose me. He chose you, too. Just as we are.

The last week, I started getting a little worried. It was Monday and my husband didn't have a game to umpire yet. "God, you know if there's no umpiring, then no pizzas. I could pay for them out of my pocket, but I trust you with the funds." Tuesday afternoon, my husband called and told me that he received a call to umpire and the pay would be more than the usual fee. Never early, never late, but always on time!

So the sixth week we celebrated with more expensive, delicious three-meat pizzas, as opposed to pepperoni or cheese. "God can do anything, you know—far more than you could ever imagine or guess or request in your wildest dreams!" (Ephesians 3:20). That was God all right, always showing up and showing out.

In our last meeting, I no longer had to prod them to talk. I saw a new air of confidence. It was refreshing.

As I was leaving on the last day of school, a grandmother of one of the members stopped me in the parking lot. She said, "Aren't you the lady that had the RSVP Club? I just wanted you to know how much it meant to my granddaughter. She has always felt like a misfit, and she *finally* feels like she's a part of something. I can never thank you enough! She saved the invitation card. It meant so much to her!"

I smiled and gave her a hug. It's nice to make a difference. I like this passage: "He gave them power to ... tenderly care for the bruised and hurt lives" (Matthew 10:1). There are a lot of people in your life who are bruised and hurt. God has given you the power to care for them. Ask Him for a plan. Ask Him to let you see people through His eyes.

He will answer and you will never be the same.

Questions

1. Will God give you wisdom to know how to handle situations in your life? (a)

2. What do we need in order to get an answer? (b)

3. Has God ever given you a plan to help someone who looked lonely? If so, what was the plan?

4. How did the action impact you? How do you think it impacted them?

5. Do you believe that God cares about "nobodies"? (c, d)

6. Is there a blessing for the people who give special consideration to the outcasts? (e)

7. Real religion ignores the homeless and loveless. True or false? (f)

8. Are we obligated to help the weak? (g)

Scriptural Answers

(a) "If you want to know what God wants you to do, ask him, and he will gladly tell you, for he is always ready to give a bountiful supply of wisdom to all who ask him; he will not resent it" (James 1:5 LB).

(b) "If you don't ask with faith, don't expect the Lord to give you any solid answer" (James 1:8 LB).

(c) "Hosea put it well: I'll call nobodies and make them somebodies; I'll call the unloved and make them beloved. In the place where they yelled out, 'You're nobody!' they're calling you 'God's living children'" (Romans 9:25–26).

(d) "Down-and-outers sit at God's table and eat their fill" (Psalm 22:26).

(e) "Invite some people who never get invited out, the misfits from the wrong side of the tracks. You'll be—and—experience a blessing. They won't be able to return the favor, but the favor will be returned—oh, how it will be returned!—at the resurrection of God's people" (Luke 14:13–14).

(f) "Real religion, the kind that passes muster before God the Father, is this: Reach out to the homeless and loveless in their plight, and guard against corruption from the godless world" (James 1:27).

(g) "Those of us who are strong and able in the faith need to step in and lend a hand to those who falter, and not just do what is most convenient for us. Strength is for service, not status. Each one of us needs to look after the good of the people around us, asking ourselves, 'How can I help?'" (Romans 15:1–2).

49
Have you ever loved enough to lose?

My friend Gwen invited me over to play a board game called Clue. Also invited were her sister, Georgette, her daughter-in-law, LaJuana, and her thirteen-year-old granddaughter, Legacy. LaJuana and I had played the game before, but the others had to learn as they went along.

Clue is a game of elimination and deductive reasoning based on clues you get as the game progresses. The players must find out which room a murder was committed in, whodunit, and which weapon they used. Gwen won early in the first game. Her eyes lit up and her competitive juices flowed as she realized her guesses were correct.

A second game ensued, but for me at least, it quickly ended. When I made my official accusation, Georgette realized that she had overlooked a card of hers that she should have shown me. Consequently, it caused me to make an incorrect guess. Oh well, I could still enjoy the game as I watched them plot their strategies.

When it was Georgette's turn, she immediately made a wild accusation which eliminated her from the game, too. A couple of turns later and LaJuana was also eliminated. Gwen and Legacy were the only remaining participants, but we all had to stay at the table to show our cards to the accuser.

Forty minutes later, Gwen had gathered in all of her clues. We were waiting for her to scream in delight once again as she announced her accusation and looked in the envelope containing the solution. However, she made the wrong guess. Georgette, LaJuana, and I were shocked—we *knew* she had all the facts. Legacy won because she was the only player left in the game. Needless to say, Legacy was pleasantly surprised.

The next day I talked to Georgette. She told me that she had guessed incorrectly because it didn't seem fair for her to stay in the game since she was the reason I'd lost. I told her that I respected her noble gesture. Then I added, "I suspect that Gwen threw the game so Legacy could win. Isn't that cool that we love each other that much?"

It's so easy to be kind to each other, but do we always make that choice? Does our pride get in the way, making us insist on winning the game or the argument? How many times have we argued with a friend or a spouse over an insignificant fact only to win the argument, but lose the friendship? I've heard Joyce Meyer say, "Being right is highly overrated." I agree.

I used to think differently, though. I would often argue with my husband or my kids. My veins would bulge on my neck and I would smile knowingly as I made my point and proved it with all sorts of backup. But really, what was the point? *Yay, I'm right!* Who cares? No one wants to live with a know-it-all, or a win-it-all, or, for that matter, a sore loser.

As new Christians, we must seem like caterpillars, inching along in life and making slow progress. As we read the Bible, our thinking starts to change. We see things differently and our inner being starts to undergo a metamorphosis. We start to look more like Christ in our thoughts and actions. People notice a difference. Or *do* they?

If we've changed according to God's plan, we are no longer consumed with a mentality of "Ha ha, in your face, I'm better and smarter than you." We can give all our belongings to the poor, but if we don't have love, then our actions won't fly. "We ... are being transformed into his likeness" (2 Corinthians 3:18 NIV). A beautiful change.

Speaking of change, that's the word the Holy Spirit put in my heart early one morning. *Change.* I didn't know what He meant. *Who am I supposed to change?* I thought. I started looking at the people all around me. *Lord, he could use some change; her, too.* Creflo Dollar's television show is called *Changing your World*. Was I supposed to watch his show? It seemed everywhere I turned, preachers were emphasizing the word "change." Was this some type of national theme?

After a two-year process of elimination and deductive reasoning, I was ready to formulate an accusation. All the clues pointed to me. *I* was the one God wanted to change. He wanted me, the caterpillar, to change into the selfless, giving butterfly. Well, it's been a process, and I know He's not finished with me, but I'm making progress.

> If I could speak in any language in Heaven or on earth, but didn't love others, I would only be making meaningless noise like a loud gong or a clanging cymbal ... If I gave everything I have to the poor and even sacrificed my body, I could boast about it; but if I didn't love others, I would be of no value whatsoever. Love is patient and kind. Love is not jealous or boastful or proud or rude. Love does not demand its own way. Love is not irritable, and it keeps no record of when it has been wronged. It is never glad about injustice but rejoices whenever the truth wins out. Love never gives up, never loses faith, is always hopeful, and endures through every circumstance.
> —1 Corinthians 13:1, 3–7 NLT

God is love. If we want to be more like Him, then we must show our love for one another. Not just in the big ways, but in the little ways, too.

For instance, you could take yourself out of a game that you ruined for someone else. Or you could allow a novice to win at a board game so she doesn't become discouraged. *Love is patient and kind.*

Sometimes the best way to win in a relationship is to lose arguments—not all, but some. Conceding to the other person may give them freedom to concede their point in the future. *Love does not demand its own way.* I wish I had learned that earlier in my marriage. Presenting my arguments strongly gave no room for my husband to voice his opinion. Then I would become upset because he would not tell me his opinion on many family issues.

You might not want to make such a big deal about your son's long hair. By the time he hits his mid-twenties, it will be normal-length again. Sometimes a critical eye hurts worse than a stinging tirade. So we shouldn't pride ourselves in keeping our mouths shut, but turn around and give them the old evil eye every time they pass by. *Love is not jealous or boastful or proud or rude.*

There are many ways to win by losing. Don't rejoice when you win a minor battle; Satan is still fighting a fierce war to conquer your children.

Many relationships have been ruined by a hurtful rude statement that could have been avoided if you had looked at your children with love in your eyes. I had an acquaintance who kicked her eighteen-year-old daughter out of her house because she refused to make her bed. We should let the punishment fit the crime. She won the battle, but at what cost? "For the whole law can be summed up in this one command: 'Love your neighbor as yourself.' But if instead of showing love among yourselves you are always biting and devouring one another, watch out! Beware of destroying one another" (Galatians 5:14–15 NLT).

Ezekiel says, "I will give you a new heart and new desires, and I will put a new spirit in you. I will take out your stony heart of sin and give you a new obedient heart" (Ezekiel 36:26 NLT). God is the only one who can change our hearts. He will give us a new, obedient, loving heart if we ask Him. He will heal our relationships if we obey His words.

In Paul's first letter to the Corinthians he said, "There are three things that will endure—faith, hope, and love—and the greatest of these is love" (1 Corinthians 13:13 NLT). Jesus lost His life, but gained the world. Love always wins.

Questions

1. Have you ever worked or lived with a know-it-all? Was it a pleasant experience? (a)

2. Have you ever been around someone who would make rude remarks, then say, "I'm joking"? How did you feel about that? (b)

3. Is it easy for you to see others' faults, yet be oblivious to your own? (c)

4. If we ask Jesus into our hearts, should our old way of doing things be different from our new, God-fashioned life? In what way? (d)

5. Making yourself look better than others makes for a great working environment. True or false? (e)

6. A wise person will be peace-loving and considerate of others. True or false? (f)

7. What do you think this Scripture means: "For whoever wants to save his life will lose it, but whoever loses his life for me will save it" (Luke 9:24 NIV)?

Scriptural Answers

(a) "Know-it-alls don't like being told what to do; they avoid the company of wise men and women" (Proverb 15:12).

(b) "People who shrug off deliberate deceptions, saying 'I didn't mean it, I was only joking,' are worse than careless campers who walk away from smoldering campfires" (Proverbs 26:18–19).

(c) "It's easy to see a smudge on your neighbor's face and be oblivious to the ugly sneer on your own" (Luke 6:41).

(d) "Since, then, we do not have the excuse of ignorance, everything—and I do mean everything—connected with that old way of life has to go. It's rotten through and through. Get rid of it! And then take on an entirely new way of life—a God-fashioned life, a life renewed from the inside and working itself into your conduct as God accurately reproduces his character in you" (Ephesians 4:22–24).

(e) "Whenever you're trying to look better than others or get the better of others, things fall apart and everyone ends up at each other's throats" (James 3:16).

(f) "But the wisdom that comes from heaven is first of all pure; then peace loving, considerate, submissive, full of mercy and good fruit, impartial, and sincere" (James 3:17 NIV).

50

Have you ever needed a harvest?

When our sons were young, we thought it would be a great idea to have a vegetable garden in our backyard. Our neighbor, Mr. Rice, graciously tilled the hard ground for us. Then we decided which vegetables we wanted to grow: bell peppers, cucumbers, tomatoes, green onions, squash, and my personal favorite, loose leaf lettuce. Mr. Rice had introduced us to a fabulous salad recipe, which was one of our main reasons for starting a garden. This was in the days before we were aware of cholesterol, but it is a recipe that I want to eat when I get to heaven, where our bodies will be perfect, with no worry about clogging our arteries.

You may be curious, so I'll go on a rabbit trail and give you the recipe: *Cook bacon. Save the grease. Pluck and wash the loose leaf lettuce from your garden. Grab some green onions while you are there. Gently tear the lettuce, cut the onions, and break the pieces of bacon. Place them in a bowl and drizzle hot bacon grease over the mixture until the lettuce wilts a little, then add vinegar.* Voila! Best salad ever. My mouth is watering.

Okay, back to the story. We chose seeds and plants for our garden, and then our sons planted them in the rich soil. Aaron, Nathan, and Paul were willing and eager to oblige. One of the boys asked, "Mom, can we eat the seed?"

I laughed and said, "No, don't eat the seed or we won't have anything left to put in the ground." He reluctantly complied. In no time, our sons had planted everything.

My husband put a chicken wire fence around the perimeter to keep our dogs out. The garden looked so beautiful with its freshly plowed and planted rows that we even put a birdbath (made of a trash can lid) beside it.

I told my kids that the garden would take a while to grow. However, they felt two days was plenty of time. "Where's the food? I'm hungry. Are you sure we did it right, Mom?" I looked at the seed packages that we had placed at the ends of some of the rows. "Yep, we did it right." Every morning, I went straight to our soil patch, hoping to find something green. *Anything.* Oh, the green onions were sticking up. The tomato plants were there. The tiny bell pepper plants. But I wanted to see progress, real progress.

Finally one day, I saw the dark brown soil had parted and an itty-bitty speck of green was splitting through. It was so small that I needed a magnifying glass to make sure I was seeing growth, not just a stray leaf that had blown onto our dream. I ran into the house to get the boys. We were ecstatic!

The next day, there were more. It didn't take long for the plants to start sprouting like crazy. I had wondered if one seed was enough for each desired plant, but here they were in living color, proof that we had read and followed the instructions correctly. My sons had put the correct amount of seed in the holes and planted them at the right depth. We had watered them perfectly: not too much, not too little, just right.

We played the waiting game. Sure there were little seedlings, but nothing edible yet. Wait, wait, wait. Not every vegetable progressed at the same rate. Some had a lot of greenery, but took longer to produce edible fruit. The tomatoes had to ripen on the vine.

But the day finally came! The family harvested the fruits of our labor. There's nothing like a plentiful harvest. We even shared with our neighbor, Mr. Rice. The garden lasted until the plants turned yellow and went to seed. We had the garden for only one year, but it was a wonderful learning experience. Our sons still talk fondly about our backyard garden.

Throughout the Bible, God uses the concept of planting seeds and reaping a harvest. After the flood, the Lord promised that "As long as the earth endures, seedtime and harvest … will never cease" (Genesis 8:22 NIV). Joyce Meyer has a unique way of saying it: Seed, *tiiiiiime*, and harvest. With his parables, Jesus spoke about things that people were familiar with so they could get a better grasp on the spiritual world. I'm going to make an attempt to show you what God has shown me.

For one thing, I listen to saints who have knowledge in this field. I heard that one preacher asked Oral Roberts to tell the most profound principle that he garnered from the Bible. Oral Roberts is highly respected, so my ears perked up; my heart wants to learn from this godly man. I'm sure you've anticipated his answer: seedtime and harvest.

Next, I decide what I want in my spiritual harvest. If I've run out of hope, I sow hope in someone's life. If I'm depressed, I sow positive actions into a depressed life. If I need a new vehicle and can't figure out how to afford it, God instructs me to let someone borrow my truck as a seed-planting for my truck harvest. When I'm praying for a new, better-paying job for my husband, I give someone else money to help them get to their job interview across the country. I have been impressed to take large bags of deer meat to several people who were out of work. As I left their houses, God said, "You and your children will never be hungry." And we haven't been. I've given people money for gas. Afterward, God whispered to me, "You'll always have money for gas."

You see, when I wanted tomatoes, I didn't plant watermelons. If I wanted lemons, I didn't plant an oak tree. Sometimes your harvests are quick, but mostly they take *tiiiiiime.*

Have you planted the seeds of God's word in your children and wondered what went wrong? Don't worry. God has a promise. "Train a child in the way he should go, and when he is old he will not turn from it" (Proverb 22:6 NIV). The seeds you planted a long time ago will eventually sprout. We plant the seeds, and then we water them with our prayers and Scriptures.

Are you worried about the future of the world? *How will my children be fed in the future?* Read this: "I have been young and now am old, yet have I not seen the [uncompromisingly] righteous forsaken or their seed begging bread" (Psalm 37:25 AB).

Don't think you have any seed? "Now he who supplies seed to the sower and bread for food will also supply and increase your store of seed and will enlarge the harvest of your righteousness. You will be made rich in every way so that you can be generous on every occasion and through us your generosity will result in thanksgiving to God" (2 Corinthians 9:10–11 NIV). So you see, He's got you covered.

There is something else I learned about gardening: little sucker branches will appear on a tomato plant, for example. You prune them because they suck nutrients out of the fruit and take it to a useless, unproductive area.

God gave me a wonderful example of how pruning helps us. I was walking in my neighborhood and looked up to see the most majestic, twenty-foot tall purple crepe myrtle I had ever seen in my life. God whispered to me: "If you'll let me have your son, I will make him fruitful like this tree." I was speechless. I continued on my walk and lo and behold, the lady who lived at that house came out and talked to me. "Isn't it beautiful?! It's hard to believe it, but a few years ago, the freeze got it. We thought it was dead. But we pruned the branches down to four feet tall and hoped for the best. Now look at it!"

Sometimes there are things in your life that sap every ounce of fruitfulness. You're so drained that any fruit you produce is hard and knotty. Let God prune the sucker branches from your life. There's fresh fruit He wants you to bear. Don't deny the pruning shears; embrace them.

I've heard people ask, "How do you know when a blessing is a seed, or when it is a harvest?" When the seed that I have in my hand is not enough to meet *my* need, but is enough to meet someone else's need, then I know I am supposed to bless someone with this seed. If I need a job, but I don't know how to make a connection, I help someone else make a connection for their job. If I want my needs for this world met, I help someone with their needs.

One time, God asked me, "Well, are you going to eat or plant your seed?" I thought back to my son's question the year that we grew our garden and I knew exactly what God meant. Was I going to use my blessing to make myself happy for a day, or was I going to plant my blessing in a neighbor's life and reap a bountiful harvest that would last for a long time?

It seems contradictory to this world's logic, but it's perfectly logical to God. "I don't think the way you think. The way you work isn't the way I work. God's Decree. For as the sky soars high above earth, so the way I work surpasses the way you work, and the way I think is beyond the way you think" (Isaiah 55:8 9). Scatter your seeds outside your own backyard and *waaaiiiiiit* for the harvest.

Questions

1. If God is our gardener, what is our landscape? (a)

2. What kind of fruit should we have in our spiritual garden? (b)

3. What type of harvest should we expect if we sow kindness and mercy?

4. What a person plants, he will harvest. True or false? (c)

5. What type of harvest should we expect if we sow selfishness? (d)

6. If you get tired of doing good, tired of waiting for the harvest, should you give up? (e)

Scriptural Answers

(a) "In simple humility, let our gardener, God, landscape you with the Word, making a salvation-garden of your life" (James 1:21).

(b) "What happens when we live God's way? He brings gifts into our lives, much the same way that fruit appears in an orchard—things like affection for others, exuberance about life, serenity. We develop a willingness to stick with things, a sense of compassion in the heart, and a conviction that a basic holiness permeates things and people. We find ourselves involved in loyal commitments, not needing to force our way in life, able to marshal and direct our energies wisely" (Galatians 5:22).

(c) "Don't be misled: No one makes a fool of God. What a person plants, he will harvest" (Galatians 6:7).

(d) "The person who plants selfishness, ignoring the needs of others—ignoring God!—harvests a crop of weeds. All he'll have to show for his life is weeds! But the one who plants in response to God, letting God's

Spirit do the growth work in him, harvests a crop of real life, eternal life" (Galatians 6:8).

(e) "So let's not allow ourselves to get fatigued doing good. At the right time we will harvest a good crop if we don't give up or quit" (Galatians 6:9).

51

Have you ever needed a word from God?

Randy was riding his Honda 110 Scrambler motorcycle and he zoomed past my house. I was just getting on my bicycle, and I started waving frantically, trying to flag him down. I was in panic mode. When the band rode to out-of-town football games, it was customary for boys to ask girls to sit by them on the school bus. The word was that a guy I was not too fond of was going to ask me to sit by him. When I saw Randy whiz past me, I thought, *Hey, if I ask Randy to sit with me, I will have the perfect excuse to say no to Ronald.* Randy was quite shy and I assumed he would never get up the nerve to ask any girl, so I figured I had to take the initiative. I knew Randy enough to see that he was a likable fellow. We were both in the tenth grade and played the French horn at Plainview High School in Plainview, Texas.

When we caught up to each other at a vacant lot a block from my house, I told Randy about my predicament. He was more than willing to oblige and, as they say, the rest is history. We dated for almost four years, and then we married at the ripe old age of nineteen after our first year of college.

About four months after we married, Randy's parents, Bill and Betty Witt, informed us that they would be moving 120 miles away to Dumas, Texas. We were surprised, but we realized that we still had my mom and dad living in the same town.

Two weeks later, my parents, Raymond and Betty Phillips, told us that they would be moving to a city which was thirteen hours away. Needless to say, Randy and I were in shock!

There we were, two newlyweds with both our families telling us that they would be moving a billion miles away. Not literally, of course, but it might as well have been that far. I was feeling really down, so I started praying. I said, "God, I am *so* sad. I really need an encouraging word. Both of our families are moving and we won't have anybody related to us living nearby. My heart is breaking."

I heard God say in that still, small voice, "Read your Bible." I got my Living Bible out and it fell open to Psalms 45. When I got to verses 10 and 11, I couldn't believe my eyes. It said, "I advise you, O daughter, not to fret about your parents in your homeland far away. Your royal husband delights in your beauty. Reverence him, for he is your lord." I instantly felt the most wonderful peace. It was a stark contrast from the turmoil I had been feeling before. My unrest never came back. When moving day for both sets of parents came, I was at total peace. My attitude changed from that of being a dutiful daughter to one of embracing the title of wife.

Oh, I forgot to tell you the other verse that caught my eye that day: "Your sons will someday be kings like their father. They shall sit on thrones around the world!" (Psalm 45:16 LB). When I read that, I had the uncanny feeling that I wasn't just reading a Scripture, but a prophecy. Somehow, I knew that all of our children would be boys—and they were. Now they may not sit on thrones around the world, but two of our sons live in Texas and one lives in Utah, so that's pretty close. Maybe the thrones are for when we all get to heaven.

Do you have a problem that has you crying or at least scratching your head? Maybe you just need peace like I did thirty-eight years ago. Well, I've got news for you: God is only a prayer away. Tell Him what your problem is, listen to the quiet voice that guides you, and read His Word for comfort. Before long, your tears will turn to joy and that one word from God will last you a lifetime.

Questions

1. Whom should we turn to when we have a problem that we can't solve? (a)

2. God will ignore your cry for help. True or false? (b)

3. If God gives a solution to your problem, should you obey Him? What can you expect as a result of obedience? (c)

4. Have you ever needed a word from God? Write about your experience.

5. Do you believe that worry will solve your problems? (d)

6. When you marry someone, whom are you supposed to put first, your spouse or your parents? (e)

Scriptural Answers

(a) "See, God has come to save me! I will trust and not be afraid, for the Lord is my strength and song; he is my salvation" (Isaiah 12:2 LB).

(b) "Listen closely to my prayer, O God. Hear my urgent cry. I will call to you whenever trouble strikes, and you will help me" (Psalms 86:6–7 LB).

(c) "I run in the path of your commands, for you have set my heart free" (Psalms 119:32 NIV).

(d) "Don't worry about anything; instead, pray about everything; tell God your needs and don't forget to thank Him for His answers. If you do this you will experience God's peace, which is far more wonderful than the human mind can understand. His peace will keep your thoughts and your hearts quiet and at rest as you trust in Christ Jesus" (Philippians 4:6–7 LB).

(e) "Therefore shall a man leave his father and his mother, and shall cleave unto his wife: and they shall be one flesh" (Genesis 2:24 KJV).

52

Have you ever needed an intercessor?

A twenty-pound object fell on the big toe of my left foot. It hurt when it happened, but I was amazed at how easily I could walk on it the next day. I wore oversized shoes which allowed my toe ample room and went on with my daily routines. However, three weeks later, my toe was still twice as fat as it was ordinarily. I finally conceded to get it checked out. Dr. Harris ordered an x-ray and shared the results. I was quite surprised to find out the bone had broken all the way through, right underneath my cuticle. He wanted me to see a specialist.

When I went to see Dr. Schimmel, I tried to ask a question but it came out vague and rambling. I knew what I wanted to ask him, but I couldn't explain it properly, so he wasn't able to answer properly. His nurse, Karol, listened intently to what I was saying (or trying to say). She promptly turned to the doctor and said, "Mrs. Witt wants to know if her nail bed is injured."

I felt so relieved; Karol had phrased my question perfectly. It seemed so simple after she'd translated my question that I wondered why I had to have help. *Why couldn't I phrase it properly so the doctor could answer my question?*

Dr. Schimmel said, "Oh, I see. Your nail bed is fine. Put an adhesive bandage across your toenail so you don't accidently rip the nail loose, and keep wearing those shoes. They are perfect." I was amazed at the nurse and the doctor's relationship. Karol came between the doctor and me to interpret our communication; she was an intercessor. He welcomed and heeded her words. My words were unclear, but her words were crystal clear.

Have you ever tried to pray to God, but felt like you couldn't exactly put into words what you wanted to say? You knew in your heart what you were trying to say but the words just didn't come out right. Or maybe you didn't even know how to pray about a situation. *Should I change jobs or stay where I am? Do I discipline my child or show mercy? Where are you, God? They hurt me. My child has cancer.*

Did you know that we have someone who will interpret your heart's cry? Jesus said, "I will ask the Father and He will give you another Helper, that He may be with you forever; that is the Spirit of truth, whom the world cannot receive, because it does not see Him or know Him, but you know Him because He abides with you and will be in you" (John 14:16–17 NASB). The Spirit of truth is the Holy Spirit that abides in us and goes to the Father to translate our deepest thoughts, questions, and fears.

The Bible says, "In the same way, the Spirit helps us in our weakness. We do not know what we ought to pray for, but the Spirit himself intercedes for us with groans that words cannot express. And He who searches our hearts knows the mind of the Spirit, because the Spirit intercedes for the saints in accordance with God's will" (Romans 8:26–27 NIV).

We don't need to be consumed with offering up the correct prayers to God. The Holy Spirit can interpret our thoughts and groanings and He lets the Father know exactly what we are trying to say. We can pour our hearts out with tears enough to fill a bucket, and everything will be perfectly understood and heeded.

Karol was an intercessor for me and told the doctor my concerns. The Holy Spirit is an intercessor for me and tells the Father my concerns. It's a beautiful relationship.

QUESTIONS

1. What is our best source of written instruction from God? (a)

2. Is the Bible our only help in life? (b)

3. What if you don't have a Bible with you and you can't remember what you learned about the Lord? How can you be reminded of everything? (c)

4. Does Jesus intercede to the Father for us? What qualifies Him? (d)

5. We should never ask God to make us wise about spiritual things. True or false? (e)

6. Have you ever been unable to pray, yet had the Holy Spirit intercede for you? How could you tell?

7. Is it possible to grieve the Holy Spirit? (f)

8. What will happen if the Holy Spirit gives us advice, but we don't listen? (g)

Scriptural Answers

(a) "Your words are so choice, so tasty; I prefer them to the best home cooking. With your instruction, I understand life" (Psalm 119:105).

(b) "I will instruct you (says the Lord) and guide you along the best pathway for your life; I will advise you and watch your progress" (Psalm 32:8 LB).

(c) "But the Counselor, the Holy Spirit, whom the Father will send in my name, will teach you all things and will remind you of everything I have said to you" (John 14:26 NIV).

(d) "But because Jesus lives forever, he has a permanent priesthood. Therefore, he is able to save completely those who come to God through him, because he always lives to intercede for them" (Hebrews 7:24–25 NIV).

(e) "We have kept on praying and asking God to help you understand what He wants you to do; asking Him to make you wise about spiritual things" (Colossians 1:9 LB).

(f) "And do not grieve the Holy Spirit of God" (Ephesians 4:30 NIV).

(g) "But my people would not listen to me … so I gave them over to their stubborn hearts to follow their own devices" (Psalms 81:11–12 NIV).

53

Have you ever needed help?

September 4, 2011, was Labor Day weekend. I got a text from my son Aaron, but it wasn't the text I was expecting. It was short and to the point, giving three main facts: fire, pray, don't call yet. They'd had about three hours' notice, but didn't take the threat seriously until the last hour when they could see *and* smell the smoke. The wind could have shifted and they would have been out of danger. But that didn't happen. Hurricane winds came in from the coast and started whipping at around thirty miles per hour.

Each person in the family grabbed seven days' worth of clothes. Thankfully, this was a Sunday so they were all at home. If it had been a normal weekday, Aaron and Laura would have been at work in Bastrop, and with the fire separating them, Skyler (nine) and Ayla (five) would have been at school in Smithville. They scooped up all their medications, a few precious pictures, and their computer which contained pictures and important data. They grabbed their two dogs, Sadie (a dachshund) and Tink (a miniature Chihuahua), then they got into their vehicles and headed down the gravel driveway. They looked back at their house and prayed that God would save their home. Laura's parents, Corliss and Andy, who lived on the same property, followed behind them.

Their friends Mark and Evelyn in Smithville invited all of them to stay at their house that night. Since they didn't want to get too far from home, the invitation was accepted. They learned from the broadcasts the next day that the fire was worse, so they headed for our other son's house. Paul had invited them to stay with him in Waco, Texas, a safe distance from all harm, two hours away. *Normally* it would have been a two-hour trip, but this day it took the three-car entourage five hours because of all the detours and traffic.

On my end of the world in Pine Bluff, Arkansas, I called friends, family, and church members, and asked them to pray for Aaron's family and his in-laws. Randy and I weren't able to communicate with them until they got out of the area because the cell phone towers had burned down, but we knew at least that they were out of the worst line of fire.

In Waco, Paul took off two days of work to assist them in any way he could. He coached a select baseball team of eleven-year-olds, so he texted the parents to solicit clothes for Aaron's family. He also texted one of his former coaches at Baylor, Mitch Thompson. Within one hour, they had collected twenty-four large bags of clothes and toys. Aaron and his family were overwhelmed with gratitude at the response.

I offered to bring Skyler and Ayla to Pine Bluff so that Aaron could concentrate on decisions and phone calls they would have to make. I was pleased with their answer, though: "Mom, thanks for the offer, but the kids are all we have left in the world. We need to have them close to us right now." I found out later that they had thought I would be upset, but the opposite was true. I was extremely proud.

I talked to someone in the office at our church to keep them posted about the fire. They said they would pray and relay the message to our church members, but I never heard anything from anyone. I was okay, though. I rationalized that they were praying and didn't give it much thought at the time.

On Saturday, September 10, Aaron, Laura, and the kids watched Paul coach his baseball team as they slaughtered an opposing team. Then they headed back to Bastrop. There, a fabulous family that they were friends with—Mason, Alexandria, and their children—opened their home to the whole group. That meant a total of ten people (six adults, four kids, two dogs, and one cat) in a small three-bedroom, two-bathroom house. I asked God to bless that wonderful family. Aaron's entourage arrived at Mason and Alexandria's house on Saturday night.

Aaron and Andy, his father-in-law, couldn't get past the road barriers to get to their houses until Tuesday, the thirteenth. When they finally got to their property, their homes were *completely* burned to the ground. The only thing salvageable was a nativity statue of Joseph and a cross necklace. Figure that! A whole lifetime of memories and collections had gone up in smoke. Everything was reduced to ashes. They were not alone, though. Over 34,000 acres and more than 1,600 homes were destroyed in the Bastrop County Complex fire.

Meanwhile, back in Pine Bluff, I was struggling. The devil had started jumping in my mind. I kept telling people about Aaron's family in Bastrop, and the usual response was, "Oh, that's terrible! I'll be sure to pray for them." But I wanted them to *do* something.

I called our church office and reported the fact that Aaron's home had been destroyed. I asked them to put it in the bulletin. More people told me they were praying for my son and his family. I was happy about that because I knew that prayers move the heart of God. But I still wondered why no one offered to help them.

In spite of the catastrophe, I decided to count my blessings. Aaron called and said, "Mom, the best thing that came out of this tragedy was getting to know Paul better. I left home when I was nineteen and he was fourteen. He's really turned into an awesome man!" That warmed my heart.

I was also happy that the kind people in Waco had rallied around them with so many clothes and toys. They had such an overflow that they were able to pass on numerous bags to other families in need.

The fact that their lives were spared was the best blessing. That's the most important thing, anyway, isn't it?

It should have been, but to be honest, I was hurt because I wanted someone to *do* something. What I really needed was help with my attitude. I cried. I tried so hard to shake the feeling, but it was a battle. I didn't like feeling this way. My emotions were raw at this time. Looking back, I can now see that I was overly sensitive.

"For you, the righteous God, look deep within the hearts of men and examine all their motives and their thoughts" (Psalm 7:9 LB). God was examining me, and I was not so sure that He was pleased.

I talked to my mom and she said, "Sherry, you're just human."

I talked to my friend. She said, "Did you ever *ask* anyone for help or did you just ask them to *pray*? I'm sure people would help if you just asked them."

Uh oh! That's where I had made my mistake. I wasn't specific like Paul was. I knew down deep in my heart that the congregation would have helped me in any way that I asked.

God brought to my mind this Scripture: "Stop judging others, and you will not be judged. Stop criticizing others, or it will all come back on you. If you forgive others, you will be forgiven" (Luke 6:37 NLT). God brought back to my memory the times that people had told me of tragedies in their lives and I had said the exact same thing: "I'll pray for you." Prayer really is the *very* thing that moves the heart of God! I have the most awesome church family in the world and I know that they touched God's heart. I repented of my judgmental, criticizing spirit and I asked God to forgive me. My whole attitude changed.

One night, I woke up at 1:00 a.m. I couldn't go back to sleep, so I turned the television on to VTN, a religious television station in Arkansas. I drifted in and out of sleep, but I jolted awake right before someone said, "Give and it shall be given to you." I looked this up later and found it in Luke 6:38, right after the stop-judging Scripture.

God started talking to me. "I did not say give to certain people and I will have those same people give back to you. Give to the people I tell you to, and then I will take care of who gives to you." That sounded familiar. In fact, that's what I told other people.

"You do not have because you do not ask God" (James 4:2 NIV). God is the one to meet my son's needs. I wanted help from my choices, but God's plans are always exceedingly better than my choices. Besides, I got to thinking, *If I wanted a lawn swing for my birthday yet never told my husband that, I would have no right to be upset with him if he didn't buy it for me. He's not a mind reader. The people I was so hurt by had never been asked to help or told that we had a need besides prayer.*

Meanwhile, as my mind was fighting this inner battle, God was working behind the scenes. We were not aware that a new church, Journey Lorena, was having its first inaugural service in a small town twelve miles south of Waco. The youth pastor Mark Williams, whose son Caleb was on Paul's baseball team, told Pastor Cory Smith about their need. He asked his congregation if they would vote to give their entire first offering to Aaron and his family. The seventy-seven people in the congregation unanimously said yes!

Afterward, Pastor Cory, Pastor Mark, and Paul drove the two-hour trip from Lorena to Bastrop fourteen days after the fire to present them with the check. Aaron cried, Paul cried, and I cried when I found out—it was $5,000! Matthew says, "This is your Father you are dealing with, and he knows better than you what you need" (Matthew 6:8). God was *really* showing out. Amazing!

I needed help with my attitude and Aaron needed help with his resources. God, in His own way, provided for both. The prayers of the beautiful people in my church may have been the prayers that God answered, since my attitude wasn't right. Aaron's insurance wouldn't even begin to cover a down payment on a new house, but Journey Lorena's extremely generous gift made it possible. Our wonderful brothers and sisters in Christ helped beyond our wildest dreams.

Solomon said, "A friend is always loyal and a brother is born to help in time of need" (Proverb 17:17 NLT). Aaron's brother Paul helped him when he needed it most. Paul remembered to ask for help with their resources when I forgot. Mason and Alexandria and Mark and Evelyn opened their homes when they could have shut their doors.

I know that the next time the devil invites me to a pity party, I'm going to read him this scripture: "Be careful! Watch out for attacks from the Devil, your great enemy. He prowls around like a roaring lion, looking for some victim to devour. Take a firm stand against him, and be strong in your faith. Remember that your Christian brothers and sisters all over the world are going through the same kind of suffering you are" (1 Peter 5:8–9 NLT). I want Satan to know that I'm aware of his tactics.

You see, I didn't really want to write this story because it revealed my personal flaws. The devil wants us to cower and hide our human frailty. But exposing it to light may help me avoid Satan's snare in the future. Satan wants us to believe his lies, but God wants us to grow and to help others who go through the same trials. When Satan rears his ugly head, stomp it with some powerful Scriptures, and *he* will be the one who cowers. God will always win.

If my story feels similar to anything you've experienced in your life and you need help, too, I give you this advice:

Pray to God about anything you need. He hears your prayers.
Be specific when you need help.
Realize that God works through people who may surprise you.
List your blessings.
Find Scriptures to comfort you.
Trust God.
Enjoy your life while God is at work. We are not alone.

QUESTIONS

1. Have you ever been upset at someone, then later realized it was your attitude that was stinky, not their actions? (a)

2. God is our source of real help. True or false? (b)

3. If you want something from someone, should you be direct and ask them or should you just give hints?

4. Should you be direct with God, or should you give Him hints? (c)

5. Do you feel that your plans are better than God's plans? (d)

6. Write down a time that God had to give you an attitude adjustment. Did you like your new attitude better? (e)

7. Do we have a promise from God that He will give the righteous their desires? What verse do you depend on? (f)

8. A storm or fire may destroy a good person's home and a bad person's home, but what gives the righteous hope? (g)

9. Have you ever had unrelenting disappointment until a sudden good break turned your life around? Write down your personal story. (h)

Scriptural Answers

(a) "God can't stand pious poses, but he delights in genuine prayers" (Proverb 15:8).

(b) "Real help comes from God. Your blessing clothes your people" (Psalm 3:8).

(c) "Don't bargain with God. Be direct. Ask for what you need" (Luke 11:10).

(d) "In his heart a man plans his course, but the Lord determines his steps" (Proverb 16:9 NIV).

(e) "You were taught … to put off your old self, which is being corrupted by its deceitful desires to be made new in the attitude of your minds; and to put on the new self, created to be like God in true righteousness and holiness" (Ephesians 4:22–24 NIV).

(f) "What the wicked dreads will overtake him; what the righteous desire will be granted" (Proverb 10:24 NIV).

(g) "The prospect of the righteous is joy, but the hopes of the wicked come to nothing" (Proverb 10:28 NIV).

(h) "Unrelenting disappointment leaves you heartsick, but a sudden good break can turn your life around" (Proverb 13:12).

54

Have you ever noticed a flaw?

Having recently put on a few pounds, I asked my friend if she was disappointed in me. She looked at me strangely and asked, "Would you hate me if I quit smoking and gained thirty pounds?" I didn't answer, but I understood what she meant. You don't love people because of their outer beauty, but because of their inner beauty.

I've always been self-conscious of my large nose. Every time I meet someone, I think they're privately thinking, *My, what a big nose you have.* You know, like Little Red Riding Hood said to the Big Bad Wolf.

One day, I was a substitute teacher in a seventh-grade class, and I gave them the assignment of writing a colorful story. I was reading their stories out loud when about two sentences in, I realized Tyeshia's story was about me. I almost stopped midsentence, but I heard God tell me to keep reading. I felt the anticipation building in the room. I guess she had told the other students what to expect.

She had written her story about a teacher who helped the police locate drugs because of her ability to smell strong odors with her large nose. They put the big-nosed teacher on the police force as a police dog. I knew that Tyeshia was upset with me because I had sent her to the principal for an infraction of the rules a few days earlier. I felt she had written the story as payback and was trying to embarrass me. There was a time when I would have been upset about the story. I probably would have cried. But this time, I just smiled. Actually, she had written the story quite comically, and I even laughed.

I've made peace with my nose.

A few months later, I allowed Tyeshia to read *this* story, which includes *her* story about the big-nosed teacher. She put her hand over her mouth and exclaimed, "You knew that story was about you?! How come you're not mad at me?"

I flashed a big grin and held out my arms in a grandiose fashion. "Because I'm unique!"

We both had a good laugh.

Later that same day, Ray made fun of the large scar on Albert's neck, and I overheard Tyeshia say, "Hey, leave him alone, he's unique!" and that ended the squabble. I understood why God had me finish the story in the classroom that day when everything inside me was screaming for me to stop. There were lessons to be learned that were more important than just writing a colorful story.

Jeremiah says, "Before I formed you in the womb I knew you [and] approved of you [as my chosen instrument] and before you were born I separated and set you apart, consecrating you" (Jeremiah 1:5 AB). So there you have it! God made you and me exactly the way He wanted us. In His eyes, we are *perfect*. He approved of us, flaws and all.

I know that my husband loves me, but it caught me by surprise a few years ago when he said, "You're beautiful." I had heard what he said, but I wanted to hear it again, so I asked him to repeat what he had just said. I don't know what made me ask this, but I also said, "Could you be more specific?" He went on to explain: "You've been a great mom for our kids and a great mom for your kids at school. Best of all, you have and always will be the wife of the world to me." I didn't *feel* beautiful, but he *saw* me as beautiful.

After that, I was speechless. I had no idea he was thinking that. How many times have you felt inferior because of your buckteeth, big ears, crooked toes, or bald head? Outer features are not real beauty; they are only the house for the soul. In the February 2011 edition of *Guideposts*, Laura Mercier, a makeup artist and creator of her own cosmetics line, said, "Beauty is not generic. Quite often the thing that makes you memorable is the thing that makes you different."

Is an elephant criticized because it is heavy and has a funny-looking nose? How about a lion? Is it less majestic because it has a large fluffy mane around its neck? Have you considered the crocodile? Exactly how many teeth does it have, anyway? What if all those beautiful creatures gathered in heaven to complain about their supposed flaws? I imagine God's reply might be, "You've got to be kidding! That's what makes you unique. I designed you like that for a reason. You are beautiful. I love you."

I recently purchased a tea cart to use as a writing desk. I found it at a used furniture store. As I looked it over, I saw where it had been broken and glued. At first I thought: "Oh no, a flaw." Then I looked it over again. It was exactly what I wanted. It had wheels and two drop-down sections, and it was just the right height for me to have some serious writing sessions. I smiled in the store as I went to purchase my cherished table. The flaw didn't make it unusable; it made it unique. Just like me. I've gained weight, I've got a big nose, I've sinned, I've lied, and I've lost my temper. I'm flawed just like the table. But the Master carpenter looks at my flaws and He calls me unique. He calls me beautiful.

And that's what God said to me one day as I looked in the rearview mirror of my car. "Sherry, you are beautiful and I love you." Satan wants you to beat yourself up. That's what he intends. But God can turn your physical and spiritual flaws into a victory march if you help others who walk where you have been and let them know that God will bring them out. "God of all healing counsel! He comes alongside us when we go through hard times, and before you know it, he brings us alongside someone else who is going through hard times so that we can be there for that person just as God was there for us" (2 Corinthians 1:3–4). He repairs your life. What Satan meant for evil, God will turn to good.

"The way I think is beyond the way you think" (Isaiah 55:9). Look at yourself through Jesus's eyes. Look at others through Jesus's eyes. Instead of WWJD (What Would Jesus Do?), I prefer WWJT (What Would Jesus Think?).

You are beautiful. You are unique.

QUESTIONS

1. Do you have any physical flaws that make you feel inferior? Are you able to look at yourself through God's eyes? (a)

2. Is it a good idea to compare ourselves with others? (b)

3. A robust body is a sign of an unsound mind. True or false? (c)

4. If you have a spiritual weakness, should you just give in to it? (d)

5. Should we confess our sins to God? (e)

6. Do you think your flaws separate you from God's love? (f)

7. Should we broadcast each other's flaws (physical and spiritual) to others, or should we cover each other in love? Why? (g)

8. How does God look at you? (h)

Scriptural Answers

(a) "God rewrote the text of my life when I opened the book of my heart to his eyes" (Psalm 18:24).

(b) "That means we will not compare ourselves with each other as if one of us were better and another worse. We have far more interesting things to do with our lives. Each of us is an original" (Galatians 5:26).

(c) "A sound mind makes for a robust body, but runaway emotions corrode the bones" (Proverb 14:30).

(d) "Don't allow love to turn into lust, setting off a downhill slide into sexual promiscuity, filthy practices, or bullying greed. Though some tongues just love the taste of gossip, Christians have better uses for language than that. That kind of talk doesn't fit our style. Thanksgiving is our dialect" (Ephesians 5:3–4).

(e) "When anyone is guilty in any of these ways, he must confess in what way he has sinned" (Leviticus 5:5 NIV).

(f) "I'm absolutely convinced that nothing—nothing living or dead, angelic or demonic, today or tomorrow, high or low, thinkable or unthinkable—

absolutely nothing can get between us and God's love because of the way that Jesus our Master has embraced us" (Romans 8:38–39).

(g) "Above all, love each other deeply, because love covers a multitude of sins" (1 Peter 4:8 NIV).

(h) "You're beautiful from head to toe, my dear love, beautiful beyond compare, absolutely flawless" (Song of Songs (Solomon) 4:7).

55
Have you ever overcome a failure?

I'm sure you know that many famous people dealt with failures early in their lives. To name a few:

- Thomas Edison failed in more than 9,000 experiments before he perfected the first successful light bulb.
- Abraham Lincoln failed at twelve major events in his life before he was elected sixteenth president of the United States.
- Michael Jordan, one of the most prolific basketball players of all time, was cut from his tenth-grade basketball team because he "lacked skills."

Since my book is about my life situations, I'll tell you about some failures I'm familiar with. They're not very profound, but they make my point.

I must begin by telling you that not all failures are supposed to be overcome. For instance, there was the time I auditioned to be a cheerleader in the fourth grade. I didn't make the squad, and you know what? All of the private lessons and hard work in the world would never have made me a Dallas Cowboys Cheerleader. I'm five-foot-two and I don't enjoy yelling *or* flips.

Or how about the time I went to work for a distributorship? They had me taking merchandise orders and sending out trucks by my second hour on the job. By noon, I told them that I appreciated the chance to work for them, but I was going to fire myself. I told them that they didn't even have to pay me for the half-day of work. Believe me, nobody stopped me! But at least I had the sense to know to get out. Some things you know you weren't born to do.

But now I want to tell you about my son Nathan. When he was in high school he took Chemistry. He had a lot of trouble with that class. It seemed no matter how hard he tried, he couldn't grasp anything that was being taught. He went to his counselor and was told that if he could make a D in the class, it wouldn't affect his graduation because all his other grades were so high. Nathan struggled, but he managed to eke out a C-. Yay!

Nathan headed to college and decided to major in nursing. But in order to do that, he had to take a chemistry class. I thought, *Oh, no! That dreaded subject again! How could he pass college chemistry if he struggled with it in high school? Maybe he could get a tutor. God, please help him with this course. Help his brain to comprehend.*

"If any of you lacks wisdom, he should ask God, who gives generously to all without finding fault, and it will be given to him" (James 1:5 NIV). There it was in a nutshell: ask God for wisdom, He will give it to you, and He won't be mad at you. I like James. Nathan was lacking, so I was asking.

By the end of the course, Nathan had an epiphany. "Mom, I'm really good at chemistry! I want to change my major!"

Wow, what a turnaround! "Are you serious? What happened?!"

"I don't know. It just seems like I get it now. It's hard to explain."

But *I* knew what happened: God generously gave.

My husband, Randy, asked Nathan, "How will you ever be able to get a job with a degree in chemistry?" That must have put some doubts in Nathan's head.

But God graciously gave Nathan determination and extreme wisdom in this field. He ended up taking over fifteen chemistry courses and excelling at them all. He graduated with honors, and got a job offer before he even graduated. He has lived and worked in Arkansas, Indiana, and Utah. He has even created a better method to look for a compound that was causing issues for his company. Because his discovery would benefit others, they flew him to a Dallas convention to give a presentation explaining his procedure to other chemists in his field. Not too bad for a C- high school chemistry student.

"Who are those who fear the Lord? He will show them the path they should choose. They will live in prosperity, and their children will inherit the Promised Land" (Psalms 25:12–13 NLT). I'm glad God showed Nathan the right path, because if it had been up to my husband and me, we might have persuaded him down a different pathway. Sometimes we think we are so smart in our guidance, but we could be wrong. We should pray for God to guide our children, not for Him to make them listen to us.

I look back in awe at how Nathan's life took an unexpected turn. What if he had been afraid of chemistry because of his high school grade? What if God had never been consulted? What if Nathan had agreed with Randy that there were no good jobs for a chemistry major? When I see a student in the classroom discouraged with their bad grades, I always tell them about my son and his victory. You see, not all heroes are in sports.

Look in the Bible at Jonah, who ran from his assignment to preach to Nineveh. Then he went back and preached to them. The whole city was saved from God's wrath (Jonah 3). And Peter, who denied Christ three times in less than twenty-four hours (Matthew 26:69–75), then came back to preach on the day of Pentecost, when 3,000 were baptized (Acts 2:1–41). God still believed in them. What if Jonah and Peter had said, "It's no use; I've already disappointed you, God. I'm a failure." We would not have known about victory after defeat from God's point of view.

Have you had a failure in your life? Do you want to try again? I've heard that the only true failure in life is the failure to try. Ask God for wisdom. He will give it to you, and He won't be mad when you ask. He won't hold your failures against you. Remember Edison, Lincoln, Jordan, Jonah, and Peter. And also remember my fantastic son, Nathan!

QUESTIONS

1. Write down several failures that you've experienced and overcome.

2. Should we face a challenge head-on? How do you handle a new challenge? (a)

3. Do you feel that it is important to keep your spirits up when you've been crushed? (b)

4. If you lack confidence after a failure, what could you say? (c, d, e)

5. When you delight yourself in the Lord, He will turn His back on you if you stumble. True or false? (f)

6. Are you tired of all your problems and trials? Could God be trying to teach you something? (g)

7. Should we share our testimonies with others or just keep them to ourselves because it is embarrassing? (h)

Scriptural Answers

(a) "Anyone who meets a testing challenge head-on and manages to stick it out is mighty fortunate. For such persons loyally in love with God, the reward is life and more life" (James 1:12).

(b) "A healthy spirit conquers adversity, but what can you do when the spirit is crushed?" (Proverb 18:14).

(c) "So we say with confidence, 'The Lord is my helper; I will not be afraid. What can man do to me?'" (Hebrews 13:6 NIV).

(d) "God made my life complete when I placed all the pieces before him. When I got my act together, He gave me a fresh start" (Psalm 18:20)

(e) "God, make a fresh start in me, shape a Genesis week from the chaos of my life. Don't throw me out with the trash, or fail to breathe holiness in me; bring me back from gray exile, put a fresh wind in my sails!" (Psalms 51:10–12).

(f) "If the Lord delights in a man's way, he makes his steps firm; though he stumble, he will not fall, for the Lord upholds him with His hand" (Psalms 37:23–24 NIV).

(g) "We can rejoice, too, when we run into problems and trials, for we know that they are good for us—they help us learn to be patient. And patience develops strength of character in us and helps us trust God more each time we use it until finally our hope and faith are strong and steady. Then, when that happens, we are able to hold our heads high no matter what happens and know that all is well, for we know how dearly God loves us" (Romans 5:3–5 LB).

(h) "What a wonderful God we have ... who so wonderfully comforts and strengthens us in our hardships and trials. And why does he do this? So that when others are troubled, needing our sympathy and encouragement, we can pass on to them this same help and comfort God has given us" (2 Corinthians 1:3–4 LB).

56

Have you ever overlooked a diamond in the rough?

There's a town in Arkansas where you can look for diamonds. My husband and I took our kids there once when they were young. On Interstate 30 near Arkadelphia you will see a sign that reads "Crater of Diamonds State Park at Exit 73." Travel thirty-nine miles to Murfreesboro and you will come to an area that might surprise you. It is basically rows of dirt that the park rangers regularly plow. People are allowed to bring spoons, shovels, anything with which to dig, and everyone comes with hope that they will find the next big diamond.

We had a lot of fun that day. We found a few clumps of fool's gold, but no diamonds. The park rangers explained to us that a diamond doesn't appear the same in the ground as it does after the jeweler has cut the stone to reflect the light. I'd say "lumpy rock" is a better description. In fact, it looks pretty rough, hence the phrase, "diamond in the rough."

I had a thought as we drove away that day. *I wonder if this place was just a gimmick? There may have been diamonds here before, but I doubt there are any more left. Oh well, the kids had fun.*

But throughout the years, there have been many articles in our local newspaper about diamond finds at that same location. Not just small finds, but diamonds worth big bucks. How did we miss them? They were there all the time. I guess I was wrong.

Did you know that there are diamonds all around you, but you might not have noticed them? I'd like to share with you about some real-life diamonds I almost overlooked.

Patrick and Charles were twins who were smaller than the other kids on the T-ball team. They had not developed coordination skills yet. If you've ever seen a mare give birth to a colt, and then watched the colt awkwardly taking its first steps, then you understand what the twins looked like when they ran. The rules required everyone to play, so there was no getting around it—they had to play.

My seven-year-old son, Paul, was also on the team. Jason and my older sons, Aaron and Nathan, were their coaches. The kids on the team were all stellar athletes, except for the twins. I told Aaron and Nathan, "Your team will only be as strong as your weakest link (links, in this case), so you'll need to work on the twins' skills extra hard. You can never tell when the game might depend on them."

So work they did: they took turns training them on their running, hitting, and catching skills. Anything to help. I even remember them chasing the twins down the base path, trying to encourage them to speed it up.

They saw improvement in the twins, but on some days, well, it was back to the basics. The team ended up winning first place that season, but now the postseason tournament was coming up. They had great success and the championship came down to one last game. The score was tied, there was one out, and it was the bottom of the last inning when one of the twins came up to bat. I heard sighs in the stands. I knew what they were thinking, because I was thinking it, too. *Here's a quick out. Even if he hits it, he'll never make it to first base.*

But he did hit it, and he did make it to first. The other team made a bad throw and "Safe!" was what we heard. The stands erupted in unison. Then someone hit the ball to the outfield. "Run!" we screamed, and run he did. That little boy ran as fast as his short legs would go!

Now there were two runners. The next batter hit the ball, but he was out at first. With two outs, one twin was on third and the other twin was batting: a coach's worst nightmare. The other team's fans were cheering; our fans were shuddering. With all the calmness of a major league ballplayer, the twin hit the ball toward third base. The pitcher ran over, picked up the ball, and threw it as hard as he could to first. Unbelievably, *that* twin was safe!

"*Oh, no!* What about the *other* twin on third? Did he run? Aaron sent him in!"

Sheep Ears   279

It seemed like everything went silent and in slow motion. The twin running, the throw to home, the missed catch, and the tap of the twin's foot as he hit home plate. "Safe!" screamed the umpire. Everyone went wild! Our two little diamonds in the rough had saved the game! Whoever would have thought on that first day of practice that *they* would be the heroes of the championship game?

I reflected back to that summer day when Patrick and Charles were heroes, diamonds, if you will. I can't remember which one was one batting or which one was running home, but that doesn't matter. It was a glorious day that I will never forget.

Another diamond was a sixth grader named Mario. He always sat away from the other students, sullen and dejected. "A happy face means a glad heart; a sad face means a breaking heart" (Proverb 15:13 LB). I felt prompted to talk to him. "Why are you always so sad, Mario? Do you not have anything to be happy about? What's wrong?"

"Kids make fun of me. They call me Scarface."

He did have a few small scars on his forehead, but to be honest, I hadn't been aware of them until his comment. "My mom told me she doesn't even notice them," Mario said as he halfheartedly smiled and lowered his eyes. But to him, the scars must have seemed gargantuan. He also told me his father had died from a staph infection four months before his birth. This young man might have felt like a loser, but I saw someone who looked like a diamond. He mentioned to me that what he *really* wanted to be was a writer. Hmm. Right down my alley.

I showed Mario my tablet where I wrote my stories. His eyebrows raised and I saw a little glimmer of hope. I said, "Write from your heart and let the words flow. Your stories might not be so great in the beginning, but they will definitely get better."

The next day, I brought him new pencils, a big eraser, a pencil sharpener, and a writing tablet just like mine. I made him promise to let me read some of his stories, and he agreed. I detected a little more sparkle in his eyes.

The following day, I was anxious to see if Mario had written anything in his tablet. I was assisting another student as he walked into the classroom. When I glanced in his direction, I smiled as I noticed that his furrowed brow had lifted. Instead, the handsome Mario was in his place, the one his mother saw, and the one that I saw. As I got closer, I observed that his writing tablet was open and placed neatly on the corner of his desk. It seemed like he was hoping that I would take notice.

"Wow, I see you wrote a story! Do you mind if I read it?"

"No, ma'am," he said, as he bit the corner of his lip. Then he gingerly handed me the tablet. Out of the corner of my eye, I could see him glancing nervously at me as I read. His story had a ghoulish beginning with a hint of intrigue, like the *Goosebumps* books. I praised Mario and finally saw the huge smile that I had been waiting to see. He faithfully brought the writing tablet to class until the end of school that year. He even shared his writing paper with some of the other aspiring writers in the classroom.

Will Mario be a famous writer one day? I don't know. But I do know that for at least a while, he quit thinking about the scars. Maybe he realized that underneath that lumpy rock was a diamond.

God discovered diamonds in the rough. He found stuttering Moses, who led the Israelites out of Egypt. He found Rahab the Harlot, who saved the spies that Joshua sent to Jericho. She ended up in Jesus's lineage. Jesus picked a band of fishermen to propel the gospel. And He got the greatest persecutor of Christians in His day, Paul, to write a major part of the New Testament. It sounds like a lot of diamonds could easily have been overlooked. Like the father of the prodigal son declared upon his son's return home, "He was lost and has been found" (Luke 15:24 NASB).

I think of how bizarre it is for God to use me to write a book. I had only two years of college and I worked as a teacher's aide for sixteen years. I haven't had the best education or the fanciest job in the world. But God sent two people into my life who saw me as a diamond instead of a lumpy rock. They were Dr. Robert Muhumuza and Gwen Terry. Dr. Muhumuza listened to my stories and encouraged me to write them down. Gwen pushed me. "Keep writing," she said. "Read your stories to me. They encourage me." Patricia Jones, Claudia Escudero, my husband, and many others cheered me on, too. Without their encouragement, I would have stopped writing. The Holy Spirit guided me with every word I wrote. I didn't see it, but they did. The rough edges were chipped away by the Master jeweler.

Guess what? I still look for diamonds, only not in Murfreesboro. They're in the classroom, in the neighborhood, and in the pews at church.

So if you see someone who is a little rough around the edges, don't pass them by. They may be the diamond that the world has been looking for. Give them encouragement. Cheer them on. See what God sees: diamonds that shine, reflections of the Father.

*As a special treat, here is a free download of the single "Polish Me" by Gene White, a.k.a. BGWhyte. He wrote this song after reading "Have you ever overlooked a diamond in the rough?"

Questions

1. Name some people who were rough diamonds that God found and polished to be used in his work. What made them seem incapable by the world's standards? (a, b, c, d, e)

2. What did God see in David that made Him take notice? (f)

3. Does God look at the outward appearance of people he uses for His service? If not, then what does He look at? (g)

4. Why do you think God chooses the lowly things of the world to accomplish great things? (h)

5. Has there been anyone in your life who encouraged you when you felt "lumpy"? Who were they? How did they spur you to action?

6. Have you discovered any diamonds whom other people overlooked? How did you encourage them?

Scriptural Answers

(a) "'But Lord,' Gideon asked, 'how can I save Israel? My clan is the weakest in Manasseh, and I am the least in my family'" (Judges 6:15 NIV).

(b) "'[Jericho] and everything in it is under a holy curse and offered up to God. Except for Rahab, the harlot—she is to live; she and everyone in her house with her, because she hid the agents we sent'" (Joshua 6:17).

(c) "So [Elijah] ... went to Zarephath ... he met a woman, a widow, gathering firewood. He asked her, 'Please, would you bring me a little water in a jug ... bring me something to eat?' She said, 'I swear, as surely as your God lives, I don't have so much as a biscuit. I have a handful of flour in a jar and a little oil in a bottle ... After we eat it, we'll die'" (1 Kings 17:10–12).

(d) "[Zacchaeus] wanted desperately to see Jesus, but the crowd was in his way—he was a short man and couldn't see over the crowd. So he ran on ahead and climbed up in a sycamore tree so he could see Jesus when he came by. When Jesus got to the tree, he looked up and said, 'Zacchaeus, hurry down. Today is my day to be a guest in your home'" (Luke 19:3–5).

(e) "He chose David his servant and took him from the sheep pens; from tending the sheep he brought him to be the shepherd of His people Jacob, of Israel his inheritance" (Psalms 78:70–71 NIV).

(f) "[David's] good heart made him a good shepherd; he guided the people wisely and well" (Psalm 78:72)

(g) "But God told Samuel, 'Looks aren't everything. Don't be impressed with his looks or stature. I've already eliminated him. God judges persons differently than humans do. Men and women look at the face; God looks into the heart'" (1 Samuel 16:7).

(h) "He chose the lowly things of this world and the despised things ... to nullify the things that are, so that no one may boast before him" (1 Corinthians 1:28–29 NIV).

57

Have you ever planted seeds?

One day, as I walked by a seventh-grade student, I felt God say, "She's a court reporter." I had noticed earlier that she was able to do her work with lightning speed, but I'd never given it much thought. I turned around and asked Kayla if she had ever thought of being a court reporter. She giggled and replied, "I don't even know what that is." I explained what it was and she said, "Yeah, I might like that." It just so happened that I knew Judge Jodi Dennis. I mentioned to her what had happened that day. She said to give her court reporter, Sha, a call. Judge Dennis said that she would allow Kayla to shadow Sha for a day to see how Kayla liked it. I was shocked!

I went to our principal, Ms. Hatley, and told her what was proposed. She said that she needed to call Kayla's mother for permission. Everyone loved the idea and the day was set up, thanks to Ms. Hatley, Judge Dennis, and Sha. It's so nice to know people who really care.

Kayla spent the whole day in court and came back with a clear sense of a court reporter's job. I thought she would have returned all bright-eyed and excited with story after story of things that had happened during the day. Maybe she would discover this was a great vocation for her to pursue. But she simply related the bare facts to me blandly, and never mentioned the visit again.

At first, I was a little disappointed at her lackluster response, and then I remembered that my assignment was to obey and let God fulfill His plan. Will Kayla become a court reporter? I honestly don't know. I do know that a seed was planted. All I can do is follow God's leading. If I missed the mark, it's not because I didn't try. God wants obedience. Only the future will tell. Some people plant seeds, some water, and some harvest.

"[Paul] planted the seed, Apollos watered it, but God made it grow. So neither he who plants nor he who waters is anything, but only God, who makes things grow. The man who plants and the man who waters have one purpose, and each will be rewarded according to his own labor. For we are God's fellow workers; you are God's field, God's building" (1 Corinthians 3:6–9 NIV).

So I may have planted a seed, and Judge Dennis, Sha, and Ms. Hatley may have watered it, but only God will make it grow, if that's His will.

The next year I walked past Ron, a sixth grader who had trouble reading, and I heard God say, "He's a car mechanic." I stopped dead in my tracks, turned to him and said, "Ron, have you ever thought of being a car mechanic when you grow up? Mechanical work doesn't require a lot of reading and I bet you would be awesome at it."

Ron grinned and said, "I don't know, Mrs. Witt. I'll think about it."

Ron was an amazing young man with above-average artistic ability. One of his drawings of President Obama had been displayed at the White House. However, Ron was on the pre-primer level of reading.

I didn't mention it again until about five months later. I said, "Ron, did you think any more about being a car mechanic?"

His eyes lit up! "Oh, yeah, Mrs. Witt, I forgot to tell you. My mom's car broke down and I watched the man the whole time he worked on it. You know, I think I *would* like to work on cars."

Will he become a mechanic? I don't know. I'm just a farmer planting seeds. You can be a farmer, too. You don't even have to get your hands dirty. Just listen to the prompting with your sheep ears. It's not as hard as you might think.

Questions

1. Has God ever prompted you to plant a seed of encouragement in someone's life? Was it flavored with love? (a)

2. Have you ever felt like God wanted you to encourage or inspire someone, yet you were too shy to do so? How should we handle that situation? (b)

3. It's best to keep your mouth shut and mind your own business. True or false? Why? (c)

4. How big will your harvest be if you plant no seeds? (d)

5. Will every seed you plant grow? Why or why not? (e)

6. Must our seeds be large (and wordy) to be effective? (f)

Scriptural Answers

(a) "We continually remember before our God and Father your work produced by faith, your labor prompted by love, and your endurance inspired by hope in our Lord Jesus Christ" (1 Thessalonians 1:3 NIV).

(b) "If we love God, we will do whatever He tells us to. And He has told us from the very first to love each other" (2 John 1:6 LB).

(c) "Don't just think about your own affairs, but be interested in others, too, and in what they are doing" (Philippians 2:4 LB).

(d) "A farmer too lazy to plant in the spring has nothing to harvest in the fall" (Proverb 20:4).

(e) "'What do you make of this? A farmer planted seed. As he scattered the seed, some of it fell on the road, and the birds ate it. Some fell in the gravel; it sprouted quickly but didn't put down roots, so when the sun came up it withered just as quickly. Some fell in the weeds; as it came up, it was strangled by the weeds. Some fell on good earth, and produced a harvest beyond his wildest dreams'" (Matthew 13:3–8).

(f) "Though (the mustard seed) is the smallest of all your seeds, yet when it grows, it is the largest of garden plants and becomes a tree, so that the birds of the air come and perch in its branches" (Matthew 13:32).

58

Have you ever prayed like a child?

My friend Tammy told me an amazing story that transpired at Ridgway Christian School where she worked. It was 7:30 a.m., and the senior high girls were having basketball practice. The ball was passed to Cady, and as she pivoted to pass the ball to a fellow teammate, something in her knee gave out and she fell to the ground. The team gathered around her and gasped at the sight. Her left knee cap was not on top of her joint where it should be; it was on the side of her leg. They got her an ice pack to reduce the swelling while Cady's coach called 911. As they waited for the ambulance, the coach laid her hands on top of the ice pack and the team chanted, "Jesus! Jesus! Jesus!"

Their worship leader, Vickie, walked in on them and said a short prayer for Cady as the girls bowed their heads. Many were so sickened by the sight of her knee that they vowed to never, *ever* go into the medical field.

The medics carried Cady out on a stretcher, but when they took the ice off of her knee at the hospital, Cady's knee cap was back in the proper position. The doctor was surprised; he said that the only way her kneecap could have been at the side of her leg was if the ligament had snapped, and it was impossible for the kneecap to go back to its proper location without surgery. Amazing! He dismissed Cady and she went back to school that day.

The girls were telling Tammy how horrible Cady's knee had looked, but they became speechless as Cady walked in the door of the classroom.

Not only was she walking free of crutches, she had also walked up the stairs to get there! It was a modern-day miracle that those faith-filled girls will never forget.

"Every good and perfect gift is from above, coming down from the Father of the heavenly lights" (James 1:17 NIV). Those are very powerful words that we need to remember as we celebrate our blessings.

God hears our praise. He's not worried about lengthy prayers. Have you ever wondered what Jesus thought about the length of prayers? Jesus talked about the teachers of religious law who piously walked around loving their honored seats in the synagogues: "They shamelessly cheat widows out of their property, and then, to cover up the kind of people they really are, they make long prayers in public. Because of this, their punishment will be the greater" (Mark 12: 40 NLT).

Jesus loves children. Why? I'm guessing because they have not been clouded with junk. They take God at His word. "I assure you, anyone who doesn't have [a child's] kind of faith will never get into the kingdom of God" (Mark 10:15 NLT). *The Message* phrases it "the simplicity of a child." Flowery words are not impressive to God. Sincere gratitude and love are what He desires. That short prayer by Cady's teammates—"Jesus! Jesus! Jesus!"—was sufficient.

A friend named Monica shared with me an incident about her daughter, Kaneeshia, who is a junior at Pine Bluff High School. They had just moved into a new house, a big improvement over their former house, which was in a rough neighborhood. While on the catwalk at the school, Kaneeshia said to her classmate, "This is what you do when God does something good in your life." She screamed, "Thank you, Jesus!" at the top of her lungs.

It was contagious. Students on the catwalk and those below joined in with hearty, "Thank you, Jesus!" cries that rang across the campus. I can only imagine God saying to the angelic hosts, "Listen to that! Praise from my children. I love it! I love it! I love it!"

Simple, child-like faith is the key to God's heartstrings. Jesus said, "You may ask me for anything in my name, and I will do it" (John 14:14 NIV). Do you believe Jesus's Word? Then you're ready to trust and pray like a child.

When my three sons were little, we taught them to pray. I am thankful that they have also taught *their* kids to pray. When my grandkids, Skyler and Ayla, visited during the summer, I enjoyed observing them in their sweet innocence. Their fresh perspective was enlightening. I think we could all learn from them.

For example, we went to buy snow cones from a vendor. As we were leaving the parking lot, four-year-old Ayla spouted, "We need to say something to God." It tickled me because she had already thanked me, but she knew instinctively to thank God, too. From her viewpoint, if anything was great, it must be from God. Both kids clasped their hands and said in unison, "Thank you, God!" then devoured their cones.

A few days later, after purchasing toys at the Dollar General, Skyler and Ayla gave me a big hug and hearty thanks. Back in the truck, before we left the parking lot, Ayla said, "Let's pray." Once again, I was caught off guard and amazed by her statement. This time she expanded her prayer: "Thank you, God, for these awesome toys! Amen."

One day we were looking for the remote control. I saw nine-year-old Skyler with his eyes closed and his hands clasped. I stopped in my tracks. "What are you doing, Sky?"

"I'm praying for God to help us find the remote," he replied matter-of-factly. And about four minutes later, we did find it. *Now why hadn't I thought of that?*

On one of our jaunts around the neighborhood, Skyler was about three houses ahead of us when I noticed him hop off his scooter, walk up to a gorgeous purple crepe myrtle tree, pause, then get back on his ride and wait for Ayla and me. As we approached, he blurted out, "Don't worry, Grandma Sherry, I already thanked God for the beautiful flowers." I thought that was really cool.

One of my fondest episodes happened the night that Skyler was sick. He and Ayla had been attending Vacation Bible School at Summit Baptist Church. On Wednesday night his tummy was rumbling, and eventually he threw up. I told him we would stay home, but he claimed he was much better and insisted on attending VBS. I warned the ladies at the sign-in table that he wasn't feeling well and I gave them my phone number in case he got worse. I went across the street to attend the midweek service at my church and watched my phone for calls.

Sure enough, about ten minutes later, my phone vibrated. He was sick again. When I arrived, one of the ladies carried Skyler out to the car. "I can tell he really *is* sick. I feel so bad for him," she said. I didn't want to take Ayla out of her class so I went back across the street and sat in a chair in the vestibule at First Assembly of God. I texted my friend, Gwen, and asked her to pray for Skyler. He sprawled under my chair wanting to be left alone.

I placed my cell phone in my purse on the floor and within five minutes, he asked me if he could play a video game on my phone. I said, "Skyler, are you feeling better?"

He replied, "Yes, I think I am." He stood up, looking bright-eyed and bushy-tailed, as my mom used to say.

I hugged him and exclaimed, "Skyler, Jesus healed you!"

He took a few quick steps away from me, threw both hands in the air, and screamed, "I—love—God!" It was a beautiful prayer of thanks from a sincere nine year old boy.

He wanted to go back to VBS. As we walked in the door, the women looked at the chipper Skyler and asked what had happened. He shrugged his shoulders and nonchalantly replied, "God healed me." Their mouths were agape.

He never was sick again.

My grandchildren's pure, sweet responses to wonderful things in their lives caused me to reflect on my own responses to wonderful things in *my* life. Who do I thank for my raise at work? Of course, I thank my boss, but it's important to thank God, also. As I drive off the parking lot with my new truck, do I say "Wow! I love my new truck!" or do I say "Thank you, God, for my awesome truck?" I *should* say both. I can imagine Jesus smiling as the words come freely from my mouth. Just like a child.

Ayla and Skyler felt thanks welling up in their spirits and they expressed their gratitude and love to God. I'm thankful that my grandkids' voices refresh my thoughts of God. Cady's friends called on the name of Jesus, and He heard their cry. Kaneeshia shouted praise—no apologies, no long soliloquies, just calling the name of Jesus.

Another incident occurred once when I was sitting in church by J'Mille and her three-year-old son. Pastor Bell prayed before his sermon, ending with "Amen." Kaleb picked up on it and with all the fervor of an anointed child of God, proclaimed, *"Aaaamen.* Thank you, Jesus!" He put the rest of us grown folks to shame. I watched as numerous adults turned their heads and gave approving smiles.

Have you prayed like a child lately? "Enter with the password: 'Thank you!' Make yourselves at home, talking praise. Thank him. Worship him" (Psalm 100:4). Let go of all your inhibitions. Talk to Him from your inner being. There's a child that lives within us all. Thank Him for blessings throughout your day. To quote Ayla, "We need to say something to God."

Think like a child, believe like a child, and pray like a child.

Questions

1. Children are very complex; when they pray or talk about God, they get nervous and question God's actions. True or false? (a)

2. Do you believe children praise God without inhibitions? Should we follow their example? (b)

3. What two attitudes will give God the greatest pleasure when we come to Him in prayer? (c)

4. When children want something from you, do they give hints or do they ask directly? Should we be direct with God? (d)

5. If your children cry to you for help, do you ignore them? If you cry to God for help, will He ignore you?(e)

6. Give some examples of short, simple prayers you have prayed. (f)

7. Do you believe God heard you? (g)

Scriptural Answers

(a) "'Mark this: Unless you accept God's kingdom in the simplicity of a child, you'll never get in'" (Luke 18:17).

(b) "You have taught the little children to praise you perfectly. May their example shame and silence your enemies!" (Psalm 8:2 LB).

(c) "Enter his gates with thanksgiving and his courts with praise; give thanks to him and praise his name" (Psalm 100:4 NIV).

(d) "So I say to you: Ask and it will be given to you; seek and you will find; knock and the door will be opened to you. For everyone who asks receives; he who seeks finds; and to him who knocks, the door will be opened" (Luke 11:9–10 NIV).

(e) "I love the Lord, for he heard my voice; he heard my cry for mercy. Because he turned his ear to me, I will call on him as long as I live" (Psalms 116:1–2 NIV).

(f) "The cords of death entangled me; the anguish of the grave came upon me; I was overcome by trouble and sorrow. Then I called on the name of the Lord: 'O Lord, save me!'" (Psalms 116:3–4 NIV).

(g) "The Lord is gracious and righteous; our God is full of compassion. The Lord protects the simple-hearted; when I was in great need, he saved me" (Psalms 116:5–6 NIV).

59

Have you ever provoked someone?

There were times in my life that my parents criticized me. I didn't like what they said, but now I'm glad they spoke up *and* I'm glad I listened. "Don't refuse to accept criticism; get all the help you can" (Proverb 23:12 LB).

There were also times that I was provoked. I did not like that, and I never saw any benefit to it. "Fathers, do not provoke or irritate or fret your children, lest they become discouraged and sullen and morose, and feel inferior and frustrated. [Do not break their spirit]" (Colossians 3:21 AB). To provoke means to make angry, to vex.

If you've ever watched the television dance competition *Dancing with the Stars*, you'll know about their grading scale. A 1 is lousy; a 10 is fantastic. I will attempt to create my own grading scale: 1 is mild criticism, and 10 is fully provoked. For example, if you walked by a Rottweiler behind a fence and commented, "My, that sure is a big dog with a scary bark," that would be a 1. If you ran up and down the fence, clanging a stick until the Rott went berserk, that would be a 10.

As I go through my list, you might reflect on provocations that have occurred in your life.

- When I was in the fifth grade, I broke my right arm just above the elbow. The doctor put my arm in a straight cast. It was rather heavy. When the cast was removed, my parents noticed that I no longer swung my right arm when I walked. It irritated me whenever they reminded me to swing both arms. Later, I was glad they cared enough to point it out. I'd give that a 1.

- When I was in the third grade, my dad forced me to eat my sweet peas. I could not leave until my plate was clean. I probably stayed at the table for two hours. I almost threw up. I couldn't stand them then, and I can't stand them now. At the time, I didn't like asparagus, squash, meatloaf, spaghetti, or French fries, either. I now eat them all, except for sweet peas. He ruined my taste forever because he forced the issue. I'd give that an 8 or 9.

- When I was in the fourth grade, I took piano lessons. The teacher repeatedly hit my knuckles with a conductor's baton when I messed up. After the third lesson, I refused to go again. I feel like I could have been a good pianist. After all, my mom and dad are great musicians. But something died in me that third day. I'd give that a 10.

- As a seventh grader, I developed a habit of talking in a high-pitched voice. It aggravated me when my parents would say, "Sherry, talk deeper." I would have to repeat my sentence in a lower tone. After recently seeing a woman on television with an annoyingly high-pitched, twangy voice, I'm now *exceedingly* grateful for their reminders. In the seventh grade, I would have given that an 8, but now, I would say it was a 1 and give big thanks.

- When Paul was twelve, he and his friend did something that I deemed "really bad." I started to give him a whooping, but somewhere along the way, it turned into an all-out body thrash. I had gotten out of control. My anger soared. Nathan even screamed, "Mom, that's enough!" I regretted losing control. I've since apologized. Paul said, "Thanks, Mom. That means a lot." I was wrong. Sadly, I give myself a 10.

- When Paul was sixteen, I set out to teach him how to drive a standard transmission car. After about ten clunky attempts, he stormed out of the car, stood at my door and said, "Get out! I can't drive this stupid thing!" I crossed my arms and said, "Then I guess I'll sit here all night, because if you don't drive us home, we're staying." He was mad, all right, but he learned how to drive a stick shift that day. Later when one of his friend's vehicles got stuck in the mud, he was able to drive the standard truck to pull him out. He said he was really glad I had forced him to learn that day. I guess that would be a 5.

- When Aaron was nineteen, he developed diabetes. He was enrolled in SEARK, a junior college in our town. His plan was to complete two years in Pine Bluff, then transfer to Conway, which was sixty miles away. But I guess I peered over his shoulder one too many times. "Are you sure you need to eat that? Have you taken your shot yet? How many carbohydrates is that?" I'm sure he must have been frustrated. He ended up moving to Conway earlier than he had originally planned. I'm guessing that would be an 8. Sorry, Aaron.

- When Nathan was nineteen, I was looking for something. I looked in drawers and in the attic. I went to look under his bed while he was doing homework on top of his bed. I pulled out a box and discovered a whiskey bottle. "Is this yours?" "Nope," was his reply. I called my husband into Nathan's room. "Randy, is this yours?" It was a silly question, because neither my husband nor I drink. "No, I don't know whose it is," Randy said. I asked, "Would you mind pouring it out?" Randy gladly complied and we never mentioned it to Nathan again. We could have ranted and raved, but God gave us wisdom that day. About ten years later, Nathan told me that if I had made a big scene, it would have made everything worse. I guess that day I got a 1.

- I knew a sixth grade boy who oozed with basketball talent. He was fast, had a good jump shot, a smooth three-pointer, and could weave in and out of traffic on the court. His father coached him. But his father made him hate the game. No matter how well Asa played, screaming and ranting was all he got from the man that he loved. Asa refused to play the next year. His mom told me that it was easier for him to quit basketball than to face his dad's wrath and disappointment. I'd give that a 10+.

Maybe you can relate to some of these. Maybe you've even laughed a little. My desire is for you to realize that there is a fine line between helping someone and provoking them. A helpful criticism may improve them, but provoking does damage. Sometimes it's reversible, but most of the time, it's not.

This does not apply just to children. It applies to grown-ups, too. We are to encourage and guide each other through our weaknesses, not bash and embarrass each other to the point of giving up. Let's get off our holier-than-thou pedestals. Show new Christians the love of God, not judgmental words that provoke them to feel inferior and frustrated.

"But the fruit of the Spirit is love, joy, peace, patience, kindness, goodness, faithfulness, gentleness, and self-control ... Let us not become conceited, provoking and envying each other" (Galatians 5:22–23, 26 NIV).

There is another definition of "to provoke" that I like: to bring about, to start into action, to call forth. "And let us consider one another to provoke unto love and to good works" (Hebrews 10:24 KJV). That sounds good. Instead of associating anger with the word "provoke," let's provoke those in our world to love and care for each other. As the saying goes, show them how, and if necessary, use words.

Questions

1. If you unjustly provoke people, what kind of harvest will you reap? (a)

2. What should you do with a troublemaker in the classroom, at church, or at work—tolerate them or kick them out? (b)

3. If you are provoked to anger, how should you handle yourself? (c)

4. When you offend a brother, is it easy or hard to win back the friendship? Why? (d)

5. If you know a hot-tempered man who provokes everyone around him, should you always rescue him when he gets into trouble? Explain your answer. (e)

6. Do you believe parents have the right to continually scold and nag their children? Why or why not? (f)

7. What is the best way to handle yourself when you are tempted to act the wrong way? (g)

8. Do you provoke with anger or provoke unto love and good works?

Scriptural Answers

(a) "The unjust tyrant will reap disaster and his reign of terror shall end" (Proverb 22:8 LB).

(b) "Kick out the troublemakers and things will quiet down; you need a break from bickering and griping!" (Proverb 22:10).

(c) "Smart people know how to hold their tongue; their grandeur is to forgive and forget" (Proverb 19:11).

(d) "It is harder to win back the friendship of an offended brother than to capture a fortified city. His anger shuts you out like iron bars" (Proverb 18:19 LB).

(e) "A hot-tempered man must pay the penalty; if you rescue him, you will have to do it again" (Proverb 19:19 NIV).

(f) "And now a word to you parents. Don't keep on scolding and nagging your children, making them angry and resentful. Rather bring them up with the loving discipline the Lord himself approves, with suggestions and godly advice" (Ephesians 6:4 LB).

(g) "But remember this—the wrong desires that come into your life aren't anything new and different. Many others have faced exactly the same problem before you. And no temptation is irresistible. You can trust God to keep the temptation from becoming so strong that you can't stand up against it, for He has promised this and will do what He says. He will show you how to escape temptation's power so that you can bear up patiently against it" (1 Corinthians 10:13 LB).

60

Have you ever read a different version?

When my sons were young, I would read them a story from the Bible and then they would perform different scenes from that story. They had a blast when they re-enacted the stories of Daniel in the Lion's Den, David and Goliath, and Jonah and the Whale. It didn't take me long to figure out that the King James Version of the Bible was difficult, not only for me to read, but also for them to understand. Since words like "thee," "thou," and "fret" were not in their vocabulary, I spent more time explaining than reading. So I looked for a version or a paraphrase that they could comprehend, one in everyday language. I discovered *The Living Bible*, and we were all happy.

As they grew older, we studied Proverbs because of the profound wisdom Solomon gave us. They were Words to live by.

Recently, while in a doctor's office, I read from Proverbs in the King James Bible that was in the waiting room. It was very difficult to read. Here is a comparison of the two versions:

> My son, let not them depart from thine eyes: keep sound wisdom and discretion: So shall they be life unto thy soul, and grace unto thy neck.
>
> —Proverbs 3:21–22 KJV

Have two goals: wisdom—that is, knowing and doing right—and

common sense. Don't let them slip away, for they fill you with living energy, and are a feather in your cap.

—Proverbs 3:21–22 LB

The wise heart shall be called prudent: and the sweetness of the lips increaseth learning.

—Proverb 16:21 KJV

The wise man is known by his common sense, and a pleasant teacher is the best.

—Proverb 16:21 LB

The beginning of strife is as when one letteth out water: therefore leave off contention, before it be meddled with.

—Proverb 17:14 KJV

It is hard to stop a quarrel once it starts, so don't let it begin.

—Proverb 17:14 LB

Do you see what I mean? My friend Tricia is in a book club. Their last book was *A Tale of Two Cities* by Charles Dickens. She reported that she had only skimmed the book because it was so deep. Some of the other ladies had had the same response: too complex.

In my opinion, if you give a child or a new Christian the King James Version, it may be the same as giving them *The Tale of Two Cities* for their first reading experience. They might skim it, set it aside, and not read it because it is too deep.

It may be more effective to use a different version of the Bible. Other favorite versions of mine are *The Message* and *The New International Version*. Later on, as you progress, the King James Version might become perfect for you.

You can't relate to a book if you don't understand what it says, now can you? If you try some other versions and parallels of the Bible, you may find out that you love reading it after all.

Questions

1. We have no responsibility to our kids and grandkids to tell them about God. True or false? (a)

2. Do you share your faith in God with others in your family? (b)

3. Is it advisable to understand the meaning of Bible passages or should you just skip over the hard parts? (c)

4. When you tried a different version of the Bible, did it give you a better understanding of the Word?

5. Have you asked God to help you understand the Bible? (d)

6. When we read the Bible, we should pray for insight into the words of wisdom. True or false? (e)

Scriptural Answers

(a) "But watch out! Be very careful never to forget what you have seen God doing for you. May His miracles have a deep and permanent effect on your lives! Tell your children and grandchildren about the glorious miracles He did" (Deuteronomy 4:9 LB).

(b) "I know how much you trust the Lord, just as your mother Eunice and your grandmother Lois do; and I feel sure you are still trusting Him as much as ever" (2 Timothy 1:5 LB).

(c) "As Ezra read from the scroll ... the Levites went among the people and explained the meaning of the passage that was being read" (Nehemiah 8:7–8 LB).

(d) "Help me understand these things inside and out so I can ponder your miracle-wonders. My sad life's dilapidated, a falling down barn; build me up again by your Word" (Psalms 119:27–28).

(e) "God, teach me lessons for living so I can stay the course. Give me insight so I can do what you tell me—my whole life one long, obedient response. Guide me down the road of your commandments; I love traveling this freeway! Give me a bent for your words of wisdom, and not for piling up loot" (Psalms 119:33–36).

61

Have you ever received a new name?

When my son Nathan got his puppy from an animal shelter, he asked them what her name was. They said they called her "Penny" because she had a copper spot on her back that resembled a penny. But when Nathan took her home, the name just didn't fit. He tossed around several names, then settled on "Jackie" because he thought she was a Jack Russell terrier. The name seemed to fit her personality.

When Nathan went to our hunting club, there was a dog there named "Lil' Red" who was used as a deer dog. Her job was to flush the deer out of the woods. Lil' Red got lost during a hunt. Two months later, they found her howling a mournful cry and horribly emaciated. Lil' Red was returned to her wire cage where she would remain until the next hunt. Nathan couldn't stand for her to lead such a sad life, so he adopted her and took her to his safe, comfortable house and nursed her back to health.

When Nathan moved to Indiana a year later, my husband and I inherited both dogs because he would be living in a hotel indefinitely. Jackie's name stayed the same, but somehow, I never could get used to the name Lil' Red. Since we were now her masters, I tried to think of a new name for her.

We had once had a dog named Brownie who was one of the sweetest dogs ever. Her death had hit us hard. Every time I looked at Lil' Red, I almost called her Brownie. She had the same temperament, the same face, and even the same brown-and-white coloring. Eventually, I started calling her Brownie.

My husband questioned the name change. I tried to call her Lil' Red, but Brownie just felt natural. Randy finally gave in because he knew that it would make me happy. At first, Brownie didn't recognize her name, but she eventually figured it out.

When our third dog came onto the scene, she had no name. She had been roaming the streets, unkempt and starving not just for food, but for love. I knew I needed to give her a name. *How about Cujo? No, that's terrible; she looks too sweet.* Then I looked at her and said, "How about *Mollie*?" She cocked her head sideways, as if to say, "What did you call me?"

I said it again. "Hey, Mollie." She wagged her tail as if to say, "Yeah, I like that name." And Mollie fit perfectly.

I heard the testimony of Christine Caine. She told of her shocking discovery at age thirty-three: she was adopted. After a search, she found her birth certificate. It said only "Unnamed #2508." Upon further research, she found out that the social worker's report said, "unwanted." When she was older, the biggest university in Australia sent her a document telling her that she was "unqualified" to be a youth leader.

Basically, she had been labeled "unnamed," unwanted," and "unqualified." Not exactly desirable descriptive words. Her adoptive parents named her Christine. They wanted *and* loved her. She is now on staff at Hillsong Church, probably the largest church in Sydney, Australia. Her story is on the website YouTube.

It would have been easy to feel defeated about those terrible adjectives used to describe her. However, she had a firm foundation in Jesus Christ and she knew that God had created her with a plan and a purpose. She drew strength from Psalms: "You made all the delicate, inner parts of my body, and knit them together in my mother's womb" (Psalm 139:13 LB). Christine said that she may not have known the facts surrounding her conception, but she knew the truth of God's Word.

My husband's paternal grandfather, Christopher, was one of the crushed in spirit. His mother had died when he was only six months old and his father had abandoned him, so he roamed the streets of Ringwood, England. His sister, Emily, married a man in the United States, and she sent for Chris to join her. At the young age of eleven, Chris pursued a new start to his life in the land of the free and the home of the brave. He caught a ship out of Liverpool and headed for New York. He was on a lower deck, surrounded by thousands, yet all alone. Food was scarce. Their only restroom was a bucket. He was scrawny and he fought for every morsel he could find, falling to the ground for just a crumb.

Shortly after boarding the ship, Christopher noticed a strange sight: a black man. He had never seen anything like him and out of curiosity he followed the man to the hull of the ship. After snooping and shadowing this stranger for a while, they struck up a friendship. Teako was the caretaker of the animals on the ship. He had plenty of food for himself. Christopher volunteered to help if Teako would only share some of his food.

I imagine that he must have admired the scrappy little kid. He probably said something like, "Stick with me, son, and we'll make it to the other side. I'll help you." Teako shared his food with little Chris on the month long trip. They shared space with the animals on the boat. The hull of the ship smelled rancid—a horrible mixture of vomit, urine, and feces—but at least Chris had food. And a friend.

He never left Teako's side, and on board the ship, his name gradually evolved from little Chris to little Teak. True to Teako's promise, they made it safely to America on February 23, 1915. Randy's grandfather has a brick with his name on it, Melton Christopher Teak Witt, at Ellis Island. Although Christopher never again saw the man who had saved his life, he didn't want to forget the sacrifice that was made to nurture him. He gave honor to his savior by taking his nickname.

My dogs had been rejected, but we took them in. Now they are well loved and have a safe home. It took them a while to recognize their names, but now the old names are long forgotten.

Two different people in my life in a six-month period called me "Kathy." It dawned on me that maybe it was a new name that God was giving me. I looked up the name. It means pure. I liked that.

God changed Abram's name to Abraham, Sarai's name to Sarah, Jacob's name to Israel, and Simon's name to Cephas (Peter). I can just imagine God changing Gideon's name from Chickenheart to Boldheart.

Christine Caine said that her daughter was told by a classroom bully that she was "dumb and ugly." Her reply? "That's not true. My daddy says I'm intelligent and beautiful."

She heard her father's words and believed. Now hear *your* Father's words and believe. "I am holding you by your right hand—I, the Lord, your God—and I say to you, Don't be afraid; I am here to help you ... I am the Lord, your Redeemer" (Isaiah 41:13–14 LB).

What name do you answer to? Incompetent, unlovable, outsider? How about stupid, jerk, or ugly? When asked why He was eating and drinking with crooks and sinners, Jesus said, "Who needs a doctor: the healthy or the sick? I'm here inviting outsiders not insiders—an invitation to a changed life, changed inside and out" (Luke 5:31–32).

If you have been mislabeled, God wants to change your name, also. He calls you beautiful, creative, intelligent, and youthful. Do you recognize Him when He calls you? He beckons you to His safe arms. "The Lord is close to the brokenhearted and saves those who are crushed in spirit" (Psalm 34:18 NIV). "Praise the Lord, O my soul and forget not all his benefits who forgives all your sins and heals all your diseases, who redeems your life from the pit and crowns you with love and compassion who satisfies your desires with good things so that your youth is renewed like the eagle's" (Psalms 103:2–5 NIV).

Are you willing to forget the name that hurt you? Jesus sacrificed His life to give you a new name, one that fits perfectly. Receive Jesus into your heart. He has a safe house where He will nurture you back to health. He's calling.

> Instead of unnamed, He calls you Beautiful.
> Instead of unwanted, He calls you Beloved.
> Instead of unqualified, He calls you Capable.

Receive a new name from your Savior.

Questions

1. Which do you believe is more desirable: a good name or riches? Why? (a)

2. A good name is symbolic of a good reputation. How do you earn a good name? (b)

3. You are special and God knows you by name. True or false? (c)

4. When Moses asked God what His name was, what did He say? What do you think His name means? (d)

5. Why did God change Abram's name? (e)

6. Why did God change Sarai's name? (f)

7. One day, if we overcome, will we all receive a new name? (g)

Scriptural Answers

(a) "A good name is more desirable than great riches; to be esteemed is better than silver or gold" (Proverb 22:1 NIV).

(b) "Let love and faithfulness never leave you; bind them around your neck, write them on the tablet of your heart. Then you will win favor and a good name in the sight of God and man" (Proverbs 3:3–4 NIV).

(c) "For I know you well and you are special to me. I know you by name" (Exodus 33:17).

(d) "But Moses protested, 'If I go to the people of Israel and tell them, "The God of your ancestors has sent me to you," they won't believe me. They will ask … "What is His name?" Then what should I tell them?' God replied, "I Am the One Who Always Is. Just tell them, 'I Am sent me to you'" (Exodus 3:13–14 NLT).

(e) "Nor shall your name any longer be Abram [high, exalted father]; but your name shall be Abraham [father of a multitude], for I have made you the father of many nations. And I will make you exceedingly fruitful and I will make nations of you, and kings will come from you" (Genesis 17:5–6 AB).

(f) "And God said to Abraham, As for Sarai your wife, you shall not call her name Sarai; but Sarah [Princess] her name shall be. And I will bless her and give you a son also by her. Yes, I will bless her, and she shall be a mother of nations; kings of peoples shall come from her" (Genesis 17:15–16 AB).

(g) "He who has an ear, let him hear what the Spirit says to the churches. To him who overcomes, I will give some of the hidden manna. I will also give him a white stone with a new name written on it, known only to him who receives it" (Revelation 2:17 NIV).

62

Have you ever refused a gift?

Jesus told us, "Freely you have received, freely give" (Matthew 10:8 NIV). I've experienced the joy of giving, but recently God let me experience the joy of receiving.

It began when my friend Rose told me about a business venture. She was so excited about her idea, but she lacked the funds to make it possible. When I prayed for God to somehow provide the money for her, He laid it on *my* heart to supply the money. I talked to my husband about it and he agreed with me that it was the right thing to do.

The amount was actually more than we had available to give. A few days before my offer, I had told her how our salary had just decreased by more than $700 a month; my husband's salary had decreased 10 percent and I had recently retired from my second job. God instructed me to not take anything from our savings; it should be a sacrifice. I wrote a check for half the amount, with a promise to God to give her the balance by the next month. We had no idea where the money was going to come from, but I have heard it said that if God puts it in your heart; He will put it in your hand. I had found that to be true in the past, so I had no doubt this time. I just didn't know *how* He was going to do it.

Within two weeks, my husband had to travel to Alabama to work at a job site. He was paid by the hour, and they were trying to meet a deadline, which would require a lot of overtime hours. In one week, even with the 10 percent pay cut, he had cleared more than double his salary. The balance was paid in full!

The next week, I found out that I was getting a bonus at work. All right! God, you sure didn't waste any time in *that* harvest! I started to plan where to spend our extra moolah: our property taxes, our vacation time with our grandkids. I consulted God. "God, what do *You* think?"

"Give it to Rose."

"*What*? You know that Rose tried to refuse the money before. Now you want us to humiliate ourselves by trying to give her *more*? Please God, don't ask us to do that!" God was not persuaded.

The next day I revealed our offer. It happened just like I thought it would. Rose refused adamantly. I knew what God had told me, but I couldn't put water in a sealed container. I wanted to cry, but I didn't in Rose's presence. I asked her to pray over the matter and see what God told her. I never felt that her pride was what prevented her from taking the gift. I thought she was afraid that it was too much of a sacrifice for us to make.

I went home and really cried. The next day didn't go so well, either. I came home after work and fussed at God. "Why are you doing this? Are you trying to ruin a friendship? I *knew* that Rose would refuse, and she *did*!"

Then I heard God speak to my heart: "I'm trying to teach Rose something." That was all He said.

"Well, that's good to know. But I hope she learns it quickly. I don't like dissention."

About an hour later the phone rang. "I would be glad to accept the money. But God told me to sow some seeds into your life. I'm giving you a pair of my diamond earrings and a Louis Vuitton purse."

I wanted to protest. The gifts were too fancy and expensive. But God stopped me. "How can you sow into other people, but refuse *their* seed-gift?" *I get it, God. I cannot expect to freely give if I cannot freely receive. Maybe the lesson wasn't just for her. It was for me, too.*

Amazingly, my husband's 10 percent pay cut was totally restored two weeks after we gave Rose her second monetary gift and received the earrings and the purse. Coincidence? I think not.

I remembered when Abraham's servant looked for a wife for Isaac in the city of Nahor. He prayed for a sign to confirm the right maiden. He met Rebekah, who offered to draw water for all ten of his camels, which was a hard, tedious chore. Seriously, can you imagine the magnitude of that task? Believe it or not, that *was* the sign he had asked for. He knew she was a woman who was not afraid of work and one who was compassionate. That part is not in the Bible, but it's my opinion. This sign cinched the deal. Ten camels heavily laden with jewels set in solid gold and silver, clothing, and valuable presents were what he offered Rebekah and her family (Genesis 24). How ridiculous would it have been if she had watered the camels, yet refused the gifts? Sometimes a refusal to accept a gift will close the door on a future blessing.

The Queen of Sheba traveled for miles to visit King Solomon. She brought four and a half tons of gold, sack after sack of spices, and precious stones to shower him with wealth. He in turn gave the Queen of Sheba all of her desires: treasures from his royal stash (1 Kings 10:10–13). She had brought some really nice and expensive gifts for King Solomon, but how ludicrous would it have been for her to refuse *his* gifts? He would have been insulted, and rightly so. I'm allowed to give to you, but you're not allowed to give to me? That wouldn't be right, now would it?

Recall the story of the woman who came to Jesus two days before he was crucified. She had an alabaster box filled with perfume which she poured over His head. He didn't say, "Woman, sell your perfume and give the money to the poor." However, that's what the guests at the table advised. In fact, Judas Iscariot left the room determined to betray Him after that insult. But Jesus welcomed the gift. It was worth a year's wages, but He chose to receive the gift (Mark 14:3–11).

I mow the yard of my neighbor to the left. It makes me happy to see the joy in Linnie's face as she looks at the freshly cut grass. John, my neighbor to the right of us, scatters seed all over our yard to give it that luscious look. It is beautiful! I smile as I watch the seeds sprout. I bless her, he blesses us.

If Jesus says, "Freely you received, freely give," then someone must be on the receiving end. The next time someone wants to bless you, take some advice from Rebekah, King Solomon, and Jesus. I know I'm not in the same category as them, but take some advice from me, too. Receive with joy. Let them *see* how happy they made you.

We are not to be like a sponge mop that is squeezed so hard that all the water is sucked out of it, but it never receives the refreshing, revitalizing fluid that keeps it vibrant.

You've been given a gift from God. Perhaps it's singing, painting, or writing, or perhaps it's playing a musical instrument or repairing cars. Maybe you have the gift of encouraging or listening to people. Have you accepted the gift, or have you refused His covering for your talent?

God once told me that I was a writer, but I didn't believe Him. The most I had ever written were letters to my children. How could God possibly perceive me as a writer? I would tell stories from my life and friends would encourage me to write them down. Was it a form of false flattery? I didn't know. Then one day, God said, "If you don't start writing, I'm going to give it to someone else." "It" was the gift. I received it on December 24, 2010, and I've been writing ever since. I looked at it as an early Christmas present.

God will give you the grace to complete your gifted assignment. You may say, "It's too late for me." I was fifty-five years old when I accepted my gift. Colonel Sanders was sixty-five when he started his chicken restaurant franchise. You may have heard of Kentucky Fried Chicken. Moses was eighty years old when God asked him to lead the Israelites out of Egypt.

You may think you are too young. But Joash was seven years old when he began to reign as the king of Judah (2 Chronicles 24:1). Josiah was eight years old when he became king of Jerusalem (2 Kings 22:1). Scholars say that Jeremiah was between the ages of thirteen and seventeen when God called him to be a prophet. Jeremiah argued with God, "O Lord God ... I can't do that! I'm far too young! I'm only a youth!" (Jeremiah 1:6 LB). Guess what God's reply was? "Don't say that ... for you will go wherever I send you and speak whatever I tell you to. And don't be afraid of the people, for I, the Lord, will be with you and see you through" (Jeremiah 1:7–8 LB).

You are *not* too young or too old. You are just right. God will see you through. Accept your gift. God wants to bless the world with your talent—if not the world, at least your corner of the world. He has a job for you to do. Repeat this Scripture until you believe it: "I can do all things through Him who strengthens me" (Philippians 4:13 NASB).

Don't refuse the gift.

Sheep Ears

Glorious Day[2]

God gave Jesus.
Accept,
Rejoice.

Brilliant light
Shouts
Enter.

The Gift

God relinquished Son.
I receive the sacrifice.
Blood bought, free at last.

Dazzling white, gold streets,
Rubies, sapphires, amethysts.
Don't refuse the gift.

---

2 After writing "Have you ever refused a gift?" God had a strange request of me: write a haiku poem about the story. I had no idea what a haiku was, so I looked up the information on the Internet. It seemed like a strange and foreign thing for me to do, however I was willing to give my best attempt. There were two types of haiku: modern and traditional. God never specified which kind to write, so I wrote two poems. They are my best attempt. I'm sure they are far from perfect. Maybe God is wanting to show someone that even if you feel that you are incapable of performing a task that God asks you to do, *if you are willing*, He will give you the power to complete his request.

Guide

Spring is coming soon,
God's words spring even faster,
Guide my hands to write.

Say, I think it's getting easier. Yay, God!

QUESTIONS

1. When you receive a gift from someone, how do you feel? (a)

2. Do you act thankful and bless them for the gift, or do you refuse it? (b)

3. God has given each one of us a special gift. True or false? (c)

4. What should we do with the gift God has given us? (d)

5. What happens to the person who is given a gift from God, yet is unfaithful with their gift? Write down your thoughts. (e)

6. Have you been faithful with the gift God gave you?

SCRIPTURAL ANSWERS

(a) "Receiving a gift is like getting a rare gemstone; any way you look at it, you see beauty refracted" (Proverb 17:8).

(b) "And now I have it all—and keep getting more. The gifts you sent ... were more than enough, like a sweet-smelling sacrifice roasting on the altar, filling the air with fragrance, pleasing God no end. You can be sure that God will take care of everything you need, his generosity exceeding even yours in the glory that pours from Jesus" (Philippians 4:18–19).

(c) "But that doesn't mean you should all look and speak and act the same. Out of the generosity of Christ, each is given his own gift" (Ephesians 4:7).

(d) "Each one should use whatever gift he has received to serve others, faithfully administering God's grace in its various forms" (1 Peter 4:10 NIV).

(e) "To those who use well what they are given, even more will be given, and they will have an abundance. But from those who are unfaithful, even what little they have will be taken away" (Matthew 25:29 NLT).

63
Have you ever robbed God?

I began tithing when I was a little girl. There was a girl's club at our church called Missionettes, and in order to earn a badge, we needed to have a record of our tithe. I received an allowance of one dollar a week. Therefore, I plunked ten cents into the offering plate. I did this every week for as long as I can remember. As my allowance increased, my tithe increased. I never questioned the principle; after all, they taught us that it was in the Bible.

When my husband and I got married, it was a no-brainer to tithe, so we joyfully gave. After all, you should always be a cheerful giver. "Each man should give what he has decided in his heart to give, not reluctantly or under compulsion, for God loves a cheerful giver" (2 Corinthians 9:7 NIV).

You can imagine my surprise when I read a book written by an author who took a different slant on tithing. Basically, she implied that you should be free to do with your tithe whatever you feel you should do. You could use your tithe to go on vacation to Hawaii since God wants you to rest. Or get your car fixed with the money, because after all, you do need the car to drive to church, don't you? Maybe taking your boss out to eat with the money would be acceptable. After all, praying before you eat is a testimony that you love God.

Those may not have been her exact words, but that was what I got out of it. It could be that I read into it what I wanted to believe. I thought, *Well, well, well, I guess I've been looking at this all wrong.* This gal must know what she's talking about since she wrote a book, right? So we jumped on board. We had a lot of fun for a while, but there was always a gnawing feeling that we were cheating God. That was the Holy Spirit pricking our consciences.

We practiced that theory, but it didn't last long.

Some time later, I had another bright idea: only pay once at the end of the month. It made perfect sense; we were still paying the tithes, but just using one check. I don't believe God liked that way either. "Honor the Lord by giving Him the first part of all your income, and He will fill your barns with wheat and barley and overflow your wine vats with the finest wines" (Proverbs 3:9–10 LB). I didn't have a barn or any wine vats, but I did have a bank account and a refrigerator and as far as I could tell, nothing was overflowing at our house. We concluded our experiment with last-part tithing when the car broke down, the kids got sick, and the washing machine overflowed.

What does God say about tithing? I'm glad you asked that. Listen to these Scriptures:

"I am God—yes, I Am. I haven't changed. And because I haven't changed, you, the descendants of Jacob haven't been destroyed. You have a long history of ignoring my commands. You haven't done a thing I've told you. Return to me so I can return to you," says God-of-the-Angel-Armies.

"You ask, 'But how do we return?'

"Begin by being honest. Do honest people rob God? But you rob me day after day."

"You ask, 'How have we robbed you?'

"The tithe and the offering—that's how! And now you're under a curse—the whole lot of you—because you're robbing me. Bring your full tithe to the Temple treasury so there will be ample provisions in my Temple. Test me in this and see if I don't open up heaven itself to you and pour out blessings beyond your wildest dreams. For my part, I will defend you against marauders, protect your wheat fields and vegetable gardens against plunderers." The Message of God-of-the-Angel-Armies.

"You'll be voted 'Happiest Nation.' You'll experience what it's like to be a country of grace." God of the Angel-Armies says so.

—Malachi 3:6–12

What a beautiful promise—but it is conditional. "Tithe" means 10 percent. "Offering" I interpret to mean gifts to people, or money above the 10 percent. "Test me"—I think you know what that means. "Pour out blessings and defend you" is the good part. And how about "voted 'Happiest Nation'"? I can't help but smile when I think of everyone in our nation tithing. Now that's an awesome thought!

That's as plain as it gets, folks. So my husband and I give our tithe to the church we attend. We give to missions, to people, and to other ministries as an offering above our tithe. And we also give every week from our "first part."

But now there's another matter. Should you tithe off the net or gross of your paycheck? That's another good question. Our pastor, Gary Bell, challenged everyone in the church to increase their giving, and if after a few months God did not prove Himself, the church would refund their money. I felt kind of smug as I sat in my pew, because I knew we had been faithful in our giving. But then I heard the small voice: "Why don't you tithe off your gross income instead of the net?" Gulp. "It might be a little harder for us, but that was definitely You speaking, God. Okay, I'll do it! After all, You did say bring your *full* tithe. I think that does mean to tithe on our gross income." That first week was a little hard, but after that, it was a breeze. And you know what? God has opened up heaven and He has poured out blessings beyond our wildest dreams.

Do you want lots and lots of blessings? Maybe you need to test God. He's given you permission. Do you have some wild dreams? He has ways to supersede anything you could imagine. But he's waiting on you.

Don't rob God.

Questions

1. Has anyone ever persuaded you to experiment with variations of tithing? How did it work out for you? Should we listen to God or man? (a)

2. Do you hoard your treasures here on earth or do you stockpile treasures in heaven? (b)

3. God just wants our money; he doesn't care about our motives. True or false? (c)

4. Can a Christian tithe perfectly, yet still be considered a hypocrite? (d)

5. We need money to get along in life, but why should we be free from the love of money? (e)

6. Write down a blessing you feel you got as a direct response to increased giving. Is this Biblical? (f)

7. How would you handle tithing if your spouse did not agree with it?

8. Is it a good idea to listen to teachings that contradict what you know is right? (g)

Scriptural Answers

(a) "Peter and the other apostles replied: 'We must obey God rather than men!'" (Acts 5:29 NIV).

(b) "Don't hoard treasure down here where it gets eaten by moths and corroded by rust or—worse!—stolen by burglars. Stockpile treasure in heaven, where it's safe from moth and rust and burglars. It's obvious, isn't it? The place where your treasure is, is the place you will most want to be and end up being" (Matthew 6:19–21).

(c) "We justify our actions by appearances; God examines our motives" (Proverb 21:2).

(d) "Yes, woe upon you, Pharisees, and you other religious leaders—hypocrites! For you tithe down to the last mint leaf in your garden, but ignore the important things—justice and mercy and faith. Yes, you should tithe, but you shouldn't leave the more important things undone" (Matthew 23:23 LB).

(e) "Keep your lives free from the love of money and be content with what you have, because God said, 'Never will I leave you; never will I forsake you'" (Hebrews 13:5).

(f) "The one who blesses others is abundantly blessed; those who help others are helped" (Proverb 11:25).

(g) "Stop listening to teaching that contradicts what you know is right" (Proverb 19:27 LB).

64
Have you ever said "never"?

While growing up, I periodically heard the phrases "never say never" and "never criticize someone because it could happen to you." In the Bible we read, "Do not judge, or you too will be judged" (Matthew 7:1 NIV). I was caught off guard recently when I was confronted by the Holy Spirit. I was guilty.

I was watching a show that reenacted a scene from the Bible: soldiers were mocking and berating Jesus Christ before His death. "So you call yourself King of the Jews! Liar!! How dare you say you're the Son of God! This is anarchy!" As I watched the television, I thought to myself, *I would never mock anyone.* Immediately the Holy Spirit reminded me of a scene in my life when I was in junior high.

There was a girl named Debra Kay who was a habitual liar. She attended the youth group in our church and was attending a mini-camp with us. We caught her in several lies on the bus trip, but there was one whopper of a lie that really got me. She said she had eaten chocolate-covered ants when she went to New York. *Well, this is the last straw! Who ever heard of such a thing?*

I made up my mind that I was going to call her bluff on her ridiculous lies once and for all. I plotted with some other girls to get a chocolate candy bar, melt it, and mold it into little balls around some dead ants. We were going to make her prove that she lied, because we *knew* she wouldn't eat them. A counselor heard about what was going on, stopped the confrontation, and made us apologize to the tearful Debra Kay. Oh, we apologized with our mouths, but in my case at least, I didn't mean it. I wanted her lying to *stop.*

After that incident, I don't remember seeing Debra Kay at our youth group very often. I thought, *Good riddance,* in my self-righteous, preteen mind. Some time later, I heard someone else talking about something they had eaten that was unusual: *chocolate covered ants.* Oh, no! Was there really such a thing? I had thought it was a lie. I wanted to apologize to Debra Kay, but I couldn't find her. So I let it go, until God reminded me of it. I said I would never mock anyone, but I had already done so. My hideous actions could have steered her away from God.

When we repent, God does not remember our sins anymore. However, God remembered *that* incident just like it was yesterday because I hadn't confessed my sin to God. I cried as He flashed the scene in my mind. Psalm 32:6 says, "Now I say that each believer should confess his sins to God when he is aware of them, while there is time to be forgiven. Judgment will not touch him if he does" (LB). I asked God to forgive my sin and to work in Debra Kay's heart to woo her to heaven, not because of my actions, but in spite of them. I was a stumbling block to her. I learned that the hard way. Paul said, "We try to live in such a way that no one will be hindered from finding the Lord by the way we act, and so no one can find fault with our ministry" (2 Corinthians 6:3 NLT).

When I was nineteen years old, my husband and I married. My youngest brother, Tony, was four, and my sister, Michelle, was eighteen months old. I gave a lot of good advice (in my opinion) to my parents as I watched them make what I thought were mistakes raising my siblings. *I would never do that with my kids,* I thought. My mom would just smile a strange smile when I gave her such jewels, and I didn't understand what they implied until I started having children of my own. Now I get it. You can read all the books you want on child rearing, but there's nothing like a dose of real-life medicine.

Phooey on all my great wisdom. I'm sorry I judged my parents. It wasn't as easy as I thought.

If you're reading this and are thinking, *That doesn't relate to me,* let me ask you these questions:

- Have you ever criticized a woman who took her husband back after an infidelity?
- Have you ever looked at someone with a disability or an illness and thought, *Quit being a crybaby, it's not that bad?*

- Have you ever thought of a friend whose child was in jail, *You didn't do a good job raising him?*

Again, I say phooey. We have no idea how we will act if tragedy hits us. Peter told Jesus that he would *never* forsake him, yet he denied Christ three times before the cock crowed. Paul held the coats of the men who stoned Stephen as he became the first Christian martyr. Yet after they repented, Peter preached and brought multitudes to Christ, and Paul wrote thirteen books of the New Testament.

I'm confident that God has now forgiven me since I repented. My slate is clean. Pride caused me to judge Debra Kay. It caused me to judge my parents. It affected Peter and Paul. It affects everyone. "If anyone respects and fears God, he will hate evil. For wisdom hates pride, arrogance, corruption, and deceit of every kind" (Proverb 8:13 LB).

Let's be wise. Get out of the judgment seat, and let God be the judge of those around you. Repent when you need to. Ask God to bring to your memory any unresolved issues. I wouldn't want to be anyone's stumbling block, and I know you wouldn't, either.

QUESTIONS

1. Have you ever mocked anyone? Did you later regret your actions?

2. Instead of criticizing and being catty to others, how should a Christian act? (a)

3. Our wrong attitudes and actions could hurt our witness and actually turn others away from God. True or false? (b)

4. What does the Bible warn may happen to us if we think, *I would never act like that?* (c)

5. If you know someone who has given another person grief, should you exclude them from your life permanently, or should you forgive and comfort them once they realize and repent of their error? Explain. (d)

6. If you have been mocked or criticized, how should you respond? (e)

7. How did Jesus respond to the men who crucified him? (f)

Scriptural Answers

(a) "For, dear brothers, you have been given freedom: not freedom to do wrong, but freedom to love and serve each other. For the whole Law can be summed up in this one command: 'Love others as you love yourself.' But if instead of showing love among yourselves you are always being critical and catty, watch out! Beware of ruining each other" (Galatians 5:13–15 LB).

(b) "Try to stay out of all quarrels and seek to live a clean and holy life, for one who is not holy will not see the Lord ... Watch out that no bitterness takes root among you, for as it springs up it causes deep trouble, hurting many in their spiritual lives" (Hebrews 12:14–15 LB).

(c) "So be careful. If you are thinking, "Oh, I would never behave like that"—let this be a warning to you. For you too may fall into sin" (1 Corinthians 10:12 LB).

(d) "I don't want to be harder on him than I should. He has been punished enough by your united disapproval. Now it is time to forgive him and comfort him. Otherwise, he may become so bitter and discouraged that he won't be able to recover. Please show him now that you still do love him very much" (2 Corinthians 2:6–8 LB).

(e) "But I tell you: Love your enemies and pray for those who persecute you" (Matthew 5:44 NIV).

(f) "Jesus prayed, Father, forgive them, for they know not what they do" (Luke 23:34 AB).

65

Have you ever said, "Okay God, talk to me"?

One Sunday I woke up with a plan. I told God that this was going to be His day to speak to me. So I did everything I could think of to give Him an open door: I went to church with pen in hand, ready to write words of wisdom, I read my Bible all afternoon, I didn't turn on the television, I meditated and prayed.

Nothing.

It was as if I had settled in my recliner, popcorn in hand, ready to watch a good movie, but the television wouldn't work. Actually, the television worked fine, it just wasn't connected to the power source.

It was a very frustrating day, because I had really expected to hear from God. "Where are You? Don't You know I'm trying to write a book about hearing from God? Are You messing with me?" Very disappointed, I went to bed. I thought, *Well, maybe I'll have an enlightening dream. After all, He does speak through dreams.*

I woke up the next morning and to my dismay, I recalled no dreams. However, my remote had fallen off the bed, and as I reached down to get it, my eyes landed on some old copies of *National Geographic*. I wasn't sure why I picked them up (they were about five years old), but after looking at them, I got an idea for a door I was supposed to decorate at school. I had been mulling over different ideas in my head for about five days and coming up blank. Within fifteen minutes, I had the sketch for the whole design. I gathered all the supplies I needed: scissors, markers, magazines, shipping tape. I lacked only an Exacto knife to cut the pictures out of the magazines. Scissors would not have worked for the job I had in mind.

At the office, my principal, Ms. Hatley, asked me and Mrs. Morris, another paraprofessional, if we would get the parenting center into presentable shape during second period. The people from the State were coming to inspect our school. *Oh well, my project can wait.*

As I went to my first period assignment, Mrs. Taylor and I were talking and she pointed out how she had put contact paper on her counter. As I admired it, I said, "How did you get the lines so perfect?"

She nonchalantly replied, "Oh, with an Exacto knife."

My ears perked up when she said that. "Would you mind if I borrowed it?" Amazed at how God had so easily provided what I needed, I shared my story with her. She had worked at the school for two years, yet had only decided to apply contact paper the day before I would need an Exacto knife. Unusual.

When Mrs. Morris and I went to the parenting room, we found it in disarray, with wallpaper coming off the walls and boxes of junk everywhere. My eyes kept being drawn to the falling wallpaper. What could be done? It was an eyesore. Suddenly it dawned on me: the shipping tape! I had worked in the school system for sixteen years and this was the first day that I had brought shipping tape—and the first day I had needed it! We taped the wallpaper to the wall and it looked fantastic.

Wait a minute ... I was seeing a pattern: the falling remote, the magazines, the idea for the door, the Exacto knife, the tape. It was only 9:30 a.m. and my cup was running over. The whole day went like that. It was like those pop-ups on your computer that surprise you out of nowhere. Except these weren't annoying; they were little gifts from God. God knows what you need before you even ask. I could imagine God smiling as the day unfolded, a twinkle in His eye, hoping I would get the message.

At the end of the day, I heard God speak to me in that still, small voice. He wasn't mad; He was teaching me. I'm the type of person who learns better when you show me instead of just telling me. He said, "I'm not like your beloved dog Mollie. You command her to sit, shake, high five, lie down, crawl. I'm not like that. You don't tell Me when to speak, give Me directions, or demand My attention." That was all He said, but I got the point.

"I will instruct you and teach you in the way you should go; I will counsel you and watch over you. Do not be like the horse or mule, which have no understanding, but must be controlled by bit and bridle or they will not come to you" (Psalms 32:8–9 NIV).

No, I don't want to be led like a horse with a bit. That hurts. I'd rather be like a horse that is neck-rein trained: you feel a gentle touch and you obey. If you listen closely, you will hear and see that God speaks to you all day. Maybe you've never realized it. Pay attention. I believe He's saying more than you thought.

Questions

1. Have you ever approached God with the wrong attitude? How did that work out for you? Is your attitude important? (a)

2. Is God only concerned about our big issues? Explain your answer. (b)

3. When we approach God in prayer, how should we act? (c)

4. Does God get angry with us if we're not perfect? Should we find comfort in the fact that God is happy when we try to do the right thing (even if it comes out wrong)? (d)

5. Does God want us to ask him about things that concern us? (e)

6. Have you ever had an answer to your need before you even prayed about it? How is this possible? (f)

7. After you pay attention to God's voice, what should you do? (g)

8. Has God said anything to you today? If He has spoken to you, how did He speak?

Scriptural Answers

(a) "Now change your mind and attitude to God and turn to him so he can cleanse away your sins and send you wonderful times of refreshment from the presence of the Lord" (Acts 3:19 LB).

(b) "Let him have all your worries and cares, for he is always thinking about you and watching everything that concerns you" (1 Peter 5:7 LB).

(c) "Be still before the Lord and wait patiently for him" (Psalm 37:7 NIV).

(d) "Many sorrows come to the wicked, but abiding love surrounds those who trust in the Lord. So rejoice in him, all those who are his, and shout for joy, all those who try to obey him" (Psalms 32:10–11 LB).

(e) "This is God's Message, the God who made earth ... 'Call to me and I will answer you. I'll tell you marvelous and wondrous things that you could never figure out on your own'" (Jeremiah 33:2–3).

(f) "Remember, your Father knows exactly what you need even before you ask him!" (Matthew 6:8 LB).

(g) "First pay attention to me, and then relax. Now you can take it easy—you're in good hands" (Proverb 1:33).

66

Have you ever sat under an overpass?

On a trip to watch my son Paul play baseball at Baylor University, I noticed a shabby woman under an overpass. She had a baby stroller and I wondered if the poor child needed food and milk. I thought it would be a great idea to go to McDonald's and buy them a meal.

While standing in line, I felt God urge me to buy myself a meal to eat with them on the slanting cement slab. I gave a mental gulp and agreed to do what He asked of me. Now this wasn't a secluded area, but on South University Parks Drive, which was the street the ballpark was on. I fleetingly wondered if my son would be embarrassed if he saw me with my dining partner at our roadside cafe. I wondered if the ballplayers' parents would think I was a nutcase. But my love for God and His instructions won out.

I purchased the two largest meals McDonald's had to offer with a large bottle of milk for the baby and headed back to the underside of the overpass. I was relieved to find that she was still there. I parked my car off the shoulder of the road and proceeded up the slow ascent. With each step I took, God spoke to me. "What good is it to just offer this lady a meal? What she needs is companionship. Don't do all the talking. She needs to feel like someone cares about her. Take your time and be a friend."

I got a little teary eyed as I got closer. However, I was quite surprised to find out that the "baby" was actually a dog. I felt betrayed for a second, but dismissed my personal thoughts and focused on God's mission. She was very receptive to the meal and the fellowship. We talked for about thirty minutes and had a grand time. I got a smudge on my pants that never came out. I always smile when I see it because it reminds me of the day God asked me to sit under the overpass.

Was God's request outrageous? No. I can recall Jesus going to eat with a contemptible tax collector named Zacchaeus. He also asked a Samaritan woman for a drink of water. "The Samaritan woman, taken aback, asked, "How come you, a Jew are asking me, a Samaritan woman, for a drink? (Jews in those days wouldn't be caught dead talking to Samaritans.)" (John 4:9). Jesus modeled the Father's heart.

Jesus told his followers what to expect when we get to heaven. He said,

> Then the King will say to those on his right, "Enter, you who are blessed by my Father! Take what's coming to you in this kingdom. It's been ready for you since the world's foundation. And here's why:
> I was hungry and you fed me,
> I was thirsty and you gave me a drink,
> I was homeless and you gave me a room,
> I was shivering and you gave me clothes,
> I was sick and you stopped to visit,
> I was in prison and you came to me."
> Then those "sheep" are going to say, "Master, what are you talking about? When did we ever see you hungry and feed you, thirsty and give you a drink? And when did we ever see you sick or in prison and come to you?" Then the King will say, "I'm telling the solemn truth: Whenever you did one of these things to someone overlooked or ignored, that was me—you did it to me."
> —Matthew 25:34–40

That last sentence is hard to ignore. "Whenever you did one of these things to someone overlooked or ignored, that was me—you did it to me." I finally got it. God was not asking me to fellowship with that shabby ignored lady that day. He was asking me to fellowship with Him, the Loving Father who cares for everyone, wherever they are and whoever they are.

"Live in harmony with one another. Do not be proud, but be willing to associate with people of low position. Do not be conceited" (Romans 12:16 NIV).

I keep in mind that if it weren't for the grace of God, it could be me under the overpass. If God asks you to feed the hungry, visit the sick, or come to the prisoner, don't be miffed. He's really inviting you to an audience with the King.

Questions

1. Your care for others is the measure of your greatness. True or false? (a)

2. Do you believe God is pleased when we share what we have with the needy? Why or why not? (b)

3. Write down some times you have helped the less fortunate. Did you feel that God was pleased with you?

4. Why should we not walk away from someone who deserves help? (c)

5. Is there a difference between a person in need and a lazy Christian? Write your thoughts.

6. How should we treat a lazy Christian? (d)

7. Should we treat a lazy Christian like they are an enemy? (e)

Scriptural Answers

(a) "Now came an argument among them as to which of them would be greatest ... But Jesus knew their thoughts, so he stood a little child beside him and said to them, 'Anyone who takes care of a little child like this is caring for me! And whoever cares for me is caring for God who sent me. Your care for others is the measure of your greatness'" (Luke 9:46–48 LB).

(b) "Don't forget to do good and to share what you have with those in need, for such sacrifices are very pleasing to him" (Hebrews 13:16 LB).

(c) "Never walk away from someone who deserves help; your hand is God's hand for that person" (Proverb 3:27).

(d) "Stay away from any Christian who spends his days in laziness and does not follow the ideal work we set up for you ... It wasn't that we didn't have the right to ask you to feed us, but we wanted to show you, firsthand, how you should work for your living. Even while we were still there with you we gave you this rule: 'He who does not work shall not eat'" (2 Thessalonians 3:6, 9–10 LB).

(e) "If anyone refuses to do what we say ... notice who he is and stay away from him, that he may be ashamed of himself. Don't think of him as an enemy, but speak to him as you would to a brother who needs to be warned" (2 Thessalonians 3:14–15 LB).

67
Have you ever seasoned with salt?

Have you ever noticed that salt is one of the smallest ingredients in a recipe or on a label? You would think that means that it is insignificant or unimportant, but you would be wrong. Try leaving it out of a recipe and you'll wonder why the food doesn't taste as good as it normally does. Paul wrote, "Let your conversation be always full of grace, seasoned with salt, so that you may know how to answer everyone" (Colossians 4:6 NIV). But what does that mean? I didn't understand that passage until I read it in *The Message*: "Be gracious in your speech. The goal is to bring out the best in others in a conversation, not put them down, not cut them out."

Going by that description, I would say that my mom is the saltiest person I know. I have only heard positive words come out of her mouth. I can't ever remember her raising her voice in anger. My dad was normally the disciplinarian at home, but there was one time that she attempted to spank my brother and me. I felt so sorry for her feeble attempt that I wet my fingers, made fake tears run down my face, and feigned a weak cry.

My dad was a pastor; my mother was a pastor's wife. She would play the piano in most of the services, but was very low-key and never sought attention. If you've never been a pastor's wife, you may not relate to this next statement: It's a lonely life. Being a P.K. (Preacher's Kid), I can verify that. If a pastor's wife has a friend in the church, then criticizing eyes tear her apart. If she has a friend outside the church, well, let's just say that's even worse.

Her husband and children were generally her only network of friends. I didn't discover the full extent of this until I was married with children of my own. They confided in me about some of the cruel, vicious things that were being said to and about them. It really opened my eyes to how hypocritical some "saints" really were. It tore me up so badly that I actually prayed for my parents to move because it was more than I could bear. But through all the grief, my mom never said negative things about *them*. She bore her sorrow without malice, and when she saw these people in church, she was as nice as ever. I could tell that she wasn't faking it. She didn't say, "Now look at me, Sherry. This is how you model Christ." She just lived the life. I guess that's why it's so easy for me to forgive people who treat me wrongly. I had a good model. Not someone who stood on a soap box and shouted her own virtues, but a strong woman who was meek. They say that actions speak louder than words; it's true.

Let's get back to salt. Are you "seasoned with salt"? Are you gracious in your speech? Do you bring out the best in others? Or do you put people down and cut them out of your life if they dare to say anything negative about you? Maybe you're missing the significant ingredient in your life. It will leave you wondering what is lacking. Jesus tells us to forgive, but how are you flavoring your speech and actions?

Paul instructed the Colossians,

> So chosen by God for this new life of love, dress in the wardrobe God picked out for you: compassion, kindness, humility, quiet strength, discipline. Be even-tempered, content with second place, quick to forgive an offense. Forgive as quickly and completely as the Master forgave you. And regardless of what else you put on, wear love. It's your basic, all-purpose garment. Never be without it.
>
> —Colossians 3:12–14

That describes my mother, Betty Phillips, perfectly. I've told her privately, but I'd like to tell her so the world will know: "Mom, you're my hero. You have flavored my life with an ingredient, however small it seems, that makes me who I am today. I'm a better mother, wife, and friend because not only did I *hear* your godly speech, I also *saw* your godly actions. I love you and I strive to be just like you, as you strive to be just like Christ."

Someone is watching. Are you a good model, or an example of how *not* to act? Will the seeds that you've sown come back to haunt you or will they rise up to bless you? Time will tell. Please make good choices.

Questions

1. Have you ever noticed people in the church who say they are Christians, yet cause strife? Does this bother you? (a)

2. How do you think God feels about "religious smooth talk"? Should we make a vain talker our good friend and convince them to change? Why or why not? (b)

3. We should never forgive the people who gossip about us. It's okay to talk harshly to them. True or false? (c)

4. Should we pray for God to punish those who criticize us? How did God tell Job to handle this problem? (d)

5. If you truly forgive someone, are you able to love them without faking it? Write down your feelings. (e)

6. Do you believe we have a responsibility to show others the Christian way by our actions? Why?

7. Why is it important to forgive those who hurt us? (f)

Scriptural Answers

(a) "For I have told you often before, and I say it again now with tears in my eyes, there are so many who walk along the Christian road who are really enemies of the cross of Christ" (Philippians 3:18 LB).

(b) "Don't let yourself get taken in by religious smooth talk. God gets furious with people who are full of religious sales talk but want nothing to do with him. Don't even hang around people like that" (Ephesians 5:6–7).

(c) "Be gentle with one another, sensitive. Forgive one another as quickly and thoroughly as God in Christ forgave you" (Ephesians 4:32).

(d) "My friend Job will pray for you, and I will accept his prayer. He will ask me not to treat you as you deserve for talking nonsense about me, and for not being honest with me, as he has" (Job 42:8).

(e) "Love from the center of who you are; don't fake it ... Be good friends who love deeply; practice playing second fiddle" (Romans 12:9–10).

(f) "We try to live in such a way that no one will ever be offended or kept back from finding the Lord by the way we act, so that no one can find fault with us and blame it on the Lord. In fact, in everything we do we try to show that we are true ministers of God" (2 Corinthians 6:3–4 LB).

68

Have you ever sent your last child to college?

In the fall of 2001, my youngest son left the country for college. Actually, his school was six and a half hours away in the state of Texas, but it might as well have been in another country because that's the way it felt.

I was recently talking to a friend who was tearfully preparing for her last child to leave the nest. It brought back a flood of memories of days long ago. One of my favorite times for meaningful conversations with the boys was while we were driving. My sons and I bonded during those times. We recanted the day's trivial and monumental occurrences: he said this, you won't believe what Ms. Raines did, my best friend made fun of me today. I would be a sympathetic ear while they ranted, and a shoulder to cry on when things became unbearable. These were the times that I would guide them toward God and share my experiences, not in a preachy tone, but in an I-know-how-you-feel voice.

I remember crying hard when my last son, Paul, got his driver's license. He was elated, but I was deflated. It had suddenly hit me: no more trivial yet deep conversations on our car jaunts.

Nowadays, I see parents talking in cars and in stores on their cell phones, and I cringe as I watch their children sitting or standing silently by while they rant and talk mindlessly on the phone. I wonder if they realize they are missing that valuable training time with their kids? I feel like saying, "Please hang up your phone and talk to your children. You only get a precious few years, and then they're gone." The Bible says, "Teach … your children. Talk … when you are sitting at home, when you are out walking, at bedtime, and before breakfast!" (Deuteronomy 11:19 LB).

During my youngest son's senior year in high school, I quit my second job. We really needed the money, but memories with Paul were more important to me than the material things that we could buy. I thought, *My husband's shoes should last another year, and I can recycle and mix and match my wardrobe.* I wanted a little more time to cram more life knowledge into his heart.

I wanted to keep a tight watch over my sons when they left, but I knew that wouldn't be possible. As each son prepared to leave, we gave them more and more freedom at home. Not total freedom, but inch-by-inch; it was a testing of the waters. Sure, they were going to mess up, but who doesn't? I preferred to guide them through their good and bad choices when they were at home than to set them free all of a sudden and watch them make irrevocable decisions that could alter their lives. I've seen that happen to other kids and it's not a pretty sight.

Who's perfect in this life, anyway? We should model forgiveness the way Jesus did, and give a little leeway for imperfection. God is still molding them. Let's guide, not crush them.

A friend gave me a great book by Beth Moore, *Feathers in My Nest*, which really comforted me. It's a must-read for any mother going through child withdrawal. In fact, I've let quite a few grieving mothers borrow mine, and they all said it helped. You might want to have a large box of tissues ready when you read it, though.

Speaking of tissues, that's what I needed as each of my sons left our little nest. A little piece of my heart was ripped from my body as they each drove off to the world. Now I can say that it's okay, but at the time, it felt like I'd need open heart surgery to stop the bleeding.

After Paul left, I would leave my job at 3:00 p.m., get into bed at 3:30 p.m., and stay there until the next day. I guess you could say I was mourning. After about two weeks, I received a call. The place that I had worked before Paul's senior year had an opening, and they wanted to know if I would consider coming back to work. I was screaming, "Hallelujah! Thank you, Jesus!" in my mind as I calmly took the call. I told them I would think about it. I hung up and did a happy dance.

After a few minutes, when my emotions had settled down, I called them back and told them I would take the job. I climbed out of my deep hole of emptiness by working the front desk at Seabrook Family Christian Center, mingling with parents and their children, and sharing insights and stories of my own experiences which seemed to encourage the new generation.

I read in the Bible about Hannah and her desperate plea to have a child. "She made this vow: 'O Lord of heaven, if you will look down upon my sorrow and answer my prayer and give me a son, then I will give him back to you, and he'll be yours for his entire lifetime'" (1 Samuel 1:11 LB). So when our sons left, and my mind tormented me with thoughts of how many temptations they would face in this cruel world, I would remember Hannah's words, "I will give him back to you," and know that I had done my best. Now God had them in *His* hands.

There's a saying that I like: Give them roots to grow, and wings to fly. The roots are given over their lifetime at home, but I found that giving them their wings tends to hurt. I'll give you an example: Randy and I drove the six-and-a-half hour trip to see Paul in Waco. It was our first visit of his freshman year and we could hardly wait. He greeted us with a chilly hug, then said, "I hope you don't mind, but some of the guys and I are going to watch a high school football team play tonight. It's thirty minutes away, and we're leaving in ten minutes."

It was hard to swallow for a second. My mouth went completely dry. Then I managed to utter, "Okay."

He shot back, "What's wrong?"

"I don't know, we drove a long way to see you, and Dad and I thought we could go out to eat and visit with you." I wanted to give a lecture, but I knew this was part of the growing process. "That's okay, we're fine. Go have fun with your friends."

I wanted to cry. It hurt. But instead of crying, Randy and I went to a movie. Like I said, giving them their wings hurts a little.

About three years later, we called him to say we were twenty minutes away. We were coming to watch him play a baseball game, and we wanted to swing by to see the new apartment that he was sharing with four other baseball players. "Please Mom, *do not* come here!"

"Why?"

"You'll embarrass me! You'll give all the guys a hard time! You'll start lecturing them!" I won't go into details but I believe you can fill in the blanks.

We never would have made a scene, but I guess he felt that we wouldn't think the apartment was the best environment. I said, "Paul, I promise I'll behave. So will Dad." It took a few more minutes to convince him, but we finally got permission to visit his pad.

We walked in with big grins on our faces. We hugged everyone and did our best to ignore the cardboard boxes stapled to the walls. We took pictures of the guys as we took a short tour of the apartment. They were playing a game with quarters and I asked if I could play. "Sure, Mrs. Witt," they said. I actually won, but I gave my prize to one eager roommate. We only stayed about ten minutes, but that was plenty. Paul escorted us to the door. He silently mouthed the words, "Thanks, Mom," then we left. He called us later and said, "Y'all were great. You can come back any time you want."

There were a lot of things that I didn't like, but I've learned to not voice my opinion about everything. Teaching is meant for their time at home. After your kids leave, silence is appreciated more than anything. I had God's promise that if I trained my children properly when they were young, then when they were old, they would not depart from it (Proverbs 22:6.) Nothing was said about the in-between years, so I'm guessing that there has to be a time of finding yourself and growing your own wings.

I also have a bit of advice: text your sons if you want a reply. It's an accepted tradition for moms and daughters to talk on the phone, but it embarrasses the guys. "Is that your mommy calling?" their friends jeer. If you text, no one knows who it is, and your son can maintain his coolness.

My husband and I got reacquainted with each other and learned that it was kind of nice to have each other all to ourselves again. It's been over ten years since Paul left. He still lives in Waco, where he went to college. He recently asked Randy and me if we had ever thought about moving to Waco to be closer to him. I quickly replied, "Nope," and I actually think he was disappointed. He asked me why and I told him we loved our town, our church, our jobs, our neighborhood, and our friends. We are happy.

So I have great news for all of you parents out there: you will be okay! It may take some time for you to heal. If you raised your children in the fear and admonition of God while they were at home, give them back to God as they leave your safe house. You've given them their roots; now give them permission to fly!

Questions

1. Do you feel that you may have missed opportunities to talk with your kids because you were busy talking with others?

2. Have you ever faced a situation that left you so upset that your health suffered? Describe your emotions. Do you think others feel the same way during their grief? (a)

3. Does God listen to the prayers of the destitute? (b)

4. What is a safe house for your children? What is a safe house for a child of God? Are they similar? (c)

5. What promise do we have that if we train our children correctly, they will not turn from those teachings when they are older? (d)

6. It's hard to let your children leave the nest, but is it healthy for them to stay under your roof for their entire lives? Write down your thoughts.

7. How do you think God felt when He sent His son to earth, knowing the suffering He would go through?

Scriptural Answers

(a) "Lord, hear my prayer! Listen to my plea! Don't turn away from me in this time of my distress. Bend down your ear and give me speedy answers, for my days disappear like smoke. My health is broken and my heart is sick; it is trampled like grass and is withered. My food is tasteless, and I have lost my appetite. I am reduced to skin and bones because of all my groaning and despair ... I lie awake lonely as a solitary sparrow on the roof" (Psalms 102:1–5, 7 LB).

(b) "He will listen to the prayers of the destitute for he is never too busy to heed their requests" (Psalm 102:17 LB).

(c) "You've always given me breathing room, a place to get away from it all, a lifetime pass to your safe-house, an open invitation as your guest. You've always taken me seriously, God, made me welcome among those who know and love you" (Psalms 61:3–5).

(d) "Train a child in the way he should go, and when he is old he will not turn from it" (Proverb 22:6 NIV).

69

Have you ever served two masters?

One day, I was about to walk my dog Mollie when Linnie called me over to her front yard. As Mollie and I approached Linnie, Mollie ran to her and fell on her feet. I was okay with that, but Mollie kept breaking free of her stance by me, then running to Linnie and leaning on her body. I didn't mind Mollie being friendly, I just wanted her to obey me.

At first it didn't bother me too much, but as Linnie and I talked, Mollie kept pulling to go to Linnie. She laughed and insisted that it was okay, but I was not laughing. I told her that I did not allow my dogs to jump on or lie on other people, but Linnie kept insisting that it was fine. I quickly ended our conversation when I saw that my wishes were not honored.

As I walked away with Mollie, I kept thinking about what had just transpired. I was not a happy camper. I battled in my mind whether I was right to feel this way. *Should I make a big deal about it or not? After all, Mollie really is loveable. Linnie didn't mean any harm.* But why was it bothering me so much? I asked God what He thought and a snippet of a Scripture came to my mind. "You shall not serve two masters." I didn't remember the whole verse, but I remembered enough to make my decision.

My next thought was whether or not I should directly approach Linnie or just back away from visiting her when Mollie was with me. God brought to my memory a Scripture that I had just read: "An open, face-to-face meeting results in peace" (Proverb 10:10).

I walked a few minutes longer while I waited for my emotions to subside. I knew that I needed to come to Linnie meekly and not fly off the handle. I put Mollie in the backyard and went next door. I realized that the problem was with Mollie, not Linnie. Mollie was confused about who her master was.

As I approached Linnie's house, I prayed for God to help me say things the right way. She came to the door and said, "Hi, hon."

I cordially greeted her. Then I said, "Linnie, we need to talk. I know that you love Mollie, but she cannot serve two masters." Linnie was confused because she had no idea what had been rolling around in my mind, so I invited her to sit down.

I said, "Linnie, how would you like it if Joe-Joe (her German Shepherd) always ran to me and wouldn't obey you anymore?"

"Well, I guess I wouldn't like it."

"That's what I mean. Mollie shouldn't obey you and disregard my commands. She only needs one master."

Linnie agreed with me and we talked leisurely for about an hour. She has since honored my request and we get along fabulously. Mollie still loves Linnie and Joe-Joe still loves me, but they each know and obey their master.

At the same time that I was talking to Linnie, I was also listening to the Holy Spirit making the comparison to people. As I mulled it over, I thought of a people example instead of a dog example.

What if Mr. and Mrs. Master went to a restaurant, and as the waiter came to take their order, Mrs. Master saw a friend and went to visit them at their table. Mr. Master ordered two T-bone steaks and two baked potatoes. Then, Mrs. Master came back to the table and when her husband went to the restroom, she flagged down the waiter and ordered two plates of spaghetti with two salads, ranch dressing on the side.

The waiter, baffled, said, "Ma'am, I'm confused. Do you want me to serve both Masters?"

Naturally, Mrs. Master would say no and clear up the matter. One choice would be made and the meal would be served. That's a very simple scene, but it makes a point.

What exactly does the Bible say? Jesus states, "No servant can serve two masters. Either he will hate the one and love the other, or he will be devoted to the one and despise the other. You cannot serve both God and Money" (Luke 16:13 NIV).

Jesus was talking to the Pharisees, who loved money. But this principle will apply to anything that will separate our love from God. It could be your job, your family, your boat. It could even be your children or your spouse. Whatever you love more than God is your master, causing a divided heart.

Satan will start out slyly at the onset. It could be a promotion on your job. The promotion would mean more money but less family time, then no time for your Bible reading. Next you would be so tired that you didn't feel like going to church. Before you knew it, you would be consumed. God would be a distant thought, a faraway master who no longer quickened your heart. It's hard to obey his voice if you've let Satan feed you his lies and shower you with praise. If that happened, God would be in a corner of your heart, but not loved or spoken to, for the things of this world would have taken over.

You own your heart; you need to knock on its figurative door and say, "We need to talk. Two masters cannot be served. I choose God." If the problem is addressed, it can be resolved. The confusion will leave and everything will become clearer. You can sit down once more and fellowship with the God with whom you fell in love. He desires your undivided heart.

A dog can't serve two masters, a servant can't serve two masters, and we can't serve both God and Satan.

I like Joshua, who made this bold statement: "Serve the Lord alone. But if you are unwilling to serve the Lord, then choose today whom you will serve … But as for me and my family, we will serve the Lord" (Joshua 24:14–15 NLT). Good choice.

Questions

1. What do you do when you have a problem that you don't know how to handle? (a)

2. When we have issues, we need to pray for two things: wisdom and common sense. True or false? (b)

3. How are we to handle problems with fellow believers? (c)

4. How are we to handle ourselves around unsaved neighbors? (d)

5. Have you ever read the riot act to someone, then later realized you were totally wrong?

6. Once you are saved, does sin have to be your master? (e)

7. Do you think other Christians have had this problem, too? Who can set you free? (f)

8. How do we keep from allowing anything besides God to be our master? (g)

Scriptural Answers

(a) "When I was desperate, I called out, and God got me out of a tight spot" (Psalm 34:6).

(b) "Have two goals: wisdom—that is knowing and doing right—and common sense. Don't let them slip away for they fill you with living energy, and are a feather in your cap. They keep you safe from defeat and disaster and from stumbling off the trail" (Proverbs 3:21–23 LB).

(c) "If a fellow believer hurts you, go and tell him—work it out between the two of you. If he listens, you've made a friend" (Matthew 18:15).

(d) "Be careful how you behave among your unsaved neighbors; for then, even if they are suspicious of you and talk against you, they will end up praising God for your good works when Christ returns" (1 Peter 2:12 LB).

(e) "Sin need never again be your master, for now you are no longer tied to the law which enslaves you, but you are free under God's favor and mercy" (Romans 6:14 LB).

(f) "So you see how it is: my new life tells me to do right, but the old nature that is still inside me loves to sin. Oh, what a terrible predicament I'm in! Who will free me from my slavery to this deadly lower nature? Thank God! It has been done by Jesus Christ our Lord. He has set me free" (Romans 7:24–25 LB).

(g) "'So my counsel is: Don't worry about things—food, drink, and clothes. For you already have life and a body—and they are far more important than what to eat and wear'" (Matthew 6:25 LB).

70

Have you ever sharpened your sword?

In times past, would someone go to battle without a sword? Certainly not! Well, you have no power in life's battles without the Word inside you. "For the word of God is living and active. Sharper than any double-edged sword, it penetrates … it judges the thoughts and attitudes of the heart. Nothing in all creation is hidden from God's sight. Everything is uncovered and laid bare before the eyes of him to whom we must give account" (Hebrews 4:12–13 NIV). God's Word is our (s)Word.

So my question is, "Have you ever sharpened your sword?" Or, more literally, have you read your Bible? I mean from cover to cover—not just a Scripture here, a chapter there, reading as your pastor presents his topic for the sermon, and not making excuses like, *I've heard tons of sermons, watched all sorts of edifying preachers on TV, and read my daily devotions. Isn't that sufficient?* Wrong! For most of my life I thought that was enough, too. The Holy Spirit will help us remember what we have read, but how can He help us remember if we never read it in the first place?

How do you feel about reading CliffsNotes in order to get to the author's true intent? Ever gone to a movie made from a book and been disappointed that the director didn't do the book justice? You see what I mean. That's what I call a dull sword.

I was forty-nine before I read the Bible from cover to cover. Our pastor challenged the congregation to read it through in one year. I thought it seemed impossible at first, but I've now read it five times. I read a different version each time. *The Message* is my favorite for easy modern reading, but it's good to read them all. Four times, as I finished reading my freshly highlighted beloved Bible, God asked me to give it away. I cried the first time, but I knew it was what God wanted me to do. Each time I thought that I would be able to keep it, but when each December rolled around, He asked me to give it away.

After reading the Bible that fifth time, it seemed like something clicked in my heart. I began to see things through God's eyes. Not just things, but people: the way they feel, the way they hurt. The way that a small gesture can change an attitude.

January came, followed by February and March. We rolled into July. Then before I knew it, September arrived. *Yes, I still have my Bible!* I thought. One Sunday, a visitor came to our Sunday school class. She had gone through all sorts of drama and was asking for prayer to stay strong. There was a seat between me and the visitor. Ann, one of the teachers in the class, motioned for me to move next to the lady.

I started to have the old nudge to give my Bible away. *Surely that's my imagination. I thought I was going to keep this one, God.* But slowly, I started getting my papers out of my Bible. With tears in my eyes, I gave it to her as we prayed. I sat beside her in church and in the middle of service, she left and never came back. I never saw her again. I cried really hard that day. I knew it was right to give it to her, but I had really loved that Bible!

I convinced myself that it was a meeting designed by God. I was the "noble" person giving the visitor my prized possession. It could have been that the visitor was an angel in disguise. But do you remember the Scripture I gave you at the beginning of this story? "[The Word] judges the thoughts and attitudes of the heart." Well, I think I was being judged. I had become slack in my Bible reading. Some would call it lazy. I had my faithful, highlighted Bible to rely on. All I had to do was look up my favorite scriptures; they were so easy to find. I started to realize why God might have had me give my Bibles away. God knew my heart. My sword wasn't sharp. It was getting dull. God chastises those He loves. "Blessed is the man whom you chasten" (Psalm 94:12 NASB). So here I am, telling on myself. I took my whooping. "Break open your words, let the light shine out, let ordinary people see the meaning" (Psalms 119:130). That's me: just

Sheep Ears 347

an ordinary person. If you have trouble understanding the Bible, rely on this Scripture, like I do.

I'm starting my sixth Bible-read, still sharpening my sword, if you will. I can't fight life's battles with a dull sword, after all. So what are *you* waiting for? I promise, you will never be the same. Read, read, read, and then read some more.

"So faith comes from hearing, and hearing by the word of God" (Romans 10:17 NASB). When you need faith to believe for healing, strength to not give up, wisdom in a sticky situation, how will you really have faith if you don't have the Word to build you up? It's impossible!! Let's all sharpen our swords.

Questions

1. Do you believe reading the Bible is important on your Christian walk? Will hiding the Scriptures in your heart help when you are tempted to sin? (a)

2. Should we seek God? Why or why not? (b, c)

3. Have you ever tried to convince yourself that your motives were noble, yet had the gnawing feeling that God was reading your heart? (d) How did you feel, once you were convicted?

4. Give descriptions of how powerful the Word of God feels when it gets in you. (e, f)

5. Explain to a new Christian why they should read the Bible. (g)

6. What is your favorite weapon of Scripture?

7. The Bible is outdated and irrelevant. True or false? (h)

Scriptural Answers

(a) "I have hidden your word in my heart that I might not sin against you" (Psalm 119:11 NIV).

(b) "I love those who love me, and those who seek me will find me" (Proverb 8:17 NIV).

(c) "'When you come looking for me, you'll find me. Yes, when you get serious about finding me and want it more than anything else, I'll make sure you won't be disappointed.' God's Degree" (Jeremiah 29:13–14).

(d) "All a man's ways seem right to him, but the Lord weighs the heart" (Proverb 21:2 NIV).

(e) "Righteous chews on wisdom like a dog on a bone, rolls virtue around on his tongue. His heart pumps God's Word like blood through his veins; his feet are as sure as a cat's" (Psalms 37:30–31).

(f) "God's Word is better than a diamond, better than a diamond set between emeralds. You'll like it better than strawberries in spring, better than red, ripe strawberries" (Psalms 19:10–11).

(g) "There's more. God's Word warns us of danger and directs us to hidden treasure. Otherwise, how will we find our way?" (Psalms 19:11–12).

(h) "Heaven and earth will pass away, but my words will never pass away" (Matthew 24:35 NIV).

71

Have you ever stopped the potter's wheel?

Isaiah says, "Still, God, you are our Father. We're the clay and you're our potter: All of us are what you made us" (Isaiah 64:8). That would be nice if we allowed God to do His work, but I'll be honest: sometimes I have tried to be the potter, and the results were not pretty nor effective.

Let me elaborate. As my oldest son, Aaron, was growing up, he was very frustrating to me. Today some professionals would say that he had ADHD, but back then, everyone (including me) just called him hyperactive and irresponsible. He would forget to do his homework, or, if he did do it, he'd leave it at home. He would take three hours to do a twenty-minute homework assignment with me nagging him the whole time. He often left his coat at home. Aaron stood up while eating his meals. He couldn't sit still in the classroom. His fourth-grade teacher showed me his desk at a parent-teacher conference. Aaron was placed at the back of the room where the teacher allowed him to move freely if he felt the need. Mrs. Wynne called Aaron her "Aaron Spielberg" because of his wild imagination. But he was driving me crazy. I was always on his back and it seemed like the bad moments were outweighing the good. I loved him, but I also couldn't stand him.

I knew that wasn't how a good Christian mom should feel. How could I ever change him? He was in the fifth grade when I had a revelation: I couldn't. But I could change my attitude. I asked him to sit down one day and said, "Aaron, I love you, but it seems like I'm angry with you a lot. So starting today, that's changing. If you don't do your homework, I will not yell. You may get an F, but it's your F. If you forget your coat, you just get cold. If you don't sit down while eating, I won't say a word."

All he said was "Okay, Mom," but the look on his face said it all: relief. I stayed true to my promises.

His grades went down some, but the relationship we had lost returned to its original shape. "Clean the slate, God, so we can start the day fresh! Keep me from stupid sins, from thinking I can take over your work" (Psalm 19:13). Aaron went back to being the happy-go-lucky kid who brightened everyone's day. By the time he was a senior in high school, he had raised his grade point average to 3.0. We celebrated. He brought his grades up because it was *his* goal, not mine.

I had let him off the potter's wheel. A potter's wheel is what you put a blob of clay on. It revolves at a steady pace while the potter slowly changes its shape until it becomes what the potter sees in his imagination. I had tried to be the potter. You see, I was so busy trying to form Aaron into my vessel that I wasn't allowing God to shape Aaron into *His* vessel. I made a mess of things, but God shaped him into the awesome man who was underneath that irresponsible little boy.

He has moved up the ranks at his job and is the most caring, devoted father to his children, Skyler and Ayla. He is inspiring!

I had also put my husband on the potter's wheel. Do this, do that, don't do this, why did you say that? Nag, nag, nag. Some might say I was nitpicking—not just my words, but my tone. I was insinuating that my ideas were better than his. Not about the big stuff; that was fine. It was the little stuff, "the little foxes that spoil the vineyards [of our love]" (Song of Solomon 2:15 AB). I hoped he wouldn't read this Scripture: "A nagging spouse is like the drip, drip, drip of a leaky faucet; You can't turn it off and you can't get away from it" (Proverbs 27:15–16). I thought his silence was a weakness. I was wrong; it was strength. He was modeling Jesus. "[Jesus] held his peace and answered nothing" (Mark 14:61 KJV). I tried to stop, but my nagging just kept popping back.

Then I read the most enlightening book ever: *7 Things He'll Never Tell You ... But You Need to Know*, by Kevin Leman, a Christian author who uses humor mixed with wisdom. I read his book about five years ago and it changed my life and my thinking. I gave the book to my daughter-in-law, Sharon, and she has called me numerous times to say in her beautiful British accent, "Thank you so much for sharing that book with me. I'm sure it has helped save our marriage on more than one occasion!" He also wrote a fabulous book called *Have a New Husband by Friday*.

What does it matter if his shoes don't match his clothes when we go to church, or if he takes off his dirty clothes and leaves them in the living room? At least he goes to church and works hard to make a good living. *And anyway, Sherry, have you looked at your own pile of clothes in the bedroom?*

I began complimenting him in front of people, where he could hear me. In the past, I would brag about him to other people, but he never heard me doing so. If he went to the store for me and called three times to ask me what to get, I let it go. If he loaded the dishwasher, I no longer rearranged the dishes afterward. Who cares? The dishes got cleaned, didn't they? After reading the book, I said to myself, "All this time, I thought it was *him*, but it was actually *me* who had the problem."

Jesus said it best: "Why do you look at the speck of sawdust in your brother's eye and pay no attention to the plank in your own eye?" (Matthew 7:3 NIV). I took a long hard look in the mirror. Who besides Jesus is perfect, anyway? Randy got a new wife; therefore, I got a new husband. I embraced his manhood. Slowly, that happy-go-lucky man that I married returned. I'm happy to say that we laugh together a lot these days.

I wish I could get those years back. I can't, but I can write about them. You have no idea how beautifully God will mold your clay, if you allow Him. If you are reading this and you have multiple potter's wheels at home and you're driving yourself crazy trying to micromanage everyone's lives, do them a favor and stop! I've had people try to micromanage me and I didn't like it one bit. Let's take care of our own business. God is the only potter and He works alone.

Questions

1. Have you ever lived with or been around someone who was always trying to question or change things about you? How do you feel when you are around them? (a)

2. Since God is our model for relationships, he advises us to nag, scold, hold grudges, and avenge our wrongs. True or false? (b)

3. What's the best policy when you feel tempted to open your mouth and nag? (c)

4. What should we pray for when someone gets on our last nerve (besides wisdom in handling the situation)? (d)

5. Do you believe a disgraceful wife will affect her husband's health? Why or why not? (e)

6. What are some characteristics of a virtuous woman? (f)

7. Whom do you have on the potter's wheel?

Scriptural Answers

(a) "It is better to live in the corner of an attic than with a crabby woman in a lovely home ... Better to live in the desert than with a quarrelsome, complaining woman" (Proverbs 21:9, 19 LB).

(b) "God is sheer mercy and grace; not easily angered, He's rich in love. He doesn't endlessly nag and scold nor hold grudges forever. He doesn't treat us as our sins deserve nor pay us back in full for our wrongs" (Psalms 103:8–10).

(c) "Keep your mouth closed and you'll stay out of trouble" (Proverb 21:23 LB).

(d) "Now you can have real love for everyone because your souls have been cleansed from selfishness and hatred when you trusted Christ to save you; so see to it that you really do love each other warmly, with all your hearts" (1 Peter 1:22 LB).

(e) "A wife of noble character is her husband's crown, but a disgraceful wife is like decay in his bones" (Proverb 12:4 NIV).

(f) "A good woman is hard to find, and worth far more than diamonds. Her husband trusts her without reserve, and never has reason to regret it. Never spiteful, she treats him generously all her life long ... When she speaks she has something to say, and she always says it kindly ... Her children respect and bless her; her husband joins in with words of praise: 'Many women have done wonderful things, but you've outclassed them all!'" (Proverbs 31:10–12, 26, 28).

72

Have you ever tamed your tongue?

The day before my son Aaron turned sixteen, he was involved in an accident while playing catcher in a Senior Babe Ruth baseball game. Our team was winning by six runs in a regular season game, but the runner on third acted like it was a championship game with everything on the line. There was one out when the batter hit the ball to right field. The ball was caught, the runner on third tagged up, and Aaron got ready to receive the ball. He stood in front of the baseline about three feet closer to third base. The right fielder made a perfect throw and Aaron was going to tag the runner. An easy out.

But Tim, the runner on third, made the decision to take out the catcher, which was against the rules. He ran out of the base path and headed straight for my son. *Bam*! It was a horrific collision. Aaron fell straight back. He looked like a cardboard cutout that had been flattened by a locomotive. He didn't move. I stood up and held my breath. I thought, *It's not that cool to run out on the field when your child is hurt.* So I tried to regain my composure.

Aaron still wasn't moving. My friends urged me to go check on him. I wanted to transport myself over there like the characters on *Star Trek*. As I ran down the stairs, I saw Aaron's foot move. I breathed a sigh of relief because my first fear had been a broken neck or back. Then I heard the umpire holler, "Get some ice! There's a lot of blood!" In a flash, I was on the field. Normally, it would have taken about eight minutes from where I was running, but not that day.

We tried to figure out where the blood was coming from. His entire face was crimson. Suddenly, I heard someone in the opposing dugout yelling, "Yeah, that's right, and I'll do it *again*." Tim was taunting us while we assessed the damage. He was pounding his chest. At that point, I was shocked, but still not too concerned with what he was saying, because I was concentrating on my injured son.

We got Aaron cleaned up enough to figure out that his tongue was what had received the damage. The ice stopped the bleeding, so I decided to drive him to the hospital myself instead of waiting for an ambulance. I kept explaining to Aaron what had happened, but he kept asking me over and over. I realized later that he had a mild concussion and couldn't remember anything I told him. As I answered Aaron's questions, I was praying. "Lord, please let my son be okay, and please help there be a skilled doctor available to help him."

The hospital called in Dr. Langston, an ear, nose, and throat specialist. He said it was the worst tongue laceration he had ever seen in his life. He did a remarkable job of repairing Aaron's tongue: sixty stitches inside and outside his tongue. It was swollen so badly that he couldn't close his mouth. He lost fifteen pounds over the next two weeks. I was so thankful that God had answered both of my prayers.

We'd assumed that Tim had been thrown out of the game, possibly kicked off the team. We were dismayed to find out that no punishment had been administered and that Tim had been allowed to finish the game.

We begged Aaron not to play any more baseball that summer, but he insisted. They say that when you get bucked off a horse you should get back on it right away or you'll lose your nerve. So that's what he did. I had mixed feelings of trepidation and pride as I watched him squat behind home plate at the next game he played. I started breathing again around the third inning since he seemed okay.

Aaron made all-stars that year. He had never made all-stars before in his life. The people in the stands cheered extra loud as they called out his name. He had never been the best player on any of his previous teams, but that year everyone said that he had shown the biggest heart. And to top it off, the all-stars traveled to Alamogordo, New Mexico, and won the first-place trophy. It is a memory he will always cherish.

Aaron never got an apology from Tim. In fact, over the next couple of years, we heard that Tim got so mad in one baseball game that he stormed off the field and tore a telephone off the wall. Several people told me that they had heard him brag, "I'll be dead by the time I'm nineteen." And he was. He was involved in a gang fight and died at the scene. I was devastated. I had always prayed that Tim would find God and turn his life around.

We had already forgiven him. After all, the Bible teaches us to forgive those who trespass against us—or in Aaron's case, flatten us. But I often think of Tim's prediction that he would die by the time he was nineteen. "Those who love to talk will experience the consequences, for the tongue can kill, or nourish life" (Proverb 18:21 NLT). *The Message* puts it like this: "Words kill, words give life; they're either poison or fruit—you choose."

Aaron's tongue was injured physically, but it recovered. Tim spoke death into his own life; he didn't recover.

What words are you speaking over your life? "This marriage will never work." "My daughter will be the death of me." "Everyone in my family died of heart disease by the time they were fifty-five." "My kids are hopeless." Or are you saying, "Lord, give me insight to heal my marriage." "Help me use discernment to guide my daughter with your wisdom." "I proclaim health to my body." "I'm not giving up on my child." Death or life. Our words are powerful. The world was created with words. Our words could change the course of the world. James wrote about the tongue:

> A word out of your mouth may seem of no account, but it can accomplish nearly anything—or destroy it! ... By our speech we can ruin the world, turn harmony to chaos, throw mud on a reputation, send the whole world up in smoke with it, smoke right from the pit of hell.
>
> This is scary: You can tame a tiger, but you can't tame a tongue—it's never been done. The tongue runs wild, a wanton killer. With our tongues we bless God our Father; with the same tongues we curse the very men and women he made in his image. Cursings and blessings out of the same mouth! My friends, this can't go on.
>
> —James 3:5–10

According to James, I can't tame my tongue. But I can submit my mouth to God. As I fill my mind with Scriptures, my tongue evolves into a life-giving source instead of the failure it gravitates toward.

Words are important. What are you saying? You *do* have a choice.

Questions

1. Do you think your speech reflects your heart? (a)

2. We will not be held accountable for our words. True or false? (b)

3. Although some people sound pleasant to your face, if they have hate in their hearts, it eventually comes out. True or false? Explain. (c)

4. How does the Bible describe a person who quarrels, yells, and constantly gets into fights? (d)

5. If you have an agitator at school, at church, or at your job, what should you do? (e)

6. Is it okay to rejoice when your enemy falls? (f)

7. What kind of words come out of your mouth: positive or negative?

8. Will God honor your words and beliefs whether they are positive or negative? Write your thoughts on this. (g)

Scriptural Answers

(a) "For a man's heart determines his speech. A good man's speech reveals the rich treasures within him. An evil-hearted man is filled with venom, and his speech reveals it" (Matthew 12:34–35 LB).

(b) "And I tell you this, that you must give account on Judgment Day for every idle word you speak. Your words now reflect your fate then:

either you will be justified by them or you will be condemned" (Matthew 12:36–37 LB).

(c) "A man with hate in his heart may sound pleasant enough, but don't believe him, for he is cursing you in his heart. Though he pretends to be so kind, his hatred will finally come to light for all to see" (Proverbs 26:24–26 LB).

(d) "The selfish man quarrels against every sound principle of conduct by demanding his own way. A rebel doesn't care about the facts. All he wants to do is yell … A fool gets into constant fights. His mouth is his undoing! His words endanger him" (Proverbs 18:1–2, 6–7 LB).

(e) "Drive out the mocker, and out goes strife; quarrels and insults are ended" (Proverb 22:10 NIV).

(f) "Do not gloat when your enemy falls; when he stumbles, do not let your heart rejoice, or the Lord will see and disapprove" (Proverbs 24:17–18 NIV).

(g) "Then Jesus said to the Roman officer, 'Go on home. What you have believed has happened!' And the boy was healed that same hour!" (Matthew 8:13 LB).

73

Have you ever used a password?

Part 1

I had just returned from my son's house in Texas. Aaron and his wife, Laura, had a portable electric heater that I fell in love with. My house tends to be drafty in the winter, but at their house it was so cozy that my bones actually got warm. Back in Arkansas, I told my husband that I was going to make a beeline to Walmart to get a heater just like theirs. We really didn't have the money at the time, but you know what? I was tired of shivering. I was so relieved to find the same model they had, because it was the one for me. While in the store, I had a bright idea. *Our towels are scratchy and worn. Why not get some new towels, too?* So I picked out their best towels. They were very soft. I bought not only the bath towels, but washcloths and hand towels, too.

I drove home smiling, anticipating how warm our home would be that night. I put the packages in the house, but decided to walk the dogs before settling in for the evening. While walking, I began to praise God about the purchases and rejoiced at how happy they made me. Then a funny thing happened. I heard a gentle whisper: "That's not your heater."

"It's not? Then whose is it?" No answer. I thought, *Well, I guess I'm supposed to figure it out.*

While still walking the dogs, I called Pat Hart, the care pastor at our church who was in charge of benevolence. She said, "No, I don't know of anyone who needs a heater, but I'll check around."

I walked in the door and thought, *Well, at least I get to keep the towels.*

And the voice said, "Those aren't yours, either."

So much for that!

My husband got home that evening and asked why I hadn't opened the box. I told him it wasn't mine. I explained what God had told me, and he said, "The towels, too?" Randy knew not to question. He had seen this before. He just shook his head and grinned.

On Sunday, I approached Pat Hart to see if she had found anyone who needed the heater. "By the way, I have towels to go with it," I added.

She said, "No, but I'm still checking."

I told her that I kept hearing the name "Kathy." She said she knew a few women named Kathy, but couldn't think of anyone named Kathy who needed those items. I informed her that I had put the items in the trunk of my car, so if she ran across anyone, I would be ready.

Several more times that afternoon I heard the name "Kathy" in my spirit.

I returned to church that night and sat in my regular spot. It was a small crowd, and the pastor asked us to move to the center sections. I don't remember Pastor Bell ever making that request before or after that day. I got up and moved to the fourth pew. As I passed by an elderly woman, she said, "Oh hi, Kathy." I smiled and said, "My name is Sherry, but you can call me Kathy if you want." She told me her name was Joyce. We laughed at her mistake, and the pastor began his sermon.

I was abruptly interrupted by God. "Did you not hear what she said?"

"No, what?"

"Think."

I replayed our brief conversation. *Oh my, she called me Kathy! I can't believe I missed it!* I didn't even hear the rest of the sermon because I couldn't wait to talk to Joyce.

As everyone got up to leave, I said, "Joyce, I need to ask you something. I don't want to embarrass you, but do you happen to need a portable electric heater? I have a brand-new one, still in the box."

She smiled and simply said, "Yes, I do."

I felt kind of silly, but I thought, *Well, here goes.* "Do you happen to need some towels, too?"

"Well, *yeess*, I do," she said in her slow Southern drawl. I froze for a second, trying to take everything in.

Sheep Ears 361

I shot up a quick prayer and asked God if there was anything He wanted me to tell her. I gave her His message: "Joyce, have you ever wondered if God truly cared about you?"

"Well, yes, I have."

"I believe that God knew you needed a heater and towels and this is His way of personally letting you know that He cares about you. So when you are lonely or sad, turn on the heater, or wrap up in the towels and know that God is right there with you." I could tell that the message was meaningful to her.

As we sat in the pew, I told her how the miracle had unfolded. We were both amazed, especially by the Kathy part. As far as I knew, she was the first person who had ever called me Kathy. *How did I miss that clue when I first sat down?* Maybe God wanted me to be a detective. No, wait a minute—it was more like a password. God had given Joyce a password to give me, and I had almost missed it. But isn't that the way God works? He finds ingenious ways to get His work done.

The funny thing is, I don't believe Joyce asked for a portable heater or towels. God just knew. "For your Father knows what you need before you ask him" (Matthew 6:8 NIV). How about that?

Joyce and I went to my car and got her gifts from God. I told her that she had permission to call me Kathy. In fact, I insisted. That would be our password to remember the goodness of God.

Three months later, Pastor Bell requested prayer for Joyce. He said, "Joyce went to Florida to visit her daughter and is battling cancer." I didn't know if Joyce had already had cancer when I gave her the gifts. She didn't share that with me. But I liked to believe that when she was going through the tough times, she remembered the message from God that day in the fourth pew.

About a year later, Joyce returned. I prayed with her about the cancer. She always called me Kathy, with a gleam in her eye. It was our little secret.

She eventually had to go to a convalescent center. I visited her several times. I would feed her, read from the Bible, pray, and then we would sing songs. One chorus we sang was "Mansion Over the Hilltop." I told her there would be no need for heaters up there. We both laughed.

Slowly, she started to weaken. She couldn't recognize me at the last, but when I told her I was Kathy, she always managed a smile.

I look back with wonderment and gratitude that I was able to hear God's instructions and that He was able to use me. I know it's possible for every Christian to hear the Good Shepherd's voice. Jesus said, "I am the Good Shepherd, I know my own sheep and my own sheep know me. In the same way, the Father knows me, and I know the Father. I put the sheep before myself, sacrificing myself if necessary," (John 10:14–15). God's voice will never contradict His Word or His character. Develop a relationship with God. Talk to Him and allow Him to talk to you.

I ran into Joyce's daughter-in-law a few weeks after the funeral. They were having a garage sale. I asked Shirley if they had sold the portable heater or the brown towels. She said no, and I shared with her about my secret password with Joyce. She told me that Joyce had had a large bedroom that was drafty and that the heater had kept her toasty on those long weary nights. They had sent the heater to Kansas to keep another relative warm. Someone else in the family wanted the towels. She was so grateful to know the story so she could pass it on.

Guess what? God knows what you need, too! Perhaps you're the person who has the answer to someone's need. "Enter with the password: 'Thank you!' Make yourselves at home, talking praise. Thank him. Worship him" (Psalm 100:4). A grateful attitude will usher you into the presence of Almighty God. He will guide you in his work here on earth.

Are you willing to show kindness and pray with a stranger so someone else can say, "Thank you, God! You do care about me"? I hope so. It might not be the lady sitting next to you at church. It could be a neighbor. Or maybe it's someone in another country. But that's another story ...

QUESTIONS

1. Do you feel that God still speaks to us, or is that a thing of the past?

2. Has God (or the Holy Spirit) ever spoken to you? How did you know it wasn't your imagination? (a)

3. If you feel that God has given you an assignment, does it diminish your fear and doubt? (b)

4. How does God speak? (c)

5. Do you believe God speaks to ordinary people? (d)

6. When you are trying to make right decisions, God will turn His back on you. True or false? (e)

7. Has God ever miraculously provided you with something before you even knew you needed it? What was it?

8. Has God ever given you something similar to a password to find His will?

Scriptural Answers

(a) "Every word I've spoken to you will come true on time—God's time" (Luke 1:20).

(b) "Yes, be bold and strong! Banish fear and doubt! For remember, the Lord your God is with you wherever you go" (Joshua 1:9 LB).

(c) "I hear this most gentle whisper from One I never guessed would speak to me" (Psalm 81:5).

(d) "Every young man who listens to me and obeys my instructions will be given wisdom and good sense" (Proverb 2:1 LB).

(e) "He shows how to distinguish right from wrong, how to find the right decision every time. For wisdom and truth will enter the very center of your being, filling your life with joy" (Proverb 2:9–10 LB).

74
Have you ever used a password?

Part 2

One Sunday morning I was sitting in my Sunday school class next to my friend Mary Jo. Since she was going to Mexico that week on a mission trip with several other people, I began to pray for the group. I felt the Holy Spirit tell me to take off my necklace and earrings and pass them to her to give to someone on her trip. They were the only pieces of jewelry that I owned, besides my wedding ring, which I really valued. For one thing, the necklace and earrings were beautiful. For another, they had sentimental value because they were given to me by my sister, Michelle, as a gift for being a bridesmaid in her wedding.

I was worried because the clasp was faulty, but God said, "Just tell her about it, you don't have time to get it fixed."

"Okay, God, but who shall I tell Mary Jo to give them to?"

His answer was "Juan."

I said, "God, you've got to give me more than that. There are a lot of guys in Mexico named Juan."

Next I heard, "Matilda."

"Now that's more like it—a name that's not so common. Any messages for them?"

"Just tell them that I love them very much."

When the prayer was over, I gave Mary Jo the jewelry. I told her these explicit instructions with the passwords "Juan" and "Matilda." Not a whole lot to go on, but if you're familiar with computers, you know that a password is needed to gain further access to a program. I guess God had His own passwords for His programs.

Mary Jo was excited. It seemed like *Mission Impossible*, but we both knew that God was up to something special. She told me later that she shared the instructions with the other missionaries on the bus, and they were giddy with anticipation. "I wonder who it will be. How long will it be until she finds the recipient?" This wasn't just a missionary trip, it was a mission assignment.

Mary Jo told me all of the details of the mission:

The group arrived in Mexico and split up that first day to preach individually in small churches. After the service, Mary Jo hopped in the car with an interpreter and the pastor and his wife. As they headed to the hotel, Mary Jo remembered about the jewelry. She asked the interpreter to ask the pastor and his wife, Marco and Maria, if they knew anyone named Matilda. Maria replied, "Yes, my mother's name is Matilda."

Mary Jo's eyebrows raised a little. Then she asked, "How about Juan?"

Marco replied, "That's my father's name. How did you know?"

Turning to the pastor's wife, Mary Jo exclaimed, "Well, believe it or not, I've traveled all the way from Arkansas to give you a present. God impressed a lady to give you some beautiful jewelry with the message that He loves you very much."

Maria was in shock.

They all went up to the hotel room, where Mary Jo handed her the package. Maria laid her head on Mary Jo's shoulder and cried. Maria said that God had told her He was going to do something special for her, but she didn't know it was going to be *this* special. She told Mary Jo that her daughter's *quince años* was coming up in a few months. It's a very special coming-of-age party for fifteen-year-old girls in Mexico. Mother and daughter dress up, and friends and family celebrate with them. Maria had no beautiful jewelry to wear, and this was more than her heart could imagine.

Maria quickly put on her present from God, and Mary Jo took pictures. Her husband looked at her with a shy grin and said, "Maria, I'm falling in love all over again. You look just as beautiful as when we first met."

The other missionaries were returning to the hotel at this point. When they came in, they exclaimed, "Wow! You already solved the Matilda and Juan mystery! Praise God, Hallelujah!" They all had a party right there in the hotel. They rejoiced at how quickly Mary Jo had found her divine appointment.

Now, I ask you: How amazing is our God? "For the eyes of the Lord search back and forth across the earth, looking for people whose hearts are perfect toward him, so that he can show his great power in helping them" (2 Chronicles 16:9 LB). I believe God looked on the earth and found Maria, and He wanted to help her with her problem. For all I know, the whole mission trip was a set up for this one precious woman who had a need.

I'm so glad that I didn't worry about the clasp that day. I'm sure they got it fixed. I'm glad I was willing to let go of my sentimental jewelry. It had a bigger purpose, one set up by God. What if Mary Jo had thought, *Well, her name isn't Matilda and his name isn't Juan, so I'll just have to keep looking.* Juan and Matilda were the names (or passwords, if you will) that unlocked the passage to God's miracle.

Have you noticed that God is creative in His miracles? How about marching around a city wall once a day for six days and then seven times the seventh day, then blowing horns and having people shout until the wall collapsed (Joshua 6:6–20)? Have you ever heard of a talking donkey (Numbers 22:28)? Or paying your taxes with a coin taken from a fish (Matthew 17:27)? Now that's what I call creativity!

God can also use a password to help a lady from Arkansas find a woman in Mexico and meet her need of a beautiful necklace and earrings to wear to her daughter's *quince años* celebration. I had never even heard of that celebration, but God knew all about it and how important it was to Maria.

If God tells you to do something a little bizarre, don't be afraid. Be like Peter, who walked on the water (Matthew 14:29). Step out in faith. Get your feet wet. Someone may be waiting to hear God's personal message of love.

Questions

1. What is the password that we use to come into the presence of God? (a)

2. When Abraham's servant went to Nahor to find a wife for Isaac, what was the password phrase he wanted the future wife of Isaac to say? (b)

3. What was Rebekah's comment after she gave the servant a drink of water? Did it confirm his prayer? (c)

4. As Christians, we should be willing to give others what we have (within reason). True or false? (d)

5. When God asks us to do something for Him, is it optional? (e)

6. If God asks you to do something good for someone, is it a sin if you don't do it? Explain your answer. (f)

Scriptural Answers

(a) "On your feet now—applaud God! Bring a gift of laughter; sing yourselves into his presence ... Enter with the password. 'Thank you!' Make yourselves at home, talking praise. Thank him. Worship him" (Psalms 100:1–2, 4).

(b) "As I stand here by the spring while the young women of the town come out to get water, let the girl to whom I say, 'Lower your jug and give me a drink,' and who answers, 'Drink, and let me also water your camels'—let her be the woman you have picked out for your servant Isaac, then I'll know that you're working graciously behind the scenes for my master" (Genesis 24:13–14).

(c) "When he had satisfied his thirst she said, 'I'll get water for your camels, too, until they've drunk their fill'" (Genesis 24:19).

(d) "Sinners are always wanting what they don't have; the God-loyal are always giving what they do have" (Proverb 21:26).

(e) "So see to it that you obey him who is speaking to you … how terrible our danger if we refuse to listen to God who speaks to us from heaven!" (Hebrews 12:25 LB).

(f) "Anyone, then, who knows the good he ought to do and doesn't do it, sins" (James 4:17 NIV).

75

Have you ever wanted to be generous?

When my children were small, I prayed, "God, you know we don't make that much money. We have three small kids and I don't see any possible way to be able to afford to give them the things they will need in life. I don't see how we will afford to get them cars when they are of age. Even if we do get them cars, how will we ever afford the insurance? And what about college?"

I don't always get an immediate answer to my prayers, but this time, I did. Inside my heart, that small all-knowing voice said, "If you give money to the people to whom I ask you to give, *when* I ask you to give, I will supply all your needs." That answer was so simple, yet so profound.

There are all sorts of Scriptures in the Bible to support it, but I also knew what I had heard was right because I felt peaceful when I heard the words. I had always had a generous heart, but now I felt complete freedom to give. You see, I *wanted* to give. It's like when your kids are small you start a savings fund for the kids, but instead of putting money into an account, we invested our money in people.

Since that time, I have read Scriptures to support what God said. "Command them to do good, to be rich in good deeds, and be generous and willing to share. In this way they will lay up treasures for themselves as a firm foundation for the coming age, so that they may take hold of the life that is truly life" (1 Timothy 6:18–19 NIV). "The world of the generous gets larger and larger; the world of the stingy gets smaller and smaller. The one who blesses others is abundantly blessed; those who help others are helped" (Proverbs 11:24–25). And one of my all-time favorites, "Your Father already knows all your needs, and He will give you all you need from day to day if you live for him and make the Kingdom of God your primary concern. So don't worry about tomorrow, for tomorrow will bring its own worries. Today's trouble is enough for today" (Matthew 6:32–34 NLT).

The funny thing is, God never instructed or impressed me to give to our own kids—which is not to mean that they suffered. But God specifically wanted me to give *outside* of our family. My husband always supported my endeavors, and for that I am grateful. I never had to sneak around because God also confirmed in Randy's heart that giving was the right thing to do.

Our ten-month-old grandson, Ethan, was recently learning to walk. He could do it if he held onto his mommy's hand or if he was in his "walking train." His parents recently sent me a video of him on my phone. He was giggling as they encouraged every step. That's how God is when you start to give. He encourages you, he holds your hand. I can even imagine Him recording your actions and letting the angels watch and cheer. But that's in the beginning. Later, He may gradually ask you to increase your giving, but the rewards will also be increased. We should give because we love God though, not for the reward.

Nathan and Sharon don't expect Ethan to run in a marathon a week after he takes his first steps. God won't ask you to give more than you can handle in the beginning, either. He will train you gradually. He does expect you to improve, though. It's a progression.

I've given forty cents to a student for lunch when all I had was forty-one cents in my pocket. I can't even count the number of times I've gone to church and had God tell me to give someone all of my cash. I've given restaurant gift cards away, then gone home and eaten Spam sandwiches. Sometimes I have even said, "God, when am I ever going to keep anything for myself?"

One time a friend asked me to pray for her because the motor overheated on her truck. As I prayed for Jean, God said, "Why don't you write her a check for $400?" I remembered that I had $400 set aside to pay our property taxes, so I actually had the money in our checking account.

I wrote her a check and God generously supplied our tax money when Randy got unexpected overtime at his job. It's been two years and Jean still hugs my neck and thanks Randy and I for the help we gave when she was so desperate.

Another time, a missionary came to our church and I thought, *Okay, I'll give twenty dollars.* Then I thought, *No, I'll double that to forty dollars.* Then I felt God say in my heart, "Do you want to be outrageous? Give $400." I had to juggle my bills a little. So what? When God says to give, that's what He means.

One time we got $1,100 back on our income tax refund, and God had us give $800 to sow into a college student's life. Sure, that command would have been easy to ignore, but I had a promise from God, and He never lies. So I knew it was for my own good.

One day I was going through some old mail and I found a two-week paycheck that I had never deposited. It was six months old. I don't know how that happened. I had been wondering why I was ending up short all the time. Anyway, I had already adjusted my checkbook, so I said, "God, what do you want me to do with this windfall?" He said, "Go put the money on an account in a store that sells nice suits and tell the song director at church to go pick out a nice suit, shoes, shirt, and belt." Boy, was he happy!

Once, God had me put ten hundred-dollar bills in an envelope and give anonymously to someone. I was quite surprised because they had a house three times the size of mine and were prominent in the community. Two years later, God impressed me to tell them. They were so shocked it had been Randy and me! They said they had testified to many people about what a miracle it was, because that had been exactly the amount they had needed for a debt that they owed.

Different people had different needs, but God saw them all, and thankfully Randy and I were able to be His hand extended. It's not always convenient to give, but the action will always be rewarded. Time after time after time, God has given us back more than we'd given. You can try and try and try, but you cannot out-give God! Randy and I have discovered that our giving has gotten easier and easier because we have seen the faithfulness of God.

Our three sons all got vehicles and insurance when the time came.

Not only that, they all went to college—one for three years, and two graduated with degrees—and when they left school, they left *completely* debt-free. One attended the University of Arkansas at Conway on a disability scholarship (due to asthma), one attended the University of Arkansas at Pine Bluff on an academic scholarship, and one received a baseball scholarship to Baylor University. My husband and I worked a total of four jobs to pay the balance on *that* one, but on graduation day, all he owed was a $60 parking ticket! Thank you, God! In this day and time, that is totally amazing!

But that's not the end of the story. I'd like to tell you about a chain of events that will astound you. One day, about three years ago, there was a substitute teacher in class with me. (I'm a paraprofessional, or a teacher's aide.) We were vaguely familiar with each other, and we struck up a conversation. Charla told me that she had graduated from college and sent out about a hundred job applications. Only one place was interested in her, and it was in South Carolina. She needed $200 to fly there and was desperate. No one in her family had the money and she had exhausted all her resources. We prayed together at the end of the day for an answer, and I told her I would see her tomorrow.

I left school and went to the mall to walk. As I walked, I prayed for God to send an answer to her prayer. As I prayed, God asked, "Don't you have $200?"

I said, "Yes, in the bank."

He said, "If you hurry you can make it to the bank before it closes."

Knowing it was God, I rushed out of the mall and got two crisp hundred-dollar bills from the bank. I put them in a card and gave them to Charla the next day. She started crying and said she thought the deadline had passed. However, she called the business and they extended her deadline. Long story short: she got the job.

The very next day I got a check in the mail from my son Paul for $200. He said he knew we were having a difficult time and wanted to help us out. I was speechless. The exact amount I had given to Charla was what Paul had given to us. And he knew nothing about her situation, either. As I held his check in my hand, I felt the Holy Spirit say, "Are you going to plant this seed, or eat this seed?"

I knew what He meant. If I gave to the missionary who was going to be at church that Sunday, it would be like sowing seed into a ministry to reap a harvest. Or, I could spend the money, and by next week, I wouldn't be able to remember where it went. So with tears in my eyes—not tears of sorrow, but of joy—I dropped the money in the offering plate, knowing that this money was too precious to spend. My son had given from his heart. That's what a mother always wants to see in her son.

Miracles started happening after that. Within two weeks Paul, who did not have a job at the time, was offered a job at a bank. My husband, who had been part-owner of a business for twenty-eight years, was also offered an hourly job that would double his salary. When he quit his current job where he was a partner, he would also receive a buyout. During the time we were negotiating the buyout, I asked God, "Is there anything you want us to do with the money when we get it?" I guess God had been waiting on me to ask that question, because I got a quick reply: "Give $10,000 to David." I barely knew this young man.

I was surprised, but then again, I wasn't surprised. Months before, I had had an epiphany. It finally dawned on me that we couldn't *really* bless someone in a big way unless *we* were truly blessed. I heard a minister on television say he had given $10,000 to someone and I thought, *Hey, it would be awesome to be able to do that.* I heard another minister say, "If it is in your heart, God will put it in your hand."

"God," I said boldly, "I want to be blessed so I can be a blessing, just like Abraham" (Genesis 12:2).

David's father had died in a freak accident. I believe that we are supposed to look after orphans and widows (James 1:27). But I was still curious. "God, is there any special reason?"

"Yes. David is going to pick the wrong college because of a money situation, and I want him to choose correctly. He will make a difference in the world."

Wow, what can you say to *that*? All I could feel was humble. I told God that the only way I could do this was if my husband agreed. That would be proof that this really was God speaking and not just me going off on a wild tangent.

I approached my husband and guess what his reaction was? He laughed. It wasn't a you've-got-to-be-kidding laugh, but a wow-that's-awesome laugh. He said, "Sherry, you've never steered us wrong before and I trust you." What kind of man says that? All I know is that I'm the luckiest woman alive!

With the buyout, we had enough money to pay off our house, our car, and a consolidation loan. We gave our tithes, of course. We got a stipend for five years that we put towards our Roth IRA. We promptly set up David's money in a 529 college account, and in two years, it has increased by almost $3,000. How's that for an awesome, outrageous, most excellent God?

The apostle Paul wrote:

> God can pour on the blessings in astonishing ways so that you're ready for anything and everything, more than just ready to do what needs to be done. As one psalmist put it:
> He throws caution to the winds,
> giving to the needy in reckless abandon.
> His right-living, right-giving ways
> never run out, never wear out.
> This most generous God who gives seed to the farmer that becomes bread for your meals is more than extravagant with you. He gives you something you can give away ... so that you can be generous in every way.
> —2 Corinthians 9:8–11

That's a mighty big statement. And God's Word is good enough for me. So have you ever wanted to be generous? Start giving with what you have in your hand. Then as you give to others, God will trust you with more of His resources. I wonder how many blessings He is just waiting to give you? "The good person is generous and lends lavishly ... Heart ready, trusting in God, Spirit firm, unperturbed, ever blessed, relaxed among enemies, They lavish gifts on the poor—A generosity that goes on, and on, and on. An honored life! A beautiful life!" (Psalms 112:5, 7–9). That's a promise I like!

But God won't get busy until you get busy. What would have happened if I had told Him I couldn't help Charla get to her job interview because that would only leave $17.56 in my savings account? What would have happened if we had said, "No thank you, God, we really need to put money in our grandchildren's college fund." I doubt that the floodgates would have opened. God will take care of our grandchildren. That's the kind of God He is!

Pastor Gary Bell once said in a sermon, "You're never more like God than when you're giving. 'For God so loved the world that he gave ...'" (John 3:16 NIV). I agree.

Questions

1. Did Jesus advise us to protect ourselves from greed? (a)

2. Jesus told a parable of a farmer who had a terrific crop and said to himself, "I'll build bigger barns, then take it easy." How did God feel about his selfish attitude? (b)

3. Is there a way to be secure in a declining economy? (c)

4. When we give to needy people, our hearts should go out to them as well as our money. True or false? (d)

5. Should we be generous only to the poor, or should we give to the people God tells us to give to, regardless of their station in life? (e)

6. The Bible says that we are to get rich before we help other people. True or false? (f)

7. Will the Lord forsake someone who loves Him and is generous? What happens to their children? (g)

Scriptural Answers

(a) "Speaking to the people, [Jesus] went on, 'Take care! Protect yourself against the least bit of greed. Life is not defined by what you have, even when you have a lot'" (Luke 12:15).

(b) "But God said to him, 'You fool! This very night your life will be demanded from you. Then who will get what you have prepared for yourself?' This is how it will be with anyone who stores up things for himself but is not rich towards God" (Luke 12:20–21 NIV).

(c) "Be generous. Give to the poor. Get yourselves a bank that can't go bankrupt, a bank in heaven far from bank robbers, safe from embezzlers, a bank you can bank on. It's obvious, isn't it? The place where your treasure is, is the place you will most want to be, and end up being" (Luke 12:33–34).

(d) "Turn both your pockets and your hearts out and give generously to the poor, then your lives will be clean, not just your dishes and your hands" (Luke 11:41).

(e) "Don't show favoritism to either the poor or the great. Judge on the basis of what is right" (Leviticus 19:15).

(f) "Don't wear yourself out trying to get rich, restrain yourself! Riches disappear in the blink of an eye; wealth sprouts wings and flies off into the wild blue yonder" (Proverbs 23:4–5).

(g) "I have been young and now I am old. And in all my years I have never seen the Lord forsake a man who loves him; nor have I seen the children of the godly go hungry. Instead, the godly are able to be generous with their gifts and loans to others, and their children are a blessing" (Psalms 37:25–26 LB).

76

Have you ever wondered if color matters?

I watched an episode of *Star Trek* a very long time ago. I may get a few of the details mixed up, but I remember that the main point of the show was profound. Two men were beamed aboard the Starship Enterprise. One man's face was white on the left side and black on the right. The other man was the opposite: black on the left side and white on the right. One man felt he was far superior to the other man because he was white on the left side.

As the show progressed, it got pretty confusing trying to figure out which man was which. *Who was left-side-white, who was right-side-white? How could they be so silly as to judge each other by their right-side or left-side color? I forget which one was deemed more worthy, which one was deemed a sluggard.* By the end of the episode, I was exhausted from trying to keep straight which man was of the ruling class and which was subjugated. Sound ridiculous? It was. But I never forgot that show.

Don't you imagine God must be exhausted with the people on earth who try to make judgments about each other based on skin color? God is not boring! What beauty would there be in a solid green rainbow? What if all animals looked like Chihuahuas? What if every tree was a pine tree? What if all fish were catfish? Dull. Variety is delightful! How could anyone say that blue is the only good color and all other colors are inferior? Or that a green apple is fantastic but a red one is despicable? I hope I've made my point.

God does not see the color of a person's skin as positive or negative factors. I believe He sees variety as a good thing. In his speech on August 28, 1963, Martin Luther King, Jr. said, "I have a dream that my four little children will one day live in a nation where they will not be judged by the color of their skin, but by the content of their character." I believe that is how God judges: by the issues of the heart. David said, "Examine me, God, from head to foot, order your battery of tests. Make sure I'm fit inside and out" (Psalm 26:2).

I am white, and many of my closest friends are black. I'm so glad that I didn't stereotype them and think that I could only befriend people of my skin color. I would have missed out on the true meaning of friendship. I judged them by their character, not by which sides of their faces were white or black. As a matter of fact, I'm the lucky one; they chose me.

Five years ago, our middle son, Nathan, came to my husband and me and said he had asked his girlfriend Sharon to marry him. She was from Africa. I was really fond of her. What was there not to like? She laughed at my corny jokes!

My husband was not so congenial. After all, he had not seen the *Star Trek* episode. He had not had the blinders lifted from his eyes. I talked to my husband about the black face/white face story. I told him that Moses's wife, Zipporah, was from Ethiopia (Numbers 12:1 NKJV). I said if he estranged Nathan, it would not be pleasing to God. After all that, God said, "Now you've stated your case. Be quiet and let me work." And that's what I did. I never mentioned the upcoming marriage again. However, I did pray.

Three months later, Nathan took a job in another state, where Sharon resided. They lived about sixty miles apart. Nathan informed me that Sharon's mother was flying in from Africa and wanted to meet us. She would not allow Sharon to marry Nathan if she detected any animosity from us toward Sharon. And she wanted to observe our relationship with her in person. I mentioned the trip to Randy and much to my surprise, he agreed to go. This would mean nine hours in the car just to meet Sharon's mother. You can imagine what I was thinking. *Oh no, is he just being nice now but then he'll act berserk when we get there? Maybe this isn't such a good idea.* Nevertheless, we packed our bags and began the journey.

When we arrived, Nathan, Sharon, her mom, and I were all nervous. Randy had no idea how much was riding on this trip, but we did. Nathan, Sharon, and I went to the kitchen and started discussing supper. We were deep in conversation when we caught a glimpse of Randy and Sharon's mom. They were laughing and talking. They had no idea that we had stopped what we were doing and that we stood, mouths agape, in bewilderment. How was this happening? They seemed like long-lost buddies catching up on all the latest gossip. Amazing!

I'm so glad I was quiet when God asked me to be. I think sometimes it's tempting to keep talking and talking until it turns into "blah, blah, blah." God knows what He's doing. Solomon knew. He said that there is "a time to be silent and a time to speak" (Ecclesiastes 3:7 NIV).

God changed Randy's heart. Randy offered to walk Sharon down the aisle at their wedding. They asked my dad, a semi-retired minister, to marry them, so they flew to Texas for the ceremony.

Last December, when Randy had surgery on his rotator cuff, guess who called most often to check on him? You guessed it: Sharon. When baby Ethan was born, I visited Nathan and Sharon for two weeks to help with the baby, but guess who flew for a two-day stay, just so he could be there for Ethan's baptism? You guessed it: Randy. Sharon calls him Pops. When he talks to her, he says, "What's up, girl?" I call her daughter, she calls me mom.

So back to the title of this story. Have you ever wondered if color matters? Of course it does! Color is delightful! God knows what He's doing. As a child, I sang, "Jesus loves the little children, all the children of the world. Red and yellow, black and white, they are precious in his sight, Jesus loves the little children of the world."

It's that simple.

Questions

1. Do you believe that only one race will be allowed into heaven? Are we all one in Christ Jesus? (a)

2. What is the only thing that matters for all eternity? (b)

3. Do you feel that God is pleased when we judge people by the color of their skin? What could happen to us when we judge others? (c, d)

4. If you have been the one unfairly treated, will God give you justice? (e)

5. How did the apostle Paul handle the differences between the Jews and the Gentiles? (f)

6. Where did their feud end? (g)

7. Have you ever talked so much about an issue that you got yourself in trouble when you should have kept your mouth shut? How did that work out for you? (h)

Scriptural Answers

(a) "You are all sons of God through faith in Christ Jesus, for all of you who were baptized into Christ have clothed yourselves with Christ. There is neither Jew nor Greek, slave nor free, male nor female, for you are all one in Christ Jesus. If you belong to Christ, then you are Abraham's seed and heirs according to the promise" (Galatians 3:26–29 NIV).

(b) "In this life one's nationality or race or education or social position is unimportant; such things mean nothing. Whether a person has Christ is what matters, and he is equally available to all" (Colossians 3:11 LB).

(c) "Do not judge or you too will be judged" (Matthew 7:1 NIV).

(d) "'Think it over,' says the Lord of Hosts. 'Consider how you have acted, and what has happened as a result!'" (Haggai 1:7 LB).

(e) "He gives justice to all who are treated unfairly" (Psalm 103:6 LB).

(f) "For Christ himself is our way of peace. He has made peace between us by making us all one family, breaking down the wall of contempt that used to separate us ... he took the two groups that had been opposed to each other and made them parts of himself; thus he fused us together to become one new person, and at last there was peace" (Ephesians 2:14–15 LB).

(g) "As parts of the same body, our anger against each other has disappeared, for both of us have been reconciled to God. And so the feud ended at last at the cross" (Ephesians 2:16 LB).

(h) "Keep your mouth closed and you'll stay out of trouble" (Proverb 21:23 LB).

77

Have you ever wondered if God cared about you?

Every time I go up in an airplane, I start singing this chorus: "Who am I that You are mindful of me, that You hear me when I call?" Then I'll hum a little, then I'll sing out again when I get to this part: "It's *amaaazing!*" I had thought this song, "Friend of God," was written in the last ten years until I stumbled upon David's psalm. "When I consider Your heavens, the work of your fingers, the moon and the stars, which you have set in place, what is man that you are mindful of him, the son of man that you care for him" (Psalms 8:3–4 NIV). Now I know why that song always gets to me: it's Biblical.

David wrote that psalm from an earthly viewpoint. I experience the same feelings when I fly in an airplane. I always try to get a window seat so I can scan the beauty of the earth. As the plane begins to rise, first I see the houses and buildings, and then I see the plots of land that look like geometric drawings from a math book. Next, I see large bodies of water or mountains, depending on which geographic area I'm flying from. If it's cloudy, I get to bust through the clouds. At this point I start humming, "Here He comes rising through the clouds." I can imagine Jesus when He comes back for us, and the thrill of that glorious moment.

But it's when I am at the highest point in the ascent, when the plane levels out and it's quiet, that I get teary eyed. I look down at the earth and wonder, "How can God possibly care about Sherry Witt in Pine Bluff, Arkansas?" God keeps the constellations in the sky. He keeps the oceans contained. The air that we breathe has to be in perfect balance for us to stay alive. Yet He cares about me. *Me!* Isn't that something?

When I was a kid we would sing "He's Got the Whole World in His Hands." We would progress down to, "He's got the tiny, little baby in His hands, He's got the whole world in His hands." That song was fun to sing when I was little, but up in the plane, my mind is perplexed. I'm so insignificant in this universe, yet He hears me when I call. There could be five gazillion prayers going up to God at one moment in time, yet He can hear (and answer) each and every one. Did you know that you and I are tattooed on God's hand? Just listen to this passage: "Yet they say, 'My Lord deserted us; he has forgotten us.' Never! Can a mother forget her little child and not have love for her own son? Yet even if that should be, I will not forget you. See, I have tattooed your name upon my palm" (Isaiah 49:14–16 LB). Twenty years ago, I might say that's hard to imagine. But in this day of computers and microchips, my mind can certainly fathom the thought of every one of God's children tattooed in His palm.

Do you know how I know God cares about me? When I was a young teenager, my electric toothbrush quit working. I tried everything I could think of to get it to work. After my dad looked at it, he said, "Sherry, I think you should throw it away. It can't be fixed." I know the idea of praying for an electric toothbrush is laughable, but at that point in my life, it was important to me. You see, God knew it was important to me. Right there in the bathroom, I prayed a very simple prayer, asking God to "heal" my toothbrush. The brush immediately started buzzing and I joyfully brushed my teeth. If you ask me where that toothbrush is now, I couldn't tell you. But the lesson I learned that day has never left me. Jesus loves me.

I've had a lot of serious problems that I've prayed about in my life, but I don't worry. If God cared enough to heal my electric toothbrush, which wasn't such a big request, then He must care about my big issues, too. "What is the price of five sparrows? A couple of pennies? Not much more than that. Yet God does not forget a single one of them. And he knows the number of hairs on your head! Never fear, you are far more valuable to him than a whole flock of sparrows" (Luke 12:6–7 LB). Did you hear that? Never fear, you are far more valuable to Him than a whole flock of sparrows!

So you may well laugh when I talk about my toothbrush. I imagine God thought it was funny, too. But nothing impacted me like that first answer to prayer. That settled it in my mind once and forever. Yes, I *do* know that God cares about me! And He cares about you, too. Never forget that. When your children talk to you about a seemingly insignificant prayer, don't belittle them. Sometimes, it's the wonder of that first answered prayer that reveals God's personal love.

By the way, if I see you on an airplane, I might have to fight you for that window seat. I feel a song rising up in me!

Questions

1. Write down the first time you can remember God answering your prayer, no matter how small it may have seemed.

2. Will God teach us how to live free and light? How? (a)

3. Do you burst into song in response to God's goodness? (b)

4. Has God answered your prayer or rescued you and made you feel like singing? What song did you sing? (c, d)

5. Have you ever thought of a cloud as a flag of God's faithfulness? (e)

6. Will Jesus take care of you right to the end? (f)

7. Can anything separate us from God's love? Why or why not? (g)

Scriptural Answers

(a) "Walk with me and work with me—watch how I do it. Learn the unforced rhythms of grace. I won't lay anything heavy or ill-fitting on you. Keep company with me, and you'll learn to live freely and lightly" (Matthew 11:30).

(b) "I'm about to burst with song; I can't keep quiet about you. God, my God, I can't thank you enough" (Psalm 30:12).

(c) "I've thrown myself headlong into your arms—I'm celebrating your rescue. I'm singing at the top of my lungs, I'm so full of answered prayers" (Psalms 13:5–6).

(d) "He is my strength, my shield from every danger. I trusted in him, and he helped me. Joy rises in my heart until I burst out in songs of praise to him" (Psalm 28:7 LB).

(e) "The deeper your love, the higher it goes; every cloud is a flag to your faithfulness" (Psalm 57:10).

(f) "I couldn't be more sure of my ground—the One I've trusted in can take care of what he's trusted me to do right to the end" (2 Timothy 1:12).

(g) "For I am convinced that nothing can ever separate us from his love. Death can't and life can't. The angels won't and all the powers of hell itself cannot keep God's love away. Our fears for today, our worries about tomorrow, or where we are—high above the sky, or in the deepest ocean—nothing will ever be able to separate us from the love of God demonstrated by our Lord Jesus Christ when he died for us" (Romans 8:38–39 LB).

78

Have you ever wondered if there are any good people left in the world?

What happened to my next-door neighbor Linnie was terrible. A month before her husband's death, someone hacked into Linnie's personal bank accounts and caused a big ruckus with her money. It was during that terribly stressful time that she lost Joe, the love of her life. They had been married for fifty years.

On top of that, she also had to put down Puff, her watchdog Chow Chow, because of his old age. If that wasn't enough, the key to her gate had disappeared, which made it impossible for me to access her backyard with my lawn mower. Consequently, she hired a man to chop down the weeds in her backyard. Apparently, he came back a few days later, climbed over her fence, broke into her shed and robbed her of Joe's tools. Linnie had really been pummeled!

Six months after Joe's death, I was walking my dog Mollie when I came upon two of my dog-walking buddies, Michael with MoJo, and Kyron with King. MoJo and King were both German Shepherds, and Mollie is sort of a German Shepherd/Belgian Malinois mix. After we walked for about thirty minutes, we stopped at another yard and picked up Chico, another German Shepherd.

Michael had given Chico to a friend, but they had moved and abandoned him in the backyard for three weeks. Being an animal lover, this distressed Michael no end. Someone else now had the dog temporarily, but Michael was trying to find him a permanent home.

We were some kind of sight: three people with four large dogs. I kept thinking about what a great picture we would make. I'm five foot two, Kyron is five foot seven, and Michael is six foot one. Chico kept getting underfoot with Michael, so I offered to walk him with Mollie. I beamed as I walked down the street, proud to be in such good company. Whoever would have thought that I would one day walk down the street with four (not one, not two, not three, but four) large dogs, especially since I had been attacked by two dogs several years ago.

We came to my house, and Michael and Kyron were going to move on, but Linnie was standing outside. She scooped up her poodle, mostly in fear at the sight of the four big dogs, until she realized that I was one of the dog-walking crew.

"Hey, Linnie! What's up?" I said.

"I was just looking at all the dogs. I'm amazed they're so calm. I was just telling my sister that I wish I had a German Shepherd for protection."

At Linnie's wishful comment, Michael's eyes lit up at the prospect of finding a new home for Chico. After he explained his hopes, Linnie asked Michael and Kyron to bring Chico into her backyard and see if he felt comfortable. Chico's temporary yard did not even have a doghouse, but Linnie's yard was perfect. It had a large doghouse and plenty of running room. I was impressed that, although his dad had called him a few times to come and help his little brother with care of the yard work, Michael took the time to honor Linnie's wishes.

Linnie wondered if Chico would accept her. At first, Chico leaned on my leg, but eventually he allowed Linnie to pet him. I urged Michael and Kyron to come back later to see if Chico would adapt, but Michael held up his hand. "No, Mrs. Witt. I can do this now."

"But Michael, your dad wanted you to mow—"

He held up his hand to stop me. "Don't worry Mrs. Witt. I will do all the yard work by myself. This is important." I could tell by the look on his face that nothing I said would change his mind.

I kept MoJo and King in my front yard while they tested Chico's adaptation in the back. After about thirty minutes, they emerged from the backyard. Chico was definitely staying. "By the way, you don't have to call him Chico. He doesn't really know his name," Michael said.

We all tossed around several different names: Jose, Cujo, Joe-Joe. Linnie had always called her husband "Honey," so she felt comfortable calling her new pet protector Joe-Joe. By the end of the day, he was leaning on her, a true sign that he had adopted her as his owner.

Tears ran down Linnie's face as she talked of her beloved husband. Michael and Kyron listened as she poured out her heart. I know a lot of guys would have been squirming, trying to get out of the uncomfortable conversation, but not these two guys.

I said, "See Linnie, even though some people mistreated you, there *are* still good people left in the world." With tears still streaming down her cheeks, she nodded in agreement. The boys gave her a warm hug and I could tell that her heart was starting to mend.

I thought of the many little things that had happened to me during the past week that confirmed my belief that there *are* still good people on this planet. CleEtta gave me a large bowl of potato salad left over from a luncheon. Cammrin and Anthony, seventh grade students, fought each other to open a door for me, Gwen brought us food from their barbeque, my husband brought me coffee every morning while saying, "I love you." Jean left her seat in church to come give me a hug. Reynard, my teenage neighbor across the street, volunteered to cut some branches off my tree that were too high and thick for me to handle. His brother, Isaiah, rang the doorbell to let us know that our dog had escaped from the backyard. At a restaurant, a thug badgered a frail, elderly couple, but a guy with sagging pants told him in strong street language to leave them alone. My list could go on and on, but I think you understand.

You know, if you watch television, read the newspaper, or surf the Internet, that it's the bad things that make the news. Robbery, murder, rape, and Ponzi schemes, just to name a few. Good things are also happening everywhere; we just need to refocus our eyes.

Elijah the prophet was fed up with the stinky odor of the world. He complained, "I have been working very hard for the Lord God of the armies of Heaven, but the people have broken their covenant and have torn down your altars; they have killed every one of your prophets except me; and now they are trying to kill me, too" (1 Kings 19:14 LB). God gave Elijah instructions, then said, "And incidentally, there are 7,000 men in Israel who have never bowed to Baal nor kissed him" (1 Kings 19:18 LB).

God reminded Elijah that there were good people on the earth who still loved God as much as he did.

Elisha, the prophet that succeeded Elijah, was surrounded by troops, horses, and chariots. His servant panicked. "'Don't be afraid!' Elisha told him, 'for our army is bigger than theirs!' Then Elisha prayed, 'Lord, open his eyes and let him see!' And the Lord opened the young man's eyes so that he could see horses of fire and chariots of fire everywhere upon the mountain!" (2 Kings 6:16–17 LB).

You can find the good people in the world if you allow God to reveal them to you. I know that evil lurks everywhere, but there are also wonderful people that God places around you to brighten your life. Please join Linnie and me in saying, "There are still good people in the world." They've been there all the time. Ask God to open your eyes like He opened Elisha's servant's eyes.

Questions

1. If you see a neighbor in need, should you ignore them? Write down your feelings. (a)

2. When a religion scholar asked Jesus to define "neighbor," he answered with a parable about the good Samaritan. How would you define "neighbor"? (b).

3. When you help people who aren't able to help you back, is there a reward? (c)

4. The world says to take care of yourself and leave others alone. What is your philosophy?

5. What does the Bible say? (d, e)

6. Jesus allowed people to interrupt Him (Luke 8:40-56). Should we allow people to interrupt us? Express your thoughts.

7. Was Jesus kind to people? Is He our model? (f)

Scriptural Answers

(a) "It's criminal to ignore a neighbor in need" (Proverb 14:21).

(b) "'What do you think? Which of the three became a neighbor to the man attacked by robbers?' 'The one who treated him kindly,' the religion scholar responded. Jesus said, 'Go and do the same'" (Luke 10:36–37).

(c) "Remember, the Lord will pay you for each good thing you do" (Ephesians 6:8 LB).

(d) "Don't be selfish; don't live to make a good impression on others. Be humble, thinking of others as better than yourself. Don't just think about your own affairs, but be interested in others, too, and in what they are doing" (Philippians 2:3–4 LB).

(e) "Turn from all known sin and spend your time in doing good. Try to live in peace with everyone; work hard at it" (Psalm 34:14 LB)

(f) "And you no doubt know that Jesus ... went around doing good" (Acts 10:38 LB).

79
Have you ever wondered if your prayers mattered?

I once had a very powerful dream that answered that question. I will share my dream because I believe it may help you if you have ever pondered whether your prayers matter.

I dreamed that I saw a plainly dressed person riding an average-looking horse, running from left to right. Water twirling counterclockwise sucked them down. The water was similar to a hurricane. As I looked down from above, I could see the rider's face appear under the surface of the water, but it never broke the plane.

When I was a kid, we had a Magic 8 Ball that you could ask questions. You shook the ball and an answer would appear in a window just under the surface. That's how the rider and horse looked. I could see their faces, but everything was murky. They stayed in the eye of the hurricane and continued to float to the surface, and then go back down.

In my dream, I had an idea. Maybe I should pray for the rider the next time he floated to the surface. So that's what I did. I prayed fervently. As I prayed, a giant right hand extended from above the surface and reached down toward the rider, who then reached his hand upward. When their hands clasped, as in a handshake, the person and the horse emerged from the water triumphantly, only this time they looked regal, like horses that prance around in a stadium. The rider was wearing a red riding jacket, a red cap, and looked like royalty: majestic.

As the dream continued, I thought, *Hmm, this time I won't pray and*

I'll see what happens. The rider appeared again just under the surface, and then disappeared back under the turbulent water. I experimented again. I thought, *Okay, this time I'll pray and see what happens.* Again, the rider came to the surface and as I prayed, the hand again extended from above. The rider and his horse came out triumphantly and rode off to the right. I experimented one more time, just to make sure, with the same results. Then I woke up.

Some dreams are hard to interpret, some dreams come about as a result of eating too much pizza, but this was definitely a godly dream. I had this dream more than ten years ago and I can still remember every detail. To me, my dream was confirmation of something very, very important: *prayer matters.*

If someone comes to you and asks you to pray about something, please don't nonchalantly tell them, "I'll pray for you," but never think of them again. They may be drowning, going under, and your prayer may be the one that sends God's hand down to pull them up and bring them out triumphantly.

Sometimes people are so depressed or sick that it's hard for them to pray for themselves. I've been that way myself. It seems like my prayers get about two feet off the floor and then *splat!* They come back down again. Someone had to pray *for* me. And you need to pray *for* someone. Stop right there, wherever you are, whether it's Walmart, the hallway at school, or on the cell phone talking to someone 2,000 miles away, and pray *with* and *for* someone. It will make a difference. You have to believe that.

Some years after I had that dream, I found a Scripture that supported my revelation. "But me [God] caught—reached all the way from sky to sea; He pulled me out of that ocean of hate, that enemy chaos, the void in which I was drowning. They hit me when I was down, but God stuck by me. He stood me up on a wide-open field; I stood there saved—surprised to be loved!" (Psalms 18:16–19).

It doesn't get any better than that! The prophet Samuel said to the people, "As for me, far be it from me that I should sin against the Lord by failing to pray for you. And I will teach you the way that is good and right" (1 Samuel 12:23 NIV).

Enough said!

Questions

1. Do you believe that God will hear and answer you when you pray? Why or why not? (a, b)

2. The eyes and ears of the Lord are attentive to the _____ . (c)

3. Have you ever felt like you were drowning in your problems and couldn't keep your head above water? Tell how you felt. (d)

4. Do we have a promise that God will deliver us? (e)

5. Have you ever been snatched from the clutches of death? Describe your experience. (f)

6. If God hears your prayers and answers your prayers, should you be fearful? (g)

Scriptural Answers

(a) "In my distress I screamed to the Lord for his help. And he heard me from heaven; my cry reached his ears" (Psalm 18:6 LB).

(b) "When I pray, you answer me and encourage me by giving me the strength I need ... Though I am surrounded by troubles, you will bring me safely through them" (Psalms 138:3, 7 LB).

(c) "The eyes of the Lord are on the righteous and his ears are attentive to their cry" (Psalm 34:15 NIV).

(d) "God, God, save me! I'm in over my head. Quicksand under me, swamp water over me; I'm going down for the third time ... Rescue me from the swamp, don't let me go under for good, pull me out of the clutch of the enemy; this whirlpool is sucking me down" (Psalms 69:1–2, 14).

(e) "The righteous cry out, and the Lord hears them; He delivers them from all their troubles" (Psalm 34:17 NIV).

(f) "But me? God snatches me from the clutch of death; he reaches down and grabs me" (Psalm 49:15).

(g) "Fear not, for I am with you. Do not be dismayed. I am your God. I will strengthen you; I will help you, I will uphold you with my victorious right hand" (Isaiah 41:10 LB).

80

Have you ever wondered whose words to believe?

I loved my grandmother, Zella Irene. When she died at the age of ninety-two, she was still a pretty feisty woman. My grandfather was a contractor and she was very instrumental in his company, ordering supplies and keeping the guys in line. She also had a flower garden that she was proud of, which explains my inherent love of the outdoors. We never lived in the same town as her, so most of what I remember about her is what my mother told me. My mother said that Grandma was one of the favorites at her nursing home, because while most of the residents were grumpy, she was always positive and upbeat.

Paul Harvey once used her as an example in one of his radio shows. A burglar had broken a window in her house with the intention of robbing her. She lectured him about life, told him to change his ways, and when he was leaving, she said, "Be careful, don't cut your feet on the glass," for you see, he was barefoot.

But there is one incident I *do* recall that has adversely affected me. It stuck in my mind because it hurt me. My parents, my brother, and I had just traveled four hours to visit her. We got out of the car and ran to see her. She turned to Steve first and said, "You look so handsome! You have good thick hair and pretty Thompson teeth. Just look at that smile!"

Then she turned to me, and I just *knew* that I was going to get similar praise—but that didn't happen. "When are you going to get that stringy hair cut, and when are you ever going to get some boobs," she said as she pinched my breasts. I managed a faint smile, which exposed my tusk tooth. She stared at my imperfect teeth, said nothing, and then she turned away.

I cried in my bed that night. I felt ashamed of myself, ugly. My parents had only put positive words in my life, so I had no idea that I was subpar. But those biting words and the rejecting glance did enough harm to affect me for a long time. I looked in the mirror and saw what she saw. Yes, my hair was a little stringy, my tusk tooth messed up my smile, and at the age of eleven, I wasn't fully developed. Her words changed my perspective about myself. *She must be right. After all, she's my grandmother*, I thought.

From that moment on, whenever I looked in the mirror or looked at my pictures, I heard those words. My parents never said them, and other people never said them, but I chose to believe my grandmother's words. Maybe she was just having a bad day; I don't know. I have totally forgiven her. But when you're eleven years old and coming of age, the negative words can sound louder than the positive ones.

Looking back at pictures of me when I was younger, I now realize that I wasn't as bad-looking as I remembered. Sure, I looked goofy sometimes. For instance, I once got a perm and my hair looked like a puffy poodle's, but for the most part, I didn't look too bad. Now that I'm older, I realize that I spent my whole life believing the wrong words. Why is it easier to believe the negative? I'm not a psychologist, so I can't give you a technical explanation, but I suspect that I'm not the only person who has believed a bad report.

I recall reading in the Bible about the twelve spies who went to check out the land of Canaan. Caleb and Joshua were the only men who were confident that they could possess the land. Ten spies had negative reports: "full of warriors, descendants of giants, we felt like grasshoppers." The Israelites believed the negative words. They wept and carried on all night. They wanted to go back to Egypt.

Caleb and Joshua countered,

> "It is wonderful country ahead, and the Lord loves us. He will bring us safely into the land and give it to us. It is very fertile, a land 'flowing with milk and honey!' ... the Lord is with us and he has removed his protection from them! Don't be afraid of them!" But the

only response of the people was to talk of stoning them. Then the glory of the Lord appeared, and the Lord said to Moses, "How long will these people despise me? Will they never believe me, even after all the miracles I have done among them?"

—Numbers 14:6–11 LB

Moses pleaded for mercy from God to forgive the people for doubting Him.

Then the Lord said, "All right, I will pardon them as you have requested. But I vow ... that not one of the men who has seen my glory and miracles ... shall even see the land I promised to this people's ancestors. But my servant, Caleb, is a different kind of man—he has obeyed me fully. I will bring him into the land he entered as a spy, and his descendants shall have their full share in it."

—Numbers 14:20–24 LB

So there we have it: more cases of believing the wrong words. It may seem obvious to you that the Israelites should have believed the words of Caleb and Joshua. And I'm positive I should *not* have believed my grandmother's words. Are you guilty of the same kind of negative beliefs? Does Satan whisper nonsense in your ear, and do you choose to believe him instead of God?

Here are some examples of how Satan can plant deceit, as well as some Scriptures to shut up that filthy-mouthed liar.

- When Satan tempts me to be fearful, I choose to believe: "The wicked man's fears will all come true, and so will the good man's hopes" (Proverb 10:24 LB).

No fears—only hopes.

- When Satan whispers, "This is taking too long! God's never going to make it right," I quote Paul: "And let us not get tired of doing what is right for after a while we will reap a harvest of blessing if we don't get discouraged and give up" (Galatians 6:9 LB).

Be patient; God will redeem.

- If Lucifer screams in my ear, "The economy is spiraling, there is no way you or your kids will survive! You'll starve! Gloom is everywhere!" I square my shoulders and without any hesitation quote David's words, "I have been young and now I am old. And in all my years I have never seen the Lord forsake a man who loves him; nor have I seen the children of the godly go hungry" (Psalm 37:25 LB).

  Powerful words. God has me in his hands.

- When the Accuser throws his head back and laughs at me, when I go through troubles and injustice surrounds me, when I'm worn out and he sneers, "See, you can't last another day!" I don't despair. I listen to Isaiah's words: "How can you say that the Lord doesn't see your troubles and isn't being fair? Don't you yet understand? Don't you know by now that the everlasting God, the creator of the farthest parts of the earth, never grows faint or weary? No one can fathom the depths of his understanding. He gives power to the tired and worn out, and strength to the weak. Even the youths shall be exhausted, and the young men will all give up. But they that wait upon the Lord shall renew their strength. They shall mount up with wings like eagles; they shall run and not be weary; they shall walk and not faint" (Isaiah 40:27–31 LB).

  I know I can make it another day.

I could go on and on, but I think you understand. We all have a choice as to whose words we believe.

Are you making the right choice? My grandmother was wrong, the Israelites were wrong, and Satan is wrong. Believe God's words and teach your children the same. Tell the devil to shut up, and live the victorious life you were meant to live!

Questions

1. Should mean, harsh words come out of a Christian's mouth? Why or why not? (a)

2. Are we supposed to forgive others when they say mean things? Why or why not? (b)

3. How should we prepare ourselves to counter words that hurt us? (c)

4. Sticks and stones may break my bones, but words will never hurt me. True or false? (d)

5. One day we will have to give an account for every careless word we have spoken. True or false? (e)

6. What happens to people when you crush their spirits? (f)

7. Does God make junk? (g)

8. Can God lie? (h)

9. If we are fed lies about ourselves, we should remember that _____ is the father of lies. (i)

Scriptural Answers

(a) "Stop being mean, bad-tempered and angry. Quarreling harsh words and dislike of others should have no place in your lives" (Ephesians 4:31 LB).

(b) "Instead, be kind to each other, tenderhearted, forgiving one another, just as God has forgiven you because you belong to Christ" (Ephesians 4:32 LB).

(c) "I have thought much about your words, and stored them in my heart so that they would hold me back from sin" (Psalm 119:11 LB).

(d) "Words kill, words give life; they're either poison or fruit—you choose" (Proverb 18:21).

(e) "But I tell you that men will have to give account on the day of judgment for every careless word they have spoken. For by your words you will be acquitted and by your words you will be condemned" (Matthew 12:36–37 NIV).

(f) "A cheerful heart is good medicine, but a crushed spirit dries up the bones" (Proverb 17:22 NIV).

(g) "I praise you because I am fearfully and wonderfully made; your works are wonderful, I know that full well" (Psalm 139:14 NIV).

(h) "[God] cannot lie" (Titus 1:2 LB).

(i) "For there is no truth in [the devil] … for he is a liar and the father of lies" (John 8:44 NIV).

Epilogue

My husband Randy had a good question. "Are we even that interesting?" I didn't think so, but God took our ordinary lives and guided me as I compiled a book for ordinary people. He asked me to share examples from our lives that would show how it is possible for any Christian to hear from God. Just when I felt like giving up, and I thought that my stories were too simple, God would nudge me to share some of my stories, and people would say, "Wow, that really impacted me!"

When I was working my front desk job at Seabrook Family Christian Center, Dwight, a teenage father, was given two hundred community service hours to work because of a traffic ticket. While there, he read thirty of my stories and told me that reading them had made him decide to turn his life around. Laticia, a friend of mine, told me that she was considered the "family atheist," yet my stories gave her hope that she could also have a relationship with God.

After I let a seventh grade student read "Have you ever admitted you were wrong?" she made the comment, "I'll *never* apologize to anyone!" as she rolled her eyes. However, the next day at school as I walked into the classroom, I saw the same girl apologizing to Mrs. Taylor for something that she had done. I just smiled. I thanked God that He had helped me to make a difference in that young girl's life.

Hayden, a senior in high school, read "Have you ever deprived your kids?" His comments after reading the story were, "I realize I've been selfish. It was good to see that it took time for good things to happen."

One rainy day, I felt a strange urge to go to a garage sale. I noticed one advertised in the newspaper five blocks from my house. I keep feeling the Holy Spirit urge me to talk about my book. I did not want to, because I didn't know how it would be received. After thirty minutes of awkwardly hanging around, I finally got the words out of my mouth. The lady was very receptive, and the next thing I knew, I was offering to let her read some of the stories. I drove home and got them, let her look at the titles and she picked one out: "Have you ever had an unplanned pregnancy?" She read it, then looked up in shock. "I just found out I was pregnant and I was very resentful. I was to attend college in the fall and this pregnancy has changed everything. Since I read how you felt, and what God told you, I am going to see my pregnancy as a good thing, not a bad thing."

Katie, a beautiful twenty-year-old girl, cried as she read "Have you ever been depressed?" She looked up at me and said, "This is *exactly* what I needed. How did you know?" I didn't know but Almighty God knew.

One question that people frequently ask me is, "How did you come up with the name of your book?" While on a road trip in Kentucky with my friend Gwen, we passed a clever, unique sign on the highway that said "Used Cows." We loved the sign and I told her that I wanted a title that would be memorable, like that sign. Soon after that Gwen went to sleep, and I started talking to God.

"God, what's a good title for my book?"

He said, "What's a good Scripture about hearing from Me?"

The first one that came to my mind was, "My sheep hear my voice."

Then God asked the big question: "What do sheep hear with?"

It seemed pretty obvious at that point—with *sheep ears*. I thought, *That's it, "Sheep Ears!"*

One day, about three months later, I was looking for something on the bottom shelf of my kitchen cabinets. I reached to the back and felt something with an unusual shape. I pulled it closer so I could see what it was, and I couldn't believe my eyes. It was something that was given to my mother the day that I was born. It was a sheep with prominent ears sticking out. As I held it gingerly in my hands, God spoke to me, "This is your destiny." I broke down and cried. Of all the things that I could have saved from my birth, this little sheep was the only item that had endured more than ten moves to ten different cities. I had forgotten about it, but God had preserved this sheep to confirm my book title. Unbelievable!

I pray that *Sheep Ears* has helped you to understand the importance of listening to God, and how much we are blessed when we honor our Good Shepherd's directions.

Perhaps you have your own "Have you ever …?" stories. Please take time to write them down, before you forget. Open your heart to receive the message that God is speaking to you on your walk through aisle 3 of the grocery store, about the hurt that you were able to overcome and the innocent voice of a child who has not become hardened by the world.

Join the flock of sheep who have ears for God. Like my granddaughter Ayla said, "Listen with your listening ears." I call them your sheep ears.

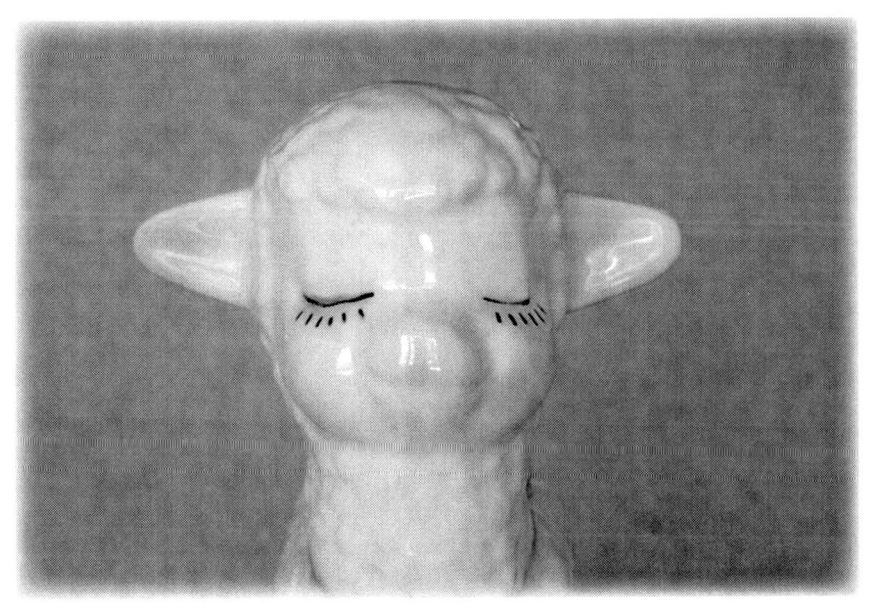

Photo by Gary Paris

This is the sheep that was given to my mother the day of my birth.

Bible Version Abbreviations

AB	*The Amplified Bible*
ESV	*English Standard Version*
GWT	*God's Word Translation*
KJV	*King James Version*
LB	*The Living Bible*
NASB	*New American Standard Bible*
NIV	*New International Version*
NKJV	*New King James Version*
NLT	*New Living Translation*

All Scripture quotations in this book unaccompanied by a version abbreviation are from *The Message* (MSG).

I used many translations and paraphrases because I have found that sometimes I garner a better understanding of how different interpretations apply to my life. Some interpretations are a little easier for me to understand and some are more potent. I've kept my heart open to receive all that God wants me to have, and I hope you will be open too.

CPSIA information can be obtained at www.ICGtesting.com
Printed in the USA
LVOW12s2347031013

355237LV00003B/7/P

9 781449 799922